132

W9-ACG-521

180 days
4 days/wk

THE **Building Christian English** SERIES

Building

Christian English

Progressing With Courage

Grade 6

Rod and Staff Publishers, Inc.

Hwy. 172, Crockett, Kentucky 41413

Telephone: (606) 522-4348

6   7   8   9   10   —   16   15   14   13   12   11   10   09   08   07

Acknowledgments

We are indebted first and most of all to God, whose blessing made possible the writing and publishing of this book.

We express gratitude to each one who was involved in this work. The original edition was written by Lela Birky and Lucy Ann Conley, and the revision by Marion W. Leinbach. Marvin Eicher and Ernest Wine were the editors, H. Lynn Martin and various others were reviewers, and most of the artwork was done by Lester Miller. We are also indebted to the teachers who used the material on a laboratory basis in their classrooms, as well as to numerous people who assisted along the way by providing finances, by encouraging those directly involved in the work, and by interceding in prayer for the work.

Various reference books were consulted in accomplishing this task, such as English handbooks, other English textbooks, encyclopedias, and dictionaries. For these too we are grateful. We have chosen to favor the more conservative schools of thought that are considered authoritative in correct English usage.

—*The Publishers*

Table of Contents

(Stars indicate Written Composition and Oral English lessons.)

Chapter 1

Understanding Sentences
Learning About Stories and Directions

Chapter 2

Working With Sentences
Understanding Paragraphs

Chapter 3

Working With Nouns
Developing Paragraphs

Chapter 4

Working With Verbs
Writing Outlines

Chapter 5

Using Verbs Correctly
Writing Reports

Chapter 6

Working With Pronouns
Writing Letters

Chapter 7

Using Correct Capitalization and Punctuation

Writing Stories

Chapter 8

Working With Adjectives

Writing Descriptions

Chapter 9

Working With Adverbs

Studying Poetry

Chapter 10

Using Prepositions, Conjunctions, and Interjections
Communicating Orally

Chapter 11

Studying Words
Using Sentence Variety

Subjects

Predicates

Clauses

Sentences

Fragments

Directions

Stories

Chapter One
Understanding Sentences
Learning About Stories and Directions

A
sentence is
a group of words that
expresses a complete
thought.

Study to shew thyself approved
unto God, a workman that needeth not to be ashamed.

2 Timothy 2:15

1. Sentences and Fragments

Imagine a school that had no teacher, or a school with a teacher but no pupils. Or what if a school had a teacher and pupils, but was without books or paper? Such a school would not be complete. It could not accomplish the work that a school should get done.

A sentence, like a school, has a job to do. Its job is to express a thought. And like a school, a sentence must be complete in order to do its work. If our writing has incomplete sentences, readers will not be able to understand our thoughts and ideas. We say, then, that a complete sentence is a group of words that expresses a complete thought.

To be complete, a sentence must have a *subject* and a *predicate*. The subject tells *who* or *what* the sentence is about, and the predicate tells what the subject does or is. Consider these complete sentences.

Brother Luke preached an inspiring sermon.
> This sentence is about *Brother Luke,* and it tells what he did—*preached an inspiring sermon.* It expresses a complete thought.

The playful kittens chased a ball of Mother's yarn.
> What is the sentence about? (the playful kittens) What did they do? (chased a ball of Mother's yarn) This is a complete sentence because it has a subject and a predicate, and it expresses a complete thought.

A group of words that does not express a complete thought is a sentence *fragment.* A group of words may be a fragment for several different reasons.

1. Sometimes a fragment does not have a subject.

    Fragment: Played in the sand.

    This group of words does not make sense because it does not say who or what played in the sand. It can be corrected by adding a subject.

    Sentence: <u>A little child</u> played in the sand.

2. Sometimes a fragment does not have a predicate.

    Fragment: The rich man Job.

    This group of words does not tell what the man Job did or was. It can be corrected by adding a predicate.

    Sentence: The rich man Job <u>lived in Uz</u>.

3. Sometimes a fragment does not have a subject or a predicate.

    Fragment: In the morning at 7:00.

    This example does not tell *who* or *what,* nor does it tell what the subject *did* or *was.* It can be corrected by adding a subject and a predicate.

    Sentence: <u>We were eating</u> in the morning at 7:00.

4. Sometimes a fragment has a verb, but it still needs a helping verb. Without a helping verb, the sentence does not make sense and is a fragment.

    Fragment: James running very fast.

    The fragment can be corrected by adding a helping verb.

    Sentence: James <u>was</u> running very fast.

Remember that every complete sentence must begin with a capital letter and end with correct punctuation.

- A sentence is a group of words that expresses a complete thought. It must have a subject and a predicate.

- A sentence fragment is a group of words that does not express a complete thought.

Class Practice

A. Tell whether each group of words is a *sentence* or a *fragment*. If it is a fragment, tell what is missing.
1. On the other side of the stream.
2. We have heard about the fire.
3. Was watching the birds.
4. Large white clouds.
5. Charles was very helpful on Saturday.
6. Brother Elvin and his children.
7. Rising above the treetops.
8. Jane going shopping with Mother.
9. He will have some left.
10. In the house or outside.

B. Make complete sentences from the fragments in Part A.

Written Exercises

A. Write whether each group of words is a *sentence* or a *fragment*. If it is a fragment, write the number from the lesson that tells what is missing.
1. Can easily open the door.
2. One of my favorite pastimes.
3. I believe God.
4. Were gathering flowers along the road.
5. Took some ducks to market.
6. Always plants her peas and onions early.
7. Moses went up the mountain.
8. Around the house.
9. Louise and Ellen were singing a new song.
10. Ruth reading a book.
11. Later in the afternoon.
12. Louanne got home before dark.

B. Make complete sentences by adding your own words to the fragments in Part A. Write the complete sentences.

Review Exercises

These exercises review things that you studied in grade 5. Writing the answers will help to prepare you for Lesson 2, which is about the predicate of a sentence.

A. Write the definition of a verb and the definition of a noun.

B. Copy all the words in this list that can be used as action verbs.

1. good	7. hard	12. split
2. scurry	8. easy	13. leader
3. bounce	9. read	14. sad
4. rejoice	10. gift	15. send
5. mountain	11. hike	16. hour
6. carry		

C. Write all the helping verbs you learned in grade 5. Write them in organized groups. (Use the index to find them in this book if you have forgotten them. Memorize them again.)

---

2. The Predicate of a Sentence

Every sentence has two main parts: the subject and the predicate. The predicate of a sentence is the part that tells what the subject does or is. We may speak of the simple predicate or the complete predicate.

The *simple predicate* is the most important part of the predicate. It is the verb in the sentence. It may be a single-word verb or several verbs together as a verb phrase. The simple predicates are underlined in the following sentences.

> An ostrich <u>runs</u> very fast.
> Two beautiful white swans <u>were floating</u> on the still surface of the pond.

To find the simple predicate in a sentence, use the following steps.

1. *Look for a word that shows action,* since most verbs are action verbs. You will remember from past years that words like *watch, call, seek, drive, run, work, sing, pray, read, talk, listen,* and *move* are action verbs. There are thousands of action verbs in our language, but most of them are easy to recognize. Use a dictionary if you are not sure whether a word can be a verb.

2. *If there is no action verb, look for a form of* be. This verb shows being instead of action. You should memorize the eight forms of *be* if you do not already know them. They are listed here.

am, is, are, was, were, be, been, being

3. *If there is no form of* be, *look for a verb that could be replaced by a form of* be. Here are the "sometimes linking verbs" that you learned in grade 5.

taste, feel, smell, sound, look, appear

Action verb: Janet <u>smelled</u> fresh bread.
Linking verb: The bread <u>smelled</u> warm and delicious.
　　　　　　　　　(It would be sensible to say "The bread
　　　　　　　　　<u>was</u> warm and delicious.")

4. *After finding the main verb, check to see if there are any helping verbs.* Look at the verb phrase *were floating.* In such a phrase, the last word is the *main verb,* and the word used before it is a *helping verb.* The simple predicate is the main verb and all the helping verbs used with it. In grade 5 you studied the helping verbs in groups, as shown here.

Forms of *be:*   am, is, are, was, were, be, been, being
Forms of *have:* have, has, had
Forms of *do:*   do, does, did
Forms of *may:*   may, might, must
Other helping verbs:
　　　　　　　　can—could, shall—should, will—would

Following the four steps, find the simple predicates in the following sentences.

Abraham believed the words of God.
His wife was an old woman.
God's promises to Abraham sounded impossible.
Many people are obeying the Bible today.

The *complete predicate* is the simple predicate and all the words that go with it to tell about the subject. In the following sentence, the simple predicate is underlined twice and the complete predicate is italicized.

Grandfather <u>*has planted*</u> *some cherry trees in the orchard.*

Has planted tells what Grandfather did. It is the simple predicate. *Some cherry trees in the orchard* goes with the simple predicate to tell more completely what Grandfather did. Thus the complete predicate is *has planted some cherry trees in the orchard.*

To find the complete predicate, find all the words that go with the verb or verb phrase to tell what the subject does or is. In most sentences, the complete predicate begins with the verb or verb phrase and the other words of the predicate come after the verb or verb phrase. In the following sentences, the simple predicates are underlined twice and the complete predicates are italicized.

> The boys <u>were riding</u> *on horses in the pasture.*
> Our God <u>is</u> *great and mighty.*
> The white and pink roses <u>smell</u> *sweet.*

Be sure to memorize the linking verbs and helping verbs listed in this lesson so that you can find the simple predicate of a sentence more easily.

- The simple predicate is the verb or verb phrase in the sentence.

- The complete predicate includes the verb and all the words that go with it to tell about the subject.

Class Practice

A. Tell which words make up the simple predicate. Then read the complete predicate of each sentence.
   1. Jesus loves all the children of the world.
   2. Noah and his sons were working on the ark.
   3. Two Roman soldiers stood in front of the tomb.
   4. The old oak tree grew very tall.
   5. The little girl looked fearful and unhappy.
   6. Pharaoh's army perished in the waters of the sea.
   7. The meek shall inherit the earth.
   8. Several lively gray squirrels are climbing up the trees.
   9. The older boys built a bridge across the brook.
   10. My other coat will be warmer than this one.

B. On the chalkboard, write the verb phrases from Part A. Underline the main verb in each verb phrase.

Written Exercises

A. Copy each complete predicate. Draw two lines under each simple predicate.
1. A little bird was singing just outside the door.
2. We shall be working here next week.
3. Your answer is correct.
4. Those little brown insects ruined the beans.
5. Amos has written us another letter.
6. These flowers have come from our garden.
7. Charlotte will be coming this evening.
8. My little dog recognizes my voice.
9. Some ants can lift a weight fifty times heavier than themselves!
10. Some ants build nests with underground rooms and passageways.
11. These flowers do smell sweet!
12. Joshua may have been there.

B. Copy each verb phrase in Part A, and underline the main verb. (Not all the sentences have verb phrases.)

Review Exercises

These exercises review things that you studied in grade 5. Answering these questions will help to prepare you for Lesson 3, which is about the subject of a sentence.

A. Write the following things.
1. The definition of a noun.
2. The definition of a pronoun.
3. The personal pronouns that are used as subjects. (See Lesson 61 in this book if you need help.)

B. Copy all the nouns that name persons. You should find twelve in all.
1. My grandfather was a farmer.
2. Her mother was a teacher, and her sister was a nurse.
3. Aunt Mary is a good cook and seamstress.
4. Brother John, our janitor, is also a good farmer.

C. Copy all the nouns that name places. You should find eight in all.
1. We didn't enjoy the large city, so we visited a farm in the country.
2. In which county of that state do you live?
3. Our family enjoyed a picnic lunch in the park.
4. On Saturday we did the cleaning at the school and the church.

D. Copy all the nouns that name things. You should find eleven in all.
1. "Get out your pencil, eraser, and tablet, and place them on your desk," instructed the teacher.
2. Use this soap and a brush to clean the floors.
3. Don't forget to polish the mirror, wash the windows, dust the furniture, and vacuum the floor.

E. Copy all the nouns that name ideas. You should find thirteen in all.
1. The Bible tells Christians to put on mercy, kindness, humility, meekness, patience, forbearance, forgiveness, and charity.
2. Proper thoughts will help you to overcome fear, gain courage, avoid evil, and do right.

F. Copy all the pronouns that are used as subjects. You should find eight in all.
1. We and they found the way.
2. He and she saw the new building.
3. You and I will fill the holes with wood putty, but he and they will do the sanding.

----

3. The Subject of a Sentence

The subject of a sentence tells *who* or *what* the sentence is about. The *simple subject* of the sentence is the main word (or words) in the subject. The simple subject is a noun or pronoun.

Find the simple subject of each sentence.

A kind, thoughtful girl helped us in the afternoon.
Who is this sentence about? It is about a girl.
Girl is the simple subject.

The waves rolled and splashed in a constant rhythm.
What is this sentence about? It is about the waves.
Waves is the simple subject.

Review the following facts about nouns and pronouns to help you find the simple subject of a sentence more easily.

1. *A noun is a word that names a person, place, thing, or idea.* Study the following examples.

> **Person:** mother, farmer, doctor
> **Place:** barn, park, city, lake
> **Thing:** door, fence, horse, desk
> **Idea:**   love, joy, cheer, faith

2. *A pronoun is a word that takes the place of a noun.* Review this list of pronouns that can be used as subjects.

I, you, he, she, it, we, they

The *complete subject* of a sentence includes the simple subject and all its modifiers. To find the complete subject, look first for the simple subject. Then find the words that modify it. In the sentence *The white lilies are blooming now,* the words *The* and *white* modify the simple subject *lilies.* So the complete subject is *The white lilies.*

In the following examples, each simple subject is underlined and each complete subject is italicized. A line is drawn between the complete subject and the complete predicate.

> *The white <u>lilies</u>* | are blooming now.
> *The low blue <u>mountains</u>* | stretched across the horizon.
> *The hot vegetable <u>soup</u>* | tasted delicious.
> <u>*God*</u> | gives us many good gifts.

In the last sentence, *God* is both the simple subject and the complete subject because this noun has no modifiers.

The simple subject and simple predicate together form the *skeleton* of a sentence. To find the skeleton, always follow these three steps.

1. Find the simple predicate (the verb).
2. Ask *who* or *what* about the verb. The answer is the simple subject.
3. Say the simple subject and simple predicate together to see if they make sense.

Use the steps above to find the skeleton of this sentence.

> Our great Lord is coming soon.

1. Find the simple predicate. The simple predicate is *is coming.*
2. Ask, "*Who* is coming?" The answer is *Lord.*
3. Say the simple subject and simple predicate together to see if they make sense: *Lord is coming.* This makes sense, so it is the skeleton.

- The simple subject is the noun or pronoun that tells *who* or *what* the sentence is about.

- The complete subject includes the simple subject and all the words that modify the simple subject. The skeleton is the simple subject and simple predicate together.

Class Practice

A. Give the simple subject and the complete subject of each sentence.
1. The tomato seeds should sprout soon.
2. Love thinks no evil.
3. Jewish scribes copied the Scriptures carefully.
4. They counted each word and letter.
5. No word was written from memory.
6. The writer pronounced each word aloud.
7. You are the light of the world.
8. A certain poor widow came into the temple.
9. She put in only two mites.
10. Jesus was pleased with her gift.

B. Give the skeleton of each sentence in Part A.

Written Exercises

A. Copy each complete subject, and underline the simple subject.

Examples: a. The five tall spruce trees stood at the end of the yard.
                b. God is love.

Answers: a. The five tall spruce <u>trees</u>
               b. <u>God</u>

1. God gave language to man.
2. He confused the languages at the Tower of Babel.
3. The world has about three thousand different languages today.
4. Our English language comes from England.
5. Many words have been adopted into English from other languages.
6. Languages do change.
7. It is generally a slow process.
8. This change is not always for the better.

9. Man is lazy and careless by nature.
10. We should put forth diligence.
11. Every person will answer for his idle words.
12. The Bible teaches carefulness in speech.
13. Several large bears lumbered through the woods.
14. Six wild geese landed on our pond last night.

B. Copy the skeleton of each sentence. Underline the simple subject once and the simple predicate twice. Draw a dividing line between the subject and the predicate.

> **Example:** The little dog was running after his little master.
> **Answer:**   dog | was running

1. Grandfather was here at noon.
2. My two white geese have come back again.
3. I missed them this morning.
4. The school was cleaned yesterday.
5. Love is always kind.
6. Mary's lemonade tastes more delicious every time.
7. The sky is very blue today.
8. An iron key opened the wooden box.
9. The native women were weaving cloth.
10. The young boy chased the pig back into the pen.

Review Exercises

Write the correct words in parentheses. Use the index in the back of this book if you need help.

1. Where shall I (lay, lie) these packages?
2. (Set, Sit) them in a place where nobody will (set, sit) on them.
3. Those tools have (laid, lain) outside all week.
4. Their owner (don't, doesn't) seem to care.
5. Father (let, left) the children (raise, rise) some chicks one summer.
6. He (taught, learned) them how to care for the chicks.
7. The children (taught, learned) many valuable things from Father.
8. The driver (let, left) the disabled car along the road.
9. It was (setting, sitting) there all night.
10. Father (raised, rose) the hood and looked at the engine.
11. "(Can, May) I please have the keys?" he asked.
12. "I'll see what I (can, may) do to help you," Father said.

4. Writing a Story About a Problem

We all like to hear or read a good story. A story catches our attention and teaches us a lesson. The Bible uses many stories to teach men about God.

You studied story writing in other grades. Do you remember these rules for writing stories?

1. Know the facts. You can never write a good story if you are not sure what happened.
2. Put things in proper order—first things first and last things last.
3. Include all the important information. Tell who, what, when, where, why, and how.
4. Stick to the main idea of the story.
5. Vary the length of your sentences.
6. Use good grammar, proper spelling, correct punctuation, and neat handwriting.

In this chapter you have studied what makes a complete sentence. Be sure to use complete sentences when you write a story.

A good story tells about a problem or difficulty someone has. This is why stories are interesting. When we read about a problem, immediately we want to know what happened next! The problem does not need to be something great or unusual. Simple, everyday problems can make good stories. Consider this example.

> **Mother sent Wilbur to the neighbors with a message. But in the neighbors' lane, Wilbur met a big, fierce-looking dog. The dog ran toward him, barking and growling.**

Did Wilbur have a problem? He certainly did! And immediately you want to know what happened next. What did Wilbur do? Did he deliver the message? Did he run home again? Was the dog really dangerous? Did it bite him?

The first part of your story must show that someone (or something) had a problem. Give facts and details to show clearly what that problem was. Make your readers want to know what happened next.

In the second part of your story, you must show how the problem was solved. What did the person do? Did it work? Was anyone hurt? How did it all end? People who read your story will not be satisfied until they know that the danger or trouble is over. Then they can relax.

Before you start writing your story, make a few notes. First, write about the basic problem; second, write notes about how the problem was solved. Include interesting details. Then arrange your notes in the order that things happened.

Use your notes to write your story. They will show you what to write and how to keep things in order. Be sure to write in complete sentences. Last of all, check your story for sentence variety and the other things listed at the beginning of this lesson. Study the following example.

Notes for a story:

1. The problem:

    Mother wanted to send message to neighbor

    Sent my little brother Wilbur with the message

    He went happily

    Big dog ran out, barking furiously

    Wilbur was too frightened to go farther

2. How the problem was solved:

    Wilbur ran home

    Mother wanted him to overcome his fear

    Sent me with him

    I showed that dog was harmless

    Spoke kindly and petted dog

    We have gone several times since

    Glad to help my little brother

The story:

Wilbur Makes a Friend

One day Mother had an important message to send to the neighbor. She asked my little brother Wilbur to take it. Wilbur went gladly. He had forgotten about Barnie, their big dog, until he got there. Suddenly Barnie ran out at him, barking furiously. Wilbur was too frightened to take another step toward the neighbor's house. He turned and ran home as fast as he could.

Mother knew that the dog was harmless, and she wanted to help Wilbur overcome his fear. She knew that I, his big brother, had already learned not to fear Barnie. So she sent me with Wilbur to deliver the message. I showed my little brother that Barnie only had a fierce bark and that he would not bite. Wilbur was relieved when the dog stopped barking as we walked toward him. I talked kindly to the dog and petted him, and finally Wilbur got up enough courage to pet him too. I had to go with Wilbur several more times before he was brave enough to go alone, but I did not mind. I was glad I could help my little brother.

Do not be too brief when you describe the problem in a story. Show how the problem was indeed a problem. Describe how things built up one upon another. For example, suppose your family was driving late one night and could not find a motel. Your story will not be interesting if you write just the bare facts, as in the following example.

Our family was traveling last summer. One day as evening approached, we began to look for a motel. Time after time we came to a motel only to see the same sign: No Vacancy. Finally we found a motel that did have room for us, and we all sighed with relief. We stopped there and spent the night resting from our long trip.

It would be much better to give details that show how the problem affected your family. Everyone was tired, the younger ones were getting fussy, and you were getting quite anxious. Show the things that made it seem like a really serious problem to your family.

Remember, the problem does not need to be something great or unusual. But it must be a difficulty that brings a feeling of concern, or the reader will not be concerned either. The following story is another version of the example above. Notice how the added details help the reader to feel what the characters felt.

Last summer our family took a trip to Virginia. As it began to grow dark, we started to look for a motel in which to spend the night. The first motel we found had a sign in large letters: No Vacancy. We drove another ten minutes before spying another motel in the distance. Hopefully we watched as we drove closer, but again we were disappointed. This motel was also full.

My little brother began crying. He was tired and wanted to stop. My mother was tired too because we had started at five o'clock that morning. Finally we saw another motel, but it also said No Vacancy. My father breathed a deep sigh as he drove on....

To write a good story, you must know the facts. You will know the facts best about things that have happened right around you. Think about something that happened to you or to someone in your family this past summer. Maybe your father had a cow that was determined to kick off the milker. Perhaps you and your mother were left stranded along the road when the car ran out of gas. Or did someone lock the keys in the car this summer? Did the weeds grow too fast for you and your sisters who were trying to keep the garden clean?

You have already met and solved a number of problems in life. Almost any one of them could be developed into an interesting story for others to read.

- A good story tells about a problem or difficulty that someone has.

- To write a story, first make and organize a set of notes. Then write in a clear and orderly manner, using complete sentences and sticking to the main idea. Use good sentence variety, good grammar, proper spelling, correct punctuation, and neat handwriting.

Class Practice

A. Ask your teacher to describe a problem he had this summer and tell how he solved it.

B. Tell about problems or difficulties you or your family faced this summer. Your ideas may help your classmates think of something to write about.

Written Exercises

A. Write notes for a story about a problem you or a friend solved this summer. First, show what the problem was. Second, write how it was solved. Arrange your details in the order they happened.

B. Write your story. Be sure to include enough details so that the reader can feel the problem with the characters. Your story should be at least as long as the story about Wilbur in the lesson.

Review Exercises

Find the fragments in the following story. Rewrite them, making complete sentences. [1] (Turn to the lesson number in brackets if you need help with these review exercises.)

Mother and I going to the store one day. Suddenly the car stopped. We were on a busy highway going up a hill! Had no power brakes and no power steering anymore. All we could do was let the car coast to a stop on the shoulder.

Mother breathed a short prayer. Then a kind driver in a pickup truck. Stopped and gave instructions to Mother. Told her to let the car roll back along the shoulder. Into the parking lot of a store. Mother thanked him for his kindness. Then she went inside and called Father, and he brought us gasoline. The next day. Father took the car to the garage to repair the fuel gauge, which had not been working properly.

---

5. More About Subjects and Predicates

The subject of a sentence may be a *noun phrase*. When it is a proper noun phrase, you can tell that the words go together because they are capitalized. In these examples the subject is underlined once.

> <u>Brother Paul Shirk</u> will lead the singing.
> <u>Mount Herman</u> is the highest mountain in Palestine.
> <u>World War II</u> ended in August 1945.

When *the* is used before a proper noun phrase at the beginning of a sentence, it is capitalized because it is the first word of the sentence. *The* is not usually part of a proper noun phrase any more than it is part of a common noun.

> The <u>Ohio River</u> flows between Ohio and Kentucky.
> **Compare:** The <u>river</u> flows between Ohio and Kentucky.

Some proper noun phrases contain small, unimportant words. These words are part of the noun phrase even though they are not capitalized. Study the following examples.

> The <u>Statue of Liberty</u> was a gift from the French people.
> <u>*Trouble at Windy Acres*</u> tells the struggles of a young boy.

Some noun phrases are made of two words that are not capitalized. You studied a few of these in grade 5. The following words are noun phrases because the two words together name the object.

post office   chain saw   blue jay

Do not think that you can use just any adjective with a noun and call it a noun phrase. Consider the difference in the following sentences.

A big black <u>dog</u> <u>bounded</u> toward us.
> The subject is *dog,* not *black dog. Black* simply describes the dog. It is not part of the simple subject.

The <u>hot dog</u> <u>tasted</u> delicious.
> The subject is *hot dog.* The two words together name the thing that is eaten. *Hot* is not an adjective telling what kind of dog tasted delicious!

Noun phrases are listed as dictionary entries. Check a dictionary when you are not sure if two words make a noun phrase.

Sometimes the simple subject of a sentence is followed by a prepositional phrase. But remember that the subject of a sentence is never found in a prepositional phrase. Look at this example.

Our <u>Father</u> in heaven <u>will supply</u> all your needs.

In heaven is a prepositional phrase. The verb is *will supply. Who* will supply? The answer is *Father.* The subject of the sentence is *Father,* not *heaven.*

In some sentences the word in a prepositional phrase would seem to make sense as the subject. But even then it is not the subject. Here is an example.

A <u>loaf</u> of bread <u>was sold</u>.

What was sold? Either *bread* or *loaf* would make sense, but the word *bread* is in a prepositional phrase. So it cannot be the subject. The subject is *loaf.*

When you look for the subject, it is good to pick out the prepositional phrases first so that they do not confuse you. The following list has some of the common prepositions that you studied in earlier grades. See Chapter 10 for a more complete list.

above	below	in	over
across	beside	inside	to
after	between	into	toward
around	by	near	under
at	down	of	up
before	for	off	upon
behind	from	on	with

To pick out a prepositional phrase, remember to find the preposition first. Then find its object by saying the preposition and asking *whom* or *what*. All the words between the preposition and the object are modifiers of the object.

When a prepositional phrase follows the subject and modifies it, the phrase is part of the complete subject. It does not belong with the predicate. In the following examples, each prepositional phrase in the complete subject is set off in parentheses. Notice that the dividing line between the complete subject and the complete predicate comes *after* any phrase that modifies the subject.

> The <u>top</u> (of the box) | <u>has blown</u> off.
> The <u>flowers</u> (on the table) | <u>are</u> from Grandmother.
> A large <u>bowl</u> (of oranges) | <u>sat</u> on the table.
> The <u>door</u> (in the back) (of the room) | <u>closed</u> with a bang.

The simple predicate in a sentence may be made up of several verbs. We call this a verb phrase. Sometimes a verb phrase is interrupted by other words. Be sure to find all the words that make up the verb phrase, but do not include any words that are not verbs. Often verb phrases are interrupted by adverbs like the following:

> not   never   ever   often   hardly   still

In the following examples, the verb phrase is underlined twice. Notice the words between the parts of the verb phrase that are not underlined.

> One warm day | <u>does</u> not <u>make</u> spring.
> He | <u>could</u> never <u>do</u> that job perfectly.
> His answer | <u>can</u> hardly <u>be</u> correct.

- The subject of a sentence may be a noun phrase.

- The subject of a sentence is never found in a prepositional phrase.

- A prepositional phrase that modifies the simple subject is part of the complete subject.

- A verb phrase may be interrupted by adverbs. Be careful not to include these words as part of the simple predicate or to miss any part of the verb phrase.

Class Practice

Read the simple subject and the simple predicate of each sentence. Then, if a prepositional phrase comes in between, read it also.

1. Flocks of geese flew overhead yesterday.
2. The tree of life was in the middle of Eden.
3. Fanny Crosby wrote many of our favorite hymns.
4. The Susquehanna River is an important river of Pennsylvania.
5. The Middle Ages ended in the 1500s.
6. The post office stood near the corner.
7. A blue jay screamed from somewhere above the trees.
8. Mrs. Brown's sister did not call today.
9. The Declaration of Independence was signed on July 4, 1776.
10. The heart of Asa was perfect all his days.

Written Exercises

Copy each sentence, and do the following things.

a. Put parentheses around any prepositional phrase in the complete subject.
b. Draw two lines under the simple predicate, and one line under the simple subject.
c. Draw a dividing line between the complete subject and the complete predicate.

1. A journey of forty days was before them.
2. The men are still working in the fields.
3. The girl in the blue dress is my sister.
4. The Red Sea stood before them.

5. King Pharaoh was bringing his army up behind them.
6. The Civil War began in 1861.
7. Yellowstone National Park is mostly in Wyoming.
8. A very swift passenger train has just gone by.
9. The lookout tower could be seen miles away.
10. John the Baptist preached in the wilderness.
11. Her sister was not helping with the doughnuts.
12. The Song of Solomon is a Bible book of poetry.
13. The picture in the book will help us with our work.
14. The answer to your question is not found in the book.
15. An angel from heaven spoke to Gideon.
16. The man of Ethiopia was reading from the Book of Isaiah.

Review Exercises

A. Copy all the words from this list that could be used as action verbs.

1. stand	5. heavy	9. shout	13. slowly
2. hunt	6. walk	10. courage	14. spin
3. teacher	7. play	11. sing	15. pray
4. memorize	8. preach	12. pay	16. sleep

B. Do the following exercises.
1. Write all the forms of *be*.
2. Write the linking verbs you learned in grade 5.
3. Write the other helping verbs in groups.
4. Write the three main steps for finding the skeleton of a sentence.

---

6. Sentences and Clauses

A *clause* is a group of words that has a skeleton. It has a subject and a verb. You can easily tell whether a group of words is a clause.

Clause: The <u>Bible</u> | <u>is</u> God's written will for man.
(has a skeleton)

Not a clause: An old <u>man</u> with a worn Bible.
(has a subject but no verb)

Since a *sentence* always contains a subject and a verb, every sentence is a clause. However, not every clause is a sentence because a clause does not always express a complete thought. Sometimes a clause is only a *fragment.* You can see that each of the following is a clause because the subject is underlined once and the verb is underlined twice. But one clause is only a fragment.

Clause that is a sentence:
> God's prophets shared His message.
> (Thought is complete.)

Clause that is a fragment:
> When the men heard God's message.
> (Thought is incomplete.)

In your writing, be especially careful to express a complete thought if you start a sentence with *when, since, because,* or a similar word. The following clauses sound much like sentences because they have subjects and verbs. But they are fragments because they fail to express complete thoughts.

> When they heard Jonah's warning.
> Since the people repented.
> Because God spared the city.

In each of these clauses, we need more information to understand the complete thought. What happened *when they heard Jonah's warning?* What took place *since the people repented?* What resulted *because God spared the city?* Can you see that each of these is a fragment?

We can make a sentence from each of these clauses by adding more words to complete the thought. The words can be placed either before or after the clause.

Sentence: The people feared when they heard Jonah's warning.
> When they heard Jonah's warning, the people feared.

Sentence: God spared Nineveh since the people repented.
> Since the people repented, God spared Nineveh.

Sentence: Jonah was angry because God spared the city.
> Because God spared the city, Jonah was angry.

Here are several more clauses that are fragments. These can be made into sentences most easily by adding words before the clauses.

Fragment: What <u>God</u> <u>would do</u>.
Sentence: <u>Jonah waited to see</u> what God would do.

Fragment: <u>That</u> <u>destroyed</u> the vine.
Sentence: <u>God sent a worm</u> that destroyed the vine.

Sometimes a clause needs a direct object to make it complete. The clause *Jane threw* does not express a complete thought. Jane threw what? A direct object must be added to make the thought complete: *Jane threw the ball.* Here are several more examples.

Fragment: I found.
Sentence: I found several Indian <u>arrowheads</u> in this field.

Fragment: Judy will bring.
Sentence: Judy will bring the <u>recipe</u>.

- Any group of words with a subject and a verb is a *clause.*

- A clause is a sentence only when it expresses a complete thought.

Class Practice

A. Say *clause* or *not a clause* for each group of words.
   1. Grandmother came.
   2. While the children were sleeping.
   3. In the evening about sunset.
   4. What did you bring?
   5. After we got there.
   6. At noon Clara and Janice.

B. Tell whether each group of words is a *sentence* or a *fragment.* If it is a fragment, tell whether it *needs a direct object* or *needs other words.*
   1. Which Mother made.
   2. Who will bring?
   3. Jonathan became ill after he was out in the rain.
   4. The sun is melting.
   5. When you come to our house next week.
   6. He cooks better than she does.

C. Add your own words to make sentences from the fragments in Part B.

Written Exercises

A. Write *clause* or *not a clause* for each group of words.
   1. Rosalie brought the cookies.
   2. In the morning at the house.
   3. Before we begin.
   4. While we were waiting for my brother.
   5. My mother and her three sisters.

B. Write *S* if the group of words is a complete sentence, and *F* if it is a fragment. If it is a fragment because it needs a direct object, also write *DO*.
   1. Because it was getting dark.
   2. While it was raining.
   3. After we have corrected our papers, we will hand them to her.
   4. This morning Ben brought.
   5. Then Brother John found.
   6. Sharon will make some cookies before we leave.
   7. Finally John found it in the bottom drawer.
   8. Where the boys were working.
   9. Before he had finished, it began to rain.
   10. Why she was crying.
   11. If the boys will help us.
   12. That grow on these bushes.
   13. Keep off the bench until the paint is dry.
   14. Always thank.
   15. Since the branch struck our car.

C. Add your own words to make sentences from eight of the fragments in Part A.

Review Exercises

Copy the part of each sentence from the *first* word of the simple subject to the *last* word of the simple predicate. If you write a prepositional phrase, put parentheses around it. [5] (Turn to the lesson number in brackets if you need help.)
   1. Jesus was born in Bethlehem.
   2. John the Baptist preached to the people about repentance.
   3. The fire from heaven burned up Elijah's offering.
   4. Ruth had followed Naomi to the land of Israel.
   5. Ruth did choose the way of God.

6. Ruth had been working hard in Boaz's field one day.
7. Brother Aden Zimmerman will speak to us on Sunday morning.
8. The desks at school were sanded.
9. Mount St. Helens erupted in 1980.
10. The volcano has erupted several times since.
11. The heat from the volcano melted much snow.
12. Floods washed away buildings, roads, and bridges.
13. Many crops were destroyed by the volcanic ash.
14. The volcano may erupt again from time to time.

7. The Four Sentence Types

Sentences are put into four classes according to how they are used. Some sentences tell something, while others ask questions. Some sentences give commands or requests. Still others express strong feeling.

In earlier grades the four types of sentences were called statements, questions, commands, and exclamations. This year you will learn their standard English names.

A *declarative sentence* declares or states a fact. It always ends with a period. Notice the fact stated by each of these sentences.

Declarative sentences: John is here now.
Jesus rose from the dead.

A declarative sentence always makes a statement that is either true or false. If it is sensible to ask whether the sentence is true or false, the sentence must be declarative. For the sentence *John is here now,* it is sensible to ask "Is this sentence true or false?" If John is here now, the sentence is true. If John is somewhere else, the sentence is false. Use this test to decide whether the following sentences are declarative.

The sunset last evening was beautiful.
Listen to the roar of that waterfall.

The first sentence above is either true or false, so it is a declarative sentence. But the second sentence tells you to do something. It is not sensible to ask "Is this sentence true or false?" So it is not a declarative sentence.

An *interrogative sentence* asks a question. It ends with a question mark. The subject may come after the verb, or it may come between the words in the verb phrase.

Interrogative sentences:

<u>Who</u> <u>wrote</u> the Book of Genesis?
<u>Are</u> the <u>children</u> ready?
<u>Will</u> the <u>boys</u> <u>paint</u> the fence?
When <u>will</u> <u>they</u> <u>begin</u>?

An *imperative sentence* gives a command or makes a request. The subject of every imperative sentence is *you*, but it is not usually stated in the sentence. An imperative sentence ends with a period.

Imperative sentences:

Sing unto the Lord a new song.
   (<u>you</u> <u>Sing</u>)
Honor thy father and thy mother.
   (<u>you</u> <u>Honor</u>)
Please bring me a glass of water.
   (<u>you</u> <u>bring</u>)

Look at the next two sentences. Both seem to give a command, do they not? But the second one is declarative because it states a fact that is either true or false.

Do your work carefully. (imperative)
You should do your work carefully. (declarative)

Sometimes a declarative, an interrogative, or an imperative sentence expresses strong feeling. It is then called an *exclamatory sentence*. An exclamatory sentence ends with an exclamation point (also called an exclamation mark).

Exclamatory sentences:

The neighbor's house is on fire!
   (states a fact)
What are we going to do!
   (asks a question)
Call the fire department!
   (gives a command)

Some exclamatory sentences have their own special form.

> What a terrible storm it was!
>> (skeleton last so that *what* comes first)

> If only Father were home!
>> (sentence that would otherwise be a fragment)

> Oh, how love I Thy law!
>> (verb before subject so that *love* is emphasized)

Learn to say and spell the name of each sentence type.

- A *declarative sentence* states a fact and ends with a period. It must be either true or false.

- An *interrogative sentence* asks a question and ends with a question mark.

- An *imperative sentence* gives a command or request and ends with a period. The subject of every imperative sentence is *you*, but it is not usually stated.

- An *exclamatory sentence* expresses strong feeling and ends with an exclamation point. Some exclamatory sentences have their own special form.

Class Practice

Tell whether each sentence is *declarative, interrogative, imperative,* or *exclamatory*. Tell what the end punctuation should be.

1. Come
2. Remember these instructions
3. You must write your name on your paper
4. Give unto the Lord the glory due His Name
5. I will praise the Lord as long as I live
6. Lead us not into temptation, but deliver us from evil
7. How sweet God's words are
8. The law of the Lord is perfect
9. The Lord by wisdom hath founded the earth
10. Where wast thou when I laid the foundations of the earth

11. When shall these things be
12. What a mighty God we serve
13. Is that so
14. Trust in the Lord with all thine heart

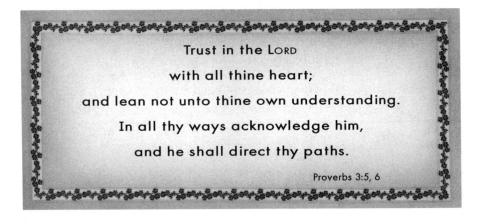

Trust in the LORD

with all thine heart;

and lean not unto thine own understanding.

In all thy ways acknowledge him,

and he shall direct thy paths.

Proverbs 3:5, 6

Written Exercises

A. Write whether each sentence is *declarative, interrogative, imperative,* or *exclamatory.* Also write the correct end punctuation. (Only three are exclamatory.)

1. Where did you learn to read so distinctly
2. The busy beavers worked on the dam
3. You must serve God with reverence
4. Samson's strength came from God's Spirit
5. What a terrible mistake he made
6. Please watch where you are going
7. Go and do thou likewise
8. A lion slew the disobedient prophet
9. David walked fearlessly toward the giant
10. Did the queen of Sheba visit Solomon
11. A small cloud arose on the horizon
12. How wicked Ahab was
13. Three brave Hebrew men refused to bow to an image
14. Was he wearing only a thin jacket
15. If only we had remembered the directions
16. Do your work correctly now

B. Describe a situation in which sentence 14 in Part A would probably be spoken as an exclamatory sentence.

Review Exercises

Write *sentence* or *fragment* to describe each group of words. If it is a fragment, write the letter of the statement that tells why it is a fragment. [1, 6] (If you need help with any review exercise, turn to the lesson numbers in brackets.)

- a. Subject is missing.
- b. Predicate is missing.
- c. Both subject and predicate are missing.
- d. Helping verb is missing.
- e. It has a subject and predicate, but thought is incomplete.
- f. Direct object is missing.

1. Sat in the shade on a comfortable chair.
2. Last week Father built a new sled for the boys.
3. Several exciting ball games.
4. Mother baked five dozen oatmeal cookies this morning.
5. In the morning before dawn.
6. When Grandfather came, we were ready.
7. Because he saw me coming.
8. In the evening Jonathan brought.
9. She carried her Bible to church.
10. Leaves falling from the trees.
11. When we finished, Father thanked.
12. Before he left, Grandfather gave us each a little book.
13. When you have finished that job.
14. Mother washing the clothes.
15. Waited a long time.
16. In the kitchen on the floor under the table.
17. Two large black cats from the neighbor's farm.
18. The children sat on the front bench.

8. Writing a Set of Directions

Think about a time when someone explained to you how to do something. Were the directions clear? Could you follow them without trouble? Did you have to ask for more explanation? We gain much help in life from the directions that others give us.

Sometimes directions are written instead of spoken. In some ways, written directions are better than oral directions because the steps are always there when you need them. You do not need to be afraid you will forget and miss a step. But written directions must be especially clear because the reader cannot ask the writer to explain something he does not understand. For that reason, you must be careful to write directions in a way that is simple to understand.

When you write a set of directions, be sure your information is correct. One inaccurate bit of information can cause the loss of valuable time, materials, or even money. One wrong measurement or ingredient in a recipe can spoil an entire dish of food. Always be sure you know how to do the thing you are trying to explain.

One of the most important things you must do to make directions clear is to tell things in the order they are to be done. Begin by making a list, step by step, of the things your reader will have to do. You might end up with a list something like this.

How to Fry an Egg

1. Get a frying pan, a pat of butter, and an egg.
2. Put pan on stove.
3. Put ½ teaspoon of butter in pan.
4. Turn burner to medium.
5. Melt butter and coat bottom of pan.
6. Break egg into pan.
7. Turn egg when clear part turns white.
8. Be careful not to break the yolk.
9. Turn off burner as soon as egg is finished.
10. Remove egg before yolk gets too hard.

Making a list of the important steps will keep you from writing mixed-up directions like this.

How to Fry an Egg

Break an egg into your frying pan. Turn the burner to medium, and place the pan on the stove. Be sure to put butter in the pan before you break the egg....

Using your list of points, write out the directions as a paragraph. Be sure to write complete sentences, not fragments. As you write, try to use sentences of different lengths. Beware of writing many short, choppy sentences. Also beware of writing just a few long sentences all strung together with *and*s. Both sets of directions below are unpleasant to read.

Sentences too long and stringy:

Get a pan, some butter, and an egg, and put the pan on the stove, and put a dab of butter into the pan. Turn the burner on medium, and then break the egg into the pan, and . . .

Sentences too short and choppy:

Get a pan, some butter, and an egg. Put the butter into the pan. Turn the burner on medium. Melt the butter. Break the egg into the pan. Let the egg sizzle a while. . . .

Your sentences should also have different beginnings. For instance, do not begin every sentence with *then* or *next*. Include other words such as *first, second, later,* and *finally.* Try to begin a few sentences with phrases like *after a while* or *in a few minutes.*

Study this example. Do the sentences have different beginnings? Do they have different lengths? Are the directions clear?

How to Fry an Egg

Get a frying pan, a pat of butter, and an egg. Put the frying pan on the stove. Put one-half teaspoon of butter into the pan, and turn the burner on medium. Stir the butter until it melts and covers the bottom of the pan. Then break the egg into the pan. After the clear part of the egg becomes white, turn the egg with a spatula. Be careful not to break the yolk. In a minute or two, turn off the burner and remove the egg before the yolk gets too hard.

When your directions are finished, read over them carefully. Is everything clear? Is everything accurate? Will the reader have any questions you did not answer? Correct any weaknesses that you find.

> • When you write directions, be sure your information is accurate. Tell things in the order they are to be done. Write in complete sentences. Use variety in sentence length and sentence beginnings.

Class Practice

Tell which one of these paragraphs gives better directions. Tell what is wrong with the poor paragraph.

Guatemalan Hot Sauce

Fry four or five bottle tomatoes in a coated pan till the tomatoes are soft. Next, fry a few hot chili peppers till they are almost black. Put the prepared tomatoes and chili peppers in a blender, and add one tablespoon coriander leaves, two small onions, and one-half teaspoon salt. Blend everything into a sauce. Try a teaspoon of the hot sauce on a plate of cooked rice. Taste only a small amount at first because it is hot! Later you can experiment with different amounts of peppers and other seasonings to suit your taste.

Guatemalan Hot Sauce

Fry four or five bottle tomatoes in a coated pan till the tomatoes are soft. Add coriander leaves, chili peppers, and onions. I think you can use garlic instead of onions if you wish. Blend the above ingredients in a blender. You must fry the chili peppers till they are black. My friend got this recipe from the natives in Guatemala. Remember to add salt, about three teaspoons. If you want it hotter, add more chili peppers. You can experiment with the amounts of other seasonings to suit your taste.

Written Exercises

A. Make a list of steps that tell how to do something. You may choose one of the following things. Be sure the steps are in the right order.
   1. How to Weave a Simple Mat
   2. How to Make a Kite
   3. How to Prepare a Garden (or Field) for Planting

4. How to Make Pancakes
5. How to Milk a Cow
6. How to Start a Lawn Mower
7. How to Clean a Paintbrush
8. How to Make Popcorn
9. How to Make Mashed Potatoes
10. How to Peel an Apple

B. Use your list from Part A to write a paragraph that gives a set of directions. Follow the instructions in the lesson, and make your paragraph clear and interesting. Write seven to twelve sentences.

Review Exercises

A. Tell which of these story beginnings is better, and why. [4]
1. Yesterday was a beautiful day. My friends and I went for a hike in the woods. We saw several unusual birds and found a clear, bubbling spring. Everyone hopped and skipped along the trail, enjoying the fresh air. Henry climbed a tall tree and said he could see our farmhouse in the distance.
2. Yesterday was a beautiful day. My friends and I went for a hike in the woods. We saw several unusual birds and found a clear, bubbling spring. The air was so clear that Henry decided to climb a tree and look around. When he was about ten feet above the ground, a branch broke and he fell to the ground. He landed on his right arm, and we all heard a muffled snap! Henry lay there groaning with pain.

B. Find the fragments in the following paragraph. Rewrite them, making complete sentences. [1]

The lion was only eight feet away! He glared at me with angry eyes. Slowly his tail moved from side to side. He looked fierce and wild. While he was crouching before me. I turned and walked to the next cage. Many interesting animals in that zoo.

9. Chapter 1 Review

Class Practice

A. Give the three steps for finding the skeleton of a sentence.

B. Answer the following questions about clauses.
1. What is a clause?
2. Is every clause a sentence?
3. What must a clause do to be a sentence?

C. Give the following verbs.
1. The forms of *be*.
2. The other helping verbs in groups.
3. The "sometimes linking verbs" that you learned in grade 5.

D. Give the answers.
1. What rules have you studied about story writing?
2. What rules should you remember when writing directions?
3. Name and describe the four sentence types.

E. Say *clause* or *not a clause* for each group of words.
1. The Grand Canyon state.
2. Here we found large areas of dry land.
3. Is mostly desert land.
4. Arizona is not completely desert land.
5. About one half of Arizona's land.
6. After the Spaniards came.

F. Tell whether each group of words is a *sentence* or a *fragment*. If it is a fragment, tell what is missing.
1. Many Indians still live in Arizona.
2. Because many people have come to Arizona.
3. The population of Arizona has increased almost fourfold since 1950.
4. My uncle once caught.
5. The cactus wren, the state bird of Arizona.
6. Have ever seen a giant cactus?
7. I drew a picture of Arizona's state flower.

G. Copy the following sentences on the chalkboard. Put parentheses around any prepositional phrase in the complete subject. Draw two lines under the simple predicate, and one line under the simple subject. Draw a dividing line between the complete subject and the complete predicate.

1. Some lakes are choked with algae.
2. It feels slimy.
3. Large quantities of algae may color a pond or lake.
4. Lake George should be cleaned up.
5. The Lake of the Ozarks was formed by a man-made dam.
6. The blue jays are plentiful here.
7. A sloth will not clean algae from his body.
8. Algae in the ocean are food for many sea creatures.

H. Tell whether each sentence is *declarative, interrogative, imperative,* or *exclamatory.* Also give the correct end punctuation.
1. Is Brazil the largest country in South America
2. Brazil is the sixth largest country in the world
3. What a large country it must be
4. Draw a map of Brazil
5. Label all the mountains and rivers
6. The Amazon River is the largest river in the world
7. Is it in Brazil
8. Part of it runs through Brazil

Written Exercises

A. Write *sentence* or *fragment* to describe each group of words. If it is a fragment, also write the letter of the statement that tells why it is a fragment.

    a. Subject is missing.
    b. Predicate is missing.
    c. Both subject and predicate are missing.
    d. Helping verb is missing.
    e. It has a subject and predicate, but thought is incomplete.
    f. Direct object is missing.

1. Arizona is sometimes called the Grand Canyon state.
2. Why didn't you bring?
3. Many Indians still live in Arizona.
4. Before Arizona became a state.
5. Most of Arizona's people.
6. The growing population.
7. People like the warm climate there.
8. Through the Grand Canyon.
9. So that we have time to hike down the mule trail.

10. The generators on Glen Canyon Dam producing large amounts of electricity.
11. Don't you think it was Noah's flood that carved out all these interesting rock formations?
12. The swirling waters may have laid down these layers of rock.
13. Could have carved out this deep canyon?
14. God showing us His greatness by the wonders of creation.

B. Copy each sentence. Put parentheses around any prepositional phrase in the complete subject. Draw two lines under the simple predicate, and one line under the simple subject. Draw a dividing line between the complete subject and the complete predicate.
1. Algae grows in oceans, lakes, ponds, and streams.
2. Microscopes must be used to see some of them.
3. Some kinds of algae are large plants with many cells.
4. Most algae are classified as plants.
5. Seaweeds are large marine algae.
6. You have never eaten algae?
7. The Japanese like a food called nori.
8. Nori is made from red algae.
9. It does taste delicious.
10. Some kinds of algae form slippery coatings on rocks.
11. A turtle may have algae on its shell.
12. The Lake of the Woods was named after the hills and forests around it.

C. Write whether each sentence is *declarative, interrogative, imperative,* or *exclamatory.* Also write the correct end punctuation.
1. Brazil has almost 175 million people
2. Is Brazil the sixth largest nation in the world
3. What a large country it is
4. Do many people live in the Amazon region
5. How thick those forests must be
6. Are many of the people Indians
7. Visit this country in South America
8. Many people in Brazil need the Word of God

―――――――――――

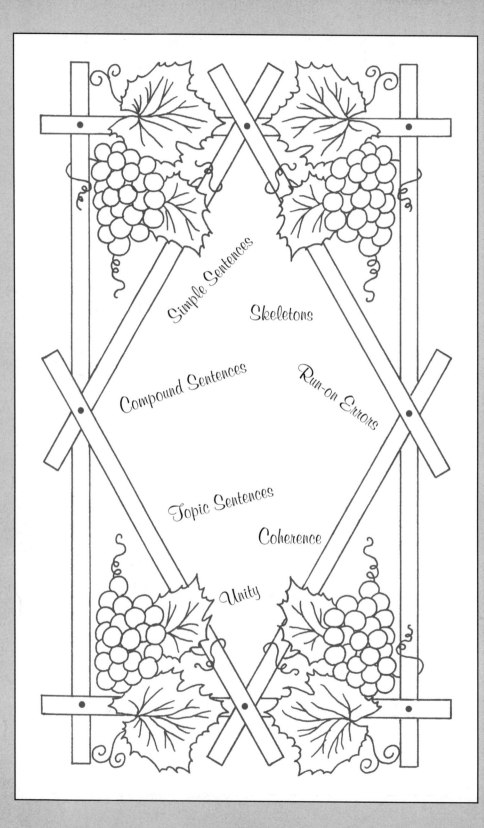

Simple Sentences

Skeletons

Compound Sentences

Run-on Errors

Topic Sentences

Coherence

Unity

Chapter Two

Working With Sentences

Understanding Paragraphs

A paragraph is a group of sentences that all deal with a single topic.

Whatsoever thy hand findeth to do, do it with thy might.

Ecclesiastes 9:10

10. Diagraming Sentence Skeletons

We often diagram a sentence to help us identify the different sentence parts. Diagraming also helps us to see clearly how the parts of the sentence work together.

The *skeleton* of a sentence is diagramed on a horizontal base line. The simple subject is put on the left half of the line, and the simple predicate is put on the right half. A vertical line separates the subject from the predicate.

$$\text{(subject)} \mid \text{(verb)}$$

Study the diagrams of the following sentence skeletons.

Crisp yellow leaves fell to the ground.

$$\text{leaves} \mid \text{fell}$$

God hears the prayers of His children.

$$\text{God} \mid \text{hears}$$

If the simple subject is a noun phrase, be sure to write the whole phrase on the base line of the diagram. This is true whether or not the noun phrase is capitalized.

Sentences with noun phrases:

Guatemala City is the largest city in Guatemala.

$$\text{Guatemala City} \mid \text{is}$$

The post office is in the center of town.

$$\text{post office} \mid \text{is}$$

Nevin L. Nissley will conduct the devotional.

$$\text{Nevin L. Nissley} \mid \text{will conduct}$$

If the simple predicate is a verb phrase, be sure to write the whole phrase on the base line of the diagram. Remember that the helping verbs you studied in Lesson 2 are always part of the verb phrase. Memorize them again if you have forgotten any.

When an adverb comes between parts of a verb phrase, do not write the adverb on the base line, since it is not part of the verb.

Sentences with verb phrases:

Karen did not see Nancy.

Karen	did see

Leon has almost finished his work.

Leon	has finished

The students are rapidly improving.

students	are improving

In many questions, part of the verb phrase comes before the simple subject and part of it comes after. Even though the verb phrase is split, the subject is placed on the left and the complete verb phrase on the right. It is helpful to reword the question as a statement before diagraming it.

Interrogative sentences:

Have you seen my brother?
    (you Have seen my brother)

you	Have seen

Do you know my father?
    (you Do know my father)

you	Do know

Is Brother Luke coming?
(Brother Luke Is coming)

Brother Luke	Is coming

Remember that *you* is understood in most commands. When diagraming such a command, write *you* in parentheses for the simple subject. If *you* is stated in the sentence, do not use parentheses.

Imperative sentences:
Rejoice evermore.

(you)	Rejoice

You start the song.

You	start

When a prepositional phrase comes between the simple subject and the simple predicate, be careful to choose the correct word for the subject. Remember, the subject of a sentence is never found in a prepositional phrase.

Sentences with prepositional phrases:
The milk in that jar is sour.

milk	is

The peaches from that tree are sweet.

peaches	are

Clever men of Gibeon deceived Joshua.

men	deceived

When you diagram sentences, be careful to keep the capital letters, but omit the punctuation marks.

- The skeleton of a sentence is diagramed on a horizontal base line. The subject is placed on the left, the predicate is placed on the right, and a vertical line is placed between them.

- If the subject or the verb is a phrase, the entire phrase is placed on the diagram.

- When the subject of a sentence is *you* understood, *you* is written in parentheses.

- The subject of a sentence is never found in a prepositional phrase.

Class Practice
Give the skeleton of each sentence, and diagram it at the chalkboard.
1. David L. Stoner has left for Ontario.
2. Many of these apples have spots on them.
3. Oh, how I love Thy law!
4. Enoch walked with God.
5. What shall I bring unto the Lord?
6. The dog could not catch the rabbit.
7. Teach me Thy way, O Lord.
8. Can a leopard change his spots?
9. The man with the cane is my grandfather.
10. Each of the children said a verse by memory.

Written Exercises
Diagram the sentence skeletons.
1. Make a joyful noise unto the Lord.
2. The Lord is my strength.
3. O give thanks unto the Lord.
4. The boys have been working hard.
5. Can your little sister ride a bicycle?
6. Brother Martin drives a black van.
7. That wren always builds her nest here.
8. I did not hear you in time.
9. Pompeii was an ancient Italian city.

10. It was completely demolished by a terrific eruption of Mount Vesuvius.
11. Mount Vesuvius erupted in A.D. 79.
12. The city was buried under heaps of ashes.
13. It was not excavated for almost 1,700 years.
14. When did the excavations begin?
15. A peasant discovered a buried wall in 1748.
16. Other men were soon digging.
17. Many of the ruins were preserved very well.
18. Houses in Pompeii had been rich and luxurious.
19. People can now visit the ruins of the city.
20. Imagine that!

Corel

Review Exercises

Write a complete sentence to answer each question. [1–6]

1. What is a noun?
2. What is a verb?
3. What is a pronoun?
4. What is a sentence?
5. What is a clause?

---

11. Compound Subjects and Predicates

A sentence may have more than one subject. Sometimes two or more nouns or pronouns are joined by a conjunction to form a *compound subject*. In the following examples, the simple subjects are underlined and the conjunctions are in boldface.

> <u>Boys</u> **and** <u>girls</u> | enjoy learning.
> <u>Paul</u> **and** <u>Barnabas</u> | were traveling in Cyprus.
> <u>You</u> **or** <u>I</u> | will have to do it.

A conjunction is a word that joins other words together. You should remember that a conjunction is one of the eight parts of speech. The three most common conjunctions are *and, but,* and *or.*

A sentence may have more than one predicate. Two or more verbs may be joined by a conjunction to form a *compound predicate*. In the following examples, the simple predicates are underlined twice and the conjunctions are in boldface.

> The deer | <u>snorted</u> **and** <u>ran</u> away.
> The missionaries | <u>preached</u> **and** <u>baptized</u> among the Gentiles.
> The dog | <u>chased</u> the rabbit **but** soon <u>lost</u> its trail.

Study the following examples to see how compound subjects and predicates are diagramed. The compound part is put on a fork, and the conjunction is put on a dotted line inside the fork.

Compound subject:

Charles and I were reading.

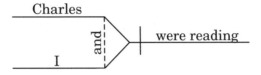

Mary, Louise, and Ruby were singing together.

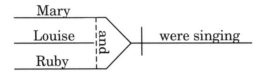

Compound predicate:

Jesus went into the temple and listened to the teachers.

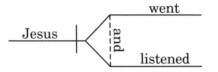

In some sentences, the two parts of a compound predicate share the same helping verb. When this happens, the helping verb is placed on the base line before the fork. This shows that the helping verb goes with both main verbs.

It was snowing or raining for several days.

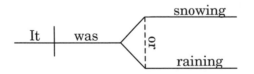

In the example above, the helping verb *was* goes with both main verbs: *snowing* and *raining*. Now notice the following sentence.

Barbara was running in the yard and fell.

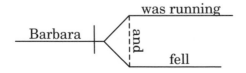

In this sentence, the helping verb goes only with the verb *running,* not with *fell.* "Barbara *was running*" is sensible, but "Barbara *was fell*" is not. Therefore, *was* is diagramed with *running.*

A sentence can have both a compound subject and a compound predicate.

Janice and her mother picked the beans and cooked them.

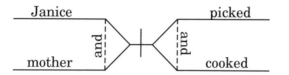

- Simple subjects joined by a conjunction form a compound subject.

- Simple predicates joined by a conjunction form a compound predicate.

- The three most common conjunctions are *and, but,* and *or.*

Class Practice

At the chalkboard, diagram the skeletons of these sentences.
1. King Agrippa talked to Paul and listened to his words.
2. The disciples fasted and prayed.
3. Rachel and Leah were sisters.
4. We have been thanking and praising God for His mercy to us.
5. Isaac and Rebekah had twin sons.
6. Paul and Barnabas were traveling and preaching.
7. The children were playing busily and forgot the time.
8. Did she draw or trace this picture?
9. She traced the outline but drew the details freehand.
10. The baby can crawl but cannot walk.
11. A robin or a wood thrush is sitting in that tree.
12. A chickadee and a junco are at the feeder.

Written Exercises

Diagram the skeletons of these sentences.
1. Ducks and geese were quacking and honking.
2. How many children came to school and studied diligently?

3. Wheat, oats, and rice are used in breakfast cereals.
4. Mars or Venus is the nearest planet to Earth.
5. Genesis and Exodus were written by Moses.
6. Jesus appeared first to Mary and was seen later by the disciples.
7. The scribes and Pharisees feared and despised Jesus.
8. The family sings and prays together every morning.
9. We can bake the fish or fry it.
10. We had found the answer but did not write it on our papers.
11. James must eat better or rest more.
12. She will not ride or walk.
13. Oranges and strawberries contain vitamin C.
14. Harold or Milton climbed the tree and rescued the kitten.
15. The goose returned, built a nest, and is now brooding the eggs.
16. A male lion measures about nine feet in length and weighs about five hundred pounds.
17. Lions and tigers usually hunt at night and sleep during the day.
18. Africa and southern Asia have lions and tigers in their forests and grasslands.
19. The Middle East and northern Africa no longer have lions.
20. In the zoo we were watching the lions and heard their roars.

Review Exercises

A. Write *declarative, interrogative, imperative,* or *exclamatory.* Also write the correct end punctuation. [7]
   1. Come and look at this beautiful bird
   2. Does a cockatoo have a beautiful song as well
   3. It greets the day with an earsplitting shriek and screams all day long
   4. You should teach it some tricks
   5. What an interesting bird it must be

B. Diagram the skeletons of the following sentences. [10]
   1. What do cockatoos eat?
   2. Please get me one for a pet.
   3. Most cockatoos can actually say a few words.
   4. The shriek of a cockatoo is very loud!

12. Simple and Compound Sentences

So far this year, you have studied only simple sentences. A *simple sentence* is made of *one* clause, having only *one skeleton.*

Mary | loved Jesus.

Mary is the subject. *Loved* is the verb. There is only one skeleton, so this is a simple sentence.

Formulas can help you to recognize simple sentences. Use letters to stand for sentence parts and a plus sign for conjunctions.

S = subject   V = verb   + = conjunction

Following is the formula for the sentence above.

S | V   = simple sentence
Mary | loved Jesus.

A sentence may have a compound subject or a compound predicate, but it is still a simple sentence. Look at these examples.

S + S | V   = simple sentence
Mary and Martha | loved Jesus.

S | V + V   = simple sentence
Mary | sat and listened to Jesus' words.

Even if a sentence has both a compound subject and a compound predicate, the sentence is still a simple sentence.

S + S | V   + V   = simple sentence
Mary and Martha | invited Jesus and served Him.

Look again at the formulas with the examples above. In each sentence, one or two subjects go with one or two verbs to form only one skeleton. This is the key to identifying a simple sentence: *one skeleton.*

A *compound sentence* is formed when *two* clauses are joined together. In a compound sentence you will always find *two skeletons,* one on each side of the conjunction. Notice the formula for a compound sentence.

S | V + S | V = compound sentence

Study these examples.

$$S \mid V \qquad\qquad + \quad S \mid V = \text{compound sentence}$$
The <u>boys</u> | <u>wanted</u> the dog, **but** <u>they</u> | <u>had</u> no money.

$$S \mid V \qquad\qquad + \quad S \mid V = \text{compound sentence}$$
<u>I</u> | <u>shall call</u> on the Lord, **and** <u>He</u> | <u>will hear</u> my prayer.

$$S \mid V \qquad + \quad S \mid V = \text{compound sentence}$$
The <u>Lord</u> | <u>is</u> high, **yet** <u>He</u> | <u>has</u> respect to the lowly.

Once again notice the formulas. Each compound sentence has two skeletons, one on each side of the conjunction.

Either of the clauses of a compound sentence could be written by itself as a simple sentence. But when they are combined into one sentence, they must be joined with both a comma and a conjunction. Some common conjunctions used to form compound sentences are *and, but, or, for, nor,* and *yet.* See how the following simple sentences are combined to make a compound sentence.

Two simple sentences:
    <u>Harold</u> | <u>saw</u> the accident. <u>He</u> | <u>told</u> his father about it.

Compound sentence:
    <u>Harold</u> | <u>saw</u> the accident, **and** <u>he</u> | <u>told</u> his father about it.

To diagram a compound sentence, diagram the two clauses side by side, with the conjunction on a dotted line between them. Here are the diagramed skeletons of the four compound sentences above.

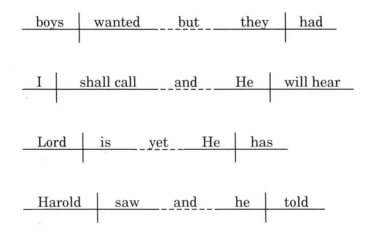

- A simple sentence has only one skeleton.

- A compound sentence has two skeletons.

- The two clauses of a compound sentence are joined by a comma and a conjunction.

- Some common conjunctions are *and, but, or, for, nor, and yet.*

- To diagram a compound sentence, diagram the two skeletons side by side, with the conjunction on a dotted line between them.

Class Practice

A. On the chalkboard, write the formula for each sentence. Tell where commas should be added.
   1. O give thanks unto the Lord for He is good.
   2. A wise man and a foolish man each built a house.
   3. Storms came and destroyed the house on the sand.
   4. Build your house on the solid rock and God will help you through all storms.

B. Diagram the skeletons of these compound sentences at the chalkboard.
   1. In Guatemala some people ride on buses, but many still walk great distances.
   2. The dirt roads are full of ruts, yet cars and trucks drive on them.
   3. The air is thin, and many visitors are not accustomed to it.
   4. You must speak Spanish, or you will need an interpreter.

C. Tell how to combine the following sentences to make compound sentences. Tell what conjunctions should be used and where commas should be placed.
   1. Frogs breathe with gills at first. They develop lungs later.
   2. Birds must eat much food. They have a high body temperature.
   3. Young amphibians live in water. Mature amphibians live on land.
   4. A bird may migrate many miles in the fall. It may stay in the same area all year.

Written Exercises

A. Combine these simple sentences to make compound sentences. Use a comma and a suitable conjunction.
1. Herons eat frogs and little fish. Ducks eat various water plants.
2. Lizards have scales. Newts have soft, moist skin.
3. Keep the windows closed. The mosquitoes will come inside.
4. Karen was bitten by many mosquitoes. Now she is miserable.

B. Diagram the skeletons of these compound sentences.
1. The sky is growing darker, and it will surely rain.
2. Aunt Rachel visited us, and we had a pleasant time.
3. He had studied the chapter carefully, yet he could not say all the verses by memory.
4. The boys took the turtle to school, and afterward they released it.

C. Write the formula for each sentence, and write whether it is simple or compound. (All commas have been omitted.)
1. Herbert and his sisters attend Meadow Valley School.
2. We had enough money but we lost it.
3. The old man and his dog were tired and hungry.
4. Jesus asked a question but the lawyer had no answer.
5. The children raked the leaves and put them on the garden.
6. Peter was put into prison and the church was praying for him.
7. We finished our work and asked the teacher for more.
8. The snow continued all night and we could not get to school the next day.
9. Science and math are Frank's favorite subjects.
10. We must hurry or we shall surely be too late.

Review Exercises

List the following items.
1. Three noun phrases
2. All the helping verbs
3. Eight common prepositions
4. Five adverbs that sometimes interrupt verb phrases

13. The Structure of a Paragraph

You have been learning about sentences. Now you will see how sentences are put together in a meaningful way. A group of sentences working together makes a paragraph.

You can easily identify a paragraph when you see one. Its first sentence is indented about half an inch from the left margin. The other sentences follow one after the other, filling up the lines. The left margin is kept straight, and the right margin is kept as straight as possible.

Why do we divide our writing into paragraphs? We make paragraphs to separate our ideas. All the sentences in one paragraph are about one main idea. When we change to another main idea, we begin another paragraph. That way the reader knows when we are moving from one thought to another. Thus, *a paragraph is a group of sentences that all deal with a single topic.*

Most paragraphs have one sentence, called the *topic sentence,* that tells what the paragraph is about. The topic sentence is usually the first sentence in the paragraph, and it clearly states what the topic is. All the other sentences develop the topic by saying more about it.

In the following paragraph, the topic sentence is underlined.

<u>The migration of salmon is one of the marvels of God's creation.</u> Every spring, large schools of ocean salmon swim upstream to lay their eggs in fresh water. Instinct guides them to exactly the same place year after year. At a rate of about two to four miles per day, the salmon swim upstream, leaping over waterfalls and clearing most obstacles in their path. They have been known to jump as high as twelve feet out of the water. When the eggs are laid, the salmon die soon afterward.

The topic of the paragraph is *the migration of salmon*. The first sentence expresses this main idea, and all the other sentences tell more about the migration of salmon.

Now look at the following paragraph. Actually, it should be two separate paragraphs because it is about two different topics. What are the two topics it develops? Where should the second paragraph begin?

> Clouds are valuable to us because they protect us from the hot sun. On a very warm summer day, you have often been glad for the shade of a friendly cumulus cloud. Like a big umbrella, it gave you a few cool minutes while you were mowing the lawn or weeding the garden. Clouds also help to keep us warm. During the day, the earth soaks up heat from the sun. But at night the ground acts as a giant radiator. The heat rays leave the earth on their way to outer space. In this way the ground loses much of its heat and can become freezing cold. But if there are clouds in the night sky, they reflect the heat rays back down to the ground to heat it again.

—Adapted from *Nature Friend*

- A *paragraph* is a group of sentences that all deal with a single topic.

- The *topic sentence* of a paragraph tells what the paragraph is about.

- The first line of a paragraph is indented, and both margins are kept as straight as possible.

Class Practice

A. Answer these questions about the paragraph below.
   1. Which is the topic sentence?
   2. How many different types of houses does the writer tell you about?

> People around the world live in different kinds of houses. In the tropical rain forest, they usually build their houses high up on poles to keep out snakes and animals. The roofs are thatched with leaves and grass. The walls are screens of palm fronds which allow cooling breezes to blow through. In the desert, many houses are made with thick mud walls and narrow windows. The walls absorb the heat of the sun and help to keep the house cool. At night, the thick walls gradually give up their heat and keep the house warm.

B. Read the three topic sentences and the rest of the paragraph below them. Decide which of the three would make the best topic sentence, and tell why the others are not suitable.
   a. The beaver has an interesting and useful tail.
   b. The tails of some animals are interesting and useful.
   c. The beaver uses his tail to steer when he swims.

   It is stiff and flat, and it looks like a paddle. It is about twelve inches long, six to seven inches wide, and three-fourths inch thick. A small part of the tail nearest the beaver's body has the same kind of fur as the body. The rest of the tail is covered with black, scaly skin and has only a few stiff hairs. The beaver uses his tail to steer when he swims. The tail is also used as a prop when the animal stands on his hind legs to eat or to cut down trees. When there is danger, a beaver slaps his tail on the water to make a loud noise and warn other beavers.

Written Exercises

A. Read the three topic sentences, and choose the best one for the rest of the paragraph below them.
   a. The orchard worker has many tasks to do in the spring.
   b. A farmer has many jobs to keep him busy.
   c. A fruit farmer has much work to do before he gets a harvest of fruit.

   In early spring he must prune his trees. He cuts out much healthy wood and any that is broken or diseased. After the trees are pruned, he must begin spraying them. Each year he sprays his trees at least four to six times. Once the fruit begins to grow, the orchard worker goes along and pulls some of the fruit from the tree. This thinning is necessary so that the remaining fruit will grow larger. Finally the worker picks the ripe fruit.

B. Use one of these topic sentences to begin a paragraph of your own. Complete the paragraph with sentences that tell more about the topic.
   1. A farmer's work may change from season to season, but he always has things to do.
   2. Pets often do strange and amusing things.
   3. Young people sometimes fail to appreciate the blessings of having an older brother or sister.

4. Earthworms, the smallest cultivators, are the farmer's friend.
5. St. Bernard dogs have helped man in important ways.
6. The habits of hummingbirds are interesting to study.

Review Exercises

Rewrite and improve the following directions. [8]

> First, bore a hole in a maple tree. Hang a bucket on a spout to catch the sap. Before that, put a metal spout into the hole you made. After you have several gallons of sap, boil the sap down until you have maple syrup. Gather the sap every day for several days. Try your delicious treat on pancakes for breakfast. It may be best to boil the sap outdoors because of the great amount of moisture that is produced.

---

14. Avoiding Run-on Errors

When two or three vehicles run into each other on the highway, the results can be terrible. Cars are ruined, property is damaged, and people are hurt or killed. Running sentences into each other has less serious results, but it is still undesirable.

How do sentences run into each other? This happens when two or more sentences are written together as one sentence without the proper punctuation between them. The result is called a *run-on error*. Can you see the sentences that have been run together in the following examples?

Run-on errors:

> A wise son maketh a glad father a foolish son is the heaviness of his mother.
>
> We have not seen her, she said she would come, is she here?

In the first example, no punctuation separates the two sentences. The second example has commas between the three sentences, but the sentences are still run together improperly.

There are three ways to correct a run-on error.

1. *End the first sentence with its proper punctuation* (period, question mark, or exclamation point), *and begin the second sentence with a capital letter.*

A wise son maketh a glad father. A foolish son is the heaviness of his mother.

We have not seen her. She said she would come. Is she here?

2. *Use a comma and a conjunction between the sentences.* This forms a compound sentence, as you studied in Lesson 12.

A wise son maketh a glad father, but a foolish son is the heaviness of his mother.

3. *Use a semicolon between the sentences.* A semicolon looks like a comma with a dot above it (;). The semicolon takes the place of both the comma and the conjunction. The following sentences are properly joined by semicolons.

It rained several inches last night; the playground is very muddy.

Laura planted the tulip bulbs; her sister watered them.

Remember the common conjunctions used in compound sentences: *and, but, or, for, nor,* and *yet.* Be sure to use both a comma and a conjunction. Simply putting commas between run-on sentences does not correct them. A comma is not strong enough to join two sentences.

Incorrect:

A wise son maketh a glad father, a foolish son is the heaviness of his mother.

Joining sentences with only a conjunction does not correct the run-on error either. Be especially careful not to write several sentences in a row, all connected with *and*s and having no commas.

Incorrect:

A wise son maketh a glad father but a foolish son is the heaviness of his mother.

We were in a hurry and Charles failed to look carefully and he almost got hit by a car.

Correct:

> A wise son maketh a glad father, but a foolish son is the heaviness of his mother.

> We were in a hurry, and Charles failed to look carefully. He almost got hit by a car.

There is one exception to this rule. When clauses are *very short* and *closely related,* they may be joined by a conjunction alone. The following sentences are written correctly even though they have no commas with the conjunctions.

> I helped him and he helped me.
> Jane wrote it and I read it.

- A *run-on error* is two or more sentences written together incorrectly.

- There are three ways to correct a run-on error.
  1. Use correct end punctuation and a capital letter.
  2. Use a comma and a conjunction.
  3. Use a semicolon.

- The words *and, but, or, for, nor,* and *yet* are common conjunctions.

- When clauses are very short and closely related, they may be joined by a conjunction alone.

Class Practice

Tell which of the following sentences have run-on errors. Tell how each one can be corrected.

1. The venders peddled their wares in the streets, the tourists bought many things.
2. In the morning there was frost on the ground by noon the weather was as warm as a summer day.
3. The food was served and it was soon gone.
4. He was short of breath he had run all the way.
5. First we picked the tea later we washed the leaves.
6. Sarah put water on the stove, she waited for it to boil.
7. Soon the water boiled, and she put the tea leaves into the kettle.
8. There may be thousands of living creatures in a drop of water we cannot see them, they are extremely small.

9. Have you ever used a microscope, you can see many tiny things in a drop of pond water you wouldn't want to drink it!

10. There are many things to learn, the world is full of the wonders of God, we should be amazed and delighted, how wise and good He is.

Written Exercises

A. Copy these sentences, and correct the run-on errors by using periods and capital letters.

1. God created the heavens and the earth He created them by His word He made them out of nothing.

2. The stars are very large and very far away, they produce enormous amounts of light and heat like the sun.

3. Toads and frogs are not reptiles but amphibians, they begin their lives in the water they are born with gills like those of fish.

4. All insects have three body parts and six legs spiders are not insects, spiders have eight legs and are different in other ways too.

5. Fish need oxygen like all animals, they have gills rather than lungs the gills allow them to breathe underwater.

B. Correct the run-on errors in these sentences by using a comma and a suitable conjunction. You do not need to copy sentences that are correct.

1. Birds are the only animals with feathers, they have no teeth.

2. The building was small and the students were few.

3. It looked like a moving haystack it was a man carrying a load of straw down the road.

4. The altitude of Guatemala City is about five thousand feet above sea level, the altitude of La Victoria is about nine thousand feet.

5. It is hot day and night on the coast of Guatemala in the mountains it is very cool at night.

6. We took the bus for the first part of our trip, we rode for several hours.

7. The clouds parted and the sun shone through.

8. Was that noise thunder was there an explosion?

C. Correct the run-on errors in these sentences by using a semicolon. Do not copy the sentences that are correct.
1. The sky was completely dark every star had disappeared.
2. Most storm clouds form high in the sky most rain starts as snow.
3. I didn't hear the telephone ring I must have been sleeping.
4. Arcturus is bright but Sirius is brighter.
5. Find the constellation Orion look for his sword and belt.
6. Learn to recognize the poison ivy plant its leaves grow in groups of three.
7. Grandfather saw a turtle in the water I saw a mud puppy by the pond.
8. Wilson A. Bentley spent over forty years examining and photographing snowflakes he never found two snowflakes that were exactly alike.

D. Correct this run-on error in all three ways taught in the lesson.

King Jehoiakim burned the roll he did not want to hear God's words.

Review Exercises

Write sentences according to the directions below.
1. Using a verb phrase containing three verbs
2. Using a form of *be*
3. Using a proper noun phrase that names a person
4. Using a proper noun phrase that names a place
5. A declarative sentence
6. An interrogative sentence
7. An imperative sentence

---

15. Word Order in Sentences

A good writer uses variety in the word order of his sentences. This makes his writing more interesting to read, and it is clearer as well.

In *normal word order,* the complete subject comes before the complete predicate.

Sentence with normal word order:
 Billowy white clouds <u>sailed across the blue sky</u>.

In *inverted word order,* the complete predicate comes before the complete subject.

Sentences with inverted word order:
 <u>Across the blue sky sailed</u> billowy white clouds.
 <u>Here come</u> the geese!

Before diagraming a sentence with inverted word order, put it in normal word order. This makes it easier to diagram.

Inverted word order:
 <u>Here come</u> the geese!

Normal word order:
 (the geese | come Here)

   geese | come

In *mixed word order,* part of the predicate comes before the subject and part of the predicate comes after. Most questions have mixed word order.

Sentences with mixed word order:
 <u>Across the blue sky</u>, billowy white clouds <u>were sailing</u>.
 <u>Then away</u> he <u>ran toward home</u>.
 <u>Where can</u> wisdom <u>be found</u>?

In the first sentence above, the adverb phrase *Across the blue sky* is part of the predicate, but it comes before the subject. In the second sentence, the adverbs *Then* and *away* modify the verb, but they come before the subject. In the question, the adverb *Where* and the helping verb *can* come before the subject.

To tell quickly if a sentence has normal, inverted, or mixed word order, find the complete subject. Then see if the complete subject comes at the beginning, at the end, or in the middle.

 Normal: <u>Two blind men</u> sat beside the road.
 Inverted: Beside the road sat <u>two blind men</u>.
 Mixed: Beside the road <u>two blind men</u> sat.

Compare the following two paragraphs. They both give the same information, but the second paragraph is much more interesting because it has good sentence variety.

Without sentence variety:

Lightning is interesting to study. Lightning strikes somewhere on the earth about one hundred times per second. It strikes the Empire State Building many times each year, but it is conducted harmlessly to the ground by its steel structure. Lightning travels about twenty thousand miles per second. A bolt of lightning may be five times hotter than the surface of the sun. A single stroke of lightning may have fifteen million volts.

With sentence variety:

What do you know about lightning? Did you know that lightning strikes somewhere on earth about one hundred times every second? It strikes the Empire State Building many times each year, but it is conducted harmlessly to the ground by the steel structure. Down streaks the lightning, traveling about twenty thousand miles per second! A single bolt of lightning may be five times hotter than the surface of the sun, and it may have fifteen million volts.

- In a sentence with normal word order, the complete subject comes before the complete predicate.

- In a sentence with inverted word order, the complete predicate comes before the complete subject.

- In a sentence with mixed word order, part of the predicate comes before the subject and part of the predicate comes after. Most questions have mixed word order.

Class Practice

A. Tell whether the word order in these sentences is *inverted* or *mixed*. Read them in normal word order. Diagram the sentence skeletons at the chalkboard.
   1. Across the stream the boys could see the excited steers.
   2. Into the narrow crack slipped the startled beetles.
   3. With his hammer, Father carefully pulled each nail.

4. In the window hung a small sign.
5. Can you see the highway from the roof?
6. Down poured the rain.
7. Kindly and tenderly Jesus spoke to the children.
8. Faithful and true are all His sayings.

B. Read the following sentences, changing them to mixed word order. Also change number 6 to inverted order.

> **Example:** The water rose rapidly after the storm.
> **Answer:** After the storm, the water rose rapidly.

1. We will study mammals tomorrow.
2. A huge black cat was peering into the window.
3. We shall search again in the morning.
4. Jesus answered the man's question with authority and clarity.
5. The rich young ruler walked sadly away.
6. A bitter wind blew across the bare fields.

Written Exercises

A. Write *normal, inverted,* or *mixed* to tell in what order each sentence is written. Diagram the skeleton of each sentence.
1. Across the river we could see the blaze.
2. Here come the boys.
3. The turtle struggled clumsily up the steep bank.
4. Was the lion in that cave?
5. Around the high walls of Jericho the Israelites marched.
6. In his tent door sat Abraham.
7. Sarah made cakes on the hearth.
8. At the door stood some visitors.

B. Rewrite these sentences, changing their word order. Write *I* or *M* to tell whether your sentence has inverted or mixed word order.
1. The hikers found a tiny stone hut yesterday.
2. I cannot see without this flashlight.
3. The deer's tails went up.
4. They ran away then.
5. The wind blew with great force.
6. An ancient building stood near the top of the hill.
7. I will trust Thee forever.

C. All the sentences in this paragraph are in normal word order. Rewrite the paragraph, changing at least three sentences to inverted or mixed word order.

Mother told Philip to bring some jars from the basement one day. He hurried to the steep, narrow stairs and started down. He found himself at the bottom about one second later. He had slid down the stairs on his back, banging his elbows on every step! Philip did not break any bones, but his elbows were very sore. He will not be in such a hurry after this.

Review Exercises

Read each group of words. If it is a complete sentence, write *declarative, interrogative, imperative,* or *exclamatory,* and write the correct end punctuation. If it is not a complete sentence, write *fragment.* [1, 7]

1. Did you ever wish you were as free as a bird
2. Do birds have chores to do
3. Yes, indeed, they do
4. They must build nests
5. Go and watch a pair of birds feeding their young
6. Cleaning, building, repairing, and many other jobs
7. What a blessing it is if children have regular chores to do
8. Prepared for a life of useful service

---

16. Unity and Coherence in a Paragraph

A paragraph is a group of sentences that develops a single topic. The topic sentence, usually the first sentence in the paragraph, gives a clear statement of what the topic is. All the other sentences support the topic sentence and say more about the topic.

When all the sentences in a paragraph tell about the same topic, the paragraph has *unity.* All the ideas fit together as one unit. But if a paragraph includes sentences that are about different topics, it no longer sticks to one main idea and its unity is broken. This makes the writing hard to understand. Imagine the reader's confusion if someone wrote a paragraph like this one.

> Our house is very large. It has fourteen rooms in all. Five of them are bedrooms. Three years ago we repaired our front porch. We have a large basement where we can play games and store our canned food. Even the attic has lots of room for storage. The kitchen is painted green and the family room is blue. This spring Father replaced several windows. We have a green bathroom. Even though our house is large, we like it because it is warm and cozy in the winter.

The topic sentence says, "Our house is very large." The next two sentences are about that topic, but the fourth sentence talks about repairing the front porch. That has nothing to do with having a large house! The next two sentences again show that the house is large because it has extra room in the attic and in the basement. But then the paragraph talks about a green kitchen, a blue family room, and replacing windows. If the writer wants to tell the reader about those other things, he may do so in other paragraphs. But he must not put these unrelated ideas into a paragraph about the size of his house.

Now find one sentence that should be taken out of the following paragraph because it spoils the unity.

> The nest building of the friendly, fluttering barn swallow has excited stable boys for thousands of years. These swooping birds bring pellets of dark, wet mud and skillfully trowel them onto the lighter-colored masonry that has dried from the day before. Who taught these aerial acrobats to choose a beam high above the cats and cattle of the barn, and to plaster their mud-and-straw nest securely to it? Cats do prowl in barns, and they would think it a feast to eat barn swallows, young or old! The reinforced stucco dwelling is completed in less than a week. Then the birds cushion the nest with soft grass and feathers and lay their five perfect eggs in it. Soon it is the home of their noisy, demanding, ever-hungry babies.
>
> —Adapted from *Nature Friend*

The sentence about cats prowling in barns does not belong in this paragraph. It does not tell about the nest building of barn swallows.

Coherence means "holding together." A coherent paragraph is one in which all the details fit together well so that the reader does not get lost or confused. There are at least three ways to make your paragraphs "hold together." You will study one way in this lesson and two more ways in the next lesson.

Give details in the order of time. Whenever you write about something that happened, tell things in the order they took place. If the order is mixed up, you might still know what you mean—but think of your poor reader! Make it easy for him. Show what was done *first,* what came *next,* what happened *after that,* and so on until everything is described.

The following two examples show how important it is to tell things in the order of time.

Paragraph with details in confusing order:

Jesus sent two disciples to bring a certain colt on which no man had ever sat. They found the colt, brought it to Jesus, and cast their garments on it. As the disciples untied it, the owners of the colt asked what they were doing. The disciples explained as Jesus had commanded them. They had found the colt tied by a door. The owners willingly let the disciples take it. So into Jerusalem went Jesus, riding on the colt.

Paragraph with details in correct order of time:

Jesus sent two disciples to bring a certain colt on which no man had ever sat. They found the colt tied by a door. As the disciples untied it, the owners of the colt asked what they were doing. The disciples explained as Jesus had commanded them. The owners willingly let the disciples take the colt. They brought it to Jesus and cast their garments on it. So into Jerusalem went Jesus, riding on the colt.

- A paragraph has unity when all the sentences tell about the topic given by the topic sentence.

- A paragraph has coherence when the sentences fit together in an orderly, sensible way.

- One way to make a paragraph coherent is to give details in the order of time.

Class Practice

A. Tell which sentences spoil the unity of this paragraph.

The Hittites were a nation in Asia Minor as early as 2000 B.C. But they disappeared from history, and in time even their name was forgotten. The Old Testament speaks of the Hittites in several different places. They are mentioned along with the Canaanites, Hivites, and Jebusites. Unbelievers laughed and said the Hittites had never existed. But in 1871 someone discovered a buried city which proved that there had indeed been a Hittite nation. People have also found an inscription that mentions Ahab, king of Israel. Later findings gave even more evidence of the ancient Hittites. These discoveries have helped to confirm that God's Word is perfectly true.

B. Tell which sentence below is the topic sentence. Tell in what order the other sentences should be written according to the order of time.
1. So he asked to buy the cave of Machpelah, which belonged to Ephron.
2. Abraham paid the price that Ephron quoted.
3. Abraham had dealings with a Hittite named Ephron.
4. At first Ephron offered to give the cave to Abraham, but later he said it was worth four hundred shekels of silver.
5. Then a record was made, clearly stating that the cave, the field, and the trees in the field were now Abraham's property.
6. When Sarah died, Abraham needed a burial place for her.

Written Exercises

A. Write the sentences that spoil the unity of this paragraph.

The Roman Empire helped to prepare the world for Christ's coming. Under the Romans, almost half of the known world at that time was united peacefully. America, of course, was unknown in those days. The Romans built many roads through the empire, which were a great help in spreading the Gospel. Most people in the Roman Empire understood Greek, so the first missionaries could preach in many different cities without having to learn new languages. The Greek language had been introduced by the Greeks, who ruled the world before the Romans. The Romans were no longer satisfied with their pagan gods, and this helped prepare them to hear the Gospel. Truly, God was directing the events of history according to His plan.

B. Use these sentences to write a paragraph in the proper form. Find the topic sentence, and write it first. Then write the other sentences in the correct order.
1. Next, catch the dog!
2. Washing a dog is not hard if you do it right.
3. Then dry him with a clean, dry towel.
4. Let him shake himself and run free again.
5. Put him into the water, and hold him tightly as you soap and scrub him.
6. Then get your other supplies.
7. First, get a tub the right size and put warm water into it.

---

17. More About Coherence

You have learned that a paragraph has *unity* when all the sentences tell about a single topic. It has *coherence* when the sentences "hold together" in an orderly, sensible way. You know that one way to make paragraphs coherent is to give details in the order of time. Now you are ready to learn two more ways of gaining coherence in paragraphs.

Give details in the order of importance or interest. When details are arranged in this way, they are usually given from the least important or interesting to the most important or interesting. This allows the writer to put the strongest point last, where the reader will be most likely to remember it. The following paragraph is written in this kind of order.

Details arranged from least important to most important:

There are several good reasons for learning a language besides English. One reason is to learn how languages compare with each other, and to discover new and interesting ways of saying things. Every language has its own peculiar expressions, and they cannot always be translated into English. A second reason is so that you can communicate with people who do not know English. Above all, knowing a second language is important for sharing the Gospel with people who speak that language.

A paragraph may also give details from the most important or interesting to the least important or interesting. But this is not as good, because it gives less emphasis to the strongest point. Compare the following paragraph with the previous sample.

Details arranged from most important to least important:
There are several good reasons for learning a language besides English. Most important, knowing a second language makes it possible to share the Gospel with people who speak that language. A second reason is so that you can communicate with people who do not know English. It is also valuable to learn how languages compare with each other, and to discover new and interesting ways of saying things. Every language has its own peculiar expressions, and they cannot always be translated into English.

Use transitional words. These are words or phrases that show how sentences are related to each other. They act as signals to tell the reader what direction the next sentence will go. Various transitional words are used to show various kinds of relationships. Some of them are listed below.

Time: first, second, next, then, finally
The potter dropped a lump of clay on the center of the wheel. Then he began molding it into the exact shape he wanted.

Addition: also, another, besides, again, further, moreover
Saul had offered a sacrifice in violation of God's law. Moreover, he had not destroyed the Amalekites as God commanded, and he had sought advice from a witch.

Contrast: but, yet, however, still, nevertheless
Ten spies said it was impossible to conquer Canaan. Two spies, however, declared that Israel was well able to take the land.

Example: for example, for instance, to illustrate
Some mammals live in the ocean, but they still breathe air. The whale, for example, must come to the surface to breathe, or it will drown.

Result: therefore, thus, so, consequently, accordingly
Christ has risen from the dead. Therefore, we have the hope that all Christians who die will rise to meet Him someday.

Notice the transitional words in the following paragraph. They help you to understand how the sentences fit together.

> Rebekah had a plan to help Jacob receive the blessing instead of Esau. She had heard Isaac telling Esau to take his weapons and hunt venison. <u>Then</u> Esau had left with his quiver and bow. Rebekah quickly commanded Jacob to fetch two kids from the flock. <u>So</u> Jacob went to bring the kids. Rebekah prepared the meat, and Jacob took it in to Isaac. <u>But</u> <u>first</u> Isaac tried to make sure that this was really Esau. <u>Finally</u> he was convinced, and he gave Jacob the blessing. When he had just finished, <u>however</u>, Esau came in from hunting. He was bitterly disappointed that he had lost the blessing. Rebekah's scheme had worked.

- Paragraph coherence can be gained by arranging details in the order of importance or interest.
- Paragraph coherence can be gained by using transitional words.

Class Practice

A. Tell which words are transitional words in the following paragraph.

> One day in 1569, a thief catcher was pursuing an Anabaptist whose name was Dirk Willems. Dirk fled over some thin ice and got across at considerable danger. Then the thief catcher tried to follow him, but he broke through the ice. Dirk could easily have escaped to safety. He realized, however, that his enemy's life was in danger. So he turned back and helped the thief catcher to get out. For this reason the thief catcher wanted to let him go. Nevertheless, the town ruler insisted that he arrest Dirk as he had promised to do. In spite of Dirk's great kindness to his enemy, this noble man was burned at the stake because of the hatred of a wicked ruler.

B. Tell whether the following sentences should be arranged in the *order of time* or the *order of importance*. Then tell in what order they should be written to make a coherent paragraph.

Topic sentence:
Always do your school homework in an orderly way, and you will have little trouble being prepared for class.

1. If there is time, you may study outside information from reference books for extra interest.
2. Then, before your mind is too tired, study any lessons that take extra concentration.
3. Last of all, clean up your work area, sharpen your pencils for the next day, and arrange your books.
4. After that, you can do the less demanding studies, such as reading and art.
5. First, make sure you have finished all the assignments that are due the next morning.

Written Exercises

A. Write the four transitional words used in the following paragraph.

The *Martyrs Mirror* is a very worthwhile book. It contains many true stories of Christians who were tortured and killed for their faith. Another feature is the pictures of many who were martyred. The book also contains numerous letters written by suffering Christians in prison. Moreover, it has a list of all the Anabaptists who suffered persecution or martyrdom from 1525 to 1660. Finally, the *Martyrs Mirror* has several confessions of faith written by Christians of various times.

B. Use the following sentences to write a paragraph in proper form, with unity and coherence. Leave out the sentence that does not belong, and write the rest of the sentences in a logical order.
   1. Put water into your pan, and light a candle.
   2. Begin by folding a piece of paper in the shape of a small square pan.
   3. Hold the pan in the flame.
   4. Did you know that you can boil water in a paper pan?
   5. Staple the corners so that water will not leak out of it.
   6. The water will get hot enough to boil, but it will keep the paper from getting hot enough to burn.
   7. A paper pan would not work very well for cooking food.
   8. Then use string to make a handle for holding the pan over a flame.

Review Exercises

Write *normal, inverted,* or *mixed* to tell in what order each sentence is written. Diagram the skeleton of each sentence. [15]
   1. That bird looks like a catbird.
   2. The mockingbird is the best imitator of all birds.
   3. On top of the pole the mockingbird danced and sang.
   4. On a nest only a foot above the ground sat the mockingbird.
   5. Some mockingbirds have imitated up to thirty bird songs in ten minutes.
   6. In the nest were six eggs.
   7. During the day and often at night he sings.
   8. He can imitate the bark of a dog, the meow of a cat, the squeak of a dry wheel, or the whistle of a policeman!

Challenge Exercises

Write a paragraph of your own, using a variety of sentence types: declarative, interrogative, imperative, and exclamatory. Vary the word order of your sentences: normal word order, inverted word order, and mixed word order. You may get ideas from the following topics.

1. A bird built a nest in the wren house I made.
2. In winter, you can attract a wide variety of birds to a feeder if you follow these simple steps.
3. I learned many things from my pet raccoon (or another pet) last summer.
4. There are many things to be thankful for on a rainy day.
5. The camel is an interesting creature.

---

18. Chapter 2 Review

Class Practice

A. Give six common conjunctions.

B. Diagram the sentence skeletons at the chalkboard.
1. Did you hear the crickets?
2. Crickets rub one wing over the other.
3. Listen to the beautiful night chorus.
4. How cheerful is a cricket's song!
5. Most kinds of crickets can hear.
6. Rose and Joan had swept and mopped the kitchen floor.
7. Martha was washing the dishes, broke a glass, and cut her finger.
8. Lightly and gracefully fluttered the butterfly.

C. Tell how to combine the following sentences to make compound sentences. Tell what conjunctions should be used and where commas should be placed.
1. I wanted the book. I did not have enough money.
2. The rain was pouring down. We got soaking wet.
3. Janet was reading. Carol was sewing.
4. Father went with us. We were too young to go alone.
5. They had to work. They would have no food.

D. On the chalkboard, write the formula for each sentence. Tell whether each sentence is *simple* or *compound*. Tell where commas should be added.

1. The snapping turtle dug a hole in the bank and laid thirty eggs.
2. A common snapping turtle may weigh twenty to thirty pounds but some giant snappers weigh sixty pounds.
3. The common snapper and the Florida snapper closely resemble each other.
4. An alligator snapper may weigh over two hundred pounds.
5. A snapping turtle depends on its strong jaws for defense for it cannot retreat into its shell.

E. Tell whether each sentence is *correct* or has a *run-on error.* Tell how to correct each run-on error.

1. We cut the sheep's wool, it was too thick for summer.
2. Mothers give their children warm winter coats God gives the sheep warm fleece for the winter.
3. The snowshoe rabbit has a brown coat in the summer, but in winter its fur becomes white.
4. Some kinds of weasels change their colors they are dark in summer and white in winter a white weasel is called an ermine.

F. Tell whether each sentence has *normal, inverted,* or *mixed* word order. If a sentence has normal word order, change it to mixed order. If it has inverted or mixed word order, change it to normal order.

1. Across the field a fox ran swiftly.
2. In the den were seven fox pups.
3. Through the woods rang the baying of the hounds.
4. Carelessly the man walked in front of the den.
5. The fox moved her pups away on the same day.
6. She must hide her pups in a safer place.
7. All through the season, the fox must hunt food for the pups.
8. Many forest animals do their hunting at night.

G. Read the following paragraph, and decide which of the three suggestions would make the best topic sentence. Tell what is wrong with the other two.

a. Before 1850, women used plants from the gardens and woods to make dye for cloth.

b. Before 1850, women used red sumac berries from the woods to make dye for cloth.

c. Before 1850, women used plants from the gardens and woods to do many household jobs.

Yellow goldenrod flowers were used to make yellow dye. Carrots also made a nice yellow. Spinach produced a green color, and beets worked fine for rose. Red sumac berries turned the cloth red, while the leaves made a fine black. If a woman needed purple cloth, she dug up the roots of dandelions. Dye was not available from stores in those days, so the people found ways to make it themselves.

H. Tell which sentences do not belong in the following paragraph.

The fruit of the apple tree gives us many delicious things. Imagine salad and some other foods without vinegar! Think of a cold drink of apple cider on a hot summer day! Try an apple in your lunch with peanut butter in the hole where you took out the core. Peanut butter icing on chocolate cake is good in your lunch too. Put apple butter on a piece of homemade bread. Doesn't the thought of apple pie and apple dumplings make your mouth water? And what would a baby do without applesauce! Of course, other kinds of baby food are also important. We know the apple is one more good thing God made for us to use right and enjoy.

I. Tell which sentence is the topic sentence. Tell in what order the other sentences should be written.

1. She hung the cloth out to dry, and finally her long, hard job was finished.

2. The next day she boiled the plant material slowly for one hour. Next, she strained the mixture to remove all the plant material.

3. Dyeing cloth in pioneer days was hard work.

4. Then she had to chop up the plant parts and soak them in water overnight.

5. First, the woman had to gather the leaves, berries, or roots that made the color of dye she wanted.

6. She added alum to prevent fading. Then she put some dampened fabric into the dye and simmered it slowly until the fabric was the shade she wanted.

J. Choose the topic sentence. Then tell in what order the sentences should be written, according to order of interest or importance.
   1. At other times, they take an accident victim to the hospital to be treated for shock, even though he is not seriously hurt.
   2. Ambulances are used for various reasons to carry sick or injured people.
   3. Then there are the helicopter ambulances, which rush a severely injured person to a hospital where specialists work on him immediately to save his life.
   4. Sometimes they simply transport a sick person from one place to another.
   5. An ambulance may rush a person to the hospital when he is critically ill, such as when he just had a heart attack.

K. Find the transitional words in this paragraph.

   Parrots are popular as pets. They are easy to tame, and they can learn to talk. Parrots can also imitate other sounds. For example, they can whistle tunes, sing songs, laugh, and cry. They can even mimic the sound of a squeaky hinge! However, parrots may carry a disease that can affect humans. For this reason all parrots must be examined by a health official before being shipped to the United States.

Written Exercises

A. Diagram the sentence skeletons.
   1. Some people in Asia keep crickets as pets.
   2. Rich people keep their crickets in tiny gold cages and carry them around with them.
   3. Their "ears" are located on their front legs.
   4. Count the number of chirps in a minute.
   5. Add forty to the number, divide by four, and then add fifty.
   6. Now you can tell the temperature in degrees Fahrenheit.
   7. Grant Marshall did have a pet cricket.
   8. Bees, ants, and crickets are insects.
   9. In the fall, crickets sometimes move into homes, hide somewhere, and sing cheerfully all night long.
   10. The aardvark is an interesting animal.
   11. Dutch settlers in Africa named it in the 1600s.
   12. Does its name mean "earth pig"?
   13. It has a snout like that of a pig, but it does not resemble a pig in other ways.

14. The aardvark is not fierce, but it can slash with its claws.

15. With its sharp claws, the aardvark slashes open ant and termite nests, and with its eighteen-inch sticky tongue, it licks them up.

16. Swiftly and silently flew the migrating birds.

B. Combine these simple sentences to make compound sentences by using a comma and a suitable conjunction.

1. Most parrots build nests in the holes of trees. Some dig burrows in the ground.

2. One of the largest parrots is the yellow-headed amazon. One of the smallest is the white-fronted amazon.

3. The yellow-headed amazon is fifteen inches long. The white-fronted amazon is only ten inches long.

4. I heard a boy whistle. Maybe it was the parrot.

C. Write the formula for each sentence, and write whether it is *simple* or *compound*. Also write the words that should have commas after them, and add the missing commas.

1. The picky parrot tasted his food and then would not eat it.

2. The chickadees and woodpeckers stopped at the suet and nibbled little pieces.

3. Downy woodpeckers eat only the suet but the chickadees and nuthatches eat the suet and seeds.

4. The lovely purple finches eat hungrily at the feeder.

5. Mother put the seeds into the feeder and Brian watched the birds come.

6. Cardinals, purple finches, and evening grosbeaks have heavy beaks and they can easily crack seeds with them.

D. Correct the run-on errors in the following sentences by using periods and capital letters.

1. Michigan is the only state that touches four of the five Great Lakes Michigan has eleven thousand lakes it is the only state that is divided into two parts.

2. Crater Lake in Oregon is the deepest lake in the United States it is 1,982 feet deep and is at the top of an inactive volcano.

3. New York City is the largest city in the United States it is the largest, busiest port in the nation people come from all over the world to see it.

E. Correct the run-on errors in these sentences by using a comma and a suitable conjunction.
   1. New Jersey is the fifth smallest state in the United States it has the largest number of people per square mile.
   2. The Erie Canal was built from Lake Erie to the Hudson River it was opened in 1825.
   3. Mules pulled barges in the early days of canals today tugboats pull large ships.

F. Correct the run-on error in each sentence by using a semicolon.
   1. Maine is the farthest east of all the states people in Maine can see the sun rise before anyone else in the United States.
   2. The Pilgrims landed at Plymouth, Massachusetts, in 1620 they held their first Thanksgiving feast in 1621.
   3. John Adams was the second president of the United States his son John Quincy Adams was the sixth president of the United States.

G. Write *normal, inverted,* or *mixed* to tell in what order each sentence is written.
   1. Early settlers in the Midwest built their houses of sod.
   2. On the Great Plains grew much grass but few trees.
   3. Since that time, people have planted many trees there.
   4. Which trees grow best on the Great Plains?
   5. Today many aspens, pines, and oaks grow in the Midwest.

H. Write the sentences that do not belong in this paragraph.

Big cities that grew up overnight in the West became small villages almost as quickly. One example is Virginia City in the dry state of Nevada. In 1859 someone discovered the Comstock Lode in Nevada, which had great amounts of gold and silver mixed together. Thousands of people rushed to Nevada, and Virginia City grew up overnight. There is also a state called Virginia. More than 300 million dollars' worth of gold and silver was taken out. But soon most of the treasure was gone, people drifted away, and Virginia City became a village. Gold had been found in nearby California about ten years earlier.

I. Write the numbers of the following sentences in the correct order to make a good paragraph. Begin with the topic sentence, which lists farm products in the order of importance. Then put the other sentence numbers in that order.

1. Millions of beef cattle are raised on huge ranches in the West.
2. The wheat-growing region extends across the Great Plains.
3. The most important farm products of the United States, in order of value, are beef cattle, milk, corn, soybeans, hogs, wheat, and cotton.
4. Almost all the country's cotton is raised in the South, the Southwest, and the state of California.
5. The nation's corn, soybeans, and hogs are produced in the Midwestern states.
6. Most of the milk is produced in the dairy belt, which extends from Minnesota to New York.

J. Write these sentences in paragraph form. Put the sentences in the correct order, beginning with the topic sentence. Add the following transitional words at suitable places: *First, Then, Finally.*

1. Keep watering it once or twice a week for a while so that it continues to do well.
2. Find a good place for it and plant it there.
3. You may want to try planting a seedling where you can enjoy watching it grow.
4. Be sure to water your seedling so that it gets a good start.
5. Find a seedling you like in a flower bed, along a fence, or in some other place that doesn't get mowed.

Details

Examples

Comparisons

Concrete

Abstract

Common

Proper

Collective

Possessive

Chapter Three

Working With Nouns

Developing Paragraphs

A
noun is a word
that names a person, place,
thing, or idea.

And whatsoever Adam called
every living creature, that was the name thereof.

Genesis 2:19

19. Recognizing Nouns

We call the things around us by their names. These names are *nouns*. *David, Chicago,* and *highway* are nouns that name a person, a place, and a thing. *Meditation, honesty,* and *illness* are nouns that name things we cannot see, but we know they exist.

A noun is a word that names a person, place, thing, or idea. The nouns in the following sentences are underlined.

> The <u>stranger</u> from the <u>city</u> bought <u>carrots</u> and <u>beans</u> from the <u>children</u> at the <u>booth</u>.
>
> The <u>harvest</u> of <u>soybeans</u> in <u>Indiana</u> and <u>Illinois</u> exceeded the <u>expectation</u> of the <u>farmers</u>.

Nouns may be concrete or abstract. A *concrete noun* is the name of something you can see or touch. It names a person, place, or thing. The names for all the objects in the world around you are concrete nouns.

Concrete nouns:

ship	hill	paper	tomato
tree	house	school	pupil

An *abstract noun* is the name of something you cannot see or touch. It names a quality, a condition, or an idea—a "thing" that has no substance. Most ideas are as real as something you can hold in your hand, even though you cannot see or touch them.

Abstract nouns:

love	memory	time	condition
concern	kindness	beauty	gravity

What are some helps for recognizing nouns? Most concrete nouns are easy to recognize because they name persons or objects. Many abstract nouns can be recognized by certain suffixes, like *-ness, -ion, -ity,* or *-ment*. In each of the following pairs, the second word is a noun made by adding one of these suffixes.

holy—holiness	pure—purity
promote—promotion	require—requirement

Spelling changes are sometimes made when noun suffixes are added. When *holy* is changed to *holiness,* the final *y* is changed to *i.* When *promote* is changed to *promotion,* the final *e* is dropped. Use a dictionary whenever you are not sure of the correct spelling.

Another help in recognizing nouns is to look for the words *a, an,* and *the.* These are called noun markers or articles. Noun markers are especially helpful in recognizing abstract nouns. In the following list, you can tell that the underlined words are nouns because it sounds right to use noun markers with them.

a <u>determination</u>   an <u>appointment</u>
the <u>friendliness</u>   the <u>dignity</u>

In the next list, the underlined words are not nouns, because they do not name objects or ideas. It does not sound right to use noun markers with them.

a <u>determine</u>   an <u>appoint</u>
the <u>friendly</u>   the <u>dignify</u>

The four *genders* of nouns are *masculine, feminine, neuter,* and *common.* Study the following definitions and examples.

Nouns of *masculine* gender refer to men and boys.

son	uncle	king	steward

Nouns of *feminine* gender refer to women and girls.

daughter	aunt	queen	stewardess

Nouns of *neuter* gender are neither masculine nor feminine.

house	chair	tree	strength

Nouns of *common* gender can be masculine, feminine, or both.

baby	child	friend	people

If you are not sure about the gender of a noun, think of a pronoun to replace it. *He* replaces masculine nouns, *she* replaces feminine nouns, and *it* replaces neuter nouns. If a noun could be replaced by either *he* or *she,* or if it names a mixed group of people, it is of common gender.

- A noun is the name of a person, place, thing, or idea.

- A concrete noun names a person, place, or thing that can be seen or touched. An abstract noun names a quality, a condition, or an idea that has no substance.

- The four genders of nouns are masculine, feminine, neuter, and common.

Class Practice

A. Read each word, and tell whether it could be used as a noun.

1. cherry	7. ask	12. school
2. James	8. warm	13. December
3. for	9. early	14. am
4. hope	10. team	15. Thompson's Market
5. hatred	11. chose	16. and
6. Dr. Jones		

B. Change each word to a noun by adding the suffix -ness, -ion, -ity, or -ment. Write the new words on the chalkboard.

1. scarce	4. require	7. complete
2. polite	5. settle	8. great
3. real	6. agree	9. relate

C. Tell which words are nouns in the following paragraph. Give the gender of each noun you find.

Many of our favorite hymns were written by Fanny Crosby. Although blinded by improper treatment of her eyes at the age of six weeks, she was always a happy child. Her cheerfulness was an inspiration to many. This woman had such a remarkable memory that at a young age she memorized the first five books of the Old Testament and the first four books of the New Testament. Poetry came to her mind quickly, and it is said that she wrote "Safe in the Arms of Jesus" in thirty minutes. Truly our lives are richer because of the hymns she contributed to mankind.

D. Give nouns as described below.
1. Three different places. **Example:** park
2. Three parts of plants. **Example:** stem
3. Three organs of the human body. **Example:** heart

Written Exercises

A. Copy only the words that could be used as nouns.

1. oh	6. sing	11. trouble	16. bless
2. desk	7. load	12. after	17. cheer
3. bill	8. hear	13. fail	18. nurse
4. shook	9. love	14. church	19. later
5. tree	10. skillful	15. joy	20. Akron

B. Make a noun from each word by adding *-ness, -ion, -ity,* or *-ment.*

1. correct	4. create	7. awful
2. complex	5. final	8. excite
3. replace	6. develop	9. careful

C. Copy all the nouns. After each one, write *M, F, N,* or *C* to tell whether its gender is masculine, feminine, neuter, or common.
   1. Cornelius was a centurion who lived at Caesarea.
   2. He was a soldier in the army of Rome.
   3. He was a devout man whose whole family feared God, and he gave much charity to his neighbors.
   4. Cornelius was in prayer one day.
   5. He saw a vision of an angel, who called his name.
   6. The angel said, "Your prayers and your charity have ascended as a memorial before God."

D. Write your own groups of nouns as described below.
   1. Four kinds of buildings. **Example:** store
   2. Four kinds of workers. **Example:** carpenter
   3. Four things that have to do with the weather. **Example:** snow
   4. Four things that have to do with church life. **Example:** hymnal

E. Write sentences with nouns that name the following items. Underline all the nouns in your sentences.
   1. A person
   2. A place
   3. A thing
   4. An idea

Review Exercises

A. Correct the run-on errors in this paragraph by using periods and capital letters. [14]

A fawn weighs three to six pounds when it is born usually there are twins or triplets the mother gives her babies rich and creamy milk without it they could not stay healthy.

B. Correct the run-on errors in these sentences by using a comma and a suitable conjunction. [14]
   1. God has given the fawn a protective coloration a fawn has no body scent for the first few days of its life.
   2. You might find a fawn seemingly all alone the mother is usually watching from a hiding place nearby.

C. Correct the run-on errors in these sentences by using a semicolon. [14]
   1. Newborn fawns usually stay in their hiding place they do not follow their mother until they can walk well enough.
   2. Those week-old fawns are not too young to run they can go as fast as thirty-five miles per hour!
   3. Deer usually run away from their enemies sometimes they stand motionless until the enemy leaves.

Challenge Exercises

Copy some Bible verses that contain abstract nouns. Underline all the abstract nouns.

---

20. Proper Nouns

All nouns can be placed in two general classes: common nouns and proper nouns. Everything about which we can speak has a common name. Many things have proper names also, but some do not.

A *common noun* is the *ordinary, general* name of a person, place, thing, or idea. For example, the noun *road* is the common name for a surface on which people drive cars.

Common nouns:
   boy   city   story   day   righteousness

A *proper noun* is the *specific, exact* name of a person, place, or thing. It distinguishes one particular thing from all others with the same common name. *Johnson Road* is a proper noun because it names one specific road and distinguishes it from all other surfaces called roads.

Proper nouns:
   James Shirk   Columbus   Lincoln   Hidden Treasure

Proper nouns are written with capital letters. Words like *uncle, city, street, river,* and *mount* are also capitalized when they are part of a proper noun. Some kinds of proper nouns are listed in groups below.

1. *Names of particular persons, including initials and titles.*

   Mark   Brother Daniel   Mr. L. W. Mason

2. *Names of towns, cities, states, counties, nations, and continents.*

   Lowville   Maryland   Germany
   Baltimore   Washington County   Europe

3. *Names of mountains, rivers, lakes, oceans, deserts, islands, and so forth.*

   Mount Rushmore   Indian Ocean
   Ohio River   Gobi Desert
   Lake Tahoe   Ellesmere Island

4. *Titles of books, newspapers, magazines, poems, stories, chapters, articles, and so forth.* An article (*a, an, the*), a conjunction (*and, but, or*), or a preposition of fewer than four letters is not capitalized unless it is the first or last word.

   Hold the Fort   A Faith Worth Dying For
   The Ninety and Nine   Water From a Rock

5. *Names of organizations, schools, churches, and other groups.*

   Charity Child Care Committee
   Bethel Christian School
   Providence Mennonite Church
   Department of Commerce
   Bethel Christian School Board
   House of Representatives

6. *Names of parks, historic sites, historic events, documents, and so forth.*

   Yellowstone National Park
   French and Indian War
   War of 1812
   Constitution of the United States
   Gettysburg Address
   Bill of Rights

7. *Calendar items such as months, holidays, and days of the week.* However, the names of seasons are not capitalized.

March	spring
Ascension Day	summer
Wednesday	fall (autumn)
	winter

8. *Names of particular ships, airplanes, trains, buildings, and monuments.*

S.S. *France*	Pentagon
Flyer	Washington Monument
Tom Thumb	Golden Gate Bridge

9. *Names of God and words referring to parts of the Bible.*

God	Pentateuch	Psalms
Jehovah	Old Testament	Ephesians
Christ	1 Kings	

10. *Brand names.* A common noun used with a brand name is not capitalized.

Post cereals	Dodge truck
Carnation milk	French's mustard

11. *Abbreviations and initials of proper nouns.*

Dept. of Education	John F. Kennedy

An adjective formed from a proper noun is a proper adjective. A proper adjective is capitalized.

India—Indian	England—English
Israel—Israelite	Bible—Biblical
America—American	

A common noun modified by a proper adjective is not capitalized.

Israelite woman	American invention

Some words can be used both as a proper noun and as a proper adjective. You must decide which it is by the way the word is used in the sentence. A proper adjective modifies another noun.

Their grandfather was an Indian. (proper noun)
Do you like this Indian food? (proper adjective)

- A common noun is the general name of a person, place, thing, or idea. A proper noun is the name of one specific person, place, or thing.

- Proper nouns are written with capital letters. These include the names, titles, and initials of specific persons; the names of cities, nations, mountains, oceans, and other geographical items; the titles of books, magazines, songs, and stories; calendar items such as months and holidays; and brand names.

Class Practice

A. Match the common nouns in the first column with the proper nouns in the second column. Write the words from the second column correctly on the chalkboard.

1. park
2. country
3. store
4. state
5. island
6. book

   a. simon's appliance and electric
   b. puerto rico
   c. glacier national park
   d. pilgrim's progress
   e. mexico
   f. south carolina

B. Tell which words below should be capitalized. Tell which words are proper adjectives.

1. The philippines is a country at the western edge of the pacific ocean.
2. A leading port is davao, but the busiest port and capital city is manila.
3. Chief islands of the philippines include bohol, cebu, leyte, luzon, negros, palawan, panay, and samar.
4. Have you ever read the book *streams of living water,* by martin carey?
5. Pizza and spaghetti are italian foods.
6. The indians attacked the jacob hochstetler family at the time of the french and indian war.
7. Father said that ascension day always comes on a thursday in the spring.

8. We like carnation powdered milk and cloister ice cream.
9. It is easier for spaniards to learn the portuguese language than it is for english people.
10. On sunday we sang the song "thine for service" from the *christian hymnal.*

Written Exercises

A. Write two proper nouns for each of these common nouns.

1. book
2. month
3. city
4. person
5. dog
6. country
7. hymn
8. state
9. president
10. lake

B. Copy and capitalize correctly.

1. mrs. n. b. benz
2. cambria, illinois
3. brother elmer martin
4. campbell's soup
5. dr. ernest h. haulk
6. friday, november 2
7. the genesee river of new york
8. independence day

C. Find each proper noun, and write it correctly.

1. An official named ashpenaz, who served king nebuchadnezzar, gave these names to the four hebrews: belteshazzar, shadrach, meshach, and abednego.

2. Ancient palestine was divided into judea, samaria, and galilee.
3. We can read about king hezekiah in three old testament books: 2 kings, 2 chronicles, and isaiah.
4. The total area of the philippines is a little more than the area of wisconsin and michigan together.
5. On luzon, the largest of the islands, a volcano named mount mayon stands close to legaspi.
6. The philippine sea, the celebes sea, the sulu sea, and the south china sea surround the philippines.
7. Sauerkraut and frankfurters came from germany.
8. I liked the chapter "a glow in the dark" the best.
9. In exodus we read how the lord helped the israelites to cross the red sea on dry land.
10. A man named john deere invented the first riding plow.
11. Grades 5 and 6 of the hopeland christian school sang "mighty army of the young" by memory.
12. The golden gate bridge, one of the largest suspension bridges in the world, crosses the entrance of the san francisco bay.
13. The *tom thumb*, one of the first locomotives to pull a passenger train, was built by peter cooper.

D. Find each proper adjective, and write it correctly.
1. Do you like kellogg's cereals?
2. Apple pie and hamburgers are american foods.
3. We like lawry's salt on popcorn.
4. The roman citizens of paul's day used the greek language for everyday speech and the latin language for legal matters.
5. The jewish people used the hebrew language in religious matters.

Review Exercises

Write whether each sentence is *declarative, interrogative, imperative,* or *exclamatory.* (Only one sentence is exclamatory.) Also write the correct end punctuation. [7]
1. Which state of the United States has the highest population
2. California has more people than any other state in the United States
3. Tell me which country of the world has the greatest area
4. Isn't the United States one of the largest countries in the world

5. Canada is larger than the United States
6. China, the most heavily populated country, has about one billion people.
7. What a crowded country that must be

---

21. Developing Paragraphs by Using Details

You have learned that a paragraph is a group of sentences that tells about one single topic. That single topic is expressed in the topic sentence. All the other sentences support the topic sentence and say more about it.

Once you have written a topic sentence, you need to show that it is true. Your goal is to convince the reader that you know what you are talking about, and that what you have said is true and worthwhile. This is what paragraph development is all about: writing things that will prove the truth of your topic sentence.

A paragraph is developed by putting details into it. Details are extremely important. They are so necessary that you cannot hope to convince anyone without them. Read the topic sentence of the following paragraph (underlined), and then read the sentences that follow. Can you tell what is wrong with the paragraph?

> Hard work brings much satisfaction. I like to work hard. Most other people like it too if they really get at it. Hard work is much better than idleness. Being idle is not as satisfying as working hard. Few things bring as much satisfaction as hard work.

In the paragraph above, all the sentences after the topic sentence merely repeat and emphasize what the topic sentence says. None of them give any details to show that the topic sentence is true. How can the writer prove that hard work is so satisfying? Has he ever experienced it himself? What has he gained by working hard? What has he suffered through idleness? The paragraph does not accomplish much, because it gives no proof that the topic sentence is really true.

The following paragraph is better. Notice how the details offer real proof that the topic sentence is true.

> <u>Hard work brings much satisfaction</u>. How good you feel when you look back over a job well done! You may also receive a compliment from your father or mother, and that is another reward. Money that you earn by working is worth more to you than money that someone gives you. A working man has a clear conscience because he has done something worthwhile and made good use of his time. He is satisfied and relaxed. Ecclesiastes 5:12 says, "The sleep of a labouring man is sweet."

When you write a paragraph, use solid facts to show that your topic sentence is true. You might also use facts to show what is wrong with an opposing idea. Be sure your statements are based on truth and not just on your opinions. The reader may challenge what you think, but it is hard to argue against solid facts. Compare the following sentences. Which set is more convincing?

> Honesty is the best way because it brings the best results. You will feel much better if you are honest than if you lie or cheat. (opinions)

> Honesty is the best way because God said it is right. The Bible pronounces a severe penalty on all liars and hypocrites. (facts)

As you learned before, the details in a paragraph must fit together well so that the reader does not get lost or confused. Remember that this is done by putting the details in some kind of logical order. They can be given in the order of time or in the order of importance or interest. Remember also to use sentence variety and good transitional words. All these things together will help to make your paragraphs meaningful, interesting, and convincing.

- A paragraph may be developed by using details. The details must show the reader that the topic sentence is true.

Class Practice

A. Which paragraph is the better one? Tell why. In your own words, briefly give the details that support the topic sentence of the better paragraph.

1.   My mother makes many sacrifices for our family. She uses much of her energy in preparing food, washing clothes, and cleaning the house. It also takes much of her energy to give us firm, loving discipline. She loses sleep to pray for us or to care for us when we are sick. It seems we cannot stop her from helping us; she seems to love doing all she can for our good. We can never show too much appreciation for the constant sacrifices of our mother.

2.   Bird watching is a worthwhile hobby. You can put up a bird feeder outside a window. You can also hang a wren house in a tree. Scientists have learned much about birds by putting bands on their legs. Arctic terns fly the eleven thousand miles between the Arctic Circle and the Antarctic Circle twice each year!

B. Choose several of the topic sentences below, and briefly give some details that could be used to develop them.
1. Every boy should have a pet of some kind.
2. It takes much work to care for a pet rabbit.
3. We have an attractive classroom.
4. You can learn much from a good book.
5. There are many interesting things to see in Egypt.
6. Alaska is an interesting place to visit.

Written Exercises

A. List briefly the details that are used to develop the topic sentence of the following paragraph.

Animals have special ways to survive through freezing cold winters. An animal's body produces plenty of heat as long as it can find food. Mammals have thick fur that helps to keep in the body heat. Birds have warm downy feathers underneath their flight feathers. Some creatures keep warm by storing fat in their bodies and hibernating in dry caves or burrows. Foxes wrap their tails around their noses like scarves. And smaller animals such as field mice build warm tunnels under the snow. Certainly God designed the animals well to withstand cold weather.

B. Write a paragraph that is developed with meaningful details. You may begin with one of the topic sentences in Class Practice, Part B. You may also use a topic sentence of your own if it is approved by your teacher.

Review Exercises

Rewrite and improve the following directions. Put the steps in proper order, and leave out the sentence that does not belong. Use transitional words, such as *first, next,* and *also.* [16, 17]

A Good Way to Study for a Chapter Test

On index cards, copy some exercises that deal with the main points of the chapter, and write the answers on the back. First read through the whole chapter. Before you start reading, make sure you have a quiet place to study. We just studied a chapter about birds, and I enjoyed it very much. Read each card several times. See if you can say all the answers without looking. If you have trouble with any cards, keep studying them until you can give all the right answers promptly.

---

22. Nouns With Regular Plural Forms

Nouns do more than merely name things. The form of a noun shows whether it is a general name (common noun) or a specific name (proper noun). For most nouns, the form also shows whether it names one or more than one. For example, a word like *king* or *queen* refers to only one person, but words like *princes* and *servants* refer to more than one person.

A noun that names only one person, place, thing, or idea is a *singular noun.* A noun that names more than one is a *plural noun.*

Singular: boy, baby, town, home, potato
Plural: boys, babies, towns, homes, potatoes

The following rules tell how to form the plurals of regular nouns.
1. The plural forms of most nouns are made by adding *-s* to the singular forms.

animal—animals   purpose—purposes

2. If a noun ends with *s, sh, ch, x,* or *z,* the plural form is made by adding *-es* so that it can be pronounced easily.

   bunch—bunches   box—boxes   quiz—quizzes

3. If a noun ends with *y* after a vowel, the plural form is made by adding *-s.* If a noun ends with *y* after a consonant, the *y* is changed to *i* and *-es* is added.

   monkey—monkeys   country—countries

4. For many nouns ending with *f* or *fe,* the *f* or *fe* is changed to *v* and *-es* is added. For others of these nouns, only *-s* is added. A few are spelled either way.

   shelf—shelves   belief—beliefs
   wife—wives   safe—safes
   scarf—scarfs *or* scarves

   Words like *belief* and *safe* have different meanings when the *f* or *fe* is changed to *v* and *-es* is added: *believes, saves. Believes* and *saves* are verbs, not nouns.

5. If a noun ends with *o* after a vowel, the plural form is made by adding *-s.* If a noun ends with *o* after a consonant, *-s* or *-es* is added. A few are spelled either way.

   patio—patios   tomato—tomatoes
   silo—silos   volcano—volcanoes *or* volcanos

   If a noun ending with *o* is a musical term, the plural form is generally made by adding *-s.*

   soprano—sopranos   alto—altos   piano—pianos

Some nouns have more than one plural form. Be sure to check the dictionary whenever you are in doubt. If the dictionary does not show any plural form, follow the rules in this lesson.

- A singular noun names only one. A plural noun names more than one.

- Check the dictionary when you need help with the spelling of a plural form.

Class Practice

A. On the chalkboard, write the correct plural form of each word. Give the number of the rule in the lesson that is followed in each case.

1. loaf
2. supply
3. solo
4. sandwich
5. grief
6. champion
7. studio
8. radish
9. tornado
10. chimney

B. In the following sentences, change all the nouns to plural forms. Make sure all the other words agree with the plural forms.

1. A mosquito buzzed around the bush and the flower.
2. The boy has a tomato in his lunch.
3. The soprano and the alto sang well during music class.
4. The child picked a beetle off the potato in this row.

Written Exercises

A. Write the plural form of each word. Check a dictionary if you are not sure of the correct spelling.

1. coin
2. sky
3. sheaf
4. trio
5. quilt
6. fly
7. box
8. echo
9. turkey
10. potato
11. thief
12. thrush
13. donkey
14. switch
15. tomato
16. cliff
17. chief
18. hero
19. guess
20. valley
21. strife
22. buzz
23. belief
24. volcano

B. Rewrite these sentences, changing each noun to its plural form. Also change other words to make them agree.

1. The box contains a bicycle for the boy.
2. Put the knife and the fork on the shelf with the spoon.
3. The roof of the house is flat.
4. The soprano and the alto will sing this note together.
5. The mosquito thrives in swamp and marsh.

Review Exercises

A. Write whether the gender of each noun is *masculine, feminine, neuter,* or *common.* [19]

1. boy
2. teacher
3. town
4. friend

5. church
6. sister
7. song
8. book

B. Write a proper noun for each noun in Part A. [20]

---

23. Nouns With Irregular Plural Forms

A few nouns have plural forms that are made in irregular ways. Study the following groups of irregular plural forms.

1. The plural forms of seven nouns are made by changing the vowels.

foot—feet	louse—lice	man—men
goose—geese	mouse—mice	woman—women
tooth—teeth		

Some of these nouns are used in compound words, such as *gentleman—gentlemen* and *dormouse—dormice.* But these seven nouns are the only root words whose plural forms are made by changing the vowels.

2. Three plural nouns end with *-en,* which is an old plural suffix.

brother—brethren   child—children   ox—oxen

Brethren is an old plural form. Today we usually use *brothers* instead.

3. Some nouns have the same form whether they are singular or plural. Most of them are names of animals.

deer—deer	swine—swine	salmon—salmon
sheep—sheep	fish—fish	trout—trout
moose—moose		

Your <u>sheep</u> <u>are</u> all here, but my <u>sheep</u> <u>is</u> missing.

4. A few nouns look like plural forms, but they are singular. There is no plural for these nouns. Because each of these nouns refers to just one thing, a singular verb is commonly used with them.

news	checkers (game)	mumps
statistics	measles	chicken pox
mathematics		

The <u>news</u> <u>is</u> encouraging. (not *are*)
<u>Measles</u> <u>is</u> a contagious disease. (not *are*)

5. Some nouns are usually considered plural whether they name one thing or more than one. Usually plural verbs are used with these nouns, and plural pronouns are used to replace them. Most nouns of this kind name something made of two main parts.

pliers	glasses (aid for eyesight)
scissors	tongs
trousers	tweezers

The <u>pliers</u> <u>have</u> been put where <u>they</u> belong.
   (*Have* and *they* are often used whether *pliers* means one tool or two.)
<u>These</u> <u>trousers</u> <u>are</u> dirty, but Mother will wash <u>them</u>.
   (*These, are,* and *them* are all plural.)

Remember to check a dictionary when you are not sure how to spell a plural form.

- Some nouns have irregular plural forms.

- Check the dictionary when you need help with the spelling of a plural form.

Class Practice

A. On the chalkboard, write the correct plural form of each word.

1. wife	5. calf	9. dairy
2. match	6. alley	10. tray
3. fox	7. army	11. buffalo
4. crutch	8. echo	12. woman

B. Tell whether each noun is *singular, plural,* or *either singular or plural.*

1. deer
2. news
3. tongs

4. salmon
5. trousers
6. molasses

7. scissors
8. mathematics
9. trout

C. Read the following sentences correctly.

1. The scissors is on the shelf.
2. Measles are uncomfortable and may be dangerous.
3. We caught twenty trouts in the cold, sparkling stream.

Written Exercises

A. For each noun, write *S, P,* or *E* to tell whether it is singular, plural, or either singular or plural.

1. swine
2. mumps
3. shears

4. measles
5. fish
6. pliers

7. mathematics
8. eyeglasses
9. headquarters

B. Copy each underlined word, and write *S* or *P* after it to tell whether it is singular or plural.

1. The grass is getting tall.
2. Grandfather has lost his spectacles.
3. White hair is a glory to old men.
4. Jesus healed leprosy and other diseases.
5. Polly has measles.
6. The boy's teeth were covered with sticky molasses.
7. Andrew has a pair of black trousers.
8. We saw a deer among the sheep.
9. Have you heard the news?
10. Mathematics is my favorite subject.

C. Write the better words.

1. Rabies (is, are) a dangerous disease.
2. Please hand me (that, those) tweezers.
3. Many (salmon, salmons) were swimming upstream.
4. The dull shears (was, were) almost useless.

Review Exercises

A. Write whether each sentence has *normal, inverted,* or *mixed* word order. Diagram the skeleton of each sentence. [15]

1. Down came the rain, sleet, and snow.

2. The next day, a farmer's wife found a weak, tired fawn beside the chimney outside her cabin.

3. She fed him apples, oatmeal, and cornmeal.

4. How tame he became!

5. She had saved his life.

B. Rewrite these sentences, changing them to normal word order. [15]

1. Around and around buzzed the bee.

2. Nearby was some green grass.

3. For several weeks the fawn lived by the side of her house.

4. Happily he joined the herd again.

---

24. Developing Paragraphs by Using Examples and Illustrations

In Lesson 21 you learned that all the sentences in a paragraph must develop the topic sentence and that this is done by using details. You need to use suitable details to convince the reader that your topic sentence is true. Many different kinds of details can be used.

Examples and illustrations are specific kinds of details used to develop a paragraph. They form pictures in the reader's mind. They help to prove that the topic sentence is true by showing the reader what something is like. Notice the examples in the following paragraph.

Paragraph developed by several different examples:

My baby sister is sweet and lovable. She is a soft, roly-poly bundle. Often when I rock her, she just falls asleep in my arms. I like to talk to her because she usually smiles when I do. Once she laughed right out loud. She has a soft, quiet baby voice even when she cries. When she does cry, of course, I usually go and ask Mother if I may hold my dear baby sister again.

Will the reader be convinced that the writer's baby sister is sweet and lovable? He should be after he reads the examples. They tell how the baby feels to the touch, and what she looks and sounds like.

The paragraph above is developed by several different examples. A paragraph may also give just one example or illustration and go into detail about that one thing. This is called an extended example or illustration. The following paragraph uses the same topic sentence as the paragraph above, but it is developed by using just one incident.

Paragraph developed by one extended example:

My baby sister is sweet and lovable. The other day I was holding her and talking to her. She liked it best when I talked to her in baby words like *coo* and *goo*. Once while she was looking right at me, I tickled her chin and said, "Goo." All at once she laughed right out loud. It was the first time she ever did that! I would not trade my baby sister for anything in the world.

Examples and illustrations will help to make your paragraphs convincing. You may give a number of different illustrations, or you may use most of the paragraph to give just one extended illustration. If you use an actual happening or example, it will do much to prove that your topic sentence is true.

- Examples and illustrations are two kinds of details that can be used to develop a paragraph.

- A paragraph may be developed by several different examples or illustrations. It may also be developed by just one extended example or illustration.

Class Practice

A. Tell which paragraph is developed by using several examples or illustrations. Tell which paragraph is developed by using only one extended example or illustration.

1.   Weather patterns in Guatemala are different from weather patterns in Pennsylvania. The mountains of Guatemala have a fairly cold climate, but down at the coast—only a few hours' drive away—the climate is always warm. Guatemala does not have spring, summer, fall, and winter. Instead, it has a rainy season and a dry season. During the dry season, the mountains have frost at night but the days can get as warm as a summer day in Pennsylvania. Weather changes can be sudden and drastic, especially during the time between seasons.

2.   Weather patterns in Guatemala are different from weather patterns in Pennsylvania. My sister and I found this out last November, when we visited some friends in Guatemala. One morning as we walked on a mountain road, the wind suddenly started blowing and a great mist rolled over us. Drops of rain began to fall. A few minutes later, the sky cleared and the sun shone brightly again. By afternoon it was as warm as a summer day, but that night we snuggled under several layers of warm blankets. The next morning there was frost on the ground!

B. What is the topic sentence in the paragraphs in Part A? In the paragraph that uses several examples, give briefly the examples that develop the topic sentence. In the other paragraph, tell what the extended illustration is.

Written Exercises

A. Write a paragraph that is developed by using several examples or illustrations. You may begin with one of the topic sentences shown below. You may also use a topic sentence of your own if it is approved by your teacher.
1. I have learned many interesting things this year.
2. I have made some careless mistakes.
3. A single act of disobedience can lead to terrible results.
4. Little brothers are very lovable.
5. We have had some interesting devotional periods this year.
6. Daniel faced a number of tests in Babylon.

B. Write another paragraph, but this time develop it by using only one extended example or illustration. Again choose one of the topics in Part A (or one that your teacher approves). You may write about the same topic as before or a different one.

Review Exercises

Write the correct words to fill in the blanks. You will not use all the words.

topic sentence	inverted	coherence	run-on
mixed	normal	unity	paragraph
compound			

1. When all the sentences in a paragraph develop one topic, the paragraph has ———.

2. In a paragraph with ———, the details fit together in such a way that the reader does not get lost or confused.
3. The ——— gives the main idea of a paragraph.
4. In a sentence with ——— word order, the complete predicate comes before the complete subject.
5. In a sentence with ——— word order, the complete subject comes before the complete predicate.
6. In a sentence with ——— word order, part of the predicate comes before the subject and part of the predicate comes after.
7. A ——— sentence has two clauses joined by a comma and a conjunction.
8. In a ——— error, two sentences are incorrectly written together as one sentence.

---

25. More Plural Nouns

Some nouns belong in special categories, and special care is needed to write their plural forms correctly. These include compound nouns, collective nouns, and nouns that have kept their foreign plural forms.

A *compound noun* is a noun made of two or more smaller words. There are three kinds of compound nouns.

Compound nouns:
1. Written as one word.

    airplane   newspaper   mailbox   gentleman

2. Written with a hyphen.

    sister-in-law   great-uncle   half-truth

3. Written as two words.

    high school   fountain pen   post office

In general, the plural form of a compound noun is made by changing the most important word (usually the last word) to its plural form.

airplanes	sisters-in-law	high schools
newspapers	great-uncles	fountain pens
mailboxes	half-truths	post offices
gentlemen		

In a few cases, both words in a compound noun are changed to the plural form.

>manservant—menservants
>woman servant—women servants

If a noun ends with *-ful,* the plural form is made by adding *-s* to *-ful.*

>cupful—cupfuls   spoonful—spoonfuls

But be careful! When *full* is a separate word, *-s* is *not* added to *full.* Study the following sentences.

>Please bring three cups full of water.
>Inside the door stood two buckets full of milk.

A *collective noun* names a group of persons or things. Read the following examples.

Collective nouns:

team	school	family
assembly	class	flock

Even though a collective noun refers to more than one, it is singular because it names *one group.* For example, the noun *team* names several people working together. Even if the team has nine people, it is one unit trying to get one thing accomplished. So we say, "Our team *has* won the game." We do not say, "Our team *have* won the game." Here are a few more examples.

>Our <u>class is</u> studying the solar system. (not *are*)
>The <u>flock</u> of sheep <u>was</u> lying near the well. (not *were*)

Of course, a collective noun also has a plural form. If it refers to more than one *group,* it is a plural noun the same as other plural nouns.

>The two <u>classes are</u> studying the solar system together.
>Several <u>flocks</u> of sheep <u>were</u> lying near the well.

Many English nouns came from foreign languages. For some of these nouns, the plural forms are spelled according to the rules in foreign languages. They do not always end with *-s* as most English plurals do. Following are a few examples, along with the pronunciations of the plural forms.

>basis—bases (bā′·sēz′)
>fungus—fungi (fun′·jī)

larva—larvae (lär′·vē)
radius—radii (rā′·dē·ī′)
parenthesis—parentheses (pə·ren′·thi·sēz′)

Some nouns with foreign plural forms also have regular plural forms. Always use your dictionary if you are not sure about the correct plural form.

radius—radii *or* radiuses
vertebra—vertebrae *or* vertebras

- The plural form of a compound noun is usually made by adding *-s* or *-es* to the most important word.

- A singular collective noun refers to a group, but it is still singular.

- Some plural forms have foreign spellings. Use the dictionary whenever you are not sure about a plural form.

Class Practice

A. Give the plural forms of the following nouns.

1. father-in-law
2. analysis
3. great-aunt
4. pupa
5. armful

6. crisis
7. bacterium
8. basketful
9. manservant
10. forefoot

B. Use a dictionary to find the two plural forms of each word. Write them on the chalkboard.

1. antenna   2. index   3. spectrum

Written Exercises

A. Write the plural form of each noun. Use the dictionary if you need help.

1. salmon
2. keyhole
3. century
4. sheaf

5. handful
6. piano
7. half
8. panful

9. eyetooth
10. mother-in-law
11. brother-in-law
12. attorney at law

B. Write the two plural forms of each noun, using the dictionary for help.

1. cactus   3. formula   5. medium
2. aquarium   4. stratum   6. focus

C. Find each incorrect plural noun, and write it correctly.
1. The class is looking up facts, using various indexs.
2. The team has found several different kinds of fungee.
3. We saw the feetprints of many deer in the vallies.
4. The ovums developed into larvaa.
5. Draw three different radises in this circle.
6. The news was sent to the two sister-in-laws who lived in other countrys.
7. The nurse found two boxesful of books on how to deal with medical crisises.

Review Exercises

A. Write the plural form of each word. Check the dictionary if you are not sure. [22, 23]

1. wolf   6. moose   11. kangaroo
2. silo   7. lady   12. pliers
3. foot   8. trio   13. glass
4. shelf   9. mouse   14. reproof
5. potato   10. fox   15. tongs

B. For each underlined noun, write S or P to tell whether it is a singular or plural noun. [22–25]
1. The sad <u>news</u> is that many in our <u>class</u> have <u>measles</u>.
2. He broke the <u>scissors</u> and bent the <u>tweezers</u> while trying to fix the <u>toy</u> for the <u>children</u>.
3. The <u>women</u> asked the <u>salesman</u> the <u>prices</u> of the new <u>trousers</u>.
4. Charles kept up with his <u>mathematics</u> even though he had <u>mumps</u>.

Challenge Exercises

Write the plural form of each noun. Use the dictionary or encyclopedia for help.

1. commander in chief   3. stimulus   5. phenomenon
2. governor-general   4. axis   6. ellipsis

26. Possessive Nouns

Read the following sentences. They both tell the same thing, but the second sentence uses fewer words. It is just as clear in meaning.

> The boils of Job made him feel miserable.
> Job's boils made him feel miserable.

The noun *Job's* makes the second sentence more clear and brief. It is a *possessive noun*. Possessive nouns show ownership or relationship. The apostrophe (') is used to form possessive nouns.

> Is this Martha's book?
> No, it is her sister's book.
> The visitor's horse is eating Mother's flowers!

Most possessive nouns are used as adjectives to modify other nouns. Usually they tell *whose*.

> Whose book is this? It is Martha's book.
> Whose horse is that? It is the visitor's horse.

Study the following rules for making the possessive forms of nouns.
1. The possessive form of a singular noun is made by adding *'s*.

> a bird's feathers   Charles's address
> the baby's fingers   our brother's letter

2. The possessive form of a plural noun that ends with *-s* is made by adding an apostrophe after the *-s*.

> our teachers' names
> the boys' seats
> a members' meeting

3. If a plural noun does not end with *-s*, the possessive form is made by adding *'s*.

> the children's room
> the mice's nests
> the deer's trails

For a word like *Moses* or *Jesus*, only an apostrophe is added because the word ends with the *zus* sound. This is done to make the possessive forms easier to pronounce.

> Moses' rod   Jesus' miracles

Study the following chart, which shows the plural and possessive forms of several nouns.

Singular	Singular Possessive	Plural	Plural Possessive
worker	worker's	workers	workers'
man	man's	men	men's
monkey	monkey's	monkeys	monkeys'
enemy	enemy's	enemies	enemies'
life	life's	lives	lives'
Filipino	Filipino's	Filipinos	Filipinos'

Most possessive forms refer to people or animals. If a noun names an inanimate object (neither person nor animal), it is not usually written in the possessive form. For those nouns it is better to use a different expression, usually a phrase with *of* or some other preposition.

The house's roof was steep.
Better: The roof of the house was steep.

Father repaired the lawn mower's engine.
Better: Father repaired the engine of the lawn mower.

The trees' leaves are changing colors.
Better: The leaves on the trees are changing colors.

- A possessive noun shows ownership or relationship. It is often used as an adjective that tells *whose.*

- An apostrophe is used to make the possessive form of a noun.

- A possessive form is not generally used for a noun that names an inanimate object.

Class Practice

A. Rewrite these expressions on the chalkboard, using possessive nouns.
1. the work of my father
2. the letters of the parents
3. the interest of the children
4. the coat of the lady
5. the feathers of the geese

B. Change each underlined phrase to the plural form, and write it on the chalkboard.
1. Our sister's cake is delicious.
2. The man's idea was excellent.
3. That louse's bite was irritating.
4. The baby's face is dirty.
5. The ostrich's feather was long.

C. Copy this chart on the chalkboard, and fill it in.

Singular	Singular Possessive	Plural	Plural Possessive
1. donkey	———	———	———
2. ox	———	———	———
3. brother	———	———	———
4. pupil	———	———	———
5. mouse	———	———	———
6. woman	———	———	———

D. Tell which of these expressions should be improved, and how.
1. the barn's walls
2. the man's gloves
3. the tractor's paint
4. the patch's color
5. the goat's horns

Written Exercises

A. Rewrite these expressions, using possessive forms.
1. the coats of the girls
2. the voice of the waiter
3. the address of Louise

B. Write the possessive form of each noun.
1. uncle   7. Alex
2. soldier   8. prince
3. babies   9. Irishman
4. animals   10. chiefs
5. rabbits   11. Doris
6. waitress   12. wolf

C. Copy and complete the chart.

Singular	Singular Possessive	Plural	Plural Possessive
1. minister	——	——	——
2. horseman	——	——	——
3. salmon	——	——	——
4. goose	——	——	——
5. fish	——	——	——
6. calf	——	——	——
7. larva	——	——	——
8. family	——	——	——

D. Improve these expressions.
1. the bed's posts
2. the stove's burners
3. the desk's drawers
4. the cabin's windows

Review Exercises

Diagram the skeletons. All but one are compound sentences. [12]
1. Snow falls in winter, and it also falls in summer.
2. Summer snow comes down as rain, for it melts on the way to the ground.
3. Snow forms directly from water vapor, but sleet forms from raindrops.
4. Sleet and hail begin as liquid rain but hit the ground as ice pellets.
5. Sometimes raindrops become colder than the freezing point, yet they do not freeze.
6. This rain freezes on contact, and it forms an icy glaze on roads, trees, and electric wires.
7. Then drivers must be very careful, or they may have serious accidents.

27. Developing Paragraphs by Comparison or Contrast

You have now studied several lessons on how to develop paragraphs. You know that all the sentences in a paragraph must develop the topic sentence and that details are important in developing a paragraph. You learned that using examples and illustrations is a good way to convince the reader that your topic sentence is true.

Giving comparisons or contrasts is another way of arranging details to develop a paragraph. When comparisons or contrasts are used, their purpose is to clarify or explain the topic so that the reader can understand it better.

Comparison is used in paragraphs to show similarities between two persons, places, things, or ideas. Such paragraphs are written to help the reader understand something by showing how it is like a common, familiar thing. When this is done, the paragraph usually tells about the more familiar thing first. See how this is done in the following paragraph.

Paragraph developed by comparison:

A hammer and the Bible are very different in size and shape, but they are alike in several ways. A hammer is a solid, unchanging tool. It can smash hard objects without being broken. When a carpenter builds a house, the hammer is one of his most valuable tools. The Bible is also solid and unchanging. Many men have tried to destroy or change it, yet it always stays the same. The Bible can break the hard hearts of sinful men. It is a valuable tool for building the church. Jeremiah surely spoke the truth when he said that God's Word is like a hammer.

This paragraph first describes a common, familiar object (the hammer) and tells about its uses. Then it shows how the Bible is similar in various ways.

Contrast is used to show differences between two persons, places, things, or ideas. When a paragraph is developed by contrast, it gives details about the ways in which two things are different. The following paragraph contrasts the personalities of two boys.

Paragraph developed by contrast:

My twin brothers, James and John, have always been as different as day and night. James was always a quiet, contented baby, but John never was! When Father took James to church, it seemed that the way he set him down was the way he stayed until Father picked him up again. But I can't tell you how many times Father had to take wiggly, squirmy John out of services for a lesson! Now that the twins are grown, what do you think they like to do? James sits patiently hour after hour working on lessons for Sunday school books. But John can run three or four different construction projects at one time without getting flustered. The twins are certainly different, but they both live useful lives for God.

There are two ways to list comparisons or contrasts. One way is to give all the points about the first thing and then all the points about the second thing. The other way is to give the comparisons or contrasts by turns, point by point. These two ways are illustrated in the paragraphs above. Compare the following lists of the points they present.

First paragraph:
1. A hammer is an unchanging tool.
2. It can smash hard objects.
3. It is valuable for building houses.
4. The Bible is an unchanging Book.
5. It can break the hard hearts of sinful men.
6. It is valuable for building the church.

Second paragraph:
1. James was a quiet, contented baby.
2. John was a restless baby.
3. Now James works on lessons for Sunday school books.
4. John can run three or four different construction projects at one time.

A paragraph must be more than just a list of comparisons or contrasts. It must also include enough details to make the comparisons or contrasts meaningful. The following paragraph is not very meaningful or interesting, because it has no details to explain the comparisons.

The Bible is like a mirror. When people look into a mirror, they can see what they look like; and when people read the Bible, they can see what their lives look like. People must look into a mirror before it can help them, and people must look into the Bible before it can help them. People don't always like what a mirror shows them, and people don't always like what the Bible shows them. So the Bible really is very much like a mirror.

In the paragraph above, every sentence that shows a comparison has two clauses that are almost the same. Sentences like these are tiresome to read. They need specific details, such as what people might see when they look into a mirror (dirty face or uncombed hair) and what they might see in their lives when they look into the Bible (pride or selfishness). Exactly how does a mirror or the Bible help a person who looks into it? What might a mirror or the Bible show people that they do not like?

Many paragraphs are developed by the use of several methods together. For example, comparison and contrast can be used in the same paragraph. In the paragraph about the hammer and the Bible, do you see the clause that shows a contrast? It is in the first sentence: "A hammer and the Bible are very different in size and shape." Whatever method you use, remember that all the sentences must develop the topic sentence and that they must be in a sensible order.

When you use comparison or contrast, end your paragraph with a concluding sentence that refers again to the comparison or contrast you have been making. Notice how this is done in each of the example paragraphs in this lesson.

- A paragraph can be developed by using comparison or contrast.

- Comparison shows similarities between things. Contrast shows differences between things.

- One way of showing comparison or contrast is to give all the points about the first thing and then all the points about the second thing. Another way is to give the comparisons or contrasts by turns, point by point.

Class Practice

A. Read the paragraph below, and do these exercises.
  1. Is this paragraph developed by comparison or by contrast?
  2. Give the comparisons or contrasts that it uses.
  3. Which method is used in this paragraph? Choose *a* or *b*.
     a. All the points about the first thing are given, and then all the points about the second thing.
     b. The comparisons or contrasts are given by turns, point by point.
  4. Read the concluding sentence, which refers again to the comparison made in the paragraph.
  5. This paragraph is about the same topic as the last sample paragraph in the lesson. Why is this paragraph better?

The Bible is like a mirror. When a person looks into a mirror, it shows him what he looks like. He can see right away if his hair is neat. When a person reads the Bible, it shows him what his life looks like to God. He can see if he is doing what God wants. Some people do not like to look into a mirror because they do not like what it shows them. They do not want to wash their faces or comb their hair. In the same way, some people do not read the Bible because they do not like what it shows about their lives. They do not want to change. A mirror helps us to keep ourselves clean and neat. The Bible helps us by showing how we can keep our lives pure in God's sight. Both a mirror and the Bible are so beneficial that we should look into them every day.

B. Choose one of these topic sentences. On the chalkboard, list some points that could be used to develop the paragraph by comparison or contrast.
1. True Christians are like sheep.
2. Joseph is an Old Testament type of Christ.
3. The Christian is like salt (or light) in the world.
4. Washing dishes is more enjoyable than weeding a garden.
5. The Bible is like a sword (or fire, rock, map, or light).
6. Butterflies are different from moths in several ways.
7. Life in New Mexico (or any state or province) is different from life in Pennsylvania (or your home state or province).
8. Dresses made from cotton fabric are better than (or not as good as) dresses made from knitted fabric.

Written Exercises

Choose one of the topic sentences in Class Practice, Part B, and write a paragraph using comparison or contrast (or both). You may choose a topic of your own if it is approved by your teacher. Do not choose a topic that is used in the lesson.

Review Exercises

Choose words from the list to answer the following questions. You will not use all the words. [16, 17]

topic sentence	finally	soon
coherence	time	first
transitional	later	unity
importance	next	form
transactional	interest	also

1. What does a paragraph have when all the sentences tell about the same topic?
2. What does a paragraph have when all the sentences fit together in an orderly, sensible way?
3. In what three kinds of order may the details of a paragraph be given?
4. What kind of words help to provide coherence in a paragraph?
5. What are six words that can be used as transitional words?

---

28. Chapter 3 Review

Class Practice

A. Tell which words in this list could be used as nouns.

1. labor	5. pray	9. quietness
2. forth	6. action	10. remember
3. singer	7. often	11. affection
4. reports	8. flight	12. different

B. Tell how to change these words to nouns by adding -ness, -ion, -ity, or -ment. Check the dictionary if you are not sure of the spelling.

1. late	3. active	5. enlarge
2. adjust	4. tranquil	

C. Tell which words are nouns in the following paragraph.

A bat is a strange-looking mammal with unusual habits and abilities. It looks somewhat like a mouse with wings. Bats sleep during the day and hunt insects at night. They hang upside down in caves or barns to sleep. Some people have a fear of bats, but bats do not usually come near people. A bat uses a special kind of sonar to keep from bumping into things. It can find its way even in the dark. Bats can see with their eyes as well as with their ears. Truly God has made the bat a most fascinating animal.

D. Give a proper noun for each of these common nouns.
1. state   3. mountain   5. friend
2. ocean   4. dog

E. On the chalkboard, rewrite these expressions, using possessive forms.
1. the hat of the man   4. the dolls of the girls
2. the hats of the men   5. the work of the waitress
3. the doll of the girl   6. the work of the waitresses

F. Which of these expressions should be improved? How should they be changed?
1. the chair's legs   4. the squirrel's nuts
2. the frog's tongue   5. the desks' tops
3. the barn's windows   6. the lantern's glow

G. Tell which of these paragraphs is better, and why. Briefly give the details that support the topic sentence of the better paragraph.

1.   "A word fitly spoken is like apples of gold in pictures of silver" (Proverbs 25:11). Apples are a valuable food. They provide important vitamins and minerals. Gold and silver are two of the most valuable metals. Iron and copper are valuable too, but not as valuable as gold and silver. Good words are really more valuable than apples, gold, and silver.

2.   "A word fitly spoken is like apples of gold in pictures of silver" (Proverbs 25:11). There are several kinds of fitly spoken words. A kind word can cheer a lonely or burdened heart. A good word of advice or instruction can prevent a costly mistake. A word of encouragement can inspire a worker to do his task with joy. Truly a word spoken in the right way at the right time is beautiful, and it is more valuable than gold or silver.

H. Read the paragraph below, and answer these questions.
1. Is this paragraph developed by comparison or by contrast?
2. Which method is used in this paragraph? Choose *a* or *b*.
   a. All the points about the first thing are given, and then all the points about the second thing.
   b. The comparisons or contrasts are given by turns, point by point.
3. Which sentence ties the end of the paragraph to the beginning?

Our Little Kubota

Our little Kubota is almost the color of a horse, and it works like a horse. As you know, a horse pulls with all four legs. Well, our Kubota pulls with all four wheels. The traction is amazing. A little feed at the beginning of the day takes a horse a long way. Fill our Kubota's tank with fuel, and it is all set to work for hours. A hardworking horse makes little noise. You hear only a creaking harness, plodding footsteps, and deep breathing. Our Kubota, even when working hard, makes little more than a pleasant purr. Yes, our little Kubota is a real workhorse.

Written Exercises

A. List nouns as described below.
1. Names of four animals. **Example:** bear
2. Names of four kinds of vehicles. **Example:** train
3. Names of four periods of time. **Example:** day
4. Names of four things a farmer might use. **Example:** harrow
5. Four nouns to illustrate the four genders.

B. Find each proper noun, and write it correctly.
1. When brother daniel lived in ontario, he was the principal at the shady grove christian school.
2. Our teacher showed us an article on the atacama desert in the magazine called *nature friend.*
3. On the first wednesday in april, the students from the london mennonite school took a test on events during the french and indian war.
4. The first truly successful steam locomotive was *the rocket,* which was built in 1829 by two english inventors named george and robert stephenson.
5. Behold, god is my salvation; I will trust and not be afraid: for the lord jehovah is my strength and my song.

C. Find each proper adjective, and write it correctly.
  1. Aspirin, the drug in bayer tablets, was first made by a french chemist.
  2. It is different from the drug in tylenol tablets.
  3. A newer kind of pain reliever is used in advil tablets.
  4. Penicillin was developed by english scientists of scottish, german, and australian backgrounds.

D. Write the plural form of each word.
  1. purpose
  2. ox
  3. trio
  4. tooth
  5. loaf
  6. glass
  7. memory
  8. belief
  9. alto
  10. deer
  11. pliers
  12. key
  13. manservant
  14. potato
  15. mosquito
  16. cupful
  17. fungus
  18. mailbox

E. Rewrite each sentence, changing all the nouns to plural forms. Include the nouns that show possession. (You will need to change some other words too.)
  1. The adventurous boy emptied his pocket.
  2. Out came a goose's feather, a deer's tooth, a paper airplane, and a card from a post office!
  3. My brother-in-law told me this story.

F. Copy and complete this chart.

Singular	Singular Possessive	Plural	Plural Possessive
1. cow	――	――	――
2. pupil	――	――	――
3. trout	――	――	――
4. man	――	――	――
5. fox	――	――	――
6. calf	――	――	――
7. city	――	――	――
8. moose	――	――	――

G. Briefly list the comparisons or contrasts from the paragraph about the Kubota tractor in Class Practice, Part H.

Action

Tenses

Helping

Forms
of Be

Verb Phrases

Transitive

Linking

Principal Parts

Book
Reports

Topical

Outlines

Sentence

Outlines

Chapter Four
Working With Verbs
Writing Outlines

A
verb is a
word that shows action
or being.

𝔅eing fruitful in every good work.

Colossians 1:10

29. Verbs

Every sentence must have a verb. The verb tells you what is happening. It tells what the subject does or is.

A verb is a word that shows *action* or *being*. These are the two main classes of verbs.

1. *Action verbs express any action that can be performed,* such as *speak, fly, walk,* and *remember.* There are so many action verbs that we could not list them all.

   Some verbs show physical action, and others show mental action.

   Physical action: jump, run, swing, slide, work
   Mental action: think, study, believe, memorize

   Have, has, and *had* are action verbs that show possession. They show that the subject of the sentence *owns* or *did own* something.

2. *The forms of* be *express being rather than action.* They give meaning to a sentence by showing that something exists or has existed. The forms of *be* are *am, is, are, was, were, be, been,* and *being.*

Sometimes two or more verbs are used together in a *verb phrase.* A verb phrase has a *main verb* and one or more *helping verbs.* The main verb is always the last word in a verb phrase. In the following sentences, the verb phrases are underlined twice.

Job | <u>was sitting</u> among the ashes.
Satan | <u>had smitten</u> him with sore boils.

Being familiar with the helping verbs will help you to recognize them quickly. You should remember these from Lesson 2.

Forms of *be:*   am, is, are, was, were, be, been, being
Forms of *have:*   have, has, had
Forms of *do:*   do, does, did
Forms of *may:*   may, might, must
Other helping verbs: can—could, shall—should, will—would

Verb phrases may be interrupted by words that are not verbs. The following words are never verbs: *not, never, hardly, always, ever,* and *surely.* These are adverbs that modify verbs.

But Job | <u>did</u> not <u>sin</u> with his lips.
His faithfulness | <u>has</u> surely <u>inspired</u> many people.

Two verbs joined by *and, but,* or *or* are compound verbs.

She <u>jumped</u> or <u>skipped</u> the whole way.
She <u>smiled</u> and <u>told</u> her teacher.

- A verb is a word that shows action or being.

- A verb phrase includes a main verb and one or more helping verbs. The helping verbs are as follows:

  Forms of *be*:   am, is, are, was, were, be, been, being
  Forms of *have*:   have, has, had
  Forms of *do*:   do, does, did
  Forms of *may*:   may, might, must
  Other helping verbs: can—could, shall—should, will—would

Class Practice

Give the verbs and verb phrases in these sentences.

1. The heavens declare the glory of God.
2. The firmament is showing His handiwork.
3. We can see God's glory in the starry skies.
4. The stars do not speak; they have no voice.
5. But they are always telling about their Creator.
6. The sun is like a strong man in a race.
7. We must observe God's creation and praise Him.
8. We can discover His law and practice it diligently.
9. God has created many interesting creatures.
10. Monstrous blue whales leap from the surface of the sea.
11. Bald eagles can soar effortlessly over the countryside.
12. Little brown squirrels fly from branch to branch.
13. In the black of night, the keen-eyed owl clearly calls, *Who-who?*
14. Silvery fish dart here and there in clear pools.

Written Exercises

A. Write whether each word is *always* a verb or *never* a verb.

1. some	5. allow	9. lose	13. subtract
2. bury	6. provide	10. certain	14. action
3. announce	7. almost	11. remind	15. discuss
4. attic	8. gradual	12. agree	16. artist

B. Copy all the verbs and verb phrases in the following sentences.
1. The swallows, robins, and wrens have returned for the summer.
2. God has given the birds various instincts.
3. Birds establish their territories and mark their boundaries.
4. Birds do not drive fence posts or hang up signs.
5. They sing at the edges of their territories instead.
6. They are warning other birds of their boundaries.
7. They must find enough food for their babies.
8. We should always speak kindly and cheerfully.
9. Sister Irene has never seen a real turtle.
10. The huge pumpkin fell onto the road and burst apart.
11. Can the boys lift the rock off the road?
12. Please erase your errors completely.

C. Use the following verbs in sentences of your own. Use each pair in the same sentence.
1. pay, take
2. remember, write

Review Exercises

Diagram the sentence skeletons. [10, 11]
1. The United States bought Alaska from Russia in 1867.
2. William H. Seward was the secretary of state, and he paid about two cents an acre for it.
3. Some people did not approve the purchase, and they called Alaska "Seward's Icebox."
4. Alaska has many valuable natural resources.
5. Huge oil reserves have been found at Prudhoe Bay along the Arctic Coast.
6. The value of Alaska's natural resources has repaid its purchase price hundreds of times over.
7. In the largest state live the fewest people.

8. In such wild country, men do not build many roads.
9. Eskimos still hunt and fish in Alaska.
10. Towering mountains and beautiful scenery attract people to Alaska.
11. Find Mount McKinley, the highest peak in the United States.
12. Great endurance is a necessity in the cold wilderness.

---

30. Principal Parts of Regular Verbs

Verbs have three main forms called *principal parts*. The principal parts are used to express different meanings. For example, if we want to tell about something that is happening now, we use one form, or principal part, of the verb. If we want to tell about something that happened yesterday or last week, we must use a different principal part. The names of the three principal parts are as follows:

First principal part: *present* form
Second principal part: *past* form
Third principal part: *past participle*

You can easily remember the three principal parts of verbs by using them in sentences like the ones below.

Present: Today I <u>write</u>.
Past: Yesterday I <u>wrote</u>.
Past participle: Every day I <u>have written</u>.

As these sentences show, the first principal part of a verb (present form) is used to speak of an action happening at the present time. The second principal part (past form) is used to speak of an action happening in the past. The third principal part (past participle) also refers to an action in the past. But the past participle must be used with the helping verb *have, has,* or *had.*

In regular verbs, the past form and the past participle are exactly the same. They are made by adding *-ed* to the present form. Be sure to spell these forms with *-ed* correctly. Study the following rules and examples.

1. If a verb ends with *e,* drop the *e* before adding *-ed.*

   Present: Today I <u>rake</u> the leaves.
   Past: Yesterday I <u>raked</u> the leaves.
   Past participle: Every day I <u>have raked</u> the leaves.

2. If a verb ends with *y* after a consonant, change the *y* to *i* and add *-ed.*

   Present: Today I <u>carry</u> the baskets.
   Past: Yesterday I <u>carried</u> the baskets.
   Past participle: Every day I <u>have carried</u> the baskets.

3. If a verb ends with *y* after a vowel, simply add *-ed.*

   Present: Today we <u>stay</u> here.
   Past: Yesterday we <u>stayed</u> here.
   Past participle: Every day we <u>have stayed</u> here.

4. If a one-syllable verb ends with a single consonant after a short vowel, double the final consonant and add *-ed.*

   Present: Today the boys <u>skip</u> this part.
   Past: Yesterday the boys <u>skipped</u> this part.
   Past participle: Every day the boys <u>have skipped</u> this part.

- Verbs have three principal parts:
  1. The first principal part (present form)
  2. The second principal part (past form)
  3. The third principal part (past participle)

- The second and third principal parts of regular verbs are made by adding *-ed* to the present form.

- The past participle must be used with the helping verb *have, has,* or *had.*

Class Practice

A. Say and spell the missing principal parts. Use *have* with the past participle. The first one is done for you.

First (Present)	Second (Past)	Third (Past Participle)
1. remember	remembered	(have) remembered
2. bloom	———	———
3. thrive	———	———
4. move	———	———
5. rely	———	———
6. obey	———	———
7. tag	———	———
8. fill	———	———

B. Say each verb or verb phrase. Tell whether the verb is the *present* form, the *past* form, or the *past participle*.
   1. Form a line along the wall.
   2. He patched the leak with some rubber.
   3. I have pressed his suit.
   4. The impact dented the side of the car.
   5. We treat him every year on his birthday.
   6. I have hemmed the new dresses.
   7. Have you identified the stranger yet?
   8. We forced the door open and entered the empty room.
   9. Trace the pattern, and pass it to me.
   10. The horses dragged the logs out of the woods.

Written Exercises

A. Copy the chart, and add the missing words. Include the helping verb
have with each past participle. The first one is done for you.

First (Present)	Second (Past)	Third (Past Participle)
1. operate	operated	(have) operated
2. count	————	————
3. change	————	————
4. vary	————	————
5. destroy	————	————
6. stop	————	————
7. journey	————	————
8. stretch	————	————

B. Copy each verb or verb phrase. Write whether the verb is the *present*
form, the *past* form, or the *past participle*.

Example: We finished all our work for today.
Answer: finished, past

1. Karen petted the poor little pup.
2. The kitten has played with the yarn a long time.
3. Have you copied all the exercises?
4. The workers stack the planks neatly.
5. This medicine has cured him of his fever.
6. The company has stored merchandise in this warehouse for several years.
7. The wise men rejoiced with exceeding great joy.
8. They had followed the star to Jesus.
9. The wise men opened their treasures.
10. They presented gold, frankincense, and myrrh to Jesus.
11. The wise men worshiped Jesus.
12. Today we also worship Jesus.
13. We hurried down that street toward the post office.
14. He has delivered your order.
15. All the sets seem complete.

Review Exercises

A. Copy the chart, and add the missing words. [22–26]

Singular	Singular Possessive	Plural	Plural Possessive
1. boy	———	———	———
2. hero	———	———	———
3. waitress	———	———	———
4. enemy	———	———	———
5. deer	———	———	———
6. baby	———	———	———
7. chief	———	———	———
8. wife	———	———	———

B. Change each underlined noun to the plural form. [22–26]

Example: The animal's cage had to be cleaned that day.
Answer: animals' cages

1. My sister's dress was lost in the baggage.
2. The fox's den was discovered.
3. The girl's room was in good order.
4. The man's hat blew off.

C. Rewrite each expression, using a possessive form. [26]
1. the voices of the children
2. the dogs of the boys
3. the miracles of Jesus
4. the meeting of the members
5. the horses of the man
6. the nests of the mice

Principal Parts of Common Verbs

(Some verbs on this chart have alternate forms.)

First	Second	Third	First	Second	Third
(Present)	*(Past)*	*(Past Participle)*	*(Present)*	*(Past)*	*(Past Participle)*
be (is)	was	(have) been	*lie	lay	(have) lain
begin	began	(have) begun	pay	paid	(have) paid
blow	blew	(have) blown	put	put	(have) put
break	broke	(have) broken	*raise	raised	(have) raised
bring	brought	(have) brought	read	read	(have) read
*burst	burst	(have) burst	ride	rode	(have) ridden
buy	bought	(have) bought	ring	rang	(have) rung
catch	caught	(have) caught	*rise	rose	(have) risen
choose	chose	(have) chosen	run	ran	(have) run
*come	came	(have) come	*see	saw	(have) seen
cost	cost	(have) cost	send	sent	(have) sent
cut	cut	(have) cut	*set	set	(have) set
dig	dug	(have) dug	shine	shone	(have) shone
*do	did	(have) done	shoot	shot	(have) shot
*drag	dragged	(have) dragged	shut	shut	(have) shut
draw	drew	(have) drawn	sing	sang	(have) sung
drink	drank	(have) drunk	sink	sank	(have) sunk
*drown	drowned	(have) drowned	*sit	sat	(have) sat
eat	ate	(have) eaten	sleep	slept	(have) slept
fight	fought	(have) fought	speak	spoke	(have) spoken
find	found	(have) found	steal	stole	(have) stolen
fly	flew	(have) flown	*swim	swam	(have) swum
forget	forgot	(have) forgotten	*swing	swung	(have) swung
freeze	froze	(have) frozen	*tag	tagged	(have) tagged
give	gave	(have) given	take	took	(have) taken
*go	went	(have) gone	teach	taught	(have) taught
hold	held	(have) held	tear	tore	(have) torn
hurt	hurt	(have) hurt	tell	told	(have) told
keep	kept	(have) kept	think	thought	(have) thought
know	knew	(have) known	wear	wore	(have) worn
*lay	laid	(have) laid	weep	wept	(have) wept
*leave	left	(have) left	win	won	(have) won
*let	let	(have) let	write	wrote	(have) written

These troublesome verbs are often used incorrectly.

31. Principal Parts of Irregular Verbs

You have studied the three main forms of verbs, which are called their three principal parts. In the last lesson you studied the principal parts of regular verbs. In this lesson you will study the principal parts of irregular verbs.

Remember the three sentences that help you to recall the principal parts of a verb.

Present:	Today I <u>talk</u>.
Past:	Yesterday I <u>talked</u>.
Past participle:	Every day I <u>have talked</u>.

For irregular verbs, the second principal part (past form) and the third principal part (past participle) are not formed by adding *-ed* as for regular verbs. Rather, they are formed in a number of different ways. Their principal parts have irregular spellings. *Ring* and *go* are two examples of irregular verbs.

Present:	Today I <u>ring</u> the bell.
Past:	Yesterday I <u>rang</u> the bell.
Past participle:	Every day I <u>have rung</u> the bell.

Present:	Today I <u>go</u>.
Past:	Yesterday I <u>went</u>.
Past participle:	Every day I <u>have gone</u>.

There is no rule to tell you how to form the second and third principal parts of irregular verbs. These forms must simply be memorized.

Many irregular verbs have three different forms, one for the first principal part, another for the second principal part, and still another for the third principal part. Study the following examples.

First (Present)	Second (Past)	Third (Past Participle)
ring	rang	(have) rung
go	went	(have) gone
break	broke	(have) broken
drink	drank	(have) drunk
fly	flew	(have) flown
know	knew	(have) known

Some irregular verbs have the same spelling for the second and third principal parts. With a few, all three forms are spelled the same. See the following examples.

First (Present)	Second (Past)	Third (Past Participle)
bring	brought	(have) brought
buy	bought	(have) bought
dig	dug	(have) dug
put	put	(have) put
set	set	(have) set

The chart before this lesson shows the principal parts of many irregular verbs. Use the chart or a dictionary whenever you do not know the correct form of a verb. If no principal parts are shown, the past and the past participle are formed in the regular way, by adding -ed. If only one principal part is shown, the past and the past participle are the same.

Memorize the three forms of irregular verbs. Remember that the past participle must always be used with the helping verb have, has, or had. The past participle is never used alone as the main verb.

- The second principal part and the third principal part of irregular verbs are formed in a number of different ways. Memorize the principal parts of irregular verbs, and always use them correctly.

Class Practice

A. Say the three principal parts for each verb in this chart. Be sure to include *have* with the third principal part.

First (Present)	Second (Past)	Third (Past Participle)
1. come	———	———
2. sing	———	———
3. give	———	———
4. see	———	———
5. know	———	———
6. go	———	———
7. bring	———	———
8. drink	———	———

B. Give the correct form of each verb in parentheses. If there is no
helping verb in the sentence, say the second principal part. If there is
a helping verb, say the helping verb and the third principal part.
1. Father has (go) to the hardware store.
2. The wise men (see) the star and followed it.
3. Herod had not (know) about the new king.
4. Micah had (write) that Jesus would be born in Bethlehem.
5. You have (sing) my favorite hymn.
6. We (begin) early this morning.
7. Mother (give) the children some fresh cookies and milk.
8. We (do) all our work early.

Written Exercises

A. Copy each verb or verb phrase. Write whether the verb is the *present*
form, the *past* form, or the *past participle*.

Example: Mother has bought some oranges.
Answer: has bought, past participle

1. Ronald has not come yet.
2. You write worthwhile letters.
3. They did their work well.
4. We know the answer.
5. My sister has gone to this school.
6. We sing this hymn often.
7. I had given them some books from this shelf.
8. They saw a moose along the road.
9. He had flown to Alaska several times.
10. They spoke about it sometimes.
11. The bells ring clearly.
12. The puppy has torn the book.
13. The boys drank all the lemonade.
14. Have you worn this dress lately?
15. Naomi and her husband had left the land of Israel.
16. Ruth spoke to Naomi with determination.
17. Orpah had gone back to her people.
18. Ruth and Naomi found rest with the people of God.

B. Write the correct form of each verb in parentheses, using the second or third principal part. Use the third principal part only when there is a helping verb, and include the helping verb in your answer.

> **Example:** Mother has (buy) some oranges.
> **Answer:**   has bought

1. The teachers have (speak) about the school trip.
2. Has he (fly) to Alaska?
3. Gary (ring) the fire alarm when he saw the smoke.
4. The puppy (tear) the book that was left on the porch.
5. The boys have (drink) the lemonade.
6. Had the children (see) the birds at the feeder?
7. Mother has (sing) our new song.
8. She has (wear) that sweater often.
9. David had (know) the memory verses from Psalm 119.
10. God has (give) many wonderful gifts.
11. The Lord (speak) to Moses on Mount Sinai.
12. He (write) on the tables of stone with His finger.
13. Ruth (go) and gleaned in the fields.
14. Boaz had (come) from Bethlehem.
15. He (speak) kind words to his workers.
16. Boaz (give) his workers a godly blessing.

C. Use the following verbs as indicated in sentences of your own.
1. the second principal part of *shake*
2. the third principal part of *know*
3. the first principal part of *taught*

Review Exercises

Write whether each sentence has *normal, inverted,* or *mixed* word order. If it has inverted or mixed order, write it in normal word order. [15]
1. At one time, cougars lived in most parts of North America.
2. With the increase of human population came the decrease of cougar territory.
3. Today most cougars are found in the western mountains.
4. Some cougars still live in the swamps of Florida.
5. In one mighty leap, a cougar can cover more than twenty feet.
6. A cougar's hind legs are longer than its front legs.
7. Because of this a cougar always appears to be walking downhill.

32. Simple Verb Tenses

Tense means "time." The tense of a verb shows whether the action has already taken place, is now taking place, or will take place at some future time. There are three simple verb tenses: the *present tense,* the *past tense,* and the *future tense.*

Be careful not to confuse the tenses of verbs with the principal parts of verbs. The *tenses* are the different *times* that verbs tell about. The *principal parts* are the different *forms* used to show the different tenses.

Verbs in the *present tense* refer to action or existence now, in the present. The *first principal part* (present form) is used for the present tense. The verb ends with *-s* if the subject is a singular noun but is not *I* or *you.*

Verbs in the present tense:

The women <u>bake</u> cookies.   They <u>see</u> George.

The woman <u>bakes</u> cookies.   She <u>sees</u> George.

Verbs in the *past tense* refer to action or existence in the past. The *second principal part* (past form) is used for the past tense. A regular verb in the past tense ends with *-ed.* For an irregular verb, the form for the past tense is spelled in various ways.

Verbs in the past tense:

Regular verbs: They <u>arrived</u> yesterday.

The children <u>learned</u> the lessons.

Irregular verbs: We <u>found</u> several kinds of wild flowers.

They <u>were</u> small and colorful.

Last summer I <u>slept</u> here.

Verbs in the *future tense* refer to action or existence that will take place in the future. The future tense is expressed by using the *first principal part* (present form) with the helping verb *shall* or *will.* In formal writing, *shall* is used with the subjects *I* and *we. Will* is used in other kinds of writing and with all other subjects.

Verbs in the future tense:

I <u>shall write</u> to her.   Rain <u>will fall</u> soon.

We <u>shall plant</u> petunias.   He <u>will bring</u> the books.

You <u>will be</u> late unless you hurry.

The following chart shows the present, past, and future tenses of two regular verbs and two irregular verbs.

Present	Past	Future
stay	stayed	will stay
journey	journeyed	will journey
freeze	froze	will freeze
bring	brought	will bring

- *Tense* means "time."

- Verbs have three simple tenses.
  1. The present tense refers to action or existence in the present. The first principal part (present form) is used for the present tense.
  2. The past tense refers to action or existence in the past. The second principal part (past form) is used for the past tense.
  3. The future tense refers to action or existence that will take place in the future. The future tense is expressed by using the first principal part (present form) with the helping verb *shall* or *will*.

Class Practice

A. Give all three tenses for each verb. The first one is done for you.

Present	Past	Future
1. arrive	arrived	will arrive
2. learn	———	———
3. stay	———	———
4. sleep	———	———
5. have	———	———
6. bring	———	———

B. Give each verb or verb phrase, and tell what tense it is.
   1. The doctor examines the cut on Marie's finger.
   2. It will not need stitches.
   3. Solomon asked the Lord for wisdom.
   4. The Lord gave him riches and wisdom.
   5. The Lord will give wisdom to all seekers of truth.
   6. Ask God for wisdom.

C. Read each sentence as it is written. Next read it in the past tense, beginning with *yesterday*. Then read it in the future tense, beginning with *tomorrow*.

1. Doris does the ironing.
2. We plant our melons.
3. Snow falls.
4. I write several letters.
5. He knows the answer.
6. I go in the morning.

Written Exercises

A. Copy the chart, and fill in all the tenses for each verb.

Present	Past	Future
1. clean	———	———
2. hike	———	———
3. carry	———	———
4. draw	———	———
5. fly	———	———
6. ride	———	———
7. move	———	———
8. obey	———	———

B. Copy the verb in each sentence. After it, write the past tense and the future tense of that verb.

> **Example:** He sings well.
> **Answer:**   sings, sang, will sing

1. My little brother sleeps soundly.
2. We have plenty of food.
3. Martha and Betty sew.
4. He brings the books with him.
5. I find nails and screws.
6. You sit near the fire.
7. We wait for him.
8. The ice floats over the dam.

C. Copy each verb or verb phrase, and write whether it is in the *present* tense, *past* tense, or *future* tense.

1. Doris copied all her exercises already.
2. A good rest will cure you.

3. Fit the pieces of the puzzle together this way.
4. Gerald burned all the trash from that room.
5. Tonight the pond will freeze over.
6. Grandmother will send the book.
7. James likes to read.
8. The Amalekites captured the wives and children of David and his men.
9. David asked God for help.
10. God answered David's prayer.
11. God will listen to the prayers of His people.
12. God always hears His children.

D. Use all three tenses of the verbs *go* and *come* in sentences of your own.

Review Exercises

A. List the eight parts of speech.

B. Name each part of speech described below. Use some names more than once.
   1. It tells *which, whose, how many,* or *what kind of.*
   2. It joins words or groups of words.
   3. It expresses strong feeling and is not related to the rest of the sentence.
   4. It names a person, place, thing, or idea.
   5. It modifies a noun or pronoun.
   6. It modifies a verb, an adjective, or an adverb.
   7. It takes the place of a noun.
   8. It tells *how, when, where,* or *to what degree.*
   9. It is a connecting word that begins a phrase.
   10. It shows action or being.

----

33. The Pattern of an Outline

An outline is an orderly arrangement of topics, subtopics, and details. Writers and speakers prepare outlines to organize their material. Readers and listeners make outlines as a help in remembering what they read or hear. An outline gives a brief summary of a composition. It shows the contents and organization of the material.

Outlines need to follow a definite pattern, as shown below.

Title of Composition

I. Topic
- A. Subtopic
- B. Subtopic
  - 1. Point
    - a. Subpoint
    - b. Subpoint
  - 2. Point

II. Topic
- A. Subtopic
- B. Subtopic

Study the following outline about olive growing. Notice how the topics, subtopics, and points are arranged in a logical order.

Growing Olives in Palestine

I. Characteristics of olive trees
- A. Thrive in rocky soil
- B. Live and bear fruit for centuries
  - 1. Bear olives only after seven years' growth
  - 2. Bear a full crop every other year

II. Harvest of olives
- A. Occurs in October
- B. Done by beating with sticks
- C. Mentioned in Scriptures
  - 1. Deuteronomy 24:20
  - 2. Isaiah 17:6

III. Uses of olives
- A. Pickled for eating
- B. Squeezed for oil
  - 1. For cooking
  - 2. For anointing
  - 3. For light

Notice how the example above follows these rules for an outline.

1. Every outline must have a title.
2. An outline is divided into topics, subtopics, points, and subpoints.
3. Topics are marked with Roman numerals.

4. Subtopics are marked with capital letters.
5. Points are marked with Arabic numerals (*1, 2,* and so on).
6. Subpoints are marked with small letters (*a, b,* and so on).
7. Each level of the outline has at least two parts. If there is an *A,* there is also a *B.* If there is a *1,* there is also a *2.* The reason is that each level indicates a division, and nothing can be divided into just one part.
8. Each level of the outline is indented.
9. The numeral or letter that marks each level is followed by a period.
10. Each topic, subtopic, and detail begins with a capital letter.
11. The topics, subtopics, and details are not stated as complete sentences. Therefore, no periods are used after any of them.

- An outline is an orderly arrangement of topics, subtopics, and details. An outline always follows a definite pattern.

Class Practice

A. Tell where these subpoints belong on the following outline.

Oranges	Plums	Tangerines
Cherries	Grapefruits	Apples

Fruits We Eat

I. Citrus fruits
   A. _____
   B. _____
   C. _____
II. Other fruits
   A. _____
   B. _____
   C. _____

B. Tell what mistakes you see in this outline.

Some States and Provinces of North America

I. States of the United States
  A. Middle Atlantic
    1. Pennsylvania
    2. New Jersey
    3. New York
  B Southern
    1. Florida
    2. Georgia
    3. Texas
  C. North Central
    1. Wisconsin
    2. North Dakota
    3. Kansas
    4. Missouri
  D. western
    1. California
    2. Utah
    3. Nevada
II. Provinces of Canada
  A. Atlantic Provinces.
    1. Newfoundland
    2. Nova Scotia
    3. Prince Edward Island
  B Prairie Provinces
    1. Manitoba
    2. Saskatchewan
    3. Alberta
  C. Pacific Province
    1. British Columbia

Written Exercises

A. Copy this outline correctly. Write the following words in their correct places. See the illustration if you are not sure where each book belongs.

Job	Micah	Mark	Major Prophets
Psalms	Nahum	Luke	Galatians
Romans	Matthew	John	Ephesians
Genesis	Joshua	Ezra	Colossians
Exodus	Judges		

Books of the Bible

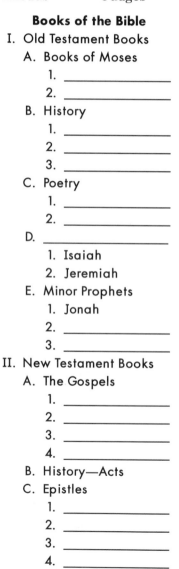

I. Old Testament Books
   A. Books of Moses
      1. _____
      2. _____
   B. History
      1. _____
      2. _____
      3. _____
   C. Poetry
      1. _____
      2. _____
   D. _____
      1. Isaiah
      2. Jeremiah
   E. Minor Prophets
      1. Jonah
      2. _____
      3. _____

II. New Testament Books
   A. The Gospels
      1. _____
      2. _____
      3. _____
      4. _____
   B. History—Acts
   C. Epistles
      1. _____
      2. _____
      3. _____
      4. _____

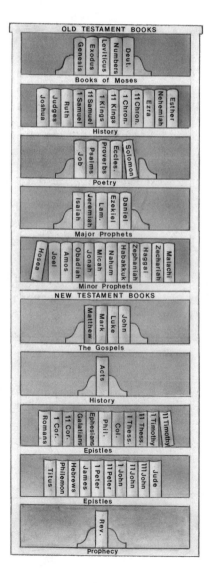

OLD TESTAMENT BOOKS

Genesis Exodus Leviticus Numbers Deut.
Books of Moses

Joshua Judges Ruth 1 Samuel 11 Samuel 1 Kings 11 Kings 1 Chron. 11 Chron. Ezra Nehemiah Esther
History

Job Psalms Proverbs Eccles. Solomon
Poetry

Isaiah Jeremiah Lam. Ezekiel Daniel
Major Prophets

Hosea Joel Amos Obadiah Jonah Micah Nahum Habakkuk Zephaniah Haggai Zechariah Malachi
Minor Prophets

NEW TESTAMENT BOOKS

Matthew Mark Luke John
The Gospels

Acts
History

Romans 1 Cor. 11 Cor. Galatians Ephesians Phil. Col. I Thess. II Thess. 1 Timothy 11 Timothy
Epistles

Titus Philemon Hebrews James 1 Peter 11 Peter 1 John 11 John 111 John Jude
Epistles

Rev.
Prophecy

B. Copy the outline below, and complete it with the following words. (You will need to provide the title.) Be sure to follow the rules in the lesson.

torch	ripsaw	hammer	sewing machine
plane	needle	pipe wrench	pipe cutter
saws	scissors	crosscut saw	

I. Tailor's tools
   A. _____
   B. _____
   C. _____
II. Plumber's tools
   A. _____
   B. _____
   C. _____
III. Carpenter's tools
   A. _____
      1. _____
      2. _____
   B. _____
   C. _____

Review Exercises

Write *true* or *false* for each sentence.

1. A paragraph is a group of sentences that tells about a single topic.
2. A paragraph has unity when all the sentences develop the topic sentence.
3. The topic sentence of a paragraph usually comes at the end.
4. In a coherent paragraph, all the details fit together well so that the reader does not get lost or confused.
5. A coherent paragraph may give details in the order of time, importance, or interest.
6. The purpose of transitional words is to produce unity in a paragraph.
7. Details in a paragraph make the topic seem less important to the reader.
8. A paragraph can be developed by using convincing details, examples and illustrations, or comparison or contrast.

Challenge Exercises

A. Make an outline like the one in Written Exercises, Part A, including all the books of the Bible.

B. Make an outline like the one in Class Practice, Part B, including all the states and provinces of North America.

---

34. Present Perfect Tense

You have learned that verbs have three main forms, called their principal parts. The following sentences are helpful for remembering the three principal parts.

Present: Today I <u>look</u>.
Past: Yesterday I <u>looked</u>.
Past participle: Every day I <u>have looked</u>.

You have also learned that verbs have three simple tenses. The *present* verb form is used for the *present tense;* the *past* form is used for the *past tense;* and the *present* form is used with *shall* or *will* for the *future tense.*

Verbs in the simple tenses:
    Present tense: The girls <u>look</u> at Orion.
    Past tense: The girls <u>looked</u> at Orion.
    Future tense: The girls <u>will look</u> at Orion.

The tenses shown above are the *simple tenses.* They are formed by using the first and second principal parts. Another set of tenses is the *perfect tenses.* They are formed by using the third principal part (past participle). The perfect tenses are shown below.

Verbs in the perfect tenses:
    Present perfect tense: The girls <u>have looked</u> at Orion.
    Past perfect tense: The girls <u>had looked</u> at Orion.
    Future perfect tense: The girls <u>will have looked</u> at Orion.

Notice that there is a perfect tense for each of the simple tenses. In this lesson you will study only the *present perfect tense*. This tense is made by using *have* with plural subjects and *has* with singular subjects except *I* or *you*.

> The children <u>have done</u> the work. (plural subject)
> Amos <u>has signed</u> the papers. (singular subject)
> Where <u>have</u> you <u>been</u>? (subject <u>you</u>)

You can recognize perfect tenses by remembering this fact: *Every verb phrase in a perfect tense includes* have, has, *or* had *as a helping verb.* You know that the helping verb *shall* or *will* always means the future tense. In the same way, the helping verb *have, has,* or *had* always means a perfect tense. If the helping verb is *have* or *has,* it is a sure sign of the present perfect tense.

Verbs in the present perfect tense:
> I <u>have eaten</u> my sandwich.
> Ann <u>has written</u> a letter.

What is "perfect" about the perfect tenses? In English grammar, *perfect* means "completed." A perfect tense speaks of completed action. Thus, a verb in the present perfect tense tells about an action that is "perfect in the present." The action is completed as of now.

> I have eaten my sandwich.
> **Meaning:** My action of eating is completed as of now.

> Ann has written a letter.
> **Meaning:** Ann's action of writing is completed as of now.

- The perfect tenses are made by using a form of *have* as a helping verb with the past participle of a main verb.

- The present perfect tense is formed by using the helping verb *have* or *has* with the past participle of a main verb.

- The perfect tenses refer to completed action. The present perfect tense refers to an action completed as of the present time.

Class Practice

A. For each sentence, say *yes* or *no* to tell whether the verb is in the present perfect tense. If it is, give the helping verb that proves it.

1. The Gospel writers have recorded many things about Jesus.
2. Jesus opened the eyes of the blind.
3. Jesus has risen from the dead.
4. Jesus ascended to heaven.
5. He has been there ever since.
6. Jesus intercedes for us.
7. All good things have come from God.
8. God created the heaven and the earth in six days.
9. He has made everything beautiful.
10. We have many reasons for praising Him.

B. Give the verb or verb phrase of each sentence in Part A. Tell whether each one is in the *present tense, past tense,* or *present perfect tense.*

C. Give the verb in each sentence. Then give its past tense and its present perfect tense.

> **Example:** Amos signs the papers.
> **Answer:**   signs, signed, has signed

1. You neglect your work.
2. The girls carry the baskets.
3. I ask this question.
4. He pushes the wagon.
5. Carl lifts the stone.
6. They print various stories.
7. We walk along the brook.
8. I do my work.

Written Exercises

A. Copy the verb or verb phrase in each sentence. Write whether each one is in the *present* tense, *past* tense, or *present perfect* tense.

1. All the students studied their lessons.
2. I have studied my lesson.
3. The sun has risen every morning.
4. It shows God's faithfulness to us.
5. Abraham lived many years ago.
6. He was a godly man.

7. James has forgotten his gloves.

8. Now he has cold hands.

9. Julie has been there a long time.

10. I have written her a long letter.

B. Write the present perfect tense of each verb in parentheses. Be sure to include the correct helping verb.

1. Mother (be) in the garden all morning.

2. We (help) her for two hours.

3. Gold and silver (be) valuable metals for many centuries.

4. Stanley (see) the Grand Canyon.

5. The geese (eat) three sacks of corn already.

6. They (grow) rapidly.

7. Luke (call) us every week.

8. The neighbors (bring) us some buns.

9. Our tomatoes (drown) because of all the rain.

10. Jesus (rise), and now He is alive forevermore.

11. Maurice (raise) rabbits for several years.

12. Finally the old dress (wear) out.

13. The operator (trace) the telephone call.

14. They (change) their number.

15. I (pay) the bill on time each month.

C. Write six sentences with the verbs *help* and *speak*. Use each word in the present tense, past tense, and present perfect tense.

Review Exercises

Copy the chart, and add the missing principal parts. Use *have* with the past participle. [30, 31]

First (Present)	Second (Past)	Third (Past Participle)
1. teach	———	———
2. destroy	———	———
3. stop	———	———
4. swim	———	———
5. shut	———	———
6. see	———	———
7. ring	———	———
8. drink	———	———

35. Past Perfect Tense

The three principal parts of verbs are used for different verb tenses. All the simple tenses are formed by using the first and second principal parts.

> **Present tense:** The birds <u>fly</u>. (first principal part)
> **Past tense:**   The birds <u>flew</u>. (second principal part)
> **Future tense:** The birds <u>will fly</u>. (first principal part)

All the perfect tenses are formed by using the third principal part. You learned about the present perfect tense in the last lesson.

> **Present perfect tense:** The birds <u>have flown</u>.

In this lesson you will study the *past perfect tense.* This tense is formed by using the helping verb *had* with the third principal part of a verb.

> **Verbs in the past perfect tense:**
> Brother David <u>had rung</u> the bell.
> Elizabeth <u>had sung</u> the song correctly.
> I <u>had heard</u> the news before you told me.

You can recognize the past perfect tense by remembering this fact: *The helping verb* had *is always used in the past perfect tense.* In the present perfect tense, either *have* or *has* may be used. But only *had* is used in the past perfect tense.

You can easily tell the difference between the simple past tense and the past perfect tense. No helping verb is used in the simple past tense. The helping verb *had* is always used in the past perfect tense.

> **Simple past tense:**
> Esau wanted the blessing, but Jacob <u>received</u> it.
> **Past perfect tense:**
> Esau wanted the blessing, but Jacob <u>had received</u> it.

Remember that the perfect tenses refer to completed action. The past perfect tense tells about an action that was "perfect in the past." The action was completed by a certain past time, which is often stated in the sentence.

> Before Father arrived, we <u>had done</u> our work.
> **Meaning:**   Our action of doing was completed by the time
>   Father arrived.

They found a flashlight, but the fox <u>had escaped</u>.
   Meaning: The fox's action of escaping was completed by the
             time they found a flashlight.

- The past perfect tense is formed by using the helping verb *had* with the past participle of a main verb.

- The past perfect tense refers to an action that was completed by a certain time in the past.

Class Practice

A. Give the verbs and verb phrases in these sentences. Tell whether each one is in the *past tense,* the *past perfect tense,* or the *present perfect tense.*
   1. David and his brother did the chores.
   2. Before we arrived, they had milked three cows.
   3. The twins have fed the calves.
   4. Saul came home after his father had found the lost donkeys.
   5. Before Saul met Samuel, God had told Samuel about him.
   6. Samuel anointed Saul to be king.
   7. Saul prophesied and praised the Lord.
   8. Have you read that story recently?

B. Give the past perfect tense of each verb in parentheses. Be sure to use the correct verb form and the correct helping verb.

   Example: The mechanic (fix) the engine before lunch.
   Answer: had fixed

   1. Harvey (go) out the door before the telephone rang.
   2. By the next morning the ship (sink).
   3. Achan (steal) some things from Jericho.
   4. The cow was dirty because she (lie) in the mud.
   5. We (have) six inches of snow before last week.
   6. Elisha (be) a farmer before he became a prophet.

Written Exercises

A. Copy the verbs and verb phrases in these sentences. Write whether the tense of each one is *past, past perfect,* or *present perfect.* (Most sentences have more than one verb or verb phrase.)

1. We assembled again after we had eaten our lunches.
2. Timothy had seen the accident, and he told us about it.
3. The boys finished before the girls had started.
4. Jane has made a small motto for Mother.
5. Saul had been a humble man before he disobeyed.
6. One thief had repented while he hung on the cross.
7. After we had sung, Brother James read a Scripture passage.
8. Long icicles have formed on the eaves.

B. Write the past perfect tense of each verb in parentheses. Be sure to use the correct verb form and the correct helping verb.

Example: The wild geese (fly) south before the cold weather came.
Answer: had flown

1. The hailstorm (destroy) many crops.
2. We (travel) through a tunnel before we stopped for lunch.
3. I (feed) the chickens before breakfast.
4. After the children (sing) three songs, the visitors left.
5. By midnight the water (rise) almost to the bridge.
6. I (know) that, but I forgot about it.
7. My older brother (wear) that coat the year before.
8. A few animals (get) sick during the cold weather.

Review Exercises

A. Change each verb in parentheses to the tense shown in italics. Be sure to use the correct helping verbs when they are needed. [32–35]

1. The girls (take) two umbrellas. *present perfect*
2. Shirley and Juanita (go) to Guatemala. *future*
3. Father (know) this man long before I met him. *past perfect*
4. This jacket (wear) out. *present perfect*
5. The girls (see) the deer. *past*
6. I could not use my tape measure because someone (break) it. *past perfect*
7. The baby (have) blue eyes. *present*
8. After I (write) the letter, I cleaned my room. *past perfect*
9. Spring (be) late that year. *past perfect*
10. I (mow) the hay after I cultivate the corn. *future*

B. Copy each word, and add the missing words. [26]

Singular	Singular Possessive	Plural	Plural Possessive
1. wolf	————	————	————
2. city	————	————	————
3. child	————	————	————
4. donkey	————	————	————
5. girl	————	————	————

C. Rewrite these expressions, using possessive forms. [26]
1. the jobs of the waitresses
2. the table of the waitress
3. the baseball bat of a boy
4. the baseballs of the boys
5. the shoes of the men

---

36. Future Perfect Tense

You have learned that the helping verbs *have, has,* and *had* are always used with the *past participle* to form the perfect tenses of verbs. In the present perfect tense, the helping verb is *have* or *has.* In the past perfect tense, the helping verb is *had.*

Present perfect tense:
He has written.
They have gone.

Past perfect tense:
He had written.
They had gone.

Another perfect tense is the *future perfect tense.* This tense is formed with the helping verbs *shall have* or *will have* and the past participle of the verb.

Verbs in the future perfect tense:
We shall have finished our work by noon tomorrow.
Sam will have left before you get here.

Whenever the helping verbs *shall have* or *will have* are used, you can be sure the verb is in the future perfect tense. Be careful not to confuse this tense with the simple future tense, in which only the helping verb *shall* or *will* is used. The helping verb *have* is not used in the simple future tense. Also, the *present* form of the main verb is used in the simple future tense, but the *past participle* is used in the future perfect tense.

> **Simple future tense:**
>> I <u>shall study</u> my lesson.
>> They <u>will work</u> six hours.

> **Future perfect tense:**
>> I <u>shall have studied</u> my lesson by noon.
>> They <u>will have worked</u> six hours by evening.

Remember that the perfect tenses refer to completed action. The future perfect tense tells about an action that will be "perfect in the future." The action will be completed by a future time that is usually stated in the sentence.

> I <u>shall have made</u> my decision before five o'clock.
>> **Meaning:**   My action of making a decision will be completed by five o'clock.

> The ministers <u>will have arrived</u> in Nigeria by noon tomorrow.
>> **Meaning:**   Their action of arriving will be completed by noon tomorrow.

- The future perfect tense is formed by using the helping verbs *shall have* or *will have* with the past participle of a main verb.

- The future perfect tense refers to an action that will be completed by a certain time in the future.

Class Practice

A. Tell whether the underlined verb phrases are in the *future tense* or the *future perfect tense.*
1. Father <u>will have decided</u> before we arrive.
2. I hope that someday this calf <u>will become</u> a cow.

3. I <u>shall have called</u> you before tomorrow evening.
4. By the time I leave, they <u>will have planted</u> four trees.
5. The glass <u>will break</u> if you drop it.

B. Give the future perfect tense of each verb in parentheses. Be sure to use the correct verb form and the correct helping verbs.

Example: We hope that we (be) at the store by Thursday.
Answer: shall have been

1. By tomorrow evening I (study) my lesson for Tuesday.
2. You (write) five letters when you have finished.
3. By Saturday, the Martins (make) six hundred cupcakes to sell.
4. Before his trip is over, Wayne (ride) on six different buses.
5. Joel (read) the three books by Saturday.
6. Before the end of the week, Sarah (bring) ten different children to Bible school.

C. Change the verb in each sentence to the future and future perfect tenses.

Example: They drive six hundred miles.
Answer: will drive, will have driven

1. They shake all the rugs.
2. The ice freezes sufficiently.
3. We sing five songs.
4. The baby drinks six bottles of formula.

Written Exercises

A. Copy each verb or verb phrase, and write whether it is in the *future* tense or the *future perfect* tense.
1. The baby will have slept two hours by four o'clock.
2. Surely Philip will have found the cows before dark.
3. By 3:00 we shall have sat in school for six hours.
4. Sheldon will feed these calves.
5. The geese will have left by next week.
6. Katie will glue the pictures onto the page.
7. A full moon will occur on Tuesday.
8. By noon tomorrow we shall have dug twenty ditches.

B. Write the future perfect tense of each verb in parentheses. Be sure to use the correct verb form and the correct helping verbs.

>**Example:** After the next load, the boys (tag) all the sheep.
>**Answer:**   will have tagged

1. If Mark gets one more mushroom, he (find) ten altogether.
2. Soon Dolores (cut) out ten dresses.
3. Laurel (draw) twenty pictures when this one is finished.
4. I (write) six poems about nature when this one is done.
5. Phyllis (give) away several bouquets by Friday.
6. By tomorrow this time, I (eat) my lunch.
7. At the end of this year, Brother John (teach) ten years.
8. We (study) three countries by the time we finish this chapter.

C. Copy the verb in each sentence, and write its future and future perfect tenses.
1. Grandmother visits all her children.
2. School begins in September.
3. Brother Joseph speaks three times at the meetings.
4. The children sleep ten hours.

Review Exercises

Copy the verb or verb phrase in each sentence. Write which tense it is: *present, past, future, present perfect, past perfect,* or *future perfect.* [32–36]

1. My cousins go to that school.
2. Dwight had thrown the ball to me.
3. Nathan's family will have left by then.
4. Marilyn forgot the price.
5. Gladys has kept the secret.
6. Robert will plant petunias.
7. The girls had sung the song well.
8. Father went to the market.
9. They have lived there for a year.
10. Nancy knows Sandra.
11. Mark will write a poem.
12. By autumn the corn will have grown tall.

37. Sentence and Topical Outlines

Outlines can be written in different forms. On a *topical outline,* each point is given as only a word or phrase. This is the kind of outline that you studied in Lesson 33. A topical outline does not have complete sentences.

On a *sentence outline,* each point is given as a complete sentence. Every sentence ends with the correct punctuation.

A writer must decide whether he will use a topical outline or a sentence outline. If some points on his outline are complete sentences, all the points should be complete sentences. Phrases should not be mixed with sentences on the same outline.

Also remember that every outline must have a title. The title gives the main idea of the outline.

Sentence outline:

Butterflies, Moths, and Skippers

I. Butterflies have special characteristics.
   A. The abdomen is narrow and straight-sided.
   B. The tips of the antennae have knobs.
   C. The head is easy to see.
   D. They sit with their wings together over their backs.
II. Moths have special characteristics.
   A. The abdomen is broad and puffy.
   B. The antennae have many different shapes.
   C. The head is usually not easy to see.
   D. They sit differently from butterflies.
      1. They sit with wings outspread like an airplane.
      2. Some sit with wings like a tent or upside-down V.
III. Skippers have special characteristics.
   A. The abdomen is much like a moth's.
   B. The antennae are far apart on the head.
   C. The wings are short and small.
   D. They are named for their fast, darting flight.
   E. They sit with their front wings together and back wings spread out.

This same outline can be shortened to a topical outline, as shown below.

Topical outline:

Butterflies, Moths, and Skippers
I. Characteristics of butterflies
   A. Narrow, straight-sided abdomen
   B. Knobbed antennae
   C. Head distinct from body
   D. Wings held together over back
II. Characteristics of moths
   A. Broad, puffy abdomen
   B. Antennae in many different shapes
   C. Head not distinct from body
   D. Wings held differently from butterfly's
      1. Outspread like airplane
      2. Held in an upside-down V
III. Characteristics of skippers
   A. Abdomen similar to moth's
   B. Antennae far apart on head
   C. Small, short wings
   D. Fast, darting flight
   E. Position of wings
      1. Front wings together
      2. Hind wings spread out

On a good outline, the points are parallel. This means each topic has a similar form. All the points in a set should start with nouns, verbs, or adjectives, or they should be alike in some other way. Sometimes all the points in a set begin with the same letter.

Suppose the main points from the outline above were written as in the following example. Can you see that the topics are not parallel?

I. Characteristics of butterflies
II. Moth characteristics
III. Skippers and their characteristics

Of course the points cannot always be perfectly parallel. But they should be made as nearly parallel as possible.

- A sentence outline has complete sentences for each point. A topical outline has only words or phrases.
- The points on a topical outline should be as nearly parallel as possible.

Class Practice

A. Reword some of the following points to make the outline parallel.

How Homes Are Heated
   I. With furnaces
      A. Wood-burning furnaces
      B. Furnaces that burn coal
      C. Some furnaces use oil.
  II. Electricity
      A. Baseboard
      B. In the ceiling
      C. Some heat and circulate water.
 III. Using energy from the sun or the earth
      A. Active solar heating
      B. Using passive solar heating
      C. Obtaining geothermal heat

B. On the chalkboard, change the outline in Part A to a sentence outline.

Written Exercises

A. Change this sentence outline into a topical outline.

Important Rivers of the World
   I. Europe has several rivers that are important for transportation.
      A. The Rhine River is the most important inland waterway of Europe.
      B. The Volga River is the longest river in Europe.
      C. The Danube River is the second longest river in Europe.
  II. Africa has some large, famous rivers.
      A. The Nile River is the longest river in the world.
      B. The Congo River is the second largest river in the world.

III. Civilizations of Asia were built around several important rivers.
   A. China has two outstanding rivers.
      1. The Yangtze River is the third longest river in the world.
      2. The Huang He River was a center of ancient Chinese civilization.
   B. Early civilizations of Mesopotamia were built around two large rivers.
      1. The Tigris River runs a fairly straight course.
      2. The Euphrates River is more winding.
   C. The Indus River was the center of an ancient civilization in India.
IV. The Mississippi and the Amazon are rivers of America.
   A. The Mississippi is the largest river system in North America.
   B. The Amazon River, of South America, is the largest river in the world.

B. Rewrite the following outline, making all the points parallel to the first one.

Important Lands of Europe
 I. Germany: Land of the Reformation
 II. Switzerland: Land where the Alps are
 III. The Netherlands: Dikes and polders are found there.
 IV. Scandinavia: where the Vikings lived
 V. Spain and Portugal: Many explorers came from this land.

Review Exercises

Copy the correct answers in parentheses.

1. Every good story tells about (a personal experience, an exciting event, a problem that was solved).
2. In a set of directions, the steps should be given (in the order they are to be done, in the order of interest, as briefly as possible).
3. Writing a good story includes all the following except (organizing notes, writing clearly, sticking to the main idea, adding all the details that come to mind).
4. Writing a good set of directions includes all the following except (making sure the information is accurate, making sure you enjoy doing what you explain, writing in complete sentences, using a variety of sentences).

5. Paragraph development can be improved in all the following ways except (using details, using examples, using a comparison, using better handwriting, using a contrast).

6. Good transitional words include all the following except (first, second, finally, then, forward, soon, next).

7. Every outline should have all the following except (a title, complete sentences, an orderly pattern, points as nearly parallel as possible).

---

38. Transitive Verbs and Direct Objects

You have learned that verbs show action or being. One kind of verb that shows action is a *transitive* verb. A transitive verb passes its action to a noun or pronoun, which is the receiver of the action. The thought of a transitive verb is not complete without a receiver of the action.

Read the following sentences. They do not seem complete, because the transitive verb has no receiver for its action. We wonder, "What did Sheila bring?" and "What did Julie throw?"

Sheila brought.   Julie threw.

A *direct object* is a noun or pronoun that receives the action of a transitive verb. A direct object usually comes after the verb and answers the question *whom* or *what*. To find a direct object, say the subject and verb together and ask *whom* or *what*. The noun or pronoun that answers the question is the direct object.

Verbs with direct objects:
Esau sold his birthright to his brother Jacob.
(Esau sold *what*? The direct object is *birthright.*)

During the storm, an angel comforted Paul.
(Angel comforted *whom*? The direct object is *Paul.*)

Paul encouraged them with the reassuring message.
(Paul encouraged *whom*? The direct object is *them.*)

A direct object is diagramed on the base line after the subject and verb, with a vertical line between the verb and the direct object. This line does not go through the base line but rests upon it.

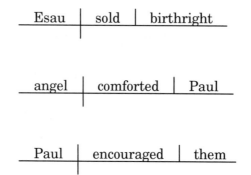

A compound direct object is diagramed on a fork after the vertical line that rests on the base line.

Jane knitted a scarf and some mittens.

If sentences have compound verbs with direct objects, they are diagramed as shown below.

We washed the dishes and folded the clothes.

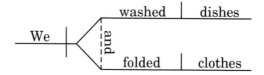

We washed and dried the dishes.

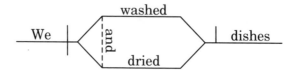

- A transitive verb passes action to another word in the sentence.

- A direct object receives the action of a transitive verb.

- A direct object is always a noun or a pronoun.

Class Practice

A. Give the transitive verbs and their direct objects. Be sure to get all the words in a verb phrase.
1. The Lord will bless His faithful people.
2. The Holy Spirit moved the prophets to speak for God.
3. God had kept Daniel safe from the lions.
4. Father passed the slow-moving vehicles.
5. Susan has written many stories and poems.

B. At the chalkboard, diagram the skeletons and direct objects of these sentences.
1. Someday Jesus will take His bride to heaven.
2. A soft answer turneth away wrath.
3. Jane read a very interesting book.
4. May we bake a white cake and some chocolate cookies?
5. Donald took the clock apart and lost the screws.

Written Exercises

A. Write the transitive verbs and their direct objects. Be sure to get all the words in a verb phrase.
1. Peter and John entered the temple.
2. Jesus healed the ten lepers.
3. God provides many good things for us.
4. We shall soon learn the answers.
5. Anna swept and mopped the floor.
6. Jesus loves you and me.
7. David was helping the neighbors for several hours.
8. The wild geese ate the corn.
9. Marcia showed the interesting picture to her friends.
10. Eldon could not find Mark and him.

B. Diagram the skeletons and direct objects of these sentences.
1. Did Ray find the keys?
2. Take this book with you.
3. Soon all the children removed their coats.
4. Please feed the calves and water the chickens.
5. The sheep and goats also need feed and water.
6. Paul and Silas came to Philippi and taught the people.

Review Exercises

Write the plural form of each noun. If a noun is always singular or is usually considered plural, simply copy it. [22, 23]

1. donkey	5. potato	9. fox	13. baby
2. chief	6. roof	10. scissors	14. measles
3. city	7. pliers	11. news	15. child
4. goose	8. mouse	12. woman	16. ox

39. Action Verbs That Are Not Transitive

You have learned that a transitive verb passes action to a receiver. A direct object is a noun or pronoun that receives the action of a transitive verb.

Harry whistled a merry tune.
> Harry whistled *what*? *Tune* is the direct object. *Whistled* is a transitive verb in this sentence because it passes action to the noun *tune*.

Not all action verbs pass action to a direct object. Sometimes an action verb is followed by an adverb instead of a direct object.

Harry whistled cheerfully.
> Harry whistled *what*? There is no word to answer this question. *Cheerfully* is an adverb that tells *how*. There is no direct object, and *whistled* is not a transitive verb in this sentence.

Sometimes an action verb is followed by a noun or pronoun in a prepositional phrase. But that noun or pronoun cannot be the direct object, for a direct object is never in a prepositional phrase.

> Harry whistled with enthusiasm.
>
>> Harry whistled *what?* There is no word to answer this question. *With enthusiasm* is a prepositional phrase that tells *how.* There is no direct object, and *whistled* is not a transitive verb in this sentence.

Study the following sentences and their diagrams. In each sentence with a direct object, the direct object tells *whom* or *what.* In each sentence without a direct object, there is no word to tell *whom* or *what.*

> Father called me.

Father	called	me

> Father called loudly.

Father	called	*(Loudly* tells *how.)*

> We often sing that song.

We	sing	song

> We often sing at school.

We	sing	*(At school* tells *where.)*

It is not hard to tell the difference between an action verb that is transitive and one that is not transitive. If a verb is transitive, it always passes action to a receiver.

> • Not all action verbs pass action to a direct object.
>
> • An action verb may be followed by an adverb or a prepositional phrase instead of a direct object.

Class Practice

A. Give the verb in each sentence, and tell whether it is *transitive* or *not transitive*. If it is transitive, also give the direct object.
   1. My cat catches mice.
   2. Sister Norma read the papers.
   3. The children were watching the birds.
   4. Joel is still standing in line.
   5. Please close the door.
   6. A small bird fell from the tree.
   7. A mouse scurried across the bare floor.
   8. We ordered a new sofa for the living room.
   9. The squirrels chattered noisily at the cat.
   10. Grace saw the little foxes in front of their den.

B. At the chalkboard, diagram the sentence skeletons and direct objects of the sentences in Part A.

Written Exercises

A. Number your paper from 1 to 16. Write only the verbs or verb phrases that are not transitive.
   1. My sisters are picking apples.
   2. Miriam can draw quite well.
   3. Everyone should sing heartily.
   4. Joshua and the Israelites conquered Jericho.
   5. Ananias could not deceive Peter.
   6. The class talked about the accident.
   7. Shirley carefully lifted the cover.
   8. Gerald and I soon smelled the smoke.
   9. The soup simmered on the burner for one hour.
   10. The cook simmered the soup for one hour.
   11. Arthur organized his desk at recess.
   12. The bird was soaring high in the blue sky.

13. The teacher assigned the next lesson.
14. Some children learn easily.
15. We traded our papers.
16. Janice traded with me.

B. Diagram the sentence skeletons and direct objects of numbers 1–10 in Part A.

C. Use each verb in two sentences, first as a verb that is transitive and then as a verb that is not transitive.
1. eat   2. read   3. play

Review Exercises

A. Copy the verb or verb phrase in each sentence. Write the present perfect, past perfect, and future perfect tenses of each verb. [34–36]

Examples: a. Peter digs worms.
b. They will see many new birds.

Answers: a. digs, has dug, had dug, will have dug
b. will see, has seen, had seen, will have seen

1. Timothy tells what happened.
2. She waits for us.
3. Richard will study diligently.
4. We begin early.

B. Copy correctly each word that needs a capital letter. [20]
1. Have you ever seen the grand canyon of arizona?
2. Long ago, produce was floated down the mississippi river in flatboats and was sold in new orleans.
3. Did the minersville christian school open this fall?
4. Do you prefer american food or italian food?
5. Are kellogg's cereals better than post cereals?
6. On friday, mrs. elizabeth d. fulton and miss barbara gauss went to see dr. fred l. frey, who is an english doctor.
7. Yesterday mr. martin w. allen and mr. ludwig m. hooke talked with brother ira d. martin.
8. dr. j. k. lee sees patients at the memphis general hospital.
9. The lord will hear when i call on him.
10. O lord, my god, in thee do i put my trust.

40. Transitive Verbs and Indirect Objects

You have learned that a transitive verb passes its action to a receiver, and that a direct object receives the action of a transitive verb. A direct object answers the question *whom* or *what* after the skeleton.

> Moses viewed Canaan from the mountaintop.
> (Moses viewed *what*? The direct object is *Canaan*.)

A transitive verb may also have an *indirect object*. An indirect object is a noun or pronoun that tells *to whom or what* or *for whom or what* the action of the verb is done. An indirect object always comes between a verb and a direct object.

subject   verb   indirect object   direct object
↓   ↓   ↓   ↓
Marilyn   wrote   her   cousin   a   letter.

To find an indirect object, first say the subject, the verb, and the direct object together. Then ask *to whom or what* or *for whom or what*. The answer will be the indirect object.

Sentences with indirect objects:

> Sister Gladys showed the class some pictures.
> > Sister Gladys showed *what*? The direct object is *pictures*.
> > Sister Gladys showed pictures *to whom*? The indirect object is *class*.

> Father bought us a good book.
> > Father bought *what*? The direct object is *book*. Father bought book *for whom*? The indirect object is *us*.

Be careful not to confuse an indirect object with a direct object.

> My sister baked me a pie.
> > Sister baked *what*? The direct object is *pie*.
> > Sister baked pie *for whom*? The indirect object is *me*.
> > My sister baked a *pie;* she did not bake *me!*

Also be careful not to confuse an indirect object with the object of a preposition. An indirect object is never found in a prepositional phrase. It never comes after a word like *to* or *for*. Compare these two sentences.

My sister baked <u>me</u> a pie. (indirect object)

My sister baked a pie for <u>me</u>. (object of preposition)

Both sentences have exactly the same meaning. But *me* cannot be an indirect object in the second sentence for two reasons.

(1) *Me* does not come between the verb and the direct object.

(2) *Me* comes after the preposition *for.*

Any sentence with an indirect object can be changed to a sentence with a prepositional phrase. Some sentences with prepositional phrases can also be changed to sentences with indirect objects. But an indirect object and the object of a preposition are never the same.

Indirect object:

The girls sent <u>Grandmother</u> some cards.

Object of preposition:

The girls sent some cards to <u>Grandmother</u>.

Indirect object:

Susan sold the <u>customer</u> from town some eggs.

Object of preposition:

Susan sold some eggs to the <u>customer</u> from town.

An indirect object is diagramed on a horizontal line beneath the base line, with a slanted line connecting the indirect object to the verb.

Diane told the children a story.

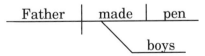

Father made the boys a rabbit pen.

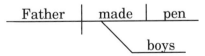

An indirect object can be compound. Study the following example.

Mother bought Karen and me a new storybook.

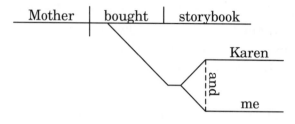

- An indirect object tells *to whom or what* or *for whom or what* the action of the verb is done.

- An indirect object is always found between the verb and the direct object in a sentence.

Class Practice

A. Tell whether each sentence has an indirect object. If it does, tell what it is.
1. Dennis and I will build Fido a house.
2. The noise must have been thunder.
3. Jesus taught His disciples many things.
4. We found the lost book in the barrel.
5. A housefly can move its wings very fast.
6. Someone has sent my brother these books.
7. He will bring the little ones a surprise.
8. The deer stood in the water near to the shore.

B. Diagram the skeletons, direct objects, and indirect objects at the chalkboard.
1. My brother carved me a whistle.
2. The Lord gave Moses the Ten Commandments.
3. Brother Lester found the visitor a seat.
4. Evelyn brought me a chocolate bar.

  5. Father gave each of the workers a check.
  6. We shall send the sick girl and boy a card.

C. Read each sentence in Part B, changing the indirect object to the object of a preposition.

D. Read the following sentences, changing the object of the preposition to an indirect object.
  1. I will give some water to the flowers.
  2. The farmer fed some hay to his steers.

Written Exercises

A. Diagram the skeletons, direct objects, and indirect objects.
  1. Aunt Sarah has baked our family a fresh blueberry pie.
  2. We are making a chart for science class.
  3. We can sell the driver some fresh vegetables.
  4. The old wagon was sinking rapidly into the mud.
  5. Brother Sensenig has given the school these lovely rosebushes.
  6. I must write the man a bill for the various repairs.
  7. Adam gave each animal a name.
  8. Marla often writes her sister a letter.
  9. This rug feels very soft.
  10. Sandra felt the soft rug too.

B. Rewrite each sentence so that the indirect object becomes the object of a preposition at the end of the sentence.
  1. Jesse fed the calves some grain.
  2. Jeffrey sent his sick cousin a card.
  3. Mother sewed Nathan a jacket.
  4. The farmer gave his cows some alfalfa hay.

C. Rewrite each sentence so that the object of the preposition becomes an indirect object.
  1. Arlene read a story to the children.
  2. We bought more feed for the chickens.
  3. The boys made a bookcase for Mother.
  4. Curtis brought the mail to Father.

Review Exercises

A. Copy each verb, and add the missing principal parts. [30, 31]

First (Present)	Second (Past)	Third (Past Participle)
1. blow	_____	_____
2. burst	_____	_____
3. hold	_____	_____
4. swing	_____	_____
5. tag	_____	_____
6. refuse	_____	_____
7. worry	_____	_____
8. knit	_____	_____

B. Copy each verb or verb phrase, and write what tense it is: *present, past, future, present perfect, past perfect,* or *future perfect.* [32–36]
   1. Mother bought two watermelons at the supermarket.
   2. I have fought a good fight.
   3. The apostle Paul had kept the faith.
   4. Jesus wept at Lazarus's grave.
   5. Jonathan has cut his finger.
   6. This costs too much.
   7. By then Laura will have drawn three horses.
   8. Will you read the new book?

---

41. Forming an Outline From a Composition

An outline is an orderly arrangement of main ideas and less important ideas. It is like a map, guiding you as you study. An outline shows how the ideas in a composition are organized. This makes it easy to see how the ideas are related to each other.

To make an outline from a composition, write in order the main idea of each paragraph. You know that the main idea of a paragraph is found in the topic sentence. The main idea of each paragraph becomes a main topic on the outline.

Study the following composition and the outline that follows it. The topic sentences are underlined.

Living in Tents in Bible Times

<u>Many people lived in tents in Bible times.</u> Genesis 4 says that Jabal was the father of those who dwelt in tents. He must have been the first tent dweller. The patriarchs lived in tents. Genesis 12 tells how Abraham pitched his tent near Bethel. In Genesis 26 we read that Isaac pitched his tent in the valley of Gerar, and in Genesis 33 we see that Jacob pitched his tent before a city of Shechem. The children of Israel lived in tents during the forty years in the wilderness. Some of them also lived in tents after they reached Canaan.

<u>How was a tent made?</u> A tent was usually made of black goats' hair. It was often in an oblong shape. Many tents had only two or three rooms. The rooms were separated by goats'-hair curtains.

<u>A tent had various furnishings.</u> Rugs were often used for floor coverings. The beds were mats that could be rolled up during the day. A piece of leather was spread out on the ground for a table. The seats were the floor. For an oven, a hollow was made in the ground and several stones were placed in it. Skin bags and leather buckets were used to carry water and other liquids.

Living in Tents in Bible Times
I. Who lived in tents
II. How tents were made
III. How tents were furnished

This simple outline does not include nearly all the details in the composition. We can go through the composition again, pick out the details that were used to develop the paragraphs, and add them to the outline. These details will be subtopics and points on the outline. Study the following outline with this added information.

Living in Tents in Bible Times
I. Who lived in tents
  A. Jabal
  B. The patriarchs
    1. Abraham
    2. Isaac
    3. Jacob

C. The Israelites
   1. In the wilderness
   2. In Canaan
II. How tents were made
   A. With black goats' hair
   B. In an oblong shape
   C. With two or three rooms
III. How tents were furnished
   A. Rugs for floor coverings
   B. Mats for beds
   C. Piece of leather for table
   D. Floor for seats
   E. Hollow in ground for oven
   F. Skin bags and leather buckets for liquids

Making an outline from a composition helps you to see the main ideas of the composition. It also helps you to see how the different ideas are related to each other. Organizing the material in this way will help you to remember it better. It will help you in your studies.

- When an outline is formed from a composition, the main idea of each paragraph becomes a main topic on the outline.

- The details used to develop the paragraphs become subtopics and points on the outline.

Class Practice

Form a sentence outline and a topical outline from the first paragraph of the composition "Mining Coal" in Written Exercises. Do this together as a class activity.

Written Exercises

Write a topical outline from the following composition. Use a Roman numeral for the main topic of each paragraph.

Mining Coal

When was coal first used? The Chinese used it already in the 300s to heat buildings and smelt metals. By the year 1000, coal was an important fuel in China. Commercial coal mining began in Europe during the 1200s, but coal was not an important fuel there until a severe shortage of wood developed in the 1600s. Then many Europeans began using coal. In North America, the Indians dug coal out of hillsides long before white men came. Some Indians used coal for baking pottery.

What kinds of mines are used to dig coal? Surface mines were used first. Indians and white pioneers simply dug coal out of hillside mines where coal was easy to get. Surface mines today are strip mines, where layers of rock and soil are stripped away to uncover the coal beneath. Underground mines came into use as coal deposits became harder to reach. In a drift mine, a tunnel is dug straight into the side of a hill to follow a coal seam. A mine with a sloping tunnel is called a slope mine. To reach coal far below the surface, a shaft mine is used. Such a mine has a tunnel going straight down into the ground, with side tunnels extending into the seams of coal.

What are some dangers of coal mining? One danger in underground mines is cave-ins. Walls and ceilings must be carefully braced so that they do not collapse. A second danger is gases such as carbon dioxide, carbon monoxide, and methane, which can cause miners to suffocate. Instruments are used to check for the accumulation of these gases, and powerful fans blow fresh air into an underground mine. When miners hit an underground river, they often face a third danger—flooding. Large pumps must be used to direct the water safely outside. A fourth danger is fire, which is sometimes caused when explosives are used in the presence of certain gases. Coal mining still has some dangers, but they are not nearly as great today as they were long ago.

Review Exercises

Read these two sets of directions, and write the title of the set that is better. Then write two reasons why it is better. [8]

How to Make a Model Volcano

It is best to do this project outside. First make a mountain of sand inside a box. Bury a small soup can up to its top in the mountain, keeping the top open. Then put two tablespoons baking soda into the can. Add several drops of red food coloring. Pour three-fourths cup vinegar over the soda in the can. Your volcano will erupt instantly!

A Model Volcano

Make a mountain of sand. Bury a can inside the mountain. Put some baking soda into the can. Pour almost a full cup of vinegar over the soda in the can. It is best to do this project outside. Put food coloring into the can. The mountain of sand should be inside the box.

Challenge Exercises

Outline the chapter you are presently studying in science or history.

---

42. The Linking Verb *Be* and Predicate Nominatives

Most verbs are words of action. But the verb *be* expresses being rather than action. *Be* is never transitive; it cannot pass action to a direct object because it does not express action. The forms of *be* are *am, is, are, was, were, be, been,* and *being.*

If an action verb is followed by a noun, the noun is usually a direct object. A form of *be* may also be followed by a noun (or a pronoun), but it is not a direct object. Look at the following sentences.

> This book is an old <u>hymnal</u>.
> My teacher was <u>she</u>.

In the sentences above, *hymnal* and *she* cannot be direct objects, because they follow forms of *be.* They are *predicate nominatives* (also called predicate nouns or pronouns). A predicate nominative is a noun or pronoun in the predicate that renames the subject.

The verbs in the sentences above are *linking verbs* rather than action verbs. A linking verb joins a word in the predicate to the subject. All the forms of *be* can be used as linking verbs.

A linking verb is like an equal sign in arithmetic. When it is followed by a predicate nominative, it shows that a noun or pronoun in the predicate is equal to the subject.

> This <u>book</u> is an old <u>hymnal</u>. (book = hymnal)
> My <u>teacher</u> was <u>she</u>. (teacher = she)

Since the subject and the predicate nominative are equal, they can usually be exchanged and the sentence still has the same meaning. Subjects and direct objects cannot be exchanged in this way.

Saul was Israel's first king. Israel's first king was Saul.
(Sentences have predicate nominatives; meaning is the same.)
Saul defeated the Philistines. The Philistines defeated Saul.
(Sentences have direct objects; meanings are different.)

A form of *be* is a linking verb only when it is the main verb. When it is used with an action verb, it is a helping verb.

Henry was chopping the wood. (*Was* is a helping verb.)
They are my brothers. (*Are* is a linking verb.)
Brother Harry has been my teacher. (*Been* is a linking verb.)

A predicate nominative is diagramed on the base line after the skeleton, with a slanted line between the verb and the predicate nominative. The slanted line leans toward the subject to show that the predicate nominative renames the subject.

They	are \ brothers

Brother Harry	has been \ teacher

A predicate nominative may also be compound.

The visitors were she and they.

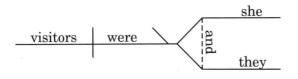

- A predicate nominative is a noun or pronoun that follows a linking verb and renames the subject.

- The forms of *be* are often used as linking verbs.

Class Practice

A. Tell whether each sentence has an *action verb* or a *linking verb*, and whether the verb is followed by a *direct object* or a *predicate nominative*.

1. Those tall trees are Douglas firs.
2. The men were planting Douglas firs.
3. Sister Eunice knows our teacher.
4. Sister Eunice will be our teacher.
5. Uncle Amos hired a good worker.
6. Uncle Amos has been a good worker.
7. Robert is the new African pupil.
8. Robert visited the new African pupil.
9. The learners will be you and I.
10. The fastest workers were he and she.

B. On the chalkboard, diagram the skeleton and the predicate nominative of each sentence in Part A that has a linking verb.

Written Exercises

A. Diagram the skeleton and predicate nominative of each sentence.

1. I am the Bread of Life.
2. Ye are the light of the world.
3. Ye shall be My people.
4. The Lord is my rock.
5. The Good Shepherd is He.
6. The Bible is the best Book.

B. Copy each verb, and write A for action or L for linking after it. Also copy each direct object or predicate nominative, and write DO or PN to tell which it is.

> **Examples:** a. The teachers will be he and she.
> b. The teachers will help us.
>
> **Answers:** a. will be—L; he—PN; she—PN
> b. will help—A; us—DO

1. The children made Mother a flower garden.
2. These little animals must be moles and shrews.
3. The first Americans were Indians.
4. Muddy water was flooding the road.
5. The nurses were she and they.

6. My little sister's favorite dessert is sherbet.
7. I shall always remember that strange man.
8. Charles is selling those people some strawberries.
9. One day this book will be a valued possession.
10. The visitors were officers and soldiers from a nearby camp.
11. They asked the minister a difficult question.
12. Every good student must be a hard worker.
13. I am he.
14. My father showed the boys the solution.

C. Four sentences in Part B have indirect objects. Write the numbers of those sentences, and write the indirect objects.

Review Exercises

A. Write all six tenses of each verb. [32–36]

Example: go
Answer: go, went, will go, have gone, had gone, will have gone

1. help   3. sleep
2. bring   4. forget

B. For each verb in parentheses, write the tense shown in italics. [32–36]
1. When I throw the ball, my dog (catch) it in his mouth. *simple present*
2. Father (dig) the ditch for the water pipes. *present perfect*
3. Be careful, or you (break) the shovel handle. *simple future*
4. The water (freeze) during the night. *past perfect*
5. I (put) it into the freezer. *present perfect*
6. Leon (ride) with us to church. *simple past*
7. The fox (run) away by the time we got there. *past perfect*
8. By Monday morning, James (go) home. *future perfect*
9. I (write) the letter by tomorrow evening. *future perfect*
10. Yesterday the swallows (come) back. *past tense*

C. Diagram the skeleton of each sentence that has a transitive verb. Include any direct object or indirect object on your diagram. [38–40]
1. John found his friend a book.
2. We hurried past the strange dog.
3. The other boys gathered wood for the fire.
4. This house was once a church building.

43. Linking Verbs and Predicate Adjectives

You have learned that a linking verb links the subject to a word in the predicate. All the forms of *be* can be used as linking verbs. The word that is linked to the subject may be a noun or pronoun that renames the subject. If so, it is a predicate nominative.

Sentences with predicate nominatives:
> That star is <u>Sirius</u>.
> My cousin is <u>she</u>.

A linking verb may also link the subject to an *adjective* in the predicate. Such an adjective is called a *predicate adjective*. A predicate adjective follows a linking verb and modifies the subject.

Sentences with predicate adjectives:
> The road is <u>rough</u>.
> > The linking verb *is* links *road* and *rough*. We know that *rough* modifies *road* because it is sensible to say *rough road*.
> You should always be <u>kind</u>.
> > The linking verb *should be* links *You* and *kind*. We do not usually say *kind you,* but *kind* does modify *You.* It tells what kind of person you should be.

There are other verbs besides the forms of *be* that can be linking verbs. In grade 5 you studied the linking verbs in the first line below. They may be called verbs of *sense* because they refer to the five senses of the body. The second line shows some more words that may be linking verbs. You should memorize all these linking verbs.

Verbs of sense: taste, feel, smell, sound, look, appear
Other linking verbs: grow, seem, stay, become, remain

> The news <u>sounds</u> good.
> > **Compare:** The news *is* good.
> The child <u>seemed</u> ill.
> > **Compare:** The child *was* ill.

Predicate adjectives are diagramed like predicate nominatives. The line before the predicate adjective leans toward the subject to show that the adjective describes the subject.

The weather feels pleasant.

<u>weather</u> | feels   \   <u>pleasant</u>

The predicate adjective may be compound.

The baby was hungry and tired.

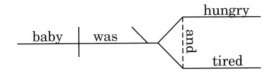

- A predicate adjective follows a linking verb and modifies the subject of the sentence.

- Linking verbs include the forms of *be* and verbs such as the following:
    taste, feel, smell, sound, look, appear
    grow, seem, stay, become, remain

Class Practice

A. Find the linking verbs and predicate adjectives in these sentences.
1. These ripe apples are sweet.
2. Our garden is hard and dry.
3. Their work usually seemed easy.
4. The sky quickly grew dark.
5. The bigger cat looked annoyed.

B. Give the linking verb in each sentence. Also give the predicate nominative or predicate adjective, and tell which one it is.
1. My little brother is a good worker.
2. This work may be too difficult for him.
3. These old nuts taste strange.
4. The trash can in the kitchen has become full.
5. Those five cattle are Father's steers.
6. The steers are becoming restless and noisy.

C. On the chalkboard, diagram the skeletons, predicate nominatives, and predicate adjectives in Part B.

Written Exercises

A. Write the linking verbs and predicate adjectives in these sentences. Be sure to get all the words in the verb phrases.
1. Goliath was extremely tall.
2. The birds in the trees sounded happy.
3. The answer will soon be clear.
4. Some of the flowers became droopy.
5. A warm sweater would feel comfortable.
6. His younger brother was growing nervous.

B. Diagram the skeletons, predicate nominatives, and predicate adjectives of these sentences. Above each predicate nominative or predicate adjective on your diagrams, write *PN* or *PA* to tell which one it is.
1. The fresh fruit tasted delicious.
2. Our old dog looks weary.
3. Their early flowers are pansies.
4. That second boy must be he.
5. The Weavers have always been friendly.
6. The next arrivals will be they.
7. Soon the thick ice becomes soft.
8. Those men were sailors.
9. Can those people be we?
10. He will probably be late today.
11. The first day seemed very long.
12. The other tall girl was she.

C. Write sentences of your own, using these verbs with predicate adjectives.
1. am   3. seem   5. look
2. was   4. sound

Review Exercises

Diagram the skeletons of only the sentences with transitive verbs. Include the direct and indirect objects on your diagrams. [38–40]
1. Alma and Betty have written their brother a note.
2. Our leader has shown us a good example.
3. Lush green plants were growing along the canal.
4. The eastern sky was growing bright.
5. That old man had been a teamster.
6. The children gathered leaves for a science project.

7. Many anxious people gathered before the doorway.
8. Our brother made the kittens a box.
9. Finally the ground became warm.
10. Jesus told His listeners many parables.
11. God shows the honest seeker the truth.
12. God's children are kind and patient.

Challenge Exercises

Follow the directions.

1. Write a sentence with a direct object and an indirect object. Diagram your sentence.
2. Write a sentence with a compound indirect object. Diagram your sentence.
3. Write a sentence with a compound predicate nominative. Diagram your sentence.
4. Write a sentence with a predicate adjective. Do not use any of the forms of *be*. Diagram your sentence.

---

44. Linking Verbs or Action Verbs?

You have learned that verbs other than forms of *be* may be linking verbs. Here are the other linking verbs you have met.

Verbs of sense: taste, feel, smell, sound, look, appear
Other linking verbs: grow, seem, stay, become, remain

The verbs shown above are not always linking verbs. Sometimes they are action verbs. They may or may not be used as transitive verbs, passing action to a direct object. Look at the following sentences.

The alarm sounded harsh.
Wesley sounded the alarm.
The alarm sounded harshly in the morning.

In the first sentence, *harsh* is a predicate adjective describing the subject *alarm*. We know that *sounded* is a linking verb because it can be replaced by a form of *be:* The alarm *was* harsh.

In the second sentence, *sounded* is not a linking verb, because it cannot be replaced by a form of *be*. It is not sensible to say, "Wesley was the alarm." *Sounded* expresses action, and *alarm* is the receiver of the action. So *alarm* is the direct object, and *sounded* is a transitive verb.

Now look at the third sentence. The verb *sounded* is not a linking verb, because it is not sensible to say, "The alarm was harshly." (*Harshly* is an adverb that tells *how*.) *Sounded* is not followed by a predicate nominative or a predicate adjective. Neither is it followed by a direct object. (*Morning* is in a prepositional phrase.) Therefore, *sounded* is simply an action verb; it does not pass the action to any word in the sentence.

So be careful. Verbs like *sound, feel, grow,* and *remain* are not always linking verbs. Sometimes they are used in these two other ways—as transitive verbs with direct objects or as action verbs that are not transitive.

Remember the test for linking verbs. If the verb can be replaced by a form of *be* without changing the meaning of the sentence, it is a linking verb.

> He <u>looked</u> sick.
> **Think:** He *was* sick. *Looked* is a linking verb because the meaning is about the same.
> He <u>looked</u> outside.
> **Think:** He *was* outside. *Looked* is not a linking verb, because the meaning is different.

Another test is to see whether the subject is doing the action expressed by the verb. If so, the verb cannot be a linking verb. Linking verbs do not express action; they simply link the subject to a predicate nominative or predicate adjective. Compare the following sentences.

> The trees grew swiftly.
> The trees grew old.

In the first sentence, the trees did the action of growing. *Swiftly* is an adverb that tells how the trees grew. There is no predicate nominative or predicate adjective. So *grew* is an action verb, not a linking verb.

The second sentence does not emphasize the action of growing. It simply says that the trees grew (became) old. The sentence could be changed to "The trees were old," and it would mean about the same. Also, the predicate adjective *old* describes the subject *trees*. So *grew* is a linking verb.

You cannot tell whether a verb is a linking verb or an action verb just by looking at the verb itself. You must also look at other words in the sentence. If there is a predicate nominative or a predicate adjective, the verb must be a linking verb. If the verb expresses action—and especially if a direct object receives the action—it must be an action verb.

- Verbs of sense (*taste, feel, smell, sound, look, appear*) and other linking verbs (*grow, seem, stay, become, remain*) are not always used as linking verbs. Sometimes they are transitive verbs with direct objects, and sometimes they are action verbs that are not transitive.

Class Practice

A. Tell whether the verb in each sentence is a *linking verb* or an *action verb*. Read each sentence that has a linking verb, replacing that verb with a form of *be*.
   1. This watermelon tastes sweet.
   2. We tasted the different kinds of cakes.
   3. The girls felt the soft, silky cloth.
   4. The cloth felt soft and silky.
   5. The twins have grown rapidly.
   6. They grew tomatoes in their garden plot.
   7. The tomatoes looked red and juicy.
   8. The floor becomes wet and slippery.
   9. The teacher sounded the bell.
   10. The bell sounded quite musical.

B. Tell whether each verb is a *linking verb,* an *action verb that is transitive,* or an *action verb that is not transitive.*
   1. John felt sick in the morning.
   2. John felt a pebble in his shoe.
   3. The new baby appeared quite healthy.
   4. Soon Jason appeared around the corner.
   5. Jonathan became David's friend.
   6. Jonathan helped his friend.
   7. Audrey looked up quickly.
   8. Loren looked cheerful.

C. On the chalkboard, diagram the skeletons, direct objects, predicate nominatives, and predicate adjectives in Part A. Label the verbs *A* for action verb or *L* for linking verb. Use *DO, PN,* or *PA* to label the direct objects, predicate nominatives, and predicate adjectives.

Written Exercises

A. Copy the verb or verb phrase in each sentence, and write *A* for action or *L* for linking after it. If it is a linking verb, also copy the predicate nominative or predicate adjective and label it *PN* or *PA*.

>   **Examples:** a. Ben tasted the cookies.
>   b. The new potatoes tasted delicious.

>   **Answers:** a. tasted—A
>   b. tasted—L; delicious—PA

1. The teacher looked into his desk.
2. Your idea sounds good to me.
3. The room looks clean.
4. The fireman sounded the alarm.
5. The pie smells delicious.
6. Your room has become a tidy place.
7. Suddenly a deer appeared on the road.
8. In a few minutes the audience grew silent.
9. Sharon remained quiet for a while.
10. I have grown many pansies.
11. Hugo has become a carpenter.
12. The work seems hard.
13. The dessert was a thick pudding.
14. Stay here by the suitcases.
15. The bananas stayed green for days.
16. Gerald appeared fearful after his experience.
17. The students remain in their seats.
18. The homemade bread tasted good.

B. Diagram the skeletons, direct objects, predicate nominatives, and predicate adjectives of these sentences.
1. Soon tiny plants appeared above the surface.
2. The plants appeared healthy.
3. The pigs grow fatter every day.
4. The farmer grows much corn for them.
5. The children looked strong and healthy.

6. Look at the beautiful sunset.
7. I will taste the soup for you.
8. It tastes rich and spicy.
9. Sick children should remain inside the house.
10. The boy remains ill.
11. I shall soon become an artist.
12. The boys look happy most of the time.
13. Feel the sticky stem of this plant.
14. She feels quite well again.

Review Exercises

Correct the run-on errors as indicated. [14]
1. Use periods and capital letters.
    a. The earth spins on its axis like a fast-moving top a person standing at the equator moves over 1,000 miles an hour most jets don't even fly that fast.
    b. The earth is also revolving around the sun it takes the earth one year to make a complete revolution the earth travels 65,600 miles per hour not even a rocket can fly that fast.
2. Use commas and suitable conjunctions.
    a. We are traveling very fast we do not get dizzy.
    b. The earth moves smoothly it never stops or makes sudden changes in speed.
3. Use semicolons.
    a. The earth is constantly moving it never stops.
    b. The sun appears to travel around the earth actually the earth is traveling around the sun.

---

45. Giving an Oral Book Report

A book report can give much valuable information. It tells what a book is about, and it also reveals how well you have read the book. If a book report is well done, it can help other people decide to read a certain book.

To give an oral book report, first choose a book that is approved by your teacher or parents. Read the whole book before you begin preparing for your report.

Make a list of points that you will cover when you give your report. Your points should include the following four kinds of information.

1. The title of the book, the name of the author, the copyright date of the book, and a place where the book can be found.
2. The setting and main characters of the book.
3. The main events in the book.
4. Your opinion of the book.

The setting is the place and time of the story. In what country, city, or state did it happen? Did it happen in recent times, in the pioneer days of America, or when? The main characters are the most important people in the story. You should give a brief description of them, and you may also include what you think of each character.

The main events of a book are the main problems that the characters faced and the way they dealt with the problems. Briefly tell what happened, but do not give the outcome. A good way to do this is to ask questions about things that happened in the book. Leave your listeners in suspense so that they will want to read the book too.

When you give your opinion of the book, tell what you enjoyed most about the story. Tell what lesson the story teaches, or give some other reason why you think others should read the book.

Write your notes briefly. Do not write every word you plan to say, but prepare to *tell* your report. It would be good to practice giving the report to someone at home.

Sample notes for an oral book report:

1. *Evangelists in Chains,* by Elizabeth Wagler
   Copyright date, 1983
   Available from Rod and Staff Publishers
2. *Setting:* Mountain valley of northern Austria during the 1500s
   Main characters: Peter Hans, a nineteen-year-old boy
                       People from his family and church
3. *Main events:* Imprisonment of Peter, his father, and others
                    Crushed dreams and hopes
                    Traveling evangelists even in chains
4. *Opinion:* A challenge to your faith and obedience
              A challenge to share the truth with others

When you give your report, remember to stand up straight, wear a pleasant expression, and speak loudly and clearly enough so that everyone can understand you easily. You should have your notes handy so that you can glance at them when you need them. But you should not have your eyes glued to your notes, to the floor, or to the back wall. Look at your listeners, and talk to *them*.

The following paragraphs show what a person might say when he gives an oral report on the book *Evangelists in Chains*.

> *Evangelists in Chains* was written by Elizabeth Wagler. It was copyrighted in 1983 and is available from Rod and Staff Publishers.
>
> This story took place in a mountain valley of northern Austria during the 1500s. The main character is a nineteen-year-old boy named Peter Hans. Other main characters are people from Peter's family and his church. His father especially was an encouragement to him as they suffered together. Peter's mother influenced him by her godly life and prayers. His sister was a Christian, and she encouraged Peter by her letters. The ministers of his church gave him hope and encouragement through their sermons in prison.
>
> Peter and his father, with some other men from their church, were captured by soldiers and put into prison for their faith. The men suffered from cold and hunger. They were no longer free to work or to be with their families. Some of the men died from the hardships of prison life. Peter's faith was tested, but it grew stronger as he faced many temptations there. His dreams and hopes seemed crushed, yet some surprises awaited him. The men became traveling evangelists even in their chains as they shared the Gospel wherever they went. What would happen to the men? Would they ever be free again? Peter learned to trust in the Lord whatever the outcome.
>
> You should read this book. It will challenge your faith. It will help you to trust the Lord as He leads in your life. It will challenge you to obey the Bible no matter what difficulties you may face. It will challenge you to share the truth with others.

- A book report gives basic information about a book. It does not tell the whole story.

- A book report may help others decide to read a certain book.

Class Practice

Answer the following questions about book reports.

1. How do book reports help other people?
2. How much of a book should you read before you give a report on it?
3. What should you do to prepare for an oral book report?
4. What four kinds of information should you give in a book report?
5. What is the setting?
6. What parts of the story should you tell? What part should you not tell?

Written Exercises

Prepare to give an oral report on a book you have read recently. Follow the directions given in the lesson.

Review Exercises

Tell whether each paragraph is developed by examples and illustrations or by comparison or contrast. [24, 27]

Paragraph A:

Mealtime Customs

Tent dwellers in Bible times had mealtime customs that were quite different from ours. We usually sit in chairs around a table, but they sat around a cloth on the ground. We eat with knives, forks, and spoons, but they washed their hands carefully before each meal and ate with their fingers. Instead of dipping soup into each person's plate, everyone ate from a large central dish with soup, sauce, or gravy in it. Our bread is in slices cut from a loaf, but theirs was paper-thin. Each person would tear off a piece of bread, dip it into the dish, and eat it. As a special sign of friendship, they would place a choice morsel of food on a little piece of bread and give it to a friend.

Paragraph B:

Early Rising

In Bible times, people in Palestine usually got up very early in the morning. Genesis 22 tells us that Abraham rose early in the morning to take Isaac to the land of Moriah. Exodus 34 says that Moses rose early to go up on Mount Sinai. Job rose early in the morning to offer sacrifices for his children. Mark wrote that Jesus rose a great while before day to pray. This habit of rising early is due partly to the climate in Palestine. For most of the year, it is cool for only a few hours after sunrise. Then the heat becomes so great that heavy work is difficult.

_____

46. Chapter 4 Review

Class Practice

A. Answer the following questions.
1. What is a verb?
2. What is a transitive verb?
3. What is a direct object?
4. What is an indirect object?
5. If a sentence has an indirect object, what else must it have?
6. What kind of notes should you write to prepare for an oral book report?
7. What four kinds of information should you include in a book report?
8. What is the setting of a story?
9. Every outline must begin with a what?
10. What word describes the points on an outline if they have a similar form?

B. Say the three principal parts of each verb. Use *have* with the past participle.

First (Present)	Second (Past)	Third (Past Participle)
1. like	———	———
2. grow	———	———
3. wear	———	———
4. burst	———	———
5. bring	———	———
6. come	———	———
7. reach	———	———

C. Give the six tenses of each verb: present, past, future, present perfect, past perfect, and future perfect.
1. begin   3. cost   5. sleep
2. choose   4. know   6. buy

D. Give the tense of each underlined verb.
1. The ice has frozen solid.
2. Sharon writes letters every Sunday.
3. Father had dug the ditch before it rained.
4. Susan will receive the recipe tomorrow.
5. Mother has prepared a meal for the visitors.
6. Lorene had done all her work beforehand.
7. By the time they leave, I shall have listed all their names.
8. Gerald kept all the notes from his classes.

E. Read each sentence, changing the indirect object to the object of a preposition at the end of the sentence.
1. My brother made his teacher a bookstand.
2. We shall take our grandmother a cake.

F. Tell how to finish the outline below with the following words. Tell how to improve the main topics so that they are parallel.

Tornadoes	Cumulus	Rain
Nimbus	Hail	Thunderstorms
Hurricanes	Blizzards	Sleet
Snow	Cirrus	Stratus

Elements of the Weather
I. Kinds of clouds
II. Precipitation and its forms
III. Storm types

Written Exercises

A. Copy all the verbs and verb phrases from the following sentences.
1. Lorraine has remembered the buns, but she forgot the butter.
2. The bread smells good, and the buns taste delicious!
3. By the time we finish, we shall have made six kinds of dough.
4. Lou Ann mixed the cakes and kneaded the bread dough.
5. Janelle had never made these cookies before.
6. We do often make them for Grandmother.
7. Erma has surely learned how by this time.
8. Ida has not been making these very long.

B. For each verb in parentheses, write the tense indicated in italics. Be sure to use the correct helping verbs.

1. The strong wind (blow) this tree down. *past*
2. Melinda (give) the package to Melody. *present perfect*
3. Merle (cut) his finger on these knives before the shield was on. *past perfect*
4. Father and the boys (dig) this ditch before the plumbers come. *future perfect*
5. Do not drop that dish, or it (break). *future*
6. By the end of the month, the price (rise). *future perfect*
7. Leah (tear) her dress before we went hiking. *past perfect*
8. The Martin family (go) to Canada. *present perfect*

C. Diagram the skeletons of the following sentences. Also diagram the direct objects, indirect objects, predicate nominatives, and predicate adjectives.

1. The children gathered leaves for an art project.
2. My brother made the rabbits a cage.
3. Aunt Mary's pumpkin pies always taste delicious.
4. Each of us tasted a piece.
5. Anna and Barbara have written their cousin a letter.
6. Finally the ground became warm.
7. The eastern sky was growing bright.
8. Many anxious people gathered before the doorway.
9. His uncle is a preacher.
10. Jesus taught the people many truths.
11. God showed Peter a vision.
12. God's children are kind and patient.

D. Here is a topical outline of the composition that follows. Copy and complete parts III and IV, choosing points from the list given.

Pictures of Jesus in the Gospels
 I. Gospel of Matthew
  A. Was apparently written to Jews
   1. Has sixty references to Jewish prophecies
   2. Has forty quotations from the Old Testament
  B. Shows Jesus as a king
   1. Wise men's search for the King of the Jews
   2. Prophecy about Jesus' triumphal entry as a king

II. Gospel of Mark
    A. Was written for Gentiles
       1. Has few references to Old Testament prophecy
       2. Explains Jewish words and customs
    B. Shows Jesus as a servant
       1. Had no time to eat
       2. Had no time to rest
III. Gospel of Luke
    A. Written for Theophilus
       1.
       2.
    B. Shows Jesus as the Son of man
       1.
       2.
       3.
IV. Gospel of John
    A. Records miracles showing Jesus as the Son of God
       1.
       2.
    B. Records words of Jesus showing His divinity
       1.
       2.

Points for parts III and IV
   "I am's" of Jesus
   Probably a Greek
   Raising of Lazarus
   Possibly a nobleman
   Healing of the man born blind
   Records His saying, "Blessed are the poor"
   Shows that Jesus helped publicans and sinners
   Times when Jesus said He was sent from God
   Shows His healing the sick and cleansing the lepers

Pictures of Jesus in the Gospels

The Gospel of Matthew shows Jesus as the King of the Jews. This Gospel was apparently written to the Jews. It has sixty references to Jewish prophecies. It also has forty direct quotations from the Old Testament. Many references show Jesus as a king. When the wise men sought Jesus, they asked, "Where is He that is born King of the Jews?" In describing Jesus' triumphal entry into Jerusalem, Matthew quoted the prophecy that says, "Behold, thy king cometh unto thee."

The Gospel of Mark shows Jesus as a servant. Its style shows that the book was written mainly for Gentiles. It contains few references to Old Testament prophecy. It carefully explains Jewish words and customs so that the reader is sure to understand them. Many passages show Jesus as a servant. Chapter 3 tells how Jesus was so busy with the multitudes that He did not have time to eat. Chapter 6 says that Jesus and His disciples had no time to rest.

The Gospel of Luke shows Jesus as the Son of man. Luke wrote this book for Theophilus, a person who is unknown today. Theophilus was probably a Greek. He may have been a nobleman because he is addressed as "most excellent Theophilus." Luke gave many examples to show Jesus' concern for needy mankind. He showed that Jesus came to help publicans and sinners. He wrote how Jesus said to His disciples, "Blessed are the poor." He showed how Jesus healed the sick and cleansed the lepers.

The Gospel of John shows Jesus as the Son of God. John recorded miracles by which Jesus' power as the Son of God is clearly seen. One such miracle is the healing of the man who was born blind. Another is the raising of Lazarus after he was dead four days. John wrote words of Jesus which show that He is divine. He recorded many "I am's" of Jesus. John also wrote about many times when Jesus said He was sent from God.

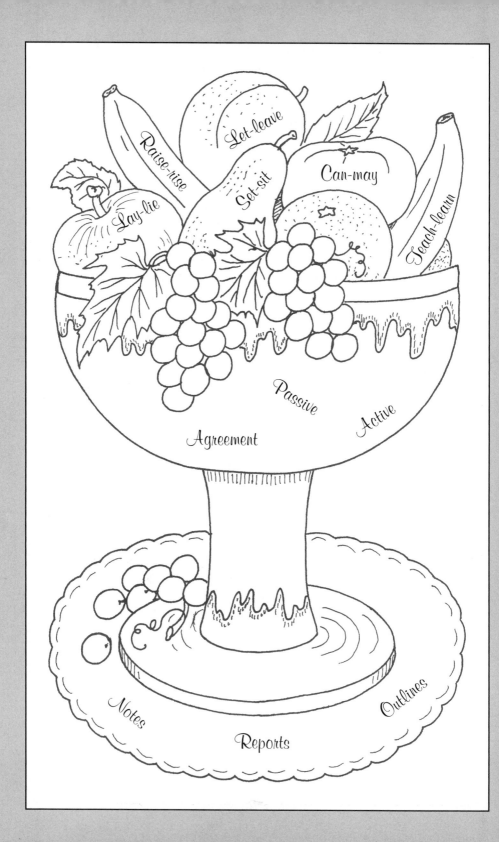

Chapter Five
Using Verbs Correctly
Writing Reports

Some verbs are very much alike, yet they have different meanings.

How forcible are right words!

Job 6:25

47. Using *Lay* and *Lie*

Some verbs are very much alike, yet they have different meanings. The verbs *lay* and *lie* are often confused. Do you know how to use them correctly? Which sentence in each of the following pairs is correct?

> The queen bee <u>lay</u> two thousand eggs in one day.
> *or* The queen bee <u>laid</u> two thousand eggs in one day.

> This drone <u>has laid</u> in the hive all day.
> *or* This drone <u>has lain</u> in the hive all day.

> The larvae are <u>laying</u> in their cells, waiting to be fed.
> *or* The larvae are <u>lying</u> in their cells, waiting to be fed.

The verb *lay* means "to put or place (something)." *Lay* is a transitive verb. Its principal parts are shown below.

Present	**Past**	**Past Participle**
lay	laid	(have) laid

The principal parts of *lay* are used correctly in these sentences.

> The masons <u>lay</u> the blocks carefully. (present form)
> (The masons *put or place* the blocks.)

> Howard <u>laid</u> his pencil down. (past form)
> (Howard *put or placed* his pencil.)

> Susan has <u>laid</u> the spoons on the table. (past participle)
> (Susan has *put or placed* the spoons.)

The verb *lie* means "to rest or recline." *Lie* is not transitive. It has three principal parts.

Present	**Past**	**Past Participle**
lie	lay	(have) lain

The principal parts of *lie* are used correctly in these sentences.

> Snow <u>lies</u> on the lawn. (present form)
> (Snow *rests* on the lawn.)

> The dog <u>lay</u> on Mother's flowers. (past form)
> (The dog *rested or reclined* on the flowers.)

> She <u>has lain</u> in bed all morning. (past participle)
> (She has *rested or reclined* in bed.)

Both *lay* and *lie* have -*ing* forms. Usually a form of *be* is used with these forms.

> The men **were** <u>laying</u> a new carpet.
> His old coat **was** <u>lying</u> on the lawn.

Whenever you must choose between a form of *lay* and a form of *lie,* you can use two tests to help you.

Test 1: *Which definition fits the sentence?* Try this test on the following sentences. Which verb is correct?

> Mother <u>lays</u> on the couch.
> *or* Mother <u>lies</u> on the couch.

Mother *rests or reclines* on the couch. She does not *put or place* anything on the couch. So the correct verb is *lies.*

> The carpenters have <u>laid</u> the floor tile.
> *or* The carpenters have <u>lain</u> the floor tile.

The carpenters have *put or placed* the floor tile. They have not *rested or reclined* the floor tile. So the correct verb is *laid.*

Test 2: *Does the sentence have a direct object?* If it does, the verb is transitive and must be a form of *lay.* If it does not, the verb is not transitive and must be a form of *lie.* Consider these sentences again.

> Mother <u>lays</u> on the couch.
> *or* Mother <u>lies</u> on the couch.

Mother lays *whom* or *what*? There is nothing to receive the action of the verb, so the verb is not transitive. The correct choice is *lies.*

> The carpenters have <u>laid</u> the floor tile.
> *or* The carpenters have <u>lain</u> the floor tile.

The carpenters have laid *what*? They have laid the *floor tile.* There is a direct object, so the verb is transitive. The correct choice is *laid.*

Notice that *lay* is the present form of *lay* (meaning "to put or place [something]"). *Lay* is also the past form of *lie* (meaning "to rest or recline"). You must be especially careful not to confuse these two different meanings of *lay.*

> You may <u>lay</u> (put) the books down.
> Yesterday Martha <u>lay</u> (rested) in bed with chicken pox.

- The verb *lay* means "to put or place (something)." *Lay* is transitive and usually passes its action to a direct object. Its principal parts are *lay, laid, (have) laid.*

- The verb *lie* means "to rest or recline." *Lie* is not transitive and never has a direct object. Its principal parts are *lie, lay, (have) lain.*

Class Practice

Tell whether the following sentences are correct. Read each sentence correctly.

1. A queen bee lays up to two thousand eggs per day.
2. The bee larvae are laying in their cells, waiting to be fed.
3. God has stretched out the heavens like a curtain and has lain the beams of His chambers in the waters.
4. The wolf also shall dwell with the lamb, and the leopard shall lay down with the kid.
5. The Lord lays up sound wisdom for the righteous.
6. Those who serve the Lord are laying up treasures in heaven.
7. The sheep laid contentedly on the green grass.
8. The flock has laid there several hours.
9. The shepherd lay the injured sheep gently on the ground.
10. Then he laid down his rod and staff.
11. A shepherd laid in the doorway of the sheepfold at night.
12. The Good Shepherd lays down His life for the sheep.

Written Exercises

A. Write the correct words in parentheses. If you write a form of *lay,* also write the direct object.

1. Snow has (laid, lain) on Mount Hood all summer.
2. The girls were (laying, lying) old newspapers between the rows of beans.
3. Gwen (laid, lay) down to rest.
4. (Lay, Lie) down, Fido.
5. The boy (laid, lay) his pack on the table while he ate.
6. My pet raccoon has (laid, lain) here on the seat to sleep.
7. The little kittens (laid, lay) in the clothes basket sleeping.

8. The mother cat had (laid, lay) them there.
9. Yesterday we (laid, lay) the carpet in the new house.
10. The contented cow (laid, lay) in the pasture, chewing her cud.
11. She has (laid, lain) there for several hours.
12. Mother (laid, lay) the sleeping baby on the bed.

B. For each blank, write the correct form of *lay* or *lie.*
1. ——— quietly while I rub your back.
2. Baby Joan is ——— in her crib.
3. Wesley has ——— his coat on this chair.
4. Please ——— this hat on the shelf.
5. The opossum ——— still until we left, pretending to be dead.
6. Grandfather has ——— many bricks in his lifetime.
7. The papers were ——— on his desk.
8. The snow did not ——— on the ground very long.

C. Write the principal parts of *lay,* and use each form in a sentence of your own.

D. Write the principal parts of *lie,* and use each form in a sentence of your own.

Review Exercises

Diagram the skeletons of these sentences. Include the direct and indirect objects, predicate nominatives, and predicate adjectives. [38–43]
1. Faith makes all things possible, and love makes them easy.
2. Mount Waialeale is the wettest place in the world.
3. Where is Mount Waialeale found?
4. This Hawaiian mountain receives about 460 inches of rainfall each year.
5. What a large amount of rainfall that is!
6. Stand up and read us your report on volcanoes.
7. By Monday I shall have read this book twice.
8. I do not always read this fast.
9. Nancy's report about constellations was excellent.
10. Beautiful mountains and valleys are found in Oregon.

48. Using *Raise* and *Rise*

The verbs *raise* and *rise* are similar in sound but different in meaning. You should not find it difficult to use them correctly.

The verb *raise* means "to cause (something) to go up or grow up." It is a regular transitive verb. Study its principal parts and the example sentences that follow.

Present	Past	Past Participle
raise	raised	(have) raised

Alma <u>raises</u> hamsters. (causes hamsters to grow up)
We <u>raised</u> the stone. (caused the stone to go up)
Father has <u>raised</u> the window. (has caused the window to go up)

The verb *rise* means "to get up or go up." *Rise* is an irregular verb and is not transitive. Study its principal parts and the example sentences that follow.

Present	Past	Past Participle
rise	rose	(have) risen

The moon <u>rises</u> early. (goes up)
Smoke <u>rose</u> above the fire. (went up)
The children <u>have risen</u>. (have gotten up)

Both *raise* and *rise* have -*ing* forms. Usually a form of *be* is used with these forms.

The men **were** <u>raising</u> a new barn after the fire.
The moon **is** <u>rising</u> in the night sky.

Since *raise* is transitive and *rise* is not transitive, you can again use two tests to help you decide whether a form of *raise* or a form of *rise* fits in a sentence.

Test 1: *Which definition fits the sentence?* Consider the following examples.

The bread in the pan <u>raised</u> slowly.
or The bread in the pan <u>rose</u> slowly.

Did the bread *go up,* or did it *cause (something) to go up?* The bread *went up,* so the correct verb is *rose.*

Test 2: *Does the sentence have a direct object?* Here are two more sentences to try.

> We <u>raise</u> our hearts in praise to God.
> *or* We <u>rise</u> our hearts in praise to God.

We raise *what*? We raise our *hearts*. The sentence has a direct object. The correct choice is the transitive verb *raise*.

- The verb *raise* means "to cause (something) to go up or grow up." *Raise* is transitive and usually passes its action to a direct object. Its principal parts are *raise, raised, (have) raised.*

- The verb *rise* means "to get up or go up." *Rise* is not transitive and never has a direct object. Its principal parts are *rise, rose, (have) risen.*

Class Practice

Tell whether the following sentences are correct. Read each sentence correctly.

1. Please raise your hand before you speak.
2. My uncle was raising turkeys for market.
3. The smoke raised above the roofs.
4. The water level is raising an inch a day.
5. The sun rose at five o'clock.
6. At what time will the sun raise tomorrow?
7. The speaker had rose to his feet.
8. Please raise your voice so that we can hear you.
9. The price of meat has raised.
10. The chicken raised its wings to fly.
11. The temperature has raised since three o'clock.
12. The bread is raising.
13. We have risen pigs and chickens.
14. We rose a little money for a colt.
15. Rise the bed while I put this caster under the leg.
16. The river has raised three inches since the rain.

Written Exercises

A. Write the correct words in parentheses. If you write a form of *raise,*
   also write the direct object.
   1. Jesus healed sick folks and (raised, rose) dead people to life.
   2. God (raised, rose) Jesus from the dead and set Him at His own
      right hand.
   3. God has (raised, risen) the believers and has made them sit
      together in heavenly places.
   4. The service was over, and the people had (raised, risen) to pray.
   5. Jesus (raised, rose) from the grave on the third day.
   6. We will (raise, rise) hymns of praise to our Creator in the days
      of our youth.
   7. In old age, a person often sleeps poorly and (raises, rises) at the
      singing of the birds.
   8. At midnight I will (raise, rise) to give thanks into Thee.

B. For each blank, write the correct form of *raise* or *rise.*
   1. The bubbles ——— to the top of the liquid.
   2. As the jellyfish searched for food, it ——— in the water and then
      sank again.
   3. Does the moon ——— in the east?
   4. Have you ——— your English score yet?
   5. Harold's scores have ——— during this marking period.
   6. Hard work ——— his scores higher than they had been.
   7. Have the farmers ——— the price of beef?
   8. Up ——— the sun like a bright orange ball.

C. Write the principal parts of *raise,* and use each form in a sentence
   of your own.

D. Write the principal parts of *rise,* and use each form in a sentence of
   your own.

Review Exercises

A. Write the correct form of *lay* or *lie* for each blank. [47]
   1. Freshwater eels ——— their eggs in the Sargasso Sea.
   2. Fishermen catch eels in nets and ——— them in their boats.
   3. Some eels are ——— in the mud when they are caught.
   4. Some fishermen ——— out bait for the eels.
   5. The eels cannot resist worms that are ——— in the water.
   6. Yesterday several eels ——— in this fisherman's net.

7. When the fishermen come, it seems that some fish ——— very still at the bottom of the river.

8. The old fisherman has ——— down to rest.

9. A young fisherman had ——— his coat here.

10. Mother ——— the good eel meat in the pan to fry.

B. Rewrite these expressions, using possessive forms. [26]

> **Example:** the net of the fisherman
> **Answer:**   the fisherman's net

1. the recipe of Mary
2. the kite of the boy
3. the bicycles of the boys
4. the tools of the men
5. the meeting of the workers

Challenge Exercises

Write a Bible story in your own words, using *lay* and *lie* or *raise* and *rise* correctly. For ideas, see Matthew 9:18–26; Mark 1:29–31; Mark 2:1–5; and John 11:1–44.

———————————————

49. Using *Set* and *Sit*

The verbs *set* and *sit* are often confused. Are the peach baskets *setting* or *sitting* on the lawn? Did Homer *set* them there, or did he *sit* them there? Learn to use the forms of *set* and *sit* correctly.

The verb *set* means "to put or place (something)," and it is transitive. Notice its irregular principal parts—they do not change at all!

Present	Past	Past Participle
set	set	(have) set

Study these sentences, which use the three principal parts of *set*.

James <u>sets</u> up the chairs for the services.
> (*puts or places* the chairs)

Alice <u>set</u> the glasses on the table.
> (*put or placed* the glasses)

They <u>have set</u> their packages on the shelf.
> (*have put or placed* their packages)

The verb *sit* means "to rest or be seated." *Sit* is an irregular verb and is never transitive. Study its principal parts and their use in the sentences below.

Present	**Past**	**Past Participle**
sit	sat	(have) sat

The boys <u>sit</u> quietly during devotions. (are seated)
They <u>sat</u> beside their mother. (were seated)
The box <u>has sat</u> on the shelf for a week. (has rested)

Usually a form of *be* is used with the *-ing* forms of these verbs.

Why <u>are</u> you <u>setting</u> the peanuts on the counter?
The congregation <u>was sitting</u> quietly during the sermon.

To decide which of these verbs is correct in a sentence, use the same tests that you learned earlier.

Test 1: *Which definition fits the sentence?* Use this test to choose the correct verb in each of the following sentences.

The baby is (setting, sitting) in a mud puddle!
(The baby is *resting,* so *sitting* is correct.)

Frank (set, sat) his books on the kitchen table.
(Frank *put* his books, so *set* is correct.)

Our Bibles should not just (set, sit) and collect dust.
(Our Bibles should not just *rest,* so *sit* is correct.)

Test 2: *Does the sentence have a direct object?* In the three sentences above, only the second one has a direct object. (Frank set *what*? Frank set *books.*) Therefore, the second sentence is the only one that should use a form of *set.* Each of the other two must use a form of *sit.*

- The verb *set* means "to put or place (something)." *Set* is transitive and usually passes its action to a direct object. Its principal parts are *set, set, (have) set.*

- The verb *sit* means "to rest or be seated." *Sit* is not transitive and never has a direct object. Its principal parts are *sit, sat, (have) sat.*

Class Practice

Tell whether the following sentences are correct. Read each sentence correctly.

1. Please sit the dishes on the table for me.
2. We set the pretty geranium in the window.
3. We all set on our blankets.
4. Everyone set down to eat.
5. The vase sat on that shelf for many years.
6. The kittens have often set on the edge of the porch.
7. We set the candles on the shelf.
8. We were setting in our chairs for three hours.
9. Set down and tell us the news.
10. We have set near the fire.
11. We had sat down to eat.
12. Sit down while I comb your hair.
13. We have sat the dishes on the table.
14. Set the butter on the table too.

Written Exercises

A. Write the correct words in parentheses. If you write a form of *set,* also write the direct object.

1. James accidentally (set, sat) on a freshly painted bench.
2. They have (set, sat) their packages on the table.
3. We have not (set, sat) here very long yet.
4. The village (sets, sits) in a deep valley.
5. We have been (setting, sitting) the table against the wall.
6. Ruth was (setting, sitting) next to me.
7. You may (set, sit) on the bench.
8. (Set, Sit) the box of chalk on the floor.
9. Where have you (set, sat) the chairs?
10. There is a box (setting, sitting) in the driveway.
11. He has (set, sat) in the vacant seat by me.
12. Now you may (set, sit) the basket on the desk.

B. Write the correct form of *set* or *sit* for each blank.

1. The four lepers outside Samaria said, "Why should we ———— here till we die?"
2. When the lepers came to the Syrian camp, the tents, provisions, and everything else were ———— just as the Syrians had left them.

3. Soon the lepers had eaten and drunk, had gotten silver, gold, and raiment, and had ——— them in a hiding place.
4. The lepers decided that they should not have ——— there selfishly enjoying themselves, but they should have shared the good news.
5. Jesus healed the blind man who ——— by the wayside begging.
6. I will ——— no wicked thing before mine eyes.
7. ——— a watch, O Lord, before my mouth; keep the door of my lips.
8. God has ——— the sun, moon, and stars in the heavens.

C. Write the principal parts of *set,* and use each form in a sentence of your own.

D. Write the principal parts of *sit,* and use each form in a sentence of your own.

Review Exercises

A. Write the correct words in parentheses. [47, 48]
1. All turtles (lay, lie) their eggs on land.
2. After the mother turtle has (laid, lain) her eggs and covered them, she leaves them.
3. The eggs (lay, lie) under the ground and are warmed by the sun.
4. Some sea turtles have (laid, lain) up to two hundred eggs.
5. The African pancake tortoise (lays, lies) only one egg at a time.
6. A baby desert tortoise hatches after (laying, lying) inside its shell for about one hundred days.
7. We watched the sun as it (raised, rose) over the sea.
8. Father (raised, rose) his hand when it was time for us to come back.
9. The sun was (raising, rising) higher and higher.
10. By noon the sun had (raised, risen) to its zenith.

B. Diagram the skeletons, predicate nominatives, and predicate adjectives. Label the predicate nominatives *PN* and the predicate adjectives *PA*. (The words in italics are noun phrases.) [42, 43]
1. That huge creature is a *grizzly bear.*
2. Mark's pet was a playful crow.

3. The *great horned owl* is dangerous to small animals like the skunk.
4. A favorite food of raccoons is frogs.
5. The *blue jay* in her painting looks lifelike.

50. Taking Notes for a Report

To be a good writer, you must learn how to take notes well. In Chapter 4 you learned about outlines. Now you are ready to take notes and make an outline from them.

First choose a topic that is interesting to you. (Your teacher can help you with this.) Then find information on your topic, using textbooks, encyclopedias, and other books from your library at school or at home. Using more than one reference source helps to make your report more informative and interesting. It is also easier to write in your own words when you must combine facts from two or more sources of information.

As you read, take notes only on information that fits your topic. For example, suppose you plan to write a report about training a dog. In your reading you find some interesting facts about feeding dogs. Should you write them down? No, because they are not related to your topic of training a dog.

The notes you write will be points that you may want to use in your report. Write down only main ideas and key words, using short phrases instead of whole sentences or paragraphs. As much as possible, write notes in your own words rather than copying someone else's writing. Write plenty of notes; it is easier to discard some than to go back through the reference books looking for more information.

Suppose you are planning to write a report called "The Habits of Alligators." In the library you find the following article—just what you are looking for! As you read it, you take notes on any ideas that you may want to include in your report. But remember, you must not take notes on facts other than those about alligators' habits—even if they are quite interesting.

The paragraphs have been numbered for easy reference. After the article is a set of notes that you might write from it.

Reference Source 1:

Learning About Alligators

1   Alligators are reptiles. They have backbones, they breathe with lungs, and they have dry, scaly skin. They thrive best where the atmosphere is hot and steamy. They live in or near freshwater swamps and lakes. In the United States, alligators live along the Gulf of Mexico and the southern Atlantic coast.

2   The jaws and teeth of an alligator are two fearsome weapons. Its teeth are heavy and sharp, and its jaw muscles are powerful enough to crush cattle bones. Surprisingly though, once an alligator's jaws are closed, a man can easily hold them shut with his hands.

3   An alligator's eyes have three eyelids. The upper and lower lids are opaque. The third lid is transparent and keeps out water when the alligator is swimming or diving.

4   Even though an alligator's ears are hidden under flaps behind the eyes, alligators can hear very well. Alligators have been trained to respond when called by name. Experienced hunters can attract alligators by making the right sounds.

5   The alligator's long, low body is shaped somewhat like a lizard's except that the alligator's body and tail are larger and thicker. A newly hatched alligator is about nine inches long. His body grows about one foot longer each year. A male alligator may grow to a length of twelve feet and a weight of five hundred pounds. In deep water an alligator tucks his legs against his body; and with mighty sweeps of his powerful tail, he swims at amazing speeds.

6   The alligator's legs and feet help him more on land than in water. The legs are short, yet he can use them to lift his body clear of the ground with just the tip of his tail touching. On land an alligator is clumsy and slow. He can move with surprising speed for a short distance, but he tires easily. His webbed hind feet are a help in paddling through shallow water.

7   An alligator spends much of his time on the banks of a stream, basking in the sun. Being cold-blooded, he needs the heat of the sun to keep warm. On extremely warm days, however, he may hide under the water, under bushes, or in a burrow or den.

8   An alligator usually digs a burrow or den in the bank of a river. He pushes into the mud with his long snout while swishing his tail back and forth to wash away the mud. He may dig a hole forty feet long, with bends as needed to avoid rocks and tree roots. At the far end, he makes a room large enough so that he can turn around.

9   In winter the alligator may hibernate in his burrow. Sometimes an alligator digs a basin in the deepest part of a pond or swamp. Such a "gator hole" contains water even in a dry season when other parts of the pond or swamp are dry. By this God-given instinct, the alligator saves himself and other animals that would otherwise die.

10   Alligators eat mostly fish. Newly hatched alligators eat small water animals such as water insects. Older alligators may attack larger animals along the shore, such as muskrats or raccoons. Rarely does an alligator attack an animal as large as a bear.

11   Alligators like marshmallows and bits of sandwiches, but it can be dangerous to feed them. When an alligator gets used to being fed, he seems to think that anything thrown at him is food. Alligators swallow many hard objects. Young alligators swallow twigs and pebbles, and older ones swallow bigger rocks and chunks of wood. In zoos they swallow things like coins or bottles. The most likely reason they swallow hard objects is to help them grind the food in their stomachs. Alligators swallow their food whole; they cannot chew.

12   Alligators do most of their feeding at night. Often they lie quietly in the water, waiting for something to catch. An alligator may use his tail to catch his food. When a school of fish passes nearby, he swirls his body into an almost complete circle. Then he uses his tail to knock the food toward his jaws. Once a chicken came too near to an alligator's tail, perhaps thinking it was a log. The alligator knocked the chicken high into the air and caught it in his jaws before it fell to the ground.

13   Alligators do not usually attack people, but a mother alligator guarding her nest can be dangerous. She remains nearby, nearly hidden in the water or bushes, guarding her nest hour after hour. But raccoons or skunks rarely get a chance to eat the eggs because not even a hungry bear wants to fight a mother alligator! When an enemy approaches her nest, she hisses a warning. If he comes closer, she will lunge forward, her mouth wide open. Once a man came too close to a nest, and he spent most of an afternoon in a tree while a mother alligator hissed at him from below.

14   God made interesting creatures when He made alligators. They are interesting to watch and study, and they are also helpful to man. But as we learn about them, we must heed their God-given instincts and keep a safe distance.

Sample notes:

The Habits of Alligators

(Paragraphs 1–6 give no information about alligators' habits.)
Paragraph 7
    Spend much time basking in sun
    Hide under water, under bushes, or in burrow or den when too warm

Paragraph 8

Dig burrow or den with long snout

Wash away mud by waving tail back and forth

Make burrow up to 40 feet long

Make large room at end

Paragraph 9

May hibernate in den in winter

Sometimes dig holes in deepest part of pond or swamp

These "gator holes" save alligators and other animals in dry weather

Paragraph 10

Eat mostly fish

Young ones eat small animals like water insects

Older ones eat animals like muskrats and raccoons

Paragraph 11

Like to eat marshmallows and sandwiches

Swallow hard objects like rocks and pieces of wood, perhaps to grind their food

Swallow food whole because they cannot chew

Paragraph 12

Catch food mostly at night

Lie quietly in water waiting for prey

Use tail to knock food toward mouth

Paragraph 13

Seldom attack people

Mother alligator fierce when guarding nest

Remains hidden nearby

Hisses a warning

Lunges forward with mouth open

Did you notice that some of the paragraphs have no notes taken from them? This is because those paragraphs have no information on the *habits of alligators.* Also notice that no whole sentences are copied. The notes are brief, yet there are plenty of them. The notes are separated according to paragraphs because that makes it easier to write an outline from them later.

- Notes for a report should include only the information that fits a chosen topic. They should consist of main ideas and key words that are written in phrases rather than complete sentences.

- Using more than one reference source helps to make a report more informative and interesting.

Class Practice

A. Read the second reference source about alligators. Find more information on "The Habits of Alligators." Tell your teacher what notes to write on the chalkboard.

Reference Source 2:

The Alligator

1   The American alligator lives in swamps, lakes, and marshes. It does not often leave fresh water. Alligators have webbed toes. When swimming, they fold their legs along their sides. Their long, strong tails send them swiftly through the water. They have a long, flat head, shaped so that the eyes, ears, and nose are the highest points on the head. They lie hidden in the water, breathing easily and looking like a log. Only the eyes, the ears, and the tip of the nose show. Black bony plates cover their bodies.

2   Flaps of skin keep water out of the alligator's ears. Clear eyelids cover the animal's eyes while it looks around underwater. Even the alligator's throat has a little stopper made of skin that keeps out water while its mouth is open underwater. When the mouth is closed, there is no large tooth showing as is true of the crocodile.

3   An alligator's skin is so tough that before modern rifles were invented, bullets could not penetrate it. The skin is watertight and has no sweat glands to keep his body from drying out. The color of the skin is a dull olive gray. Young alligators have yellow marks across their bodies, which fade away as they grow older. Alligator skin was once popular for making durable leather articles, such as handbags and ladies' shoes.

4   Alligators hunt food mostly at night. About three-fourths of the alligator's food is little creatures such as insects, shrimps, crabs, and crayfish. Larger animals like water birds, turtles, fish, muskrats, and snakes are eaten when the alligator is grown. In rare cases,

alligators have eaten bears. They seldom attack people.

5   Alligators are five or six years old before they have young ones of their own. In the spring the female alligator pulls together a big pile of leaves, grass, cattails, decaying vegetation, and mud. This pile may be four to seven feet wide and two to three feet high. She may work three days and nights building her nest. She digs a hole in the top of the nest pile with her back feet. There she lays her twenty-five to sixty eggs about the size of a large goose egg and then covers them over with more nesting material.

6   The eggs are incubated by heat from the sun and from decaying vegetation. God has given alligators the ability to keep the temperature of the nest just right. The female alligator stays around the nest to keep the eggs from harm because some animals, such as raccoons and skunks, would eat them. The eggs hatch in about eight weeks.

7   Mother alligators help their young alligators in several ways. Often newly hatched alligators have trouble getting from the nest pile. When they peep for help, the female alligator comes and rakes away the leaves and mud to set them free. Because many predators like to eat young alligators, the mother sometimes helps them reach the nearest water by carrying them there in her mouth or on her head.

8   Alligators know how to swim as soon as they are hatched. The young may stay in the same water hole with their mother for a year or two. Sometimes they climb on her back or the back of another alligator to sun themselves. They may eat food their mother or another alligator has caught. A large alligator that has killed a pig or some other animal swims about with big chunks hanging out of its mouth. The mother and other alligators allow the babies to come and nibble at the food hanging from their mouths.

9   Mother alligators call their young by grunting like a pig. Baby alligators cry with a moaning grunt that sounds like *umph-umph-umph* at a high pitch. After the age of four, young alligators' voices change and they begin to bellow. The sound is a little uncertain at first, but with practice the voice gets deeper and louder. An adult alligator has a throaty, bellowing roar that can be heard over a mile away.

10   When an alligator bellows, he raises his head slightly but keeps his mouth shut. He blows out his breath in a series of long, rumbling roars. An alligator's roar has been described as sounding like thunder, the voices of a thousand bullfrogs, or the rumble of a passing train. In a swamp, the bellow of an alligator can actually send tremors through the ground that can be felt.

B. Now go back to the first reference source in the lesson text. Pick out information from the first several paragraphs for a report on "The Body of an Alligator." Tell your teacher what notes you would write.

Written Exercises

A. From the first reference source, write a set of notes on "The Body of an Alligator."

B. From the second reference source, write a second set of notes on "The Body of an Alligator."

   NOTE: Save your notes from this lesson. You will need them in Lessons 53 and 56.

Review Exercises

A. Write the sentence that spoils the unity of this paragraph. [16]

   The skunk is helpful to man. A farmer might not think so when a skunk raids his chicken house and steals the eggs. A farmer boy might not think so when the skunk sprays his pet dog. Dogs should be taught to stay away from skunks, but some never learn. But the skunk finds and digs up turtle eggs, and this helps to keep down the turtle population. Since the turtle destroys young ducks and fish, the skunk is really helping man when he eats their eggs.

B. Write the numbers of the rules that you should follow for coherence in a paragraph. [16, 17]
   1. Give details in the order of time.
   2. Give details in the order of importance or interest.
   3. Join a number of sentences with *and then.*
   4. Use transitional words such as *first, second, finally, next,* and *then.*
   5. Be sure all the sentences tell about the same topic.
   6. Use transitional words such as *also, therefore, however, for this reason,* and *in spite of.*

51. Using *Let* and *Leave*

Which is correct? "Please *let* me have it" or "Please *leave* me have it"? Should you say "I *let* my books at school" or "I *left* my books at school"? Learn the meanings and correct usage of *let* and *leave.*

The verb *let* means "to allow or permit." It is an irregular verb because all three of its principal parts are the same.

Present	**Past**	**Past Participle**
let	let	(have) let

The principal parts of *let* are used correctly in these sentences.

Father <u>lets</u> us raise goats. (allows or permits)
Araunah <u>let</u> David buy his threshing floor. (allowed)
The boys <u>have let</u> the wagon roll into the pond. (allowed)

The verb *let* is always followed by another verb form. Notice the two verb forms in each of the example sentences.

Father <u>lets</u> us <u>raise</u> goats.
Araunah <u>let</u> David <u>buy</u> his threshing floor.
The boys <u>have let</u> the wagon <u>roll</u> into the pond.

The verb *leave* means "to depart, go away from, or allow to remain." Study its principal parts and the sentences illustrating their use.

Present	**Past**	**Past Participle**
leave	left	(have) left

Please <u>leave</u> as soon as possible. (depart)
We <u>left</u> the room and played outside. (went away from)
Mrs. Miller <u>has left</u> her purse here. (allowed to remain)

The *-ing* forms of *let* and *leave* are *letting* and *leaving.*

When you must choose between a form of *let* and a form of *leave,* two tests can help you decide.

Test 1: *Which definition fits the sentence?* Since both definitions include the idea of allowing, this may be hard to tell. One verb means "to allow" and the other means "to allow to remain." But if you think carefully, you should be able to choose the right one. Which of the following sentences is correct?

Please <u>let</u> the butter on the table.
or Please <u>leave</u> the butter on the table.

Shall we "allow the butter on the table" or "allow the butter to remain on the table"? The second meaning fits, so the correct verb is *leave*.

> Father <u>let</u> the children sleep late.
> *or* Father <u>left</u> the children sleep late.

You may think that *left* sounds right, but Father simply *allowed* the children to sleep late. So *let* is the correct verb.

Test 2: *Is the verb followed by another verb form? Let* is always used with another verb form, but *leave* is never used in that way. This test makes it simple to choose the right verb in the examples in Test 1.

> Please (let, leave) the butter on the table.

The sentence has only one verb form. Therefore, *leave* is correct.

> Father (let, left) the children sleep late.

This sentence has a second verb form—*sleep*. So the correct verb is *let*.

Be careful with this second test though, for sometimes the second verb form is understood.

> Father <u>lets</u> us <u>raise</u> goats.
> He will not <u>let</u> us next year.
> **Meaning:** He will not <u>let</u> us <u>raise</u> goats next year.

- *Let* means "to allow or permit." Its principal parts are *let, let, (have) let. Let* is always followed by another verb form, either expressed or understood.

- *Leave* means "to depart, go away from, or allow to remain." Its principal parts are *leave, left, (have) left.*

Class Practice

Tell whether the following sentences are correct. Read each sentence correctly.

1. Will you leave me go if I finish my work first?
2. We left her choose the material she wanted for a dress.
3. By leaving the door open, you let the cat come in.
4. Will you be leaving the children go along tomorrow?
5. Be sure to let the keys in the car.
6. The visitors left early this morning.

7. When you go, do not let your purse behind.
8. He left me use his eraser.
9. I have left the visitors come in.
10. They let Roger alone.   .
11. Have they left him stay alone?
12. What time shall we leave in the morning?

Written Exercises

A. Write the correct words in parentheses. If you write *let,* also write the other verb form.
1. Who (let, left) the door wide open?
2. The teacher has not (let, left) us whisper in school.
3. He (let, left) his books at school when he went home.
4. (Let, Leave) the people of God be joyful.
5. (Let, Leave) us walk in the light of the Lord.
6. A child (let, left) to himself brings his mother to shame.
7. Who hath ears to hear, (let, leave) him hear.
8. The shepherd has (let, left) the ninety-nine and has gone into the mountains to seek the one that is lost.
9. If your brother has something against you, (let, leave) your gift before the altar and first be reconciled to him.
10. They have not (let, left) the most important things for last.
11. The soldiers did not (let, leave) one stone upon another when they destroyed the temple.
12. The Jewish rulers (let, left) the apostles go again.
13. Jesus said, "Peace I (let, leave) with you."
14. The disciples had (let, left) their nets behind to follow Jesus.
15. The woman was (letting, leaving) her waterpot at the well to tell others about Jesus.
16. She had (let, left) Jesus give her the words of life.

B. Write the principal parts of *let,* and use each form in a sentence of your own.

C. Write the principal parts of *leave,* and use each form in a sentence of your own.

Review Exercises

A. Write the correct words in parentheses. [47–49]
1. Under God's care we can (lay, lie) down and sleep in safety.

2. The Lord (raised, rose) a deliverer to help the Israelites when they cried to Him.
3. Mary was (setting, sitting) and learning at Jesus' feet.
4. Jesus had (raised, risen) Lazarus from the dead.
5. Jesus (raised, rose) from the grave on the third day.
6. Jesus ascended to heaven and (set, sat) down at the right hand of God.

B. Copy each verb or verb phrase, and write whether it is in the *present* tense, *past* tense, or *future* tense. [32]
1. We have a pet crow.
2. Joel taught him tricks.
3. He left us at the end of summer.
4. We miss him.
5. Maybe he will come back to us.

C. Copy each verb phrase, and write whether it is in the *present perfect* tense, *past perfect* tense, or *future perfect* tense. [34–36]
1. The crow had appeared one day just before summer vacation.
2. He has made himself perfectly at home.
3. Within a week he had learned many things.
4. He has often eaten from their hands.
5. By winter he will likely have learned many more tricks.

---

52. Other Troublesome Verbs

Read the following sentence. Do you know which verb is correct?

Myron (can, may) ride my bicycle.

You cannot choose the correct verb unless you know what the sentence means. Does it mean that Myron *is able to* ride my bicycle or that Myron *has permission to* ride my bicycle? Either verb is correct, depending on the meaning that is intended.

Yet people often use *can* when it is clear that they mean *may*. *Can* means "to be able to." *May* means "to be permitted to." Develop the habit of using these verbs correctly.

I <u>can</u> understand the lesson.
(I *am able to* understand the lesson.)

Mabel <u>may</u> open the window if she <u>can</u>.

(Mabel *has permission to* open the window if she *is able to*.)

Teach and *learn* are two more verbs that are sometimes used wrong. *Teach* means "to give knowledge or instruction." *Learn* means "to gain knowledge." Your parents can *teach* you many things, but they cannot *learn* you anything. You must do the learning.

Incorrect: Father will <u>learn</u> me how to do it.
Correct: Father will <u>teach</u> me how to do it.
Correct: I will <u>learn</u> the right way.

Past forms can also cause trouble. Do you know which forms are correct in the following sentences?

The dog (dragged, drug) the boots off the porch.
I am out because Carol (tagged, tug) me.
The balloon sailed into the briers and (burst, bursted, busted).

In each sentence above, the correct past form is the first one shown. Learn the correct past forms of the following verbs.

Present	**Past**
tag	tagged (<u>not</u> tug)
drag	dragged (<u>not</u> drug)
drown	drowned (<u>not</u> drownded)
attack	attacked (<u>not</u> attackted)
burst	burst (<u>not</u> bursted <u>or</u> busted)

Another mistake is to use *of* for *have*, as in the following example.

You should of told me, and I would of come. I could of.

Of is not a verb. It is not correct to use *could of, should of,* or *would of.* These phrases come from carelessly saying *could have, should have,* and *would have.*

Incorrect: He <u>would of</u> done it if he <u>could of</u>.
Correct: He <u>would have</u> done it if he <u>could have</u>.

If you use incorrect forms, other people will know that either you cannot speak English very well or you are careless in your use of English. Learn and use the correct forms so that you can communicate clearly and effectively.

- *Can* means "to be able to." *May* means "to be permitted to."

- *Teach* means "to give knowledge or instruction." *Learn* means "to gain knowledge."

- Use the correct past forms of the following verbs: *tag—tagged, drag—dragged, drown—drowned, attack—attacked, burst—burst.*

- Use *could have, should have,* and *would have* rather than *could of, should of,* and *would of.*

Class Practice

A. Tell which sentences are incorrect. Read each sentence correctly.
   1. Mother said I can come after my work is finished.
   2. Can your baby brother walk?
   3. Can I take a jug of water to the workers?
   4. You should of paid attention during class.
   5. Can you make a whole meal by yourself?
   6. I would of come if I could of found a way.
   7. The molasses tank burst and made a terrible mess.
   8. Father learned me how to change the oil in a car.
   9. Two calves drownded in the flood.
   10. The dog drug his house into the lane.
   11. Indians attackted the Jacob Hochstetler family one night.
   12. If you don't know how to play, we can soon learn you.
   13. Maria tagged me, so I am caught.
   14. He blew up the plastic bag and busted it.
   15. A bulldozer drug the logs out of the woods.
   16. Mother taught me how to cook spaghetti.
   17. She has learned me many other things too.
   18. I learn more quickly when I listen carefully.

B. Change the verbs to the simple past tense.
   1. The pipes burst in the winter.
   2. The bull attacks the noisy dog.
   3. The flood drowns the muskrats.
   4. Alma quickly tags Priscilla.
   5. The chain drags on the road.

Written Exercises

Write the correct words.

1. (Can, May) you get all your work done tonight?
2. (Can, May) I see the pictures in your album?
3. (Can, May) I read the letter too?
4. (Can, May) you lift that heavy box?
5. I lifted it, but I (could have, could of) hurt my back.
6. I (should have, should of) asked someone to help me.
7. We boys (would have, would of) lifted it gladly.
8. You (should not have, should not of) tried to do it alone.
9. Mother (taught, learned) me to always close the door.
10. Our class has (taught, learned) arithmetic since first grade.
11. Last year the teacher (taught, learned) us Spanish.
12. Sister Rose and her class are (teaching, learning) a poem together.
13. I'm sure Brian (tagged, tug) you, so you're out of the game.
14. Your dirty shoes have (dragged, drug) mud into the house.
15. My pretty balloon has finally (burst, bursted).
16. Dorcas used too much water and (drowned, drownded) the plants.
17. The bag fell onto the concrete and (burst, busted) open.
18. The fever (attacked, attackted) almost everyone in the town.

Review Exercises

A. Write the correct verb for each sentence. [47–51]

1. My car (let, left) me (set, sit) this morning!
2. Please (let, leave) me help you change the tire.
3. You may (set, sit) the toolbox where I had (let, left) it.
4. Do you like to (lay, lie) on the cool grass?
5. You may (lay, lie) a rug on the grass and (lay, lie) on it.
6. The men have (laid, lain) new blacktop on the driveway.
7. Ben (laid, lain) the ball beside his bat.
8. The bird that hit the window (laid, lay) still awhile, but later it flew away.
9. The papers have (laid, lain) in that box for years.
10. Grandmother has (laid, lain) a paper there every week.
11. Gerald (laid, lay) down his pencil and took up his book.
12. A good mason can (lay, lie) many bricks in a day's time.
13. (Lay, Lie) your books aside and come for lunch.

14. When the sun comes up, the temperature will (raise, rise).
15. Emily (raised, rose) her hand to ask a question.
16. Mother has (laid, lain) the wraps on the bed.
17. Scott (laid, lay) down for a nap.
18. Sharon (laid, lay) the baby into the cradle.

B. Diagram the skeletons of the following sentences. Include all the direct objects, indirect objects, predicate nominatives, and predicate adjectives. [38–43]
1. Have you ever seen a shark?
2. Some sharks have rows and rows of sharp teeth.
3. The hammerhead is a dangerous shark.
4. The *whale shark* is not dangerous, for it eats only fish and plants.
5. A *white shark* is a powerful swimmer.
6. My teacher told me a story about sharks.

---

53. Organizing Your Notes

After you have taken notes, you need to organize them before you try to write a report. Otherwise your report will simply give details in a haphazard way and will have little value or meaning.

How should you organize your notes? One of the best ways is to form an outline as you learned in Chapter 4. See how this is done with the notes from Lesson 50, which are shown below.

The Habits of Alligators

From Reference Source 1:
Paragraph 7
Spend much time basking in sun
Hide under water, under bushes, or in burrow or den when too warm
Paragraph 8
Dig burrow or den with long snout
Wash away mud by waving tail back and forth
Make burrow up to 40 feet long
Make large room at end

Paragraph 9
    May hibernate in den in winter
    Sometimes dig holes in deepest part of pond or swamp
    These "gator holes" save alligators and other animals in dry
        weather

Paragraph 10
    Eat mostly fish
    Young ones eat small animals like water insects
    Older ones eat animals like muskrats and raccoons

Paragraph 11
    Like to eat marshmallows and sandwiches
    Swallow hard objects like rocks and pieces of wood, perhaps to
        grind their food
    Swallow food whole because they cannot chew

Paragraph 12
    Catch food mostly at night
    Lie quietly in water waiting for prey
    Use tail to knock food toward mouth

Paragraph 13
    Seldom attack people
    Mother alligator fierce when guarding nest
    Remains hidden nearby
    Hisses a warning
    Lunges forward with mouth open

From Reference Source 2:
Paragraph 4
    Hunt food mostly at night
    Usually eat smaller animals
    Seldom attack people

Paragraph 5
    Female builds nest in spring
    Uses leaves, grass, cattails, decaying vegetation, and mud
    Up to 7 feet wide and 3 feet high
    Lays 25–60 eggs size of a large goose egg
    Covers eggs with nesting material

Paragraph 6
    Allows eggs to be warmed by the sun and decaying vegetation
    Stays near nest to guard eggs

Paragraph 7
   Newly hatched alligators peep for help
   Mother sets them free from nest
   Mother may carry them to nearest water in mouth or on head
Paragraph 8
   Young can swim as soon as they are hatched
   Mothers let young ones nibble food hanging from mouth
Paragraph 9
   Mothers call young by grunting like a pig
   Babies make high-pitched cry
   At four years old, voice changes; they begin bellowing
   Bellowing roar of adult can be heard over a mile away
Paragraph 10
   Bellow made by blowing out breath while keeping mouth shut
   Sounds like thunder, many bullfrogs, or passing train
   Makes ground tremble

So many notes! How will we ever organize them into something clear and meaningful? If you work one step at a time, the job will not be too difficult.

Step 1: *Identify the main idea of the notes from each paragraph.* Often you can identify the main idea in each set of notes by identifying the main idea of the paragraph from which you took the notes. If you took your notes correctly, you can easily see the original paragraph divisions. From those main ideas, decide what the main ideas are that you want to include in your report. Study the main ideas from each list of notes as shown below.

Main ideas from Reference Source 1:
   1. Keeping warm or cool enough (paragraph 7)
   2. Digging burrows, dens, and "gator holes" (paragraphs 8 and 9)
   3. Eating habits (paragraphs 10, 11, and 12)
   4. Guarding the nest (paragraph 13)

Main ideas from Reference Source 2:
   1. Eating habits (paragraph 4)
   2. Nesting habits (paragraphs 5 and 6)
   3. Caring for young alligators (paragraphs 7 and 8)
   4. Sounds made by alligators (paragraphs 9 and 10)

Step 2: *Combine the main ideas from all the reference sources.* Decide which main ideas fit together. In the sample notes, "Guarding the nest" and "Nesting habits" go together. "Eating habits" is in both sets, so those main ideas belong together.

Step 3: *Arrange the main ideas in a logical order on an outline.* The main ideas must follow one another in a sensible way. For instance, your report might say that since alligators sometimes get too warm when they are in the sun, they dig burrows in which to cool off. So a sensible point to put after keeping warm would be one on digging burrows. Or after you mention nesting habits, it would be sensible to describe next how mothers care for their young.

There is room for some variation in the order. For instance, what should come after "Digging burrows"? It might be "Eating habits," "Building nests," or some other main idea. Whatever order you choose, be sure to arrange the main ideas in a way that is logical and meaningful.

Study the following outline, which shows only main ideas. It was made by combining main ideas as described in Step 2.

The Habits of Alligators
   I. Keeping warm or cool enough
  II. Digging burrows, dens, and "gator holes"
 III. Eating habits
 IV. Nesting habits
  V. Caring for young alligators
VI. Sounds made by alligators

Step 4: *Place the details in your notes under the main ideas where they fit.* Subtopics must be placed under the topics that they match. For instance, in the above outline you would not put the point about hibernation under "Eating habits" or "Caring for young alligators." Hibernation has to do with how alligators use their burrows, so it goes under "Digging burrows, dens, and 'gator holes.'"

Your outline does not need to include all the details that are in your notes. Keep your notes so that you can refer to them when you write your report. Your outline will give you a sense of direction when you write your report, and your notes will help you to add meaningful details.

Arranging notes in outline form is an important skill that you will find very useful in life. After you have mastered this skill, you may use it so often that it becomes a habit.

- To organize notes for a report, use the following steps.
  1. Identify the main idea of the notes from each paragraph.
  2. Combine the main ideas from all the reference sources.
  3. Arrange the main ideas in a logical order on an outline.
  4. Place the details in your notes under the main ideas where they fit.

Class Practice

Work together as a class to complete the outline "The Habits of Alligators" at the chalkboard. Write details from the notes as subpoints under the main topics where they belong.

Written Exercises

Following the steps given in the lesson, organize the notes you took on "The Body of an Alligator" to make an outline of your own. Do not throw away your notes. You will need them later when you write a report.

Review Exercises

Write *true* or *false*. [33]
1. Every outline must have a title.
2. The main topics of an outline are marked with Roman numerals.
3. A main topic begins with a capital letter, but a subtopic begins with a small letter.
4. All the points at each level of an outline are indented the same amount.
5. A period is placed after each numeral or capital letter that marks a point on the outline.
6. A period is also placed at the end of each point.

54. Agreement of Subjects and Verbs

The verb in a sentence must *agree,* or work together, with the subject. If the subject is singular, the verb must be singular; and if the subject is plural, the verb must be plural.

Singular: He walks several miles to church.
Plural: We walk quietly to our Sunday school class.

There is one main exception to this rule. A plural verb must be used when the subject is *I* or *you.*

Subject *I:*   I usually <u>walk</u> home from school.
Subject *you:* <u>You</u> often <u>walk</u> with me.

Usually you choose the correct verb form without even thinking about it. You learned that when you learned to talk! However, there are several cases when you must use special care to make sure the verb agrees with the subject.

1. *Use a plural verb with any two subjects joined by* and. A plural verb is used because the subject includes more than one.

   Incorrect: <u>Lois</u> and <u>Linda</u> <u>is</u> in the same grade.
   Correct: <u>Lois</u> and <u>Linda</u> <u>are</u> in the same grade.
   Correct: <u>Lois</u> and the <u>twins</u> <u>are</u> in the same grade.

2. *Use a singular verb with two singular subjects joined by* or. The verb is singular because only one of the subjects is performing the action.

   Incorrect: <u>Father</u> or <u>Mother</u> <u>bring</u> us to school every day.
   Correct: <u>Father</u> or <u>Mother</u> <u>brings</u> us to school every day.

3. *Be sure the verb agrees with the subject when a sentence begins with* there *or* here. *There* or *here* is not the subject, even though it begins the sentence.

   There <u>are</u> some baby <u>birds</u> in that nest.
   Here <u>is</u> a baby <u>bird</u> in this nest.

   Sometimes a sentence that begins with *there* or *here* has a compound subject. Be sure to use the correct verb form in such a sentence. Two singular subjects joined by *and* take a plural verb. Two singular subjects joined by *or* take a singular verb.

> Here <u>are</u> a <u>knife</u> and a <u>fork</u> for you. (not <u>is</u>)
> There <u>is</u> an <u>apple</u> or an <u>orange</u> in the bag. (not <u>are</u>)

Remember that the contraction *there's* stands for *there is* and is singular. Likewise, *here's* means *here is* and is singular.

> There<u>'s</u> a new <u>kind</u> of bird in our woods.
> There <u>are</u> many <u>kinds</u> of birds in our woods.

4. *Use* does *and* doesn't *with singular subjects. Use* do *and* don't *with plural subjects, compound subjects, and the pronouns* I *and* you. The most common problem with these words is the contraction *don't.* If you are not sure whether to use *don't* or *doesn't,* try *do not* or *does not* first.

> **Incorrect:** He <u>don't</u> visit us very often.
> > **Compare:** He do not visit us very often.
> **Correct:** He <u>doesn't</u> visit us very often.
> > **Compare:** He does not visit us very often.
> **Correct:** We <u>don't</u> remember what was said.
> > Marie and Karen <u>don't</u> have pencils
> > I <u>don't</u> know the answer.
> > You <u>don't</u> want a goat.

5. *Be sure the subject and verb agree when a prepositional phrase comes between them.* The verb must agree with the subject, not with the object of the preposition.

> subject   object
> ↓   ↓
> The <u>books</u> on this shelf <u>are</u> history books.

The verb agrees with the plural subject *books,* not with *shelf.* Here are two more examples.

> One <u>jar</u> of peaches <u>was</u> spoiled. (not <u>were</u>)
> Several <u>cans</u> of paint <u>were</u> sold. (not <u>was</u>)

- Use a singular verb with a singular subject, and a plural verb with a plural subject.

- Use a plural verb with two singular subjects joined by *and*.

- Use a singular verb with two singular subjects joined by *or*.

- Be sure the verb agrees with the subject when a sentence begins with *there* or *here*.

- Use *does* and *doesn't* with singular subjects. Use *do* and *don't* with plural subjects, compound subjects, and the pronouns *I* and *you*.

- Be sure the subject and verb agree when a prepositional phrase comes between them.

Class Practice

Tell which verbs are correct. Check by saying the subjects and verbs together to see if they agree.

1. There (is, are) some fish that can live out of water.
2. The mudskipper and the lungfish (do, does) not spend all their time in water.
3. The African lungfish (live, lives) in water, but it can live out of the water and breathe air for years.
4. (There's, There are) years when rivers dry up, but the lungfish (don't, doesn't) dry out, because it (roll, rolls) itself into a tight ball.
5. It (dig, digs) itself into the mud and (leave, leaves) an air hole, and then it (sleep, sleeps) till the rains come.
6. Here (is, are) some air holes.
7. One of the scientists (dig, digs) up lungfish and (send, sends) them to special aquariums and zoos.
8. A scientist or a zoo keeper carefully (unroll, unrolls) the lungfish.
9. Howard (don't, doesn't) want to lose that interesting fish.
10. One of the men (make, makes) sure the dried lungfish ball does not break.
11. After the lungfish is in water, it (don't, doesn't) waste time waking up; neither (do, does) it stay curled up.

12. It (eat, eats) much food because it (need, needs) to regain the weight it lost in the dry season.
13. A fish with brilliant colors (is, are) swimming below our ship.
14. God (have, has) made all things beautiful, and nature (help, helps) us to see His greatness.

Written Exercises

Write the simple subjects, and then write the correct words in parentheses.

1. (There's, There are) another fish that spends some time out of water.
2. This fish (don't, doesn't) even act like a fish.
3. A mudskipper (climb, climbs) trees, and it (walk, walks), (skip, skips), and (jump, jumps) around on mud flats.
4. It (don't, doesn't) have feet, but its front fins (is, are) almost like legs.
5. Here (is, are) a fish that skips so fast that a person (isn't, aren't) able to keep up.
6. A fly or a beetle (make, makes) a tasty bite for a mudskipper.
7. (Do, Does) you think that a mudskipper and a lungfish really (do, does) act like fish?
8. (There's, There are) an insect that can jump one hundred times its height.
9. Each one of the fleas (have, has) a special joint in its legs, and this joint (help, helps) it to jump.
10. The man with glasses (teach, teaches) fleas to do tricks.
11. Some of his fleas (jump, jumps) through hoops, and others (pull, pulls) little carts around.
12. Most people (don't, doesn't) like fleas, because they (is, are) hard to get rid of.
13. Fleas (have, has) hard, smooth outside skeletons, and they (slip, slips) easily through fur and fingers.
14. A dip in suds (help, helps) to get rid of fleas because they (don't, doesn't) like soap and water.
15. There (is, are) many things that men (don't, doesn't) understand.
16. Even a tiny plant or animal sometimes (present, presents) puzzling questions.
17. The God of all the earth (keep, keeps) us safe in His care.
18. The God of the heavens (love, loves) us and (care, cares) for us.

Review Exercises

A. Write all three principal parts of each verb. Use *have* with the past participle. [30, 31]

1. find
2. puff
3. slip
4. leave
5. raise
6. lie
7. lay
8. let

B. Write the correct past form of each verb in parentheses. If the helping verb *have, has,* or *had* is used in the sentence, write the helping verb and the past participle. [31]

Example: I have never (fly) in an airplane.
Answer: have flown

1. Irma has (find) the answer.
2. We (leave) some books there for you.
3. Floyd (raise) his hand.
4. My cat (lie) in the sun all morning.
5. The men have (lay) the carpet already.
6. Our visitors had (ring) the doorbell several times.
7. The mothers (bring) the children to school.
8. My dog has (dig) another hole in Mother's garden.
9. I have (tag) you, and now you are caught.
10. Mary Beth had never (wear) that dress before.
11. I (send) the letter yesterday.
12. My aunt has often (let) me help her with the baking.

55. Active and Passive Voice

You have learned that a transitive verb is an action verb that passes its action to another word in the sentence. The word that receives the action is usually the direct object.

Lot chose the best land.
Lot chose what? *Land* receives the action of the verb *chose.*

However, transitive verbs do not always pass their action to a direct object. Notice that the sentence below means exactly the same thing as the one above. But *land,* which had been the direct object, is now the subject.

The best land was chosen by Lot.

Who or what receives the action of *chosen*? The receiver is still *land.* But in this sentence, the transitive verb passes its action back to the *subject.*

You can now see that a transitive verb may pass its action to either of two receivers: the *direct object* or the *subject.* This difference in receivers is what determines the *voice* of the verb.

When a transitive verb passes its action to a direct object, the verb is in the *active voice.* The subject in such a sentence is *active;* it *performs* the action of the verb. In each of the following sentences, the subject is underlined. Notice how the subject performs the action, and the direct object receives the action.

Active voice:
A huge <u>giant</u> challenged the Israelites.

giant	challenged	Israelites

<u>David</u> chose five smooth stones.

David	chose	stones

The humble shepherd <u>boy</u> killed Goliath.

boy	killed	Goliath

When a transitive verb passes its action back to the subject, the verb is in the *passive voice.* The subject in such a sentence is not active. It is *passive; it receives* the action of the verb. In each of the following sentences, the subject is underlined. Notice how the subject receives the action of the verb rather than doing it. Also notice that the sentences do not have direct objects.

Passive voice:

The Israelites were challenged by a huge giant.

Israelites	were challenged

Five smooth stones were chosen by David.

stones	were chosen

Goliath was killed by the humble shepherd boy.

Goliath	was killed

When a simple predicate is in the passive voice, it is always a verb phrase. The helping verb is a form of *be,* and the main verb is a past participle. If any of these is missing, you can be sure that a verb is not in the passive voice. Look at the following sentences. Can you tell which one is in the passive voice?

The Philistines fled in great fear.
The Israelites were destroying their enemies.
David was praised by the women.

The first sentence does not contain a verb phrase, so it cannot be passive. The second sentence contains a verb phrase with a form of *be,* but the main verb is not a past participle. It cannot be passive either. The third sentence contains a verb phrase in which the helping verb is a form of *be* and the main verb is a past participle. So the third sentence is in the passive voice. Another proof is the fact that *David* receives the action of *praised.*

- A transitive verb may be in the *active voice* or the *passive voice.*

- When a transitive verb is in the active voice, the subject performs the action and the direct object receives the action.

- When a transitive verb is in the passive voice, the subject receives the action and there is no direct object.

- A simple predicate in the passive voice is always a verb phrase. The helping verb is a form of *be,* and the main verb is a past participle.

Class Practice

A. In each sentence, tell which word is the receiver of the action and whether that word is the *subject* or the *direct object.* Then tell whether the verb is in the *active* or the *passive* voice.
1. A large, colorful poster was drawn by him.
2. The steers are breaking the gate.
3. We found a turtle under the bridge.
4. Letters were sent by the parents.
5. Many bugs are eaten by bluebirds and swallows.
6. The children ate the doughnuts.
7. My uncle Amos lays concrete blocks.
8. The four melons were taken by the second customer.
9. I know the answer.
10. We were greeted by the new teacher.

B. In Part A, pick out the form of *be* and the past participle that is used in each sentence with a passive verb.

Written Exercises

A. For each sentence, copy the word that receives the action. Write whether it is the *subject* or the *direct object,* and whether the verb is in the *active* or the *passive* voice.
1. At the brook Cherith, Elijah was fed by ravens.
2. Ravens brought bread and meat to Elijah.
3. Later, a widow made cakes for Elijah.
4. The meal and oil were supplied by the Lord.
5. A sudden illness took the son's life.

6. He was restored to life by Elijah.
7. The child was carried back to his mother.
8. After this, the woman believed Elijah's words.

B. Copy the subject of each sentence, and write whether it is the *doer* or the *receiver* of the action. Then write whether the voice of the verb is *active* or *passive*.
1. James tears the cloth into strips.
2. The papers were gathered by us.
3. We had gathered the papers for them.
4. Someone inside raised the window.
5. Carpets are woven by Indians and Iranians.
6. Indians and Iranians have woven beautiful carpets.
7. The bus is driven by Brother Wilson.
8. The flowers were picked by them.
9. They did pick these flowers.
10. The bushes were covered by fresh white snow.

C. Copy only the verb phrases that are in the passive voice. Draw one line under the form of *be* and two lines under the past participle (the main verb).
1. The fresh white snow covered even the bushes.
2. Some money was found by my little sister.
3. My little sister found some money.
4. The class is beginning the test eagerly.
5. Moles and shrews are hunted by this cat.
6. The wrong instructions were given.
7. Mrs. Porter speaks Spanish.
8. The tree was shaken by the boys.

Review Exercises

Diagram the skeleton of each sentence. Include any direct or indirect objects, predicate nominatives, and predicate adjectives. [38–43]
1. Silkworm farms in Japan raise silkworms by the billions and mulberry trees by the millions.
2. Do silkworms eat mulberry leaves?
3. After several weeks the silkworm spins itself a cocoon.
4. Farmers send the cocoons to a factory, and big machines unwind the thin threads off each cocoon.

5. First they must unwind the thread of twenty thousand cocoons, and then they can make one pound of silk.
6. Farmers do not send all their cocoons to the factory.
7. Moths come out of some cocoons and lay hundreds of eggs.
8. Soon the eggs hatch, and more worms are spinning silk.
9. Silk is a beautiful cloth, but it is quite expensive.

---

56. Writing a Report: First Draft

You have learned how to take notes from several reference sources and use them to make an outline. Now you are ready to write a report by using the notes you took and the outline you made.

Here is a sample outline on "The Habits of Alligators." It was made by using notes taken on the two reference sources in Lesson 50.

The Habits of Alligators

  I. Keeping warm or cool enough
    A. Basking in the sun
    B. Hiding in burrows
 II. Digging burrows, dens, and "gator holes"
    A. Size and shape
    B. Usefulness
      1. Hibernation
      2. Help to other animals
III. Eating habits
    A. What they eat
      1. Mostly fish
      2. Different foods according to size
      3. Special treats
      4. Unusual objects
    B. How they catch food
      1. At night
      2. Under water
      3. With help of tail

IV. Nesting habits
    A. Construction of nest
    B. Description of eggs
    C. Fierce guarding by female
V. Caring for young alligators
    A. Setting young free
    B. Feeding the young
VI. Sounds made by alligators
    A. Mother alligators' calls
    B. Baby alligators' cries
    C. Young alligators' bellows
    D. Adult alligators' roars

How can we write a report from this outline? Reports are usually written in two drafts. The first draft is the rough, unpolished form of the report, and the second draft is the report in its finished form. This lesson deals with writing the first draft, which includes two steps.

Step 1: *Decide what to put into each paragraph.* This can be done by planning one paragraph for each topic or subtopic on the outline. So the first paragraph in the sample report will tell how alligators keep warm or cool enough.

The first sentence in a report introduces the whole report as well as the first paragraph. So the topic sentence of the first paragraph should be written in such a way that it does both. And the last sentence of the last paragraph should be written in such a way that it gives a finishing touch to your report.

Step 2: *Write your first draft.* After you write each topic sentence, develop the paragraph for each by using the information on your outline. Include interesting details from the notes you took; they are like spice in your report.

Write in complete sentences, leaving every other line blank so that you can mark changes later. In your first draft, do not worry about getting everything perfect. Concentrate on following your outline and getting the information into your report. Keep writing even if you are not satisfied with some of your sentences. The next lesson will show you how to improve your report before you write the second draft. The following sample shows the first three paragraphs of a report based on the outline.

The Habits of Alligators

If you ever see an alligator during the day, he will probably be basking in the sunshine. This creature spends much time warming himself in the sun because he is a cold-blooded animal. But sometimes an alligator gets too warm and needs to find a cool place. Then he may hide under water, under bushes, or in a burrow or den.

An alligator digs out a burrow or den by using his long snout. He washes away the mud by waving his long tail back and forth. The burrow may be as much as forty feet long and may have a large room at the end. In winter the alligator may hibernate in his burrow. He may also dig a hole in the deepest part of a swamp or pond and stay there over winter. This "gator hole" helps to save other animals when the rest of the swamp or pond dries up.

Most of the alligator's food is fish. Baby alligators eat small things like water insects, and adult alligators may eat raccoons or muskrats. Alligators in zoos or parks like to eat marshmallows and sandwiches. If anything is thrown at them, they seem to think it is food! Alligators also swallow hard objects such as rocks and pieces of wood. They do not use their teeth to chew their food, but they swallow it whole. The hard objects may help to grind the food in their stomachs.

- To begin writing a report from an outline, use the following steps.
  1. Decide what to put into each paragraph.
  2. Write your first draft.

Class Practice

A. Study the following paragraphs, which are based on the fourth main topic of the outline. Which is the better paragraph? Tell what is wrong with the other one.

1. Alligators build nests. I read once that they use mostly cattails. They probably push them together with their feet. The size of the nest is really big. She lays many eggs, too, and they are quite large. Alligators stay nearby to guard their eggs. One time I saw a picture of one with her chin right on the nest, but maybe it was a crocodile. Alligators and crocodiles do look alike in many ways.

2.   The female builds a nest by scooping together leaves, grass, cattails, mud, and decaying vegetation. Her nest may be a mound as much as seven feet wide and three feet high. In it she lays twenty-five to sixty eggs the size of a large goose egg. Then she covers the eggs with nesting material and stays nearby to guard them from predators. They are warmed by the sun and by decaying vegetation until they hatch.

B. Study the following paragraphs, which are based on the sixth main topic of the outline. Which is the better paragraph? Tell what is wrong with the other one.

1.   Alligators make a variety of sounds. Mothers call their young with a sound that sounds like a pig grunting. A baby makes a high-pitched cry until he is four years old. Then his voice changes, and he begins practicing to bellow. His bellows gradually become stronger, and finally he can roar so loudly that the ground trembles and he can be heard over a mile away! God certainly made an interesting animal when He made the alligator.

2.   Alligators make interesting sounds. Mother alligators call their babies. Baby alligators cry. Young alligators bellow. Adult alligators roar.

Written Exercises

Begin writing a report from your outline on "The Body of an Alligator." Follow the steps given in the lesson.

Review Exercises

Copy each verb or verb phrase, and write whether it is an *action* or a *linking* verb. If it is a linking verb, write the word in the predicate that is linked to the subject. [44]

1. We looked out the window.
2. The sky looked dark.
3. On Friday the sky had been cloudy all day.
4. This tastes homemade.
5. Mother tasted the soup.
6. It tasted salty.

57. Writing a Report: Second Draft

You should usually not try to write the first and second draft of a composition all at one time. It is better to lay aside the first draft at least until the next day and then come back to it. In this way, you will have a fresh view of your work and you will be better able to see what improvements are needed.

In Lesson 56 you studied the two steps for writing the first draft of a report. They are shown here.

Step 1: *Decide what to put into each paragraph.*

Step 2: *Write your first draft.*

To write the second draft of your report, follow steps 3 and 4.

Step 3: *Proofread the first draft.* This means you should look for ways to improve it. Check for mistakes in spelling, punctuation, and grammar. Reword sentences that do not read smoothly and clearly. Improve your sentence variety by making some longer sentences and some shorter sentences. Use different types of sentences and different kinds of word order. All these changes can be marked in the blank spaces that you left when you wrote your first draft. Notice the following examples.

Original:
> An alligator sometimes gets too warm. He needs to find a cool
> place. He may hide in a burrow or den.
> (choppy sentences without variety)

Revised:
> An alligator sometimes gets too warm and needs to find a cool
> place. He may hide in a burrow or den.
> (two sentences joined with compound predicate)

Revised:
> Sometimes an alligator gets too warm and needs to find a cool
> place. Then he may hide in a burrow or den.
> (sentences with varied beginnings)

Original:
> They seem to think that anything thrown at them is food.
> (declarative sentence with common word order)

Revised:
> If anything is thrown at them, they seem to think it is food!
> (exclamatory sentence with more interesting word order)

Do not be afraid to make changes. Cross out words, rewrite sentences, add ideas, and remove anything you do not like. Even the best writers mark their first drafts with many changes!

Step 4: *Write your second draft.* Rewrite the report, making the corrections you have marked. Follow the points below to give a neat, attractive appearance to your report.

1. Use composition paper rather than tablet paper.
2. If you write with ink, use either blue or black.
3. Use neat handwriting, and write on only one side of each page.
4. Center the title on the top line.
5. Leave a blank line between the title and the report.
6. Leave margins along both edges of the paper, and keep them as straight as you can.
7. Leave a margin at the bottom of each page. Do not write on the last two or three lines.
8. Follow any other directions that your teacher gives.

- To write a report from an outline, use the following steps.
  1. Decide what to put into each paragraph.
  2. Write your first draft.
  3. Proofread the first draft.
  4. Write your second draft.

Class Practice

Improve these sentences as indicated in parentheses.

1. Alligators are reptiles. Crocodiles are reptiles too. (Join into one sentence with a compound subject.)
2. A mother alligator will not leave you come near her nest. (Correct the grammar.)
3. Baby alligators eat small things like water insects, adult alligators may eat raccoons or muskrats. (Correct the run-on error.)
4. A big man put a big box on a big shelf. (Avoid repetition by using other words for *big.*)
5. The shelf and everything on it came down. (Change to an exclamatory sentence beginning with *down.*)

6. Jesus told a story about a woman. She had ten coins. (Change *she* to *who,* and join into one sentence.)

7. You can imagine how the woman felt when she lost one coin. (Change to an imperative sentence.)

8. She wondered where it could be. (Change to an interrogative sentence.)

9. The women lighted a lamp swept her house and searched carefuly for the coin. (Correct two spelling errors, and add the missing commas.)

10. She was very glad when she found the coin. (Change to an exclamatory sentence beginning with *how.*)

Written Exercises

A. Proofread the first draft of your report "The Body of an Alligator." Mark the changes that should be made. Keep your corrected first draft for your teacher to see.

B. Rewrite your report, making the changes you marked.

---

58. More About Active and Passive Voice

In Chapter 4 you studied the three simple verb tenses: present tense, past tense, and future tense. You changed from one tense to another by using a different principal part. Here is the verb *find* in all three tenses, in the active voice.

> **Active voice:**
> **Present tense:**   He <u>finds</u> his lost eraser. (present form)
> **Past tense:**   He <u>found</u> his lost eraser. (past form)
> **Future tense:**   He <u>will find</u> his lost eraser.
>   (present form with *will*)

Passive verbs also have these three tenses. But you cannot change from one tense to another by using a different principal part, for the main verb is always a past participle. Instead, you must use a different form of the helping verb *be.* See how these changes are made in the following sentences.

Passive voice:
    Present tense: His lost eraser <u>is found</u>. (present form of *be*)
    Past tense: His lost eraser <u>was found</u>. (past form of *be*)
    Future tense: His lost eraser <u>will be found</u>.
                  (present form of *be* with *will*)

Sentences can easily be changed from active voice to passive voice. To do this, reword the sentence so that the direct object becomes the subject. Change the simple predicate to a verb phrase in which the helping verb is a form of *be* and the main verb is a past participle. See how this is done in the following sentences.

direct object
↓

Active voice: Brother Charles introduced the <u>visitors</u>.

subject
↓

Passive voice: The <u>visitors</u> were introduced by Brother Charles.

Sentences can also be changed from passive voice to active voice. This is done by changing the subject to the direct object. Study this change in the following sentences.

subject
↓

Passive voice: The <u>barn</u> was rebuilt by members of the church.

direct object
↓

Active voice: Members of the church rebuilt the <u>barn</u>.

In most writing, the active voice is better because it is more direct and forceful than the passive voice. Compare the following sentences. Which one states the fact more effectively?

A good sermon was preached by Brother Noah.
Brother Noah preached a good sermon.

However, there are two cases when you may want to use the passive voice in writing. First, you can use it sometimes for the sake of variety. Second, you can use it when the doer of an action is not known or is not important in a sentence. Here are two examples.

The train was delayed for three hours.
    (We do not know what delayed the train.)

The Panama Canal was finished in 1914.
(The doer of the action is not important in the sentence.)

- To change a sentence from active voice to passive voice, change the direct object to the subject. Change the simple predicate to a verb phrase in which a form of *be* is used with the past participle of the main verb.

- To change a sentence from passive voice to active voice, change the subject to the direct object.

- In most writing, the active voice is better because it is more direct and forceful than the passive voice.

Class Practice

A. Change each verb to the past tense and the future tense, but keep them in the passive voice.
   1. Twelve barrels of water are poured onto Elijah's altar.
   2. The sacrifice, the water, and the wood are burned up.
   3. A great rain is sent from God.

B. Change these sentences to the active voice.
   1. The songbooks were distributed by Nelson.
   2. The morning message was brought by Brother John.
   3. The students were taken to the museum by the parents.
   4. A two-hour traffic jam was caused by the accident.

C. Change these sentences to the passive voice.
   1. God answered Elijah's prayer.
   2. The fire licked up even the water in the ditch.
   3. The rainstorm drenched Ahab.

Written Exercises

A. Rewrite each sentence in the past tense and the future tense, but keep the passive voice.
   1. Elijah is given strength for forty days.
   2. God's voice is heard in the cave.
   3. Rocks are crumbled by a strong wind.
   4. The ground is shaken by an earthquake.
   5. Many trees are burned by the fire.

B. Change these sentences to the passive voice.
1. God called Elijah to serve Him.
2. God protected Elijah.
3. Elijah taught the people.

C. Change these sentences to the active voice.
1. A still, small voice was heard by Elijah.
2. God was still worshiped by seven thousand people.
3. Elisha was anointed by Elijah.
4. Elijah was followed by Elisha.

D. In three of the passive sentences below, the doer of the action is named in a prepositional phrase. Such sentences would be more forceful in the active voice. In the other three sentences, the doer is not named because it is unknown or unimportant. The passive voice is better in those sentences.

Find each sentence in which the doer is named in a prepositional phrase, and rewrite it in the active voice.
1. The corn was bought by Mrs. Brown.
2. A message was sent to me.
3. My bicycle was stolen last night.
4. This package was sent from Grandmother.
5. The windows were cleaned by Sarah.
6. Dessert will be served soon.

Review Exercises

Write the correct verbs. [54]
1. Gerald always (do, does) the charts.
2. He (don't, doesn't) often forget.
3. There (is, are) several right ways to do it.
4. (There's, There are) a bluebird and a junco in that tree.
5. A sparrow or a starling (have, has) built this nest.
6. Mary and Martha (was, were) special friends of Jesus.

Challenge Exercises

Improve this paragraph by using the active voice in more of the sentences.

Jesus was followed by great crowds of people. A leper came and fell on his face before Jesus. Jesus was worshiped by the leper. "You can heal me if You are willing," he said. Jesus was moved with compassion and said, "I am willing." The leper was touched by Jesus and was healed immediately. The leper was told by Jesus to show himself to the priest and to tell no one else. But the news of Jesus' kind deed was spread abroad by the leper.

---

59. Chapter 5 Review

Class Practice

A. Give the principal parts of each verb.

Present	Past	Past Participle
1. leave	———	———
2. drag	———	———
3. tag	———	———
4. burst	———	———
5. drown	———	———
6. attack	———	———
7. teach	———	———

B. Give the correct verbs from the following list.

lay	set	can
lie	sit	may
raise	let	teach
rise	leave	learn

1. Which verbs have these meanings?
   a. To get up or go up
   b. To rest or be seated
   c. To be able to
   d. To be permitted to
   e. To cause (something) to go up or grow up
   f. To give knowledge or instruction
   g. To depart or go away from
   h. To rest or recline
   i. To allow or permit
   j. To gain knowledge

2. Which two verbs mean "to put or place (something)"?
3. Which verb is the present form of *left*?
4. Which verbs may be followed by direct objects?
5. Which verb is always followed by another verb form, expressed or understood?

C. Tell which words receive the action of the verbs. Tell whether each receiver is a *subject* or a *direct object*. Also tell whether the verb is in the *active* or the *passive* voice.
1. Rebekah covered Jacob's hands and neck with goats' skins.
2. Jacob's hands and neck were covered with goats' skins.
3. Isaac blessed Jacob.
4. Jacob was blessed by Isaac.

D. Give the correct words.
1. When you prepare to write a report, you should take —— on the information you find in reference sources.
2. You should get information from (only one, more than one) reference source.
3. You (may, must not) copy whole sentences and paragraphs.
4. You should take notes on (all the points, every point that fits your chosen topic).
5. You should organize your notes into an ——.
6. All the points in your notes (need, do not need) to be included on your outline.
7. As you write your report, you should refer to your —— and your ——.
8. You should —— your first draft by looking for ways to improve the report.

Written Exercises

A. Write all the principal parts.

Present	Past	Past Participle
1. lay	——	——
2. lie	——	——
3. raise	——	——
4. rise	——	——
5. set	——	——
6. sit	——	——
7. let	——	——

B. Write the correct words in parentheses.

1. Abraham (raised, rose) up early to go to the land of Moriah.
2. After two days he (raised, rose) his eyes and saw Mount Moriah in the distance.
3. Abraham built an altar and (laid, lay) the wood on it.
4. Abraham (let, left) the servants behind with the donkey.
5. He (let, left) Isaac carry the wood.
6. The angel said, "(Lay, Lie) not your hand upon the lad."
7. God could (of, have) (raised, risen) Isaac from the dead, but He provided a ram instead.
8. (Can, May) you remember the rest of the story?
9. (Can, May) I tell you more about Abraham tomorrow?
10. The teacher (taught, learned) the students about Abraham's prompt obedience.
11. The Bible story book is (setting, sitting) on the teacher's desk.
12. The elephants (dragged, drug) the large logs out of the jungle.
13. One baby elephant (tagged, tug) along behind its mother.
14. She would have (attacked, attackted) any person or animal that tried to hurt her baby.
15. The little elephant would not have (drowned, drownded) in the pool, for elephants are excellent swimmers.
16. An angry elephant (burst, bursted) through the forest and temporarily scattered the herd.

C. Write the subjects of the following sentences. Then write the correct words in parentheses that must agree with the subjects.

1. (There's, There are) a few stories in the Bible about twins.
2. Jacob and Esau (was, were) twin brothers.
3. There (was, were) another set of twins named Pharez and Zarah.
4. Isaac (don't, doesn't) know that the twin before him is not Esau.
5. Jacob and Rebekah (don't, doesn't) know that someday God will let Jacob be deceived by Laban.
6. (Here's, Here are) a lesson: "Be sure your sin will find you out."
7. A set of twins (is, are) mentioned in Genesis 38.
8. One of the boys (was, were) named Zarah, which means "rising" or "shining."
9. Several of the books on this shelf (tell, tells) the story.
10. The teacher of the younger grades (teach, teaches) Bible stories in reading class.

D. Copy the subject of each sentence, and write whether it is the *doer* or the *receiver* of the action. Then write whether the voice of the verb is *active* or *passive*.
1. Isaac sent Jacob to Laban's house.
2. Jacob was sent to his uncle Laban's home.
3. Laban gave Leah to Jacob for a wife.
4. Flocks were given to Jacob by Laban.

E. Rewrite each sentence in the past tense and the future tense, keeping the passive voice.
1. The sheep are led by their shepherds.
2. The trough is filled by the shepherdess.
3. The stone is removed by the strong men.

F. Change these sentences to the passive voice.
1. Esau met Jacob peacefully.
2. Jacob sent messengers to Esau.
3. Jacob protected Rachel and Joseph.

G. Change these sentences to the active voice.
1. Jacob was kissed by Esau.
2. His wives and children were presented to Esau by Jacob.
3. Jacob's gifts were accepted by Esau.

H. Write *true* or *false*.
1. You should choose a certain topic and take notes only on ideas related to that topic.
2. You should write down main ideas and key words when you take notes.
3. You should copy a few whole sentences and paragraphs when you take notes.
4. Your report will be confusing if you use more than two sources of information.
5. You should write as few notes as necessary; it is easier to find more information than to discard some notes.
6. You should carefully organize your notes before writing your report.

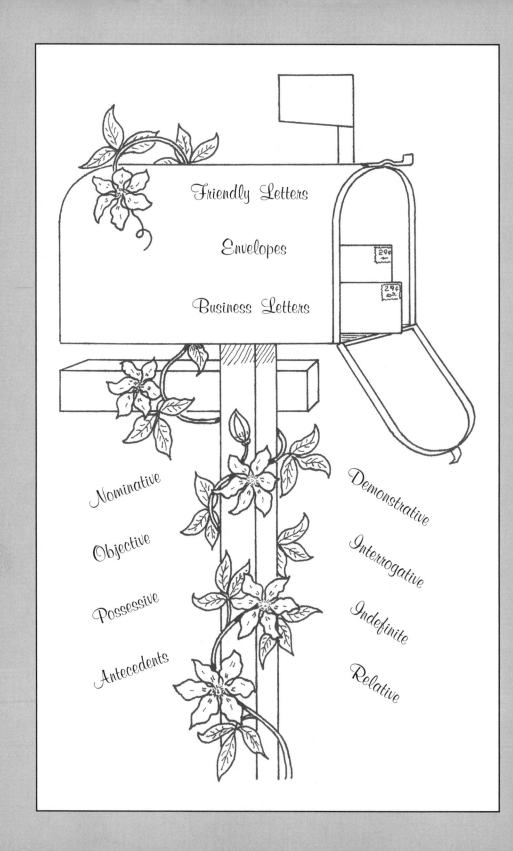

Chapter Six

Working With Pronouns

Writing Letters

A
pronoun is
a word that takes the place
of a noun.

Personal Pronouns
Nominative Case

	Singular	*Plural*
First person:	I	we
Second person:	you (thou)	you (ye)
Third person:	he, she, it	they

Objective Case

	Singular	*Plural*
First person:	me	us
Second person:	you (thee)	you
Third person:	him, her, it	them

Possessive Case

	Singular	*Plural*
First person:	my, mine	our, ours
Second person:	your, yours (thy, thine)	your, yours
Third person:	his, her, hers, its	their, theirs

(Archaic pronouns are in parentheses.)

60. Personal Pronouns

A pronoun is another of the eight parts of speech. A pronoun is a word that takes the place of a noun. We use pronouns freely, for they help to make our sentences flow smoothly. Notice how the nouns in the first sentence below are replaced by pronouns in the second sentence.

Margie saw the man drop the box.
She   saw   him drop   it.

Personal pronouns refer mainly to *persons*. You can see this when you consider the list of personal pronouns on page 264. However, some of these pronouns may refer to animals or to nonliving objects.

Personal pronouns have different forms to indicate *person, number, case,* and *gender.* These differences are explained in this lesson.

Person

Personal pronouns show three different persons: first, second, and third. *First person pronouns* refer to the person speaking (*I, we*). *Second person pronouns* refer to the person spoken to (*you*). *Third person pronouns* refer to the person or thing spoken about (*he, she, it, they*).

> I read John 3 this morning.
> (I—first person; refers to person speaking)

> What did you read today?
> (you—second person; refers to person spoken to)

> Father gave him a Bible.
> (him—third person; refers to person spoken about)

Personal pronouns have different forms according to their person. By contrast, nouns are nearly always third person. The reason is that when you speak, you use *I* or *me* instead of your own name, and *you* instead of the name of the person to whom you are speaking. If you use a noun, it usually names a person or thing that you are speaking about.

Number

Number refers to whether a pronoun is singular or plural. A word naming only one person or thing is singular; a word naming two or more persons or things is plural. You can tell by the meaning of a pronoun whether it is singular or plural.

> **Singular pronouns:** I, me, he, him, she, her, it
> **Plural pronouns:**   we, us, they, them

The pronoun *you* is different from the rest because it may be singular or plural. You must know what *you* refers to before you can tell its number.

> **Singular:** Henry, you surely do neat work. (refers to *Henry*)
> **Plural:**   Boys, where did you put my hammer? (refers to *boys*)

Case

The three cases of pronouns are *nominative, objective,* and *possessive.* The chart on page 264 shows the forms for each case. You will learn about pronoun cases in the next several lessons.

Gender

Pronouns show gender. They are *masculine, feminine, neuter,* or *common.*

Pronouns of *masculine* gender refer to men and boys.

> he   him   his

> Jacob needed to leave home. <u>He</u> went to Laban's house.

Pronouns of *feminine* gender refer to women and girls.

> she   her   hers

> Rachel was the daughter of Laban. <u>She</u> became Jacob's wife.

Pronouns of *neuter* gender are neither masculine nor feminine.

> it   its

> Jacob returned to Canaan. <u>It</u> was his homeland.

Pronouns of *common* gender can be masculine or feminine. If they are plural, these pronouns may stand for nouns of all three genders: masculine, feminine, neuter, or any combination of these.

I	you	we	they
me	your	us	them
my	yours	our	their
mine		ours	theirs

> Jacob had twelve sons and one daughter. <u>They</u> were his children.

Since a pronoun takes the place of a noun, every pronoun has an *antecedent.* The antecedent is the noun for which the pronoun stands.

> <u>Lester</u> wrote about the <u>eclipse</u>.
> <u>He</u> watched <u>it</u> through a very dark glass.
> *Lester* is the antecedent of *He. Eclipse* is the antecedent of *it.*

- A pronoun is a word that takes the place of a noun.

- *Personal pronouns* refer mainly to *persons*.

- Personal pronouns have different forms to indicate *person, number, case,* and *gender.*

- An *antecedent* is the noun for which a pronoun stands.

Class Practice

A. Replace the underlined words with personal pronouns.
   1. The storekeeper told Father and me the price of the drill.
   2. Charity and I picked the tomatoes.
   3. The drivers were ready to leave soon.

B. Tell which words are personal pronouns. Give the antecedent of each one.
   1. Jesus said to the parents of the little maid, "Weep not; she is not dead, but sleepeth."
   2. He took her by the hand and called, saying, "Maid, arise."
   3. And her spirit came again, and she arose straightway: and He commanded to give her some food.

C. Find each personal pronoun, and give its person, number, and gender.
   1. Ruth and Orpah left their native land to go with Naomi.
   2. Ruth and Orpah both wished to stay with her.
   3. After much discussion, Orpah decided that she would return to her homeland.
   4. Were many tears shed at their parting?
   5. But Ruth said, "Do not intreat me to leave you."
   6. They arrived in Bethlehem during barley harvest.
   7. Boaz showed great kindness to them.
   8. He let her glean in his fields.

Written Exercises

A. Replace the underlined words with personal pronouns.
   1. James and Doris are with Frank and Judy.
   2. The boys fed the dogs.
   3. Those children are our visitors.

4. <u>Bruce and I</u> can see <u>the men</u>.
5. This one is <u>Anna's</u>.
6. <u>Robert's</u> is on the table.
7. <u>Vernon</u> called <u>Grandfather and me</u>.
8. <u>The girls</u> helped Mother with <u>Mother's</u> work.

B. Copy the personal pronouns in these sentences, and write the person, number, and gender of each.

Example: We saw him with you.
Answer: We—first person, plural, common
            him—third person, singular, masculine
            you—second person, singular *or* plural, common

1. She and I met them.
2. Are these cards yours?
3. No, I believe they are his.
4. Where are ours?
5. They took them for her.
6. Who are they?
7. Is it she?
8. No, it is they.
9. Trust in the Lord with all your heart.
10. In all your ways acknowledge Him.

C. Copy each personal pronoun, and write its antecedent.
1. Father said he wanted to start early.
2. Did the Martins say when they will arrive?
3. Jesus asked, "Who touched My clothes?"
4. The woman was healed of her disease.
5. Jesus said to the woman, "Your faith has saved you; go in peace."
6. Jesus said to Simon, "I have something to tell you."
7. Jesus asked, "What is a man profited if he shall gain the whole world and lose his own soul?"
8. Jesus said to the disciples, "Cast your net on the right side of the ship."

Review Exercises

Copy each verb or verb phrase. After it, write the word that receives its action, and write whether the verb is in the *active* or *passive* voice. [55]

1. Twenty-two thousand men were dismissed by Gideon.
2. The Midianites were feared greatly.
3. Only three hundred vigilant soldiers helped Gideon.
4. Gideon and his men blew the trumpets and broke the pitchers.
5. The Midianites were defeated.

---

61. Pronouns in the Nominative Case

Personal pronouns have three *cases:* nominative, objective, and possessive. You may remember studying subject pronouns, object pronouns, and possessive pronouns in earlier grades. The subject pronouns are in the nominative case.

Here are the nominative case pronouns as shown on page 264. *Thou* and *ye* are in parentheses because they are the archaic forms used in the King James Bible instead of *you*. Memorize the pronouns on this chart.

Nominative Case

	Singular	Plural
First person:	I	we
Second person:	you (thou)	you (ye)
Third person:	he, she, it	they

When pronouns are used in sentences, there are two places where they must always be in the nominative case. Learn them well so that you can avoid mistakes.

1. *The* subject *of a sentence must always be in the nominative case.* Usually you have no problem choosing the correct pronoun as the subject of a sentence. Which one is correct in this sentence?

    (He, Him) offered to help us.

You know which word is correct without even thinking. But be sure you also understand the *reason* it is correct. The nominative form *he* is used because the pronoun is the subject of the sentence.

Also look at these sentences, which use the archaic forms of *you*. In each one, *thou* or *ye* is properly used because it is the subject of the sentence.

> <u>Thou</u> art my hiding place.
> <u>Ye</u> are the light of the world.

2. *A predicate nominative must always be in the nominative case.* A predicate nominative is a noun or pronoun that follows a linking verb (a form of *be*) and renames the subject of the sentence. Many people use incorrect forms for predicate nominatives, so you cannot always choose the correct word by what sounds right. Which pronouns are correct in the following sentences?

> My teacher is (he, him).
> Is your mother (she, her)?
> Our guests are (they, them).

In each sentence, the pronoun renames the subject. It is a predicate nominative, so the nominative form must be used. Remember that a subject and a predicate nominative can be exchanged and the sentence will mean the same.

> My teacher is <u>he</u>.
> **Compare:** He is my teacher.

> Is your mother <u>she</u>?
> **Compare:** Is she your mother?

> Our guests are <u>they</u>.
> **Compare:** They are our guests.

A predicate nominative is diagramed on the base line after the verb, whether it is a noun or a pronoun. A slanted line that leans toward the subject is placed before the predicate nominative to show that it refers to the subject. .

- The nominative case pronouns are *I, you, he, she, it, we,* and *they.* The archaic forms of *you* are *thou* and *ye.*

- When a pronoun is a subject or a predicate nominative, it must be in the nominative case.

Class Practice

A. Choose the correct pronouns. Tell whether each pronoun is used as a *subject* or a *predicate nominative.* Practice reading each sentence correctly.

1. Rhoda swept the floors, and (I, me) dusted the furniture.
2. Who is there? Is it (she, her)?
3. Father did the hardest parts, and (they, them) worked with us.
4. The teacher might be (she, her).
5. My cousins are (they, them).
6. Joan came soon, and (she, her) finished early.
7. The winner is (he, him).
8. The workers are (they, them).
9. James will bring the wagon, and (I, me) will help you.
10. (Thou, Thee) openest Thine hand and satisfiest the desire of every living thing.
11. O Lord, (Thou, Thee) art my refuge and my portion in the land of the living.
12. If (thou, thee) faint in the day of adversity, thy strength is small.

B. On the chalkboard, diagram the sentence skeletons, predicate nominatives, and direct objects of sentences 3–9 in Part A. Include the correct pronouns on your diagrams.

Written Exercises

A. Write the correct pronouns. After each one, write whether it is a *subject* or a *predicate nominative.*

1. (He, Him) saw the fishermen.
2. The fishermen were (they, them).
3. Jesus called them, and (they, them) left their nets.
4. (They, Them) followed Jesus immediately.

5. (They, Them) were the sons of Zebedee.
6. The writer of the Book of Revelation was (he, him).
7. The beloved disciple was (he, him).
8. It was (he, him).
9. The brothers are (they, them).
10. The fastest worker was (he, him).
11. (She, Her) was here early in the afternoon.
12. (They, Them) are polite children.
13. I saw the visitors, but who were (they, them)?
14. (He, Him) came and showed them how to do it.
15. Jason wrote the story, and (she, her) drew the pictures.
16. (They, Them) planned the schedule and called the workers.
17. Who art (thou, thee)?
18. (Thou, Thee) hast established the earth, and it abideth.
19. "The tree that thou sawest . . . is (thou, thee), O king," said Daniel.
20. Lord, (Thou, Thee) hast been our dwelling place in all generations.

B. Diagram the sentence skeletons and predicate nominatives.
1. They came on the train.
2. Was it he at the back door?
3. He is the oldest boy.
4. Mother's helper was she.

Review Exercises

A. Write each verb or verb phrase, and give the tense. [32–36]
1. Will the Lord help Gideon?
2. How were Gideon and his men encouraged in the Lord?
3. A Midianite told about his dream.
4. A cake of barley bread had upset one of the tents.
5. You have dreamed about Gideon.
6. Surely he will defeat all the Midianites.
7. God is with Gideon.
8. Before midnight, Israel will have defeated Midian.

B. Write the correct verbs in parentheses. [54]
1. There (was, were) only three hundred men in Gideon's army.
2. (There's, There are) so many Midianites that they cannot be numbered.

3. Here (is, are) several verses about Gideon.

4. (Here's, Here are) the Sunday school books you wanted.

5. Brother Gerald (don't, doesn't) teach my class every Sunday.

---

62. Pronouns in the Objective Case

Pronouns have three cases: nominative, objective, and possessive. Here are the objective case pronouns as listed on page 264. Memorize the pronouns on this chart.

Objective Case

	Singular	*Plural*
First person:	me	us
Second person:	you (thee)	you
Third person:	him, her, it	them

The pronouns *you* and *it* are the same in the objective case as in the nominative case. The archaic *thee* used in the King James Bible is the singular form of *you.*

When pronouns are used in sentences, there are three places where they must always be in the objective case. It will help you to remember what these three places are if you remember that all three are objects.

1. *A direct object* *must always be in the objective case.*

God will bless (they, them) abundantly.

The sentence skeleton is *God will bless.* God will bless *whom?* The objective form *them* must be used because the pronoun is a direct object.

In the following sentence, the archaic form *thee* is used as a direct object.

The Lord bless <u>thee</u>.

Remember that a direct object is diagramed after the verb, with a vertical line between.

subject	action verb	direct object

2. *An* indirect object *must always be in the objective case.* An indirect object comes between an action verb and a direct object, and it tells *to whom or what* or *for whom or what.*

He gave (we, us) the message.

He gave the message *to whom?* The objective form *us* must be used because the pronoun is an indirect object.

Note the use of the archaic form *thee* as an indirect object.

The Lord will give <u>thee</u> peace.

Remember that an indirect object is diagramed on a horizontal line beneath the base line, with a slanted line connecting the indirect object to the verb.

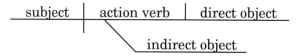

3. *The* object of a preposition *must always be in the objective case.*

The Lord has been gracious to (I, me.)

The preposition is *to.* To *whom?* The objective form *me* must be used because the pronoun is the object of a preposition.

The following sentence uses the archaic form *thee* as the object of a preposition.

The Lord make His face shine upon <u>thee</u>.

The object of a preposition is diagramed on a horizontal line beneath the base line. A slanted line connects it to the word modified by the prepositional phrase. That word may be a noun or a verb.

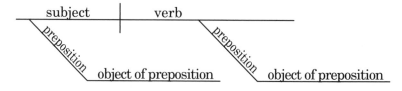

- The objective case pronouns are *me, you, him, her, it, us,* and *them.* The archaic form of *you* is *thee.*

- When a pronoun is a direct object, an indirect object, or the object of a preposition, it must be in the objective case.

Class Practice

A. Choose the correct pronouns. Tell whether each one is a *direct object,* an *indirect object,* or the *object of a preposition.* Practice reading each sentence correctly.
   1. Charles worked with (I, me).
   2. We will help (he, him).
   3. Give (she, her) the flowers.
   4. Did you give (he, him) the apples?
   5. It is a gift from (he, him).
   6. Aunt Helen wrote a letter to (she, her).
   7. The children sang three songs for (she, her).
   8. The carpenter showed (they, them) the new house.
   9. He crowneth (thou, thee) with lovingkindness and tender mercies.
  10. Unto (Thou, Thee), O Lord, do I lift up my soul.

B. On the chalkboard, diagram the sentence skeletons of sentences 1–8 in Part A. Include the direct objects, indirect objects, and prepositional phrases.

Written Exercises

A. Write the correct pronouns. After each one, write *DO, IO,* or *OP* to tell whether it is the direct object, indirect object, or object of a preposition.
   1. Ruby called (we, us) on the telephone.
   2. The experience taught (she, her) a lesson.
   3. I should pay (he, him) three dollars.
   4. Did someone warn (they, them)?
   5. Phyllis took (we, us) to the store.
   6. Give this paper to (he, him).
   7. Did you find (she, her)?
   8. Bring (I, me) the mail, please.
   9. Mother bought pretzels for (we, us).

10. A kind man gave (we, us) directions.
11. Did the medicine help (they, them)?
12. I asked (he, him) for directions.
13. Let another man praise (thou, thee), and not thine own mouth.
14. My son, keep my words, and lay up my commandments with (thou, thee).

B. Diagram the sentence skeletons, direct objects, indirect objects, and prepositional phrases.
1. Grandmother helped us with the peaches.
2. He told Sarah the story.
3. Please bring them with you.
4. Mother gave her some cookies.

Review Exercises

A. Copy each personal pronoun in Part B of Written Exercises. After each one, write its person, number, case, and gender. [60–62]

Sample answer: she—third, singular, nominative, feminine

B. Write the plural form of each noun. [22–25]

1. sky	5. roof	9. ox
2. echo	6. goose	10. fish
3. box	7. gentleman	11. moose
4. thrush	8. mouse	12. foot

---

63. Writing a Friendly Letter

How can you share news with someone you probably will not see for a long time? How can you give help or encouragement to someone who is not with you? How can you give or accept an invitation or thank someone for a favor shown when he lives far away from you? One way is to write letters. Letters written for these reasons are called friendly letters.

A friendly letter has five parts: the *heading, greeting, body, closing,* and *signature.* The heading gives the address from which you are writing, and it also gives the date. The greeting is just that—a greeting to your friend. The body of the letter is the main part, in which you write the things you have to say. The closing is your parting word or words (a sort of good-bye), and the signature is your name, showing whom the letter is from.

Greetings and closings usually follow a standard pattern. Here are some examples.

Greetings: Dear friend, Dear Cousin Mary, Dear Frank,
Closings: Yours truly, Your cousin, Sincerely,

The five letter parts are shown in the following letter.

Heading

Route 2, Box 2160
Clinton, IA 52732
April 14, 20--

Greeting

Dear Uncle Luke,

"The Lord by wisdom hath founded the earth; by understanding hath he established the heavens. By his knowledge the depths are broken up, and the clouds drop down the dew" (Proverbs 3:19, 20).

Body

I am happy to write and tell you that Father agrees to let me visit you this summer. I shall be coming to Pennsylvania in early June. (It's too soon to give an exact date.) I expect to fly to Philadelphia, and I hope you can meet me there.

I am very pleased and excited about this opportunity, and I want to thank you in advance.

Closing

Your loving nephew,

Signature

Vernon

Use correct capitalization when you write a friendly letter. The first word in the greeting of a letter and the first word in the closing must be capitalized. Capital letters are used for all proper nouns, such as the names of streets, cities, states, and months. The abbreviations *Mr.* and *Mrs.* are always capitalized. Titles of respect, such as *doctor* and *uncle,* are capitalized when they are used with names: *Doctor Merle, Dr. Merle, Uncle David.* For state names, the postal service has developed a list of two-letter abbreviations to be used with Zip Codes. These are completely capitalized and have no end punctuation. See the list at the end of this lesson.

PA 17519   MD 21719   NY 14218

Use correct punctuation in a friendly letter. In the heading, place a comma between a route number and a box number, between the name of the city and the state, and between the number of the day and the year. Do not place a comma between a house number and a street name, or between the state abbreviation and the Zip Code. Put a comma after the greeting and after the closing.

Incorrect:
1133, Maple Street
Bethel, PA, 19507
November 8 20—

Correct:
1133 Maple Street
Bethel, PA 19507
November 8, 20—

Notice where the heading, closing, and signature are written. The heading is close to the right margin. The left edge of the heading, closing, and signature are in line with each other.

The body of the letter should be written neatly and courteously. Use complete sentences, and develop your paragraphs with interesting details. Keep the left margin straight and the right margin as straight as possible.

When you write an address on an envelope, be sure to write neatly and correctly so that the letter reaches its destination. In the United States, the postal service wants the receiver's address to be printed with all capital letters and with no punctuation. Mail addressed in this way can be sorted more efficiently.

The receiver's address should be written in about the center of the envelope. It usually contains three lines. The person's name is written in the first line, the street address (or route and box number) in the second line, and the city, state, and Zip Code in the third line. If the title *Mr., Mrs.,* or *Miss* is used, it should be written before the person's name.

The sender's address should be written in the upper left corner. This is the return address, and it is arranged in the same way as the receiver's address. The following illustration shows an envelope properly addressed for mailing.

```
Vernon Martin                                    [stamp]
Route 2, Box 2160
Clinton, IA 52732



                        MR LUKE MARTIN
                        361 MAPLE DRIVE
                        NARVON PA 17555
```

- Friendly letters are written to share news, to give encouragement, to give or accept an invitation, or to thank someone for a favor shown.

- The five parts of a friendly letter are the heading, greeting, body, closing, and signature.

- A clear, courteous friendly letter is written with correct capitalization and punctuation.

Class Practice

Give the answers.

1. What are the parts of a friendly letter? Name them in the order that they appear.
2. What are three purposes for writing friendly letters?
3. Why is it important to address an envelope in clear handwriting and in good form?

4. Name the places where capitalization is always used in a friendly letter.

5. Name four places where commas are always used in a friendly letter.

6. Name two places where commas are used in addressing envelopes.

7. Where should Zip Codes be written on an envelope?

Written Exercises

A. Write each letter part correctly.

1. rachel mast
   125 pine road
   caney ky 41407

2. dear esther

3. dear aunt susan

4. loren miller

5. mr jay owens

6. miss esther martin
   route 1 box 17
   bearsville ny 12409

7. your loving friend

8. yours truly

9. your cousin

10. sincerely yours

B. Write a friendly letter to a family member or good friend who lives in another community. Prepare an envelope to go with the letter. Be clear, courteous, and neat. Here are some suggestions.

1. Invite him to your house.

2. Encourage him because he is ill.

3. Tell something interesting that has happened to you.

4. Tell him that you left something at his home during a recent visit (or that he left something at your home).

5. Thank him for something he or his family has done for you.

Review Exercises

Write *true* or *false* for each sentence.

1. A paragraph is a group of sentences that develops a single topic.

2. A paragraph has unity when all the sentences tell about one main topic.

3. You can produce unity in a paragraph by giving details in the order of time or importance, or by using transitional words.

4. A coherent paragraph is one in which all the details fit together well so that the reader does not get lost or confused.

5. Paragraphs can be developed by the use of convincing details, examples and illustrations, and comparison or contrast.

Challenge Exercises

Memorize the two-letter abbreviation for each state.

AL	Alabama	LA	Louisiana	OH	Ohio
AK	Alaska	ME	Maine	OK	Oklahoma
AZ	Arizona	MD	Maryland	OR	Oregon
AR	Arkansas	MA	Massachusetts	PA	Pennsylvania
CA	California	MI	Michigan	RI	Rhode Island
CO	Colorado	MN	Minnesota	SC	South Carolina
CT	Connecticut	MS	Mississippi	SD	South Dakota
DE	Delaware	MO	Missouri	TN	Tennessee
FL	Florida	MT	Montana	TX	Texas
GA	Georgia	NE	Nebraska	UT	Utah
HI	Hawaii	NV	Nevada	VT	Vermont
ID	Idaho	NH	New Hampshire	VA	Virginia
IL	Illinois	NJ	New Jersey	WA	Washington
IN	Indiana	NM	New Mexico	WV	West Virginia
IA	Iowa	NY	New York	WI	Wisconsin
KS	Kansas	NC	North Carolina	WY	Wyoming
KY	Kentucky	ND	North Dakota		

64. Using Pronouns Correctly

You have studied the uses of nominative case pronouns and objective case pronouns. You have learned to choose the correct word by seeing how it is used in a sentence. Usually you will have no difficulty, but there are some trouble spots, which this lesson points out to you. Form right language habits by recognizing the use of pronouns and practicing the correct forms.

One trouble spot is compound constructions. When a sentence has a compound part, you must be especially careful to use the correct pronoun. Do this by deciding what part of the sentence the pronoun is. Then you can decide whether the nominative case or the objective case should be used. Can you choose the correct pronoun for each of the following examples without reading the explanations?

Ralph and (she, her) saw them.
(Subject; use nominative *she*.)

It was Joann and (they, them).
(Predicate nominative; use nominative *they*.)

The dog bit Cheryl and (he, him).
(Direct object; use objective *him*.)

We gave Julie and (she, her) the papers.
(Indirect object; use objective *her*.)

This package is for Jerry and (they, them).
(Object of preposition; use objective *them*.)

Another help for choosing the correct word is to use the pronoun alone, without the other part of the compound construction. Study the following examples.

Ralph and (she, her) saw them.
Think: *She saw them* or *Her saw them*?
She is correct, so *Ralph and she* is correct.

The dog bit Cheryl and (he, him).
Think: The dog bit *he* or The dog bit *him*?
Him is correct, so *Cheryl and him* is correct.

A diagram can help you decide which pronoun to use. If a pronoun is diagramed as a subject or a predicate nominative, it must be in the nominative case. And if a pronoun is diagramed as a direct object, an indirect object, or the object of a preposition, it must be in the objective case.

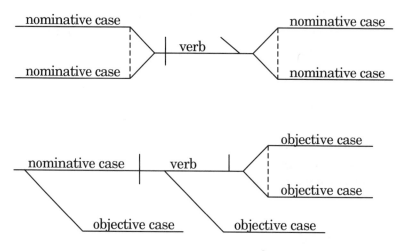

A second trouble spot is a pronoun that is followed by an appositive. An appositive is a noun that is used directly after another word to clarify it. Do you know which pronoun is correct in the following sentence?

(We, Us) girls will help Mother.

In this sentence, the pronoun is the subject and *girls* is an appositive. So the nominative case must be used: *We* girls will help.

When a pronoun is followed by an appositive, first decide what sentence part the pronoun is filling; then choose the correct pronoun. Try these examples.

(We, Us) boys are going to play baseball.
(Subject; use nominative *We.*)

Grandmother's visitors were (we, us) girls.
(Predicate nominative; use nominative *we.*)

They will not hear (we, us) boys.
(Direct object; use objective *us.*)

Charlotte gave (we, us) girls some cookies.
(Indirect object; use objective *us.*)

It will be easy for (we, us) girls.
(Object of preposition; use objective *us.*)

Saying the pronoun without the appositive is helpful in deciding which pronoun is correct.

(We, Us) boys are going to play baseball.
Think: *We are going* or *Us are going*?
We is correct, so *We boys* is correct.

It will be easy for (we, us) girls.
Think: *easy for we* or *easy for us*?
Us is correct, so *us girls* is correct.

- When a pronoun is in a compound part or is followed by an appositive, first decide how the pronoun is used in the sentence. Then choose the correct case for that use.

Class Practice

A. Tell how each pronoun is used, and then say the correct pronoun. Practice reading each sentence correctly.
1. (We, Us) children rode along.
2. Joan and (I, me) drew that picture.
3. It was (we, us) children.
4. Grandmother gave (we, us) children each an apple.
5. The speakers were Brother Amos and (he, him).
6. Grandmother helped Sara and (I, me).
7. We showed the teacher and (she, her) the butterflies.
8. Give these flowers to Sister Ellen and (she, her).
9. The letters were for (we, us) boys.
10. Uncle Jerry will teach (we, us) boys.

B. On the chalkboard, diagram the skeletons, predicate nominatives, direct and indirect objects, and prepositional phrases in the sentences from Part A.

C. Read each sentence correctly.
1. We brought Alice and she extra blankets.
2. The children went with Father and she.
3. Us boys need to start early.
4. It must be James and them.
5. The day was long for Mother and they.
6. The teacher and her had a long talk.
7. The fish in the tank could not see we visitors.
8. He got a note from Marie and I.
9. My brother and him were catching catfish.
10. I am sure it was them.

Written Exercises

A. Write the correct pronouns. After each one, write *S, PN, DO, IO,* or *OP* to tell whether it is a subject, predicate nominative, direct object, indirect object, or object of a preposition.
1. (We, Us) friends write letters often.
2. It was (we, us) boys who helped Father.
3. The children and (we, us) enjoy singing together.
4. This note is for your teacher and (he, him).
5. We told Carrie and (she, her).
6. I gave Mother and (she, her) the message.

7. Aunt Susan read to (we, us) children.
8. Uncle Joseph told (we, us) boys some stories.
9. The boys pulled the little girls and (he, him) up the hill on the wagon.
10. Uncle James pushed (he, him) and (I, me) high on the swing.
11. Uncle David gave this to (he, him) and (I, me).
12. Brother John and (he, him) led the singing.
13. It was (we, us) boys who raked the yard.
14. It was (they, them) who were here singing last night.
15. I gave Mary and (she, her) the song sheets.
16. He told (we, us) boys the way to his house.

B. Diagram the skeletons, predicate nominatives, direct and indirect objects, and prepositional phrases. Include the correct pronouns on your diagrams.
   1. (We, Us) children helped Mother all morning.
   2. It was (we, us) girls.
   3. Naomi and (she, her) came back.
   4. Naomi told Ruth and (she, her) the truth.
   5. Boaz showed kindness to Ruth and (she, her).
   6. Father told (we, us) boys.
   7. Mother gave (we, us) girls instructions.
   8. Grandfather handed the tools to (we, us) boys.

Review Exercises

A. Write whether each sentence is *declarative, interrogative, imperative,* or *exclamatory.* (There is one of each kind.) Also write the correct end punctuation. [7]
   1. Did you know that there are about two thousand different kinds of frogs known in the world
   2. Come and look at this wood frog on a log
   3. The West African goliath frog grows to be almost one foot long
   4. What a large frog that is

B. Write the correct verbs in parentheses. [47–51]
   1. The opossum (laid, lay) motionless.
   2. It has not (laid, lain) there long.
   3. The dog soon (let, left) the opossum because it looked dead.
   4. After the dog was gone, the opossum (raised, rose) its head.

5. Several edible gourds were (setting, sitting) on the table.
6. Grandmother and Grandfather had (set, sat) them there.
7. They (let, left) us keep them.
8. Nancy (laid, lay) some gourds aside.

---

65. Possessive Pronouns and Demonstrative Pronouns

You have studied personal pronouns in the *nominative case* and in the *objective case*. You are now ready to learn about *possessive case* pronouns.

Possessive Pronouns

Pronouns in the possessive case show possession or ownership. Here they are as on the chart on page 264. The words in parentheses are the archaic forms. (*Thy* is used before a consonant sound, and *thine* is used before a vowel sound.)

Possessive Case

	Singular	*Plural*
First person:	my, mine	our, ours
Second person:	your, yours (thy, thine)	your, yours
Third person:	his, her, hers, its	their, theirs

You are not likely to confuse possessive pronouns with pronouns in the other cases. But you must be careful in several other areas.

1. *Do not use an apostrophe to form a possessive personal pronoun.* Apostrophes are used to make the possessive forms of nouns, but never of personal pronouns.

Correct:	Jane's lunch, Leon's glove, book that had been Mother's
Correct:	her lunch, his glove, book that had been hers
Incorrect:	her' lunch, his' glove, book that had been her's

2. *Do not confuse possessive pronouns with contractions.* An apostrophe is used with some personal pronouns to form contractions.

Be sure to remember that they are contractions and not possessive forms. You must distinguish between the two.

Possessive Forms	Contractions
its	it's (it is)
your	you're (you are)
their	they're (they are)

Whenever you see an apostrophe used with a personal pronoun, think of the words that the contraction comes from. These sentences use the different forms correctly.

It's turning on its side.
   It's side would mean "it is side."
You're dropping some of your papers.
   You're papers would mean "you are papers."
They're painting their house a different color.
   They're house would mean "they are house."

3. *When a possessive pronoun modifies a noun, it is used as an adjective. When a possessive pronoun stands alone, it is a pronoun.*

My coat was given to Gerald.
   My is used as an adjective modifying *coat.*

The coat is now his.
   His is a pronoun standing alone.

Please give me her number.
   Her is used as an adjective modifying *number.*

I think this is hers.
   Hers is a pronoun standing alone.

Demonstrative Pronouns

Possessive pronouns are personal pronouns in the possessive case. But the *demonstrative pronouns* are in a different class altogether. They are not personal pronouns.

A demonstrative pronoun is used to point out something. The four demonstrative pronouns are *this, that, these,* and *those.*

This is my coat; that is yours.
These are my gloves; those are yours.

This and *that* are singular. *These* and *those* are plural. *This* and *these* are used to point out things nearby. *That* and *those* are used to point out things farther away.

This, that, these, and *those* are adjectives when they tell *which* about a noun. They are pronouns when they stand alone.

> <u>This</u> paper is mine. (adjective that tells which paper)
> <u>This</u> is my paper. (pronoun that means *this paper*)

> <u>That</u> book is yours. (adjective that tells which book)
> <u>That</u> is your book. (pronoun that means *that book*)

Be sure to use demonstrative pronouns correctly. Here are two rules.

1. *Do not use* here *or* there *with demonstrative pronouns.* Do not say "this here" or "that there."

> **Incorrect:**   <u>This here</u> is a little fox with soft, red fur.
> **Correct:**   <u>This</u> is a little fox with soft, red fur.

> **Incorrect:**   <u>That there</u> squirrel is a fox squirrel.
> **Correct:**   <u>That</u> squirrel is a fox squirrel.

2. *Do not use* them *as a demonstrative pronoun or as an adjective.*

> **Incorrect:**   <u>Them</u> raccoons surely are curious.
> **Correct:**   <u>Those</u> raccoons surely are curious.

- The possessive case pronouns are *my, mine, your, yours, his, her, hers, its, our, ours, their,* and *theirs.* The archaic forms of *your* and *yours* are *thy* and *thine.*

- An apostrophe is never used to make the possessive form of a personal pronoun.

- The demonstrative pronouns are *this, that, these,* and *those.*

- *This, that, these,* and *those* are adjectives when they tell *which* about a noun. They are pronouns when they stand alone.

- Do not use *here* or *there* with demonstrative pronouns.

- Do not use *them* as a demonstrative pronoun or as an adjective.

Class Practice

A. Find each possessive pronoun or demonstrative pronoun, and tell which kind it is.
1. This is my Father's world.
2. Our Father which art in heaven, hallowed be Thy name.
3. Give us this day our daily bread.
4. If ye forgive men their trespasses, your heavenly Father will also forgive you.
5. If thine enemy be hungry, give him bread to eat; ... for thou shalt heap coals of fire on his head.
6. What is that to thee? Follow thou Me.

B. Read the following sentences correctly.
1. These here are fine apples; them are no good.
2. This here wire should not be used outside. Take that there roll.
3. Carol brought them there cookies, and I brought these here.

C. Choose the correct words in parentheses.
1. (Its, It's) time for (your, you're) test.
2. (Your, You're) taking the test in (their, they're) classroom.
3. (Its, It's) about five pages long, and (your, you're) looking at the first page.
4. The longest story is (hers, her's).

D. Tell whether each underlined word is a *pronoun* or an *adjective*. If it is an adjective, tell which word it modifies.
1. These were his words.
2. These books were written by him.
3. This book is mine to keep.
4. Those are ours.

Written Exercises

A. Copy all the possessive pronouns and demonstrative pronouns, including the ones used as adjectives. After each one, write *P* or *D* to tell whether it is possessive or demonstrative.
1. This sickness is not unto death, but it is for the glory of God.
2. Their brother Lazarus had died four days before Jesus came.
3. Lord, if Thou hadst been here, my brother had not died.
4. Thy brother shall rise again.
5. Believest thou this?
6. These friends are here to weep with Mary and Martha.

7. Jesus, their Master, wept too.
8. Lazarus heard His voice and came forth.
9. Jesus told His friends to loosen the graveclothes around Lazarus.
10. These things were done to strengthen their faith.
11. Bow down thine ear, and hear the words of the wise, and apply thine heart unto my knowledge.
12. Let thine heart retain my words: keep my commandments, and live.

B. Write the correct words in parentheses.
   1. (Your, You're) time is up; (its, it's) time for lunch.
   2. (Your, You're) grades are passing; (your, you're) doing good work.
   3. (Its, It's) doors are open, and (your, you're) things are ready.
   4. (Their, They're) painting (their, they're) new house white.
   5. (His, His') typewriter is old, but it works well.
   6. (This, This here) key sticks sometimes.
   7. (Them, Those) keys should be cleaned.
   8. (That, That there) book is the one you should study.

C. Write *adj.* or *pron.* to tell how each underlined word is used. If the word is an adjective, write the word it modifies.
   1. O Daniel, has <u>your</u> God saved you from the lions?
   2. <u>My</u> God has sent His angel to shut <u>their</u> mouths.
   3. He is the living God; the kingdom is <u>His</u>.
   4. <u>His</u> kingdom will last forever.
   5. I am <u>His</u>, and He is <u>mine</u>.
   6. <u>This</u> is the true God of heaven.
   7. <u>These</u> wicked men had plotted against Daniel.
   8. The evil plan was <u>theirs</u>, and <u>that</u> was <u>their</u> punishment.
   9. God rewarded <u>His</u> servant Daniel for <u>his</u> faithfulness.
   10. I am <u>Thine</u>; save me, for I have sought <u>Thy</u> precepts.
   11. Be not wise in <u>thine</u> own eyes: fear the Lord, and depart from evil.

D. Use the following words correctly in sentences of your own.
   1. its   2. your   3. their   4. those

Review Exercises

Diagram the skeletons, direct and indirect objects, predicate nominatives, and predicate adjectives. [38–43]

1. The only marsupial in America is the opossum.
2. Opossums eat many different vegetables.
3. The girls sent Grandmother some raisin bread.
4. The date palm is a very useful tree.
5. The climate is hot and dry.

Marlin Boll

66. Indefinite Pronouns

You have learned about personal and demonstrative pronouns. A third class of pronouns is the *indefinite pronouns*. Indefinite pronouns do not refer to definite persons, places, things, or ideas.

Three Kinds of Indefinite Pronouns

1. *Some indefinite pronouns are always singular.* Here is a list of the most common singular indefinite pronouns.

each	**anybody**	**somebody**
either	**anyone**	**someone**
neither	**everybody**	**nobody**
one	**everyone**	**no one**
another		

    (*No one* is a compound pronoun spelled as two words.)

Since these pronouns are singular, they must be used with singular verb forms. (Present tense singular verbs often end with -*s*.) You will not likely use the wrong verb form in sentences like these.

Everybody has his lunch here.
Nobody walks to school.

You must be more careful in sentences where an indefinite pronoun is followed by a prepositional phrase. The verb in the sentence must agree with the *subject* of the sentence, not with the *object of the preposition.*

Incorrect: Each of the girls are bringing a recipe.
Correct: Each of the girls is bringing a recipe.
                 The verb must agree with the subject *Each,* not with *girls. Each* is singular—it means *each one. Girls* is the object of the preposition *of.*

All other words that refer to the subject must also agree with it in number. In the following sentence, which words sound correct to you?

Everybody must take (his seat, their seats).

Everybody is singular—it means every *single* body! So any words referring to the subject must be singular as well. We must say *his* (not *their*), and we must say *seat* because every person has one seat.

Everybody must take his seat.

2. *Some indefinite pronouns are always plural.* The indefinite pronouns in the following list are always plural.

   both   **few**   **several**   **many**

   Since these pronouns are plural, they must always be used with plural verb forms. (Remember that most plural verbs do not end with -*s*.) Again, be sure the verb agrees with the subject and not with the object of the preposition.

   Both come at once.

Several are here already.
Several of the children walk home from school.
Many of the leaves have fallen to the ground.

3. *Some indefinite pronouns may be singular or plural,* depending on how they are used in a sentence.

some   **any**   **none**   **all**   **most**

To decide whether a pronoun is singular or plural, you must consider the meaning of the sentence. Often your clue is in a prepositional phrase following the subject. Study the following examples.

None of the cake was eaten.
> *None* is singular because it refers to *cake,* which is singular. Use a singular verb.

None of the cookies were eaten.
> *None* is plural because it refers to *cookies,* which is plural. Use a plural verb.

Indefinite Pronouns Used as Adjectives

Many singular indefinite pronouns have a possessive form that ends with an apostrophe and *s* (*'s*). This is different from personal pronouns, which never have apostrophes in the possessive case.

Somebody's coat is lying on the grass.
One's troubles seem small compared to another's.
Do not mind everyone's business, just your own.

The possessive pronouns above are used as adjectives. Other indefinite pronouns are also used as adjectives when they come just before a noun and modify that noun. Study the following sentences.

Many people followed Jesus for the loaves and fishes. (adjective)
Many followed Jesus for the loaves and fishes. (pronoun)

Some papers are missing. (adjective)
Some of the papers are missing. (pronoun)

Another's burdens should cause us sorrow too. (adjective)

- An indefinite pronoun does not refer to a definite person, place, thing, or idea.

- The following indefinite pronouns are always singular: *each, either, neither, one, another, anybody, anyone, everybody, everyone, somebody, someone, nobody, no one.*

- The following indefinite pronouns are always plural: *both, few, several, many.*

- The following indefinite pronouns may be singular or plural, depending on how they are used in a sentence: *some, any, none, all, most.*

- An indefinite pronoun can be used as an adjective.

Class Practice

A. Say each indefinite pronoun, and tell whether it is *singular, plural,* or *either.*
1. Everyone thought somebody would do it.
2. Some needed several more.
3. A few brought some, but many didn't have any.
4. Someone left a baseball glove outside.
5. No one knew whose coat it was.

B. Some of the following sentences have mistakes. Read each sentence correctly, without changing the tense of the verb.
1. Each of the boys take a turn pitching the ball.
2. Both of the girls is a good seamstress.
3. Some of the boys can tie interesting knots.
4. None of the snow have melted yet.
5. Most of the ice cubes has been used up.
6. Everybody must bring their own lunch tomorrow.
7. Each student was sitting in their own seats.
8. Each of the students tell how to do something.

C. Tell whether each underlined word is used as a *pronoun* or an *adjective.* If it is an adjective, tell which word it modifies.
1. <u>Several</u> students memorized the Sermon on the Mount.
2. <u>Most</u> of the students can say Matthew 5:1–16.
3. <u>Many</u> students are able to recite it without error.
4. <u>None</u> have recited Psalm 119 yet.
5. <u>Someone's</u> books are on my desk.

Written Exercises

A. Write the subject of each sentence. Then write the correct verb to agree with the subject.
   1. Each of the prisoners (was, were) troubled by his dream.
   2. No one (was, were) able to interpret the dream.
   3. Neither (was, were) able to comfort the other.
   4. But someone (was, were) there who loved God.
   5. Both (was, were) told the meaning of their dreams.
   6. None of Joseph's words (fall, falls) to the ground.
   7. All of them (come, comes) true.
   8. None of the wise men (has, have) an interpretation for Pharaoh's dream.
   9. No one in the group (has, have) the answer.
  10. Nobody (is, are) able to interpret the dream.
  11. Finally somebody (remember, remembers) Joseph.
  12. Everyone (wait, waits) until Joseph is ready.
  13. Both of the dreams (is, are) told.
  14. All of the mystery (is, are) solved; God gave Joseph the answer.
  15. None of the secrets (is, are) left uncovered.

B. Write *pron.* or *adj.* to tell whether each underlined word is a pronoun or an adjective. If it is an adjective, write the word it modifies.
   1. Pharaoh said to Joseph, "God has showed you all this, and <u>none</u> are so wise and discreet as you are."
   2. <u>None</u> of the people except Pharaoh were greater than Joseph.
   3. When Joseph rode in the chariot, it was announced to <u>many</u> people, "Bow the knee."
   4. <u>No one</u> escaped the famine that came after the seven plenteous years.
   5. The famine was so severe that the people did not have <u>any</u> money left to buy food.
   6. <u>Each</u> one brought his cattle to Joseph.
   7. Soon <u>all</u> the cattle were sold.
   8. So <u>everyone</u> sold <u>all</u> his land to Joseph.
   9. Soon <u>everyone's</u> possessions were gone.
  10. Now the king owned <u>everything</u> in Egypt.
  11. <u>All</u> the people were saved from the terrible famine.
  12. God used Joseph to save <u>all</u> of them from the famine.

Review Exercises

A. Write the correct words in parentheses. [61–65]
1. Jacob and (he, him) were brothers.
2. Isaac blessed Jacob and (he, him).
3. "I am (he, him)," said Jacob.
4. Isaac gave (he, him) the birthright because he thought it was Esau.
5. "(Them, Those) wells are ours," said the herdsmen of Gerar.
6. "No, (we, us) servants dug this well, and it is (ours, our's)!" argued Isaac's servants.
7. "(Its, It's) not (your, you're) well," they said.
8. (Its, It's) the third well they had dug.
9. "(This, This here) well shall be called Rehoboth, for now the Lord has made room for us," said Isaac.
10. God has protected (we, us) children.

B. Copy the possessive nouns. After each one, write S or P to tell whether it is singular or plural. [26]
1. The shepherd's flock follows when he calls.
2. Each of the shepherds' flocks followed its own shepherd.
3. The lambs' wool is pure white.
4. The little black lamb's wool is soft.

---

67. Writing a Business Letter

Sometimes you may want to write a letter to purchase something by mail, to inquire about a purchase, or to seek information. What kind of letter should you write? A friendly letter does not serve this purpose, so a *business letter* is used.

A business letter has the same five parts as a friendly letter: *heading, greeting, body, closing,* and *signature.* In addition, a business letter also has an *inside address.* An inside address is the address of the person or company to whom you are writing.

The same rules of capitalization and punctuation are used for business letters as for friendly letters, with one exception. In a business letter, a colon rather than a comma is used after the greeting.

A business letter has a more formal greeting and closing than a friendly letter does. Here are some standard greetings used for business letters.

Dear Sir: Gentlemen: Dear Mr. Martin: Dear Madam:

Use *Dear Sir* when you do not know the person's name. Use *Gentlemen* when you are writing to a company. Some standard closings for business letters are shown below.

Yours truly,   Very truly yours,   Sincerely yours,

The body of the letter should be written neatly and courteously, using complete sentences. Keep the left margin straight and the right margin as straight as possible. Often it is good to begin the body of a business letter with these words: *I would appreciate information on . . .* or *I wish to order . . .* or *Please send me . . . .* Make the body brief and clear, and say exactly what you want. Remember that the person who reads the letter may have many letters to read each day.

Notice that the heading, closing, and signature are written in the same positions as in a friendly letter. The heading is close to the right margin. The left edge of the heading, closing, and signature are in line with each other. The left edge of the inside address is at the left margin. A blank space should be left between each letter part and the next. Such a space is especially important between the inside address and the greeting.

Heading

123 Best Road
Lehman, PA 18627
November 9, 20—

Inside Address
Pennsylvania Power and Light Company
Two North Main Street
Allentown, PA 18104

Greeting Dear Sirs:

Body
    Please send me a copy of the pamphlet *Heating the Home in Winter Weather*, which you offered with last month's billing. I would also appreciate receiving any material about home heating that you may have, which would be suitable for display on the wall of our classroom.

Closing

Sincerely,

Signature

Nancy Mellinger

A business letter is usually sent in a long business envelope rather than the smaller size commonly used for friendly letters. The receiver's address and the return address are written in the same positions as for a friendly letter. Remember that the United States Postal Service wants the receiver's address printed with all capital letters and with no punctuation, as in the following illustration.

Nancy Mellinger
123 Best Road
Lehman, PA 18627

PENNSYLVANIA POWER AND LIGHT COMPANY
TWO NORTH MAIN STREET
ALLENTOWN PA 18104

- A business letter is written to purchase something by mail, to inquire about a purchase, or to seek information.

- The six parts of a business letter are the heading, inside address, greeting, body, closing, and signature.

- In a business letter, a colon is used after the greeting. The greeting and the closing are more formal than in a friendly letter.

- The body of a business letter should be brief and clear.

Class Practice

Point out the errors in the following letter, and suggest how the body could be improved.

262, hickory view ave
new holland PA, 17557
February 2 20—

Delaware State Travel Service
630, State College road
dover de, 19901
dear Friends,

I am from sixth grade at New Holland Christian School. I would like information on your state. We are studying your state in our class. I like studying your state.

Thank you
Janice Martin

Written Exercises

A. Rewrite the business letter in Class Practice, making the needed improvements.

B. Write a business letter of your own, using one of the following suggestions. (Your teacher may need to help you find addresses.) After your work is checked, you may actually send your letter if your teacher approves.

1. Write for information about the state parks and other points of interest in a certain state. (To get an address, find an encyclopedia article on that state and look under a heading such as "Places to Visit." Often you can obtain free seals, brochures, and other interesting items.)

2. Write to the closest zoo for information on the zoo and its history.

3. Write to a local business place for information on its products and its history. Perhaps you can write to a brother in the church who has a business.

4. Write to a local place of interest, perhaps the place your class plans to visit on your school trip this year. Ask about their visiting hours, special tours, and other information that would help to make your visit enjoyable.

C. Correctly address an envelope for the business letter you wrote in Part B.

Review Exercises

Decide which of the following is *not* one of the steps in writing a report. Write the remaining steps in the correct order, and number them from 1 to 7. [50–57]

Take plenty of notes on key words and main ideas.
Write the first draft of the report.
Find several sources of information.
Decide what information may be copied word for word.
Choose a topic that is interesting to you.
Write the second draft of the report.
Write an outline based on your notes.
Proofread the first draft, and mark changes that are needed.

Challenge Exercises

Write a report on one of the following topics. Follow the rules you learned for writing reports.

1. Report on interesting things to see in a certain state of the United States.
2. Report on the behavior of a certain zoo animal of your choice (but not the alligator).
3. Report on a certain product manufactured in your area.
4. Report on a local place of interest and its history.
5. Did you send the business letter that you wrote for this lesson? If so, plan to write a report based on the information you receive.

68. Interrogative Pronouns

You know that an interrogative sentence asks a question. Can you guess the meaning of *interrogate* (in·ter′·ə·gāt′)? It means "to question." A judge may *interrogate* a person who had an accident. He may ask the following questions.

<u>What</u> is your name?   <u>Who</u> was the other driver?
<u>What</u> is your address?   <u>Whose</u> is the car you were driving?

The word *interrogative* comes from *interrogate*. An *interrogative pronoun* asks a question. *Who, whom, whose, which,* and *what* are interrogative pronouns when they introduce questions.

> <u>Who</u> can tell us the answer?
> <u>What</u> did you see in the cave?
> <u>Whose</u> is that cap on the ground?

Remember that pronouns take the place of nouns. The answer to the question introduced by an interrogative pronoun will contain the noun (or pronoun) that the interrogative pronoun stands for. In the first sentence above, *the teacher* can answer the question *who*. In the second question, *a shaggy bear* can answer the question *what*. *Teacher* and *bear* are the antecedents of the interrogative pronouns in these sentences.

An interrogative pronoun can also be used as an adjective. It is an adjective when it modifies another noun or pronoun.

> <u>Which</u> **picture** shall I buy?
> *Which* modifies *picture*.

> <u>Which</u> shall I buy?
> *Which* is a pronoun standing alone.

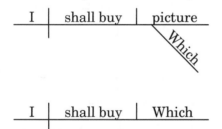

Learn to use the interrogative pronouns *who* and *whom* correctly. *Who* is in the nominative case and must be used as a *subject* or a *predicate nominative*. *Whom* is in the objective case and must be used for a *direct object,* an *indirect object,* or the *object of a preposition.*

> <u>Who</u> are the visitors? (subject)
> The man at the door was <u>who</u>? (predicate nominative)
> You told <u>whom</u>? (direct object)
> You sent <u>whom</u> the book? (indirect object)
> The package was sent to <u>whom</u>? (object of a preposition)

If you are not sure whether to use *who* or *whom* in a sentence, there is a check you can use. Try substituting *he* for *who,* and *him* for *whom.*

> You helped (*who* or *whom*?)?
> **Think:**   You helped <u>him.</u>
> **Therefore:** You helped <u>whom</u>?

> (*Who* or *Whom*?) is helping?
> **Think:**   <u>He</u> is helping.
> **Therefore:** <u>Who</u> is helping?

In many sentences with interrogative pronouns, the word order is inverted. Changing these sentences to normal word order is helpful in deciding whether *who* or *whom* is correct.

> (*Who* or *Whom*?) did you call?
> **Think:**   You did call <u>whom</u>? (direct object)
> **Therefore:** <u>Whom</u> did you call?

Do not confuse the interrogative pronoun *whose* with the contraction *who's. Whose* is a possessive form; no apostrophe is used with it. *Who's* means "who is."

> **Incorrect:** <u>Who's</u> purse is this? (means "Who is purse is this?")
> **Correct:**   <u>Whose</u> purse is this?
>   <u>Who's</u> at the door?

- The interrogative pronouns are *who, whom, whose, which,* and *what.*

- *Who* is a nominative case pronoun and is used as a subject or a predicate nominative.

- *Whom* is an objective case pronoun and is used as a direct object, an indirect object, or the object of a preposition.

- Do not confuse the interrogative pronoun *whose* with the contraction *who's.*

Class Practice

A. Find the interrogative pronouns. Tell whether each one is used as a *pronoun* or an *adjective*.
1. Who will go for us?
2. This is whose?
3. Whom shall I ask to help me?
4. You chose which little puppy?
5. Which did you bring?
6. Whose handwriting is this?
7. What did you say?
8. What number shall I use?

B. Find the interrogative pronouns, and tell whether each one is used as a *subject, predicate nominative, direct object,* or *indirect object.* (Some sentences should first be changed to normal order.)
1. Who is your teacher?
2. Your friend is who?
3. Whom did you meet?
4. This is whose?
5. Which is which?
6. Whom shall I give this?

C. On the chalkboard, diagram the skeletons, direct objects, indirect objects, predicate nominatives, and predicate adjectives of the sentences in Part B.

D. In each sentence, tell which pronoun in parentheses is correct, and tell how it is used. Practice reading the sentences correctly.
1. (Who, Whom) did you invite?
2. (Who, Whom) is she?
3. The book is for (who, whom)?
4. (Whose, Who's) reading now?
5. (Whose, Who's) voice do I hear?

Written Exercises

A. Copy the interrogative pronouns in these sentences. Write *adj.* after each one that is used as an adjective.
1. Who is your teacher?
2. Which book will you study?
3. Whom did you see at church yesterday?
4. What subjects do you have in the morning?

  5. Which is yours?
  6. This pocketknife is whose?
  7. What is the date today?
  8. Which of the boys finished first?

B. Diagram the skeletons, direct objects, indirect objects, and predicate nominatives. Also include the interrogative pronouns used as adjectives.
  1. Who was Abner's father?
  2. Whom did Elisha anoint?
  3. What lesson was Jesus teaching?
  4. Whom did you tell the story?
  5. Whose cross did Simon carry?
  6. What is a scepter?
  7. Which would you do?
  8. Which book do you want?

C. Write the correct words. Be ready to tell in class why you chose the ones you did.
  1. (Who, Whom) was the author of the wise words in Proverbs 30?
  2. (Who, Whom) did God call from a burning bush?
  3. Aaron assisted (who, whom) in his work?
  4. (Who, Whom) was the first king of Israel?
  5. The last king of Israel was (who, whom)?
  6. The Epistle to the Ephesians was written by (who, whom)?
  7. A donkey asked (who, whom) some questions?
  8. (Whose, Who's) standing in the path?
  9. (Whose, Who's) life was in danger?
  10. (Who, Whom) did Balaam finally obey?

D. Use three interrogative pronouns in sentences of your own. Use *whom* correctly in one of them.

Review Exercises

A. Write the subject of each sentence. Then write the word or words in parentheses that agree with the subject. [54, 66]
  1. (There's, There are) about twenty-eight thousand kinds of beetles in the United States and Canada.
  2. None of the beetles from the United States or Canada (is, are) as large as the beetles found in the tropics.
  3. Several of the kinds from jungles (is, are) six or more inches long!

4. Some of the natives from Cuba and Puerto Rico (tie, ties) large fireflies on their feet to light their way on mountain trails at night.
5. (Don't, Doesn't) anybody know about the bombardier beetles that can spray a foaming, bad-smelling chemical on their enemies?
6. One of the beetles (is, are) able to pull ninety times (its, their) own weight.

B. Copy the two personal pronouns in each sentence. After each pronoun, write its person, number, case, and gender. [60–65]
   1. Alice told me about them.
   2. Is it Carol's coat or yours?
   3. He brought Father and her some flowers.

69. Relative Pronouns and Relative Clauses

You have learned that the pronouns *who, whom, whose, which,* and *what* are *interrogative pronouns* when they are used to introduce questions. Now consider the following sentence.

The boy who discovered the fire ran for an extinguisher.

Is *who* an interrogative pronoun in this sentence? No, because the sentence does not ask a question. *Who* is a *relative pronoun.* Look at the sentence again, and notice two things about the relative pronoun.

1. A relative *pronoun* relates *directly to another word in the sentence.*

   The boy who discovered the fire ran for an extinguisher.

   What is the antecedent of the pronoun *who*? *Who* discovered the fire? The boy. So *who* relates to *boy,* its antecedent. A relative pronoun comes directly after its antecedent. Here are several more examples.

   Brother Brian is a man whom you can trust.
   Whom relates to its antecedent *man.*

   Grandpa, whose children are grown, loves his grandchildren.
   Whose relates to its antecedent *Grandpa.*

The young donkey, <u>which</u> had never been ridden before, was brought to Jesus. (*Which* relates to its antecedent *donkey*.)

2. *A relative pronoun introduces a* relative clause, *which modifies the antecedent of the relative pronoun.* Again consider the first example sentence. Notice that the pronoun *who* introduces a clause (a group of words with a subject and a verb).

subject | verb
The boy (<u>who</u> | <u>discovered</u> the fire) ran for an extinguisher.
The clause *who discovered the fire* modifies *boy,* telling *which* boy. Since the entire clause relates to the boy, it is a *relative clause.*

The other interrogative pronouns can also function as relative pronouns. Study the following examples; the relative clauses are in parentheses.

Interrogative:	Relative:
<u>Who</u> can do this job?	The man (<u>who</u> can do this job) will be paid well.
<u>Whom</u> should we pay?	Stephen is the man (<u>whom</u> we should pay).
<u>Whose</u> is this book?	The girl (<u>whose</u> book this is) left yesterday.
<u>Which</u> do we need?	The tool (<u>which</u> we need) is broken.
<u>What</u> did you see?	The bear (<u>that</u> I saw) was asleep.

In the last pair of sentences, notice that the interrogative pronoun *What* is replaced by the relative pronoun *that.* This is the only difference between the relative pronouns and the interrogative pronouns.

Relative pronouns: who, whom, whose, which, that

What happens if a relative clause is removed from a sentence? Since it is a separate clause, the rest of the sentence still makes sense. Study the following example.

The birds (<u>that</u> the children are feeding) are called juncos.
The birds are called juncos.

A relative clause provides more details, but the sentence is complete without it. This fact can help you to recognize relative clauses in sentences. If a clause begins with a relative pronoun and is not needed to make the sentence complete, it is a relative clause.

- The relative pronouns are *who, whom, whose, which,* and *that.*

- A relative pronoun relates directly to another word in the sentence, which is its antecedent.

- A relative pronoun introduces a relative clause, which modifies the antecedent of the relative pronoun. The relative clause can be removed from a sentence, and the sentence will still be complete.

Class Practice

A. Tell whether each underlined word is an *interrogative* pronoun or a *relative* pronoun.
  1. Everyone <u>who</u> was there saw him.
  2. <u>Whom</u> did Father meet in the city?
  3. This is the man <u>whom</u> you met yesterday.
  4. Continue in the things <u>that</u> you have learned.
  5. <u>What</u> is always the first name in the Bible list of apostles?
  6. <u>Which</u> of the roads leads to your house?
  7. The road <u>that</u> leads to our house is closed.
  8. <u>Who</u> helped the children <u>whose</u> wagon was broken down?

B. Tell which words are relative pronouns, and give their antecedents.
  1. Dorcas was a woman who was full of good deeds.
  2. The book that we read had been borrowed.
  3. You are blessed of the Lord, who made heaven and earth.
  4. A city that is set on a hill cannot be hidden.

C. Read only the relative clauses in the following sentences. Then read each sentence without the relative clause.
  1. The girl whom you saw is my niece.
  2. The book that I just read is about pioneer life.
  3. Here is a man who wants to speak with you.
  4. George will find a red cherry, which is ripe.

Written Exercises

A. Write *interrogative* or *relative* to identify each underlined pronoun.
  1. <u>Whom</u> did you meet there?
  2. The boy <u>whom</u> you met was Herbert.
  3. <u>Which</u> of the apples will you take?

4. This apple, <u>which</u> is a Winesap, is the one I want.
5. We saw a sign <u>that</u> showed us the way.
6. <u>What</u> did you ask me?
7. He <u>who</u> follows Christ shall not walk in darkness.
8. <u>Who</u> climbed into a sycamore tree to see Jesus?
9. Dorcas, <u>whom</u> Peter raised from the dead, had done many kind deeds.
10. <u>What</u> is the name of the man <u>whose</u> daughter Jesus raised to life?

B. Write each relative pronoun and its antecedent.
1. People who love the Lord obey Him.
2. This is the day that the Lord has made.
3. We know the people whom we love.
4. Those that fed the swine fled to the city.
5. The man whom Jesus healed wanted to follow Him.
6. He lived in a strange land, which was far from his home.

C. Copy only the relative clauses in these sentences.
1. Father repaired the roof, which the storm had damaged.
2. The visitor whom I met lives in Missouri.
3. Peace that passes understanding shall keep your hearts.
4. Haman was a man whose pride brought him low.
5. He has an old Bible, which is quite worn.
6. His mother, who taught him about God, was Eunice.

D. Use these relative clauses in original sentences.
1. that Sister Alice read to us
2. whom the dog bit yesterday
3. who brought the frog to school

Review Exercises

Write the word that receives the action of each verb, and label it *S* for subject or *DO* for direct object. Then write whether the sentence is in the *active* or the *passive* voice. [55]
1. Daryl has rung the bell.
2. The bell has been rung.
3. The leaves have been blown away.
4. June wrote several letters yesterday.
5. Father is planting peas.
6. The book was placed on the shelf.

70. Using Relative Pronouns Correctly

You have learned that a relative pronoun always introduces a relative clause. It is a clause because it has a subject and a verb. In many sentences, the relative pronoun is the subject of the relative clause.

> The prophet (<u>who</u> warned Jeroboam) refused his dinner invitation.
> <u>Who</u> <u>warned</u>. *Who* is the subject.

> He started for his home, (<u>which</u> was in Judah).
> <u>Which</u> <u>was</u>. *Which* is the subject.

The relative pronoun is not always the subject. It may also fill some other place in the relative clause. The relative pronoun may be a predicate nominative, a direct object, an indirect object, the object of a preposition, or a modifier. Study the following examples. The relative clauses are in parentheses.

> An old man went down the road (<u>that</u> the prophet had taken).
> <u>Prophet</u> <u>had taken</u> that. *That* is the direct object.

> The old man (with <u>whom</u> the prophet returned) had lied to him.
> <u>Prophet</u> <u>returned</u> with whom. *Whom* is the object of a preposition.

> The prophet (<u>whom</u> the old man had served a meal) was killed by a lion.
> <u>Man</u> <u>had served</u> whom meal. *Whom* is the indirect object.

> This is an example of a man (<u>whose</u> disobedience cost his life).
> *Whose* modifies <u>disobedience</u>. *Whose* is an adjective.

As you can see in the examples above, the word order in a relative clause may be inverted. Changing the clause to normal word order is helpful in deciding what sentence part the relative pronoun is.

> The sycamore tree, (<u>which</u> Zacchaeus climbed), stood along the road.
> **Normal word order:** Zacchaeus climbed which.
> *Which* is a direct object.
> Zacchaeus was changed from the cheater (<u>that</u> he had been).
> **Normal word order:** He had been that.
> *That* is a predicate nominative.

How do we know when to use the words *who, whom,* or *whose* in relative clauses? The answer is found by knowing what part of the clause the word fills. If the relative pronoun is a subject or a predicate nominative, you must use the nominative case *who*. If the relative pronoun is an object, you must use the objective case *whom*. If it shows possession, you must use the possessive form *whose*.

The man (<u>who</u> fell out the window) was Eutychus.
    <u>Who</u> <u>fell</u>. Nominative case *who* is used for a subject.

One man (<u>whom</u> Paul healed) was Publius.
    <u>Paul</u> <u>healed</u> whom. Objective case *whom* is used for a direct object.

The people (to <u>whom</u> Paul preached) listened attentively.
    <u>Paul</u> <u>preached</u> to whom. Objective case *whom* is used for the object of a preposition.

There is another rule for using relative pronouns correctly. Use *who* or *whom* in referring to people, and *which* in referring to animals or objects. *That* and *whose* may refer to people, animals, or objects.

It was Jennifer <u>who</u> helped us yesterday. (not *which*)
The lambs <u>which</u> we sold were all black. (not *whom*)
The boy <u>that</u> cleaned the floor used a broom <u>that</u> was black.
The people <u>whose</u> language was confounded had planned a tower <u>whose</u> top would reach to heaven.

- A relative pronoun can be used as several different parts of a dependent clause.

- Use the nominative case *who* when a relative pronoun is the subject or the predicate nominative in a relative clause.

- Use the objective case *whom* when the relative pronoun is the object in a relative clause.

- Use the possessive case *whose* when the relative pronoun is a modifier in a relative clause.

- Use *who* or *whom* in referring to people, and *which* in referring to animals or objects. *That* and *whose* may refer to people, animals, or objects.

Class Practice

A. Tell whether the pronoun in parentheses is used as a *subject,* a *direct object,* or the *object of a preposition.* Tell which pronoun in parentheses should be used. Then read each sentence correctly.
1. Daniel, (who, whom) prayed to God three times a day, was thrown into the lions' den.
2. King Darius, (who, whom) had not slept all night, hurried to the den early in the morning.
3. Is thy God, (who, whom) thou servest continually, able to deliver thee from the lions?
4. The God to (who, whom) Daniel prayed did save him from the lions.

B. For each sentence, decide which pronoun in parentheses is correct. Then read the sentence correctly.
1. An angel shut the mouths of the lions (who, which) were in the den.
2. The prayers (whom, which) Daniel offered faithfully were answered.
3. Our church helped the family (whose, which) house burned.
4. We enjoyed visiting with the people (whom, which) we had invited.
5. The farm was sold to the man (who, that) offered the most money.

Written Exercises

A. Write the correct pronouns in parentheses. After each one, write *S, DO,* or *OP* to tell whether it is a subject, a direct object, or the object of a preposition.
1. Eli the priest, to (who, whom) Samuel went, had not called.
2. Dorcas, (who, whom) Peter raised to life, helped the poor.
3. The Ethiopian (who, whom) was reading the Scriptures was puzzled.
4. Philip, (who, whom) knew Jesus, explained the passage to him.
5. Jesus, about (who, whom) Isaiah wrote, was the Lamb (who, whom) gave His life for all men.
6. The Ethiopian to (who, whom) Philip preached asked to be baptized.
7. Philip, (who, whom) was a deacon, baptized the Ethiopian.
8. Then the Ethiopian (who, whom) was baptized saw Philip no more.

B. Write the correct pronouns in parentheses. Write whether each pronoun refers to a *person,* an *animal,* or an *object.*
1. The animals (who, that) built this dam are beavers.
2. The Lord, (who, which) made them, taught them to work together.
3. A beaver's ax is the teeth (who, which) are in his mouth.
4. Some of the ditches (whom, that) beavers dig are thirty inches deep and eighteen inches wide.
5. These sluices, (who, which) is what the ditches are called, are made for dragging logs to the water.
6. Beavers (who, that) are younger help the older ones.
7. People (that, which) have studied beavers are amazed at their abilities.
8. My friend Jonathan, (whose, which) family traveled to the western states, has seen the beavers' large dams.
9. His brother, (who, which) writes interesting articles about beavers, has spent many hours watching them and reading about them.
10. The students, (whose, which) teacher told stories and drew pictures on the board, were also enthusiastic.

C. Use these relative clauses in original sentences. Underline the clause, and circle the word it modifies.
1. who will teach at Brownsville
2. whose money was returned
3. whom we met at church
4. which Father wanted to buy
5. that we planted in front of the house

Review Exercises

Write the correct words in parentheses. [62–68]
1. Evelyn and (she, her) wrote the stories.
2. We helped Bertha and (he, him).
3. Lois read Grandmother and (he, him) a story.
4. We translated (that, that there) story for Maria and (she, her).
5. (We, Us) girls read some stories to (they, them).
6. (Who, Whom) wrote the book?
7. For (who, whom) was the book written?
8. Some of the teachers helped (we, us) girls with our project.
9. Brother Martin showed (we, us) boys his old books.

10. Some of (them, those) books were very old.
11. Each of the girls (bring, brings) one songbook.
12. (Its, It's) cover is old and torn.

Challenge Exercises

Diagram the relative clauses from the sentences in Written Exercises, Part A. The examples given here are from the last two in Class Practice, Part A.

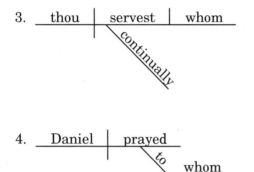

71. Courtesy and Clarity on the Telephone

The Bible says, "Let your speech be alway with grace, seasoned with salt, that ye may know how ye ought to answer every man" (Colossians 4:6). Speaking courteously and respectfully on the telephone is one way to obey this verse.

Read this telephone conversation, and study the paragraphs that follow it.

Ring! Ring!

Voice: Hello; Elam Martin's.

Sister Anna: Hello; this is Anna Yoder. May I speak with Sister Gloria?

Voice: Mother can't come to the phone just now. This is Beverly. Shall I ask her to call back, or may I take a message?

Sister Anna: Will you please take a message? At the sewing circle on Friday, we will need all the sewing machines that are available. She should bring hers along if she can.

Beverly: Okay, I'll write that down. You want Mother to bring her sewing machine along to the sewing circle on Friday.

Sister Anna: Yes, Beverly, that's correct. Thank you! Good-bye.

Beverly: Good-bye, Sister Anna.

The persons in this telephone conversation followed some important rules for using the telephone. Both parties identified themselves promptly. Beverly offered to take a message or have her mother return the call. Sister Anna said exactly what she wanted, and Beverly repeated the message and wrote it down. Sister Anna was the one who made the call, so she was the one who said "good-bye" first. Both speakers used courtesy and clear English.

When you make a telephone call, be sure you dial the right number. If you do not know a number, find it in the telephone directory or ask someone to help you find it. If you reach the wrong party, be sure to apologize. Even if the person says "That's all right," you know you have disturbed him unnecessarily.

When you are calling and no one answers right away, let the telephone ring about seven times. It is usually not necessary to let it ring much longer, unless you know that the person needs extra time to get to the telephone.

As soon as someone answers, tell who you are. You may ask a polite question such as "How are you?" but do not wait long to state the reason for your call.

When you answer the telephone, tell the caller what place he has reached and who you are. If the caller wants to speak to someone who is not available, offer to take a message. Be sure you understand the message accurately, and write it down.

Be courteous and respectful when using the telephone. In order to speak clearly, keep the mouthpiece about an inch from your mouth, and hold the earpiece lightly against your ear. Speak loudly enough so that your listener can hear you easily, but do not shout.

Do not make calls that are pointless or unnecessarily long. Be respectful of the other person's time.

If someone calls you, let him say "Good-by" first unless you must end the call for some reason. Otherwise, you may cut off the conversation before the caller has finished his business.

- Be courteous and respectful when using the telephone.

Class Practice

A. Eunice Weaver calls Jeanne Martin to get the math assignment for the next day. Show how the call should go, by having one student say the things Eunice should say and another student the things Jeanne should say.

B. Brother Carl Miller is calling your father to tell him the school board meeting this evening has been canceled. He also wants your father to relay the message to Brother Jacob Anderson. Your father is not at home, so you answer the telephone. You then call Brother Jacob and give him the message. Show how each telephone call should go by having different students say what each person should say.

Written Exercises

In your own words, write out a courteous and proper telephone conversation for Part A in Class Practice.

Review Exercises

Choose and write the one best answer for each question. [45]

1. What is the first thing you should do in preparing for a book report?
    a. Write an outline.
    b. Read the book.
    c. Take notes.
2. Which information should you *not* give in a book report?
    a. The title of the book.
    b. The name of the author and the copyright date.
    c. A description of the setting and main characters.
    d. The plot of the story.
    e. The outcome of the story.
    f. Your opinion of the book.

72. Chapter 6 Review

Class Practice

A. Name the kind of pronouns in each set. Choose from this list.

demonstrative   personal—nominative case
indefinite   personal—objective case
interrogative   personal—possessive case
relative

1. this, that, these, those
2. I, you, he, she, it, we, they
3. my, mine, your, yours, his, her, hers, its, our, ours, their, theirs
4. some, any, none, all, most, each, either, one, nobody, anyone, anybody, both, few, several, many
5. who, whom, whose, which, what
6. me, you, him, her, it, us, them
7. who, whom, whose, which, that

B. Tell whether the pronouns in each list are *always singular, always plural,* or *either singular or plural.*
1. both, few, several, many
2. each, either, neither, one, another, anybody, anyone, everybody, everyone, somebody, someone, nobody, no one
3. some, any, none, all, most

C. Read each sentence, exchanging the subject and the predicate nominative.
1. He is the fastest runner.
2. The caller at the door was he.
3. They are the cooks.
4. The seamstress was she.

D. Tell whether the underlined pronouns are *interrogative* or *relative.* Give the antecedent of each relative pronoun, and read the clause that it introduces.
1. <u>Who</u> is bringing the fruit?
2. The girl <u>who</u> is bringing the fruit will be late.
3. <u>Which</u> rabbit is yours?
4. The rabbit <u>which</u> is yours has escaped from his pen.

E. Read the following sentences correctly.
1. The rabbit who had escaped is in the window well.
2. The girl which brought the young turkey also brought a guinea hen.
3. Them chicks belong to Mary.
4. These here are John's.

F. Give the answers.
1. Name the parts of a friendly letter in the order in which they appear.
2. What part does a business letter have that a friendly letter does not have?
3. Name three reasons for writing friendly letters.
4. Why is it important to address an envelope in clear handwriting and in good form?
5. Look at the letter in Written Exercises, Part H. Is it a friendly letter or a business letter?

G. Tell how the following telephone conversation should be improved.

Ring! Ring!
"Hello," said Hilda Keppel.
"Hello. Is this the Keppels'?" asked Mrs. Brown.
"Yes."
"To whom am I speaking?
"Hilda."
"May I speak to your mother?" asked Mrs. Brown.
"No," replied Hilda.
"Can you give her a message?" Mrs. Brown asked.
"Uh-huh," replied Hilda.
"Tell her I would like to place an order for two loaves of her home-made bread next week," said Mrs. Brown.
"All right. Good-bye," said Hilda.

Written Exercises

A. Copy the personal pronouns. After each one, write its person, number, case, and gender.
1. He showed her where to find them.
2. My letter was sent to you girls and to him.
3. Our house is older than theirs.
4. "Cast thy bread upon the waters: for thou shalt find it after many days" (Ecclesiastes 11:1).

B. Copy each personal pronoun, and write its antecedent.
   1. Father wrote his name on the paper, put it into an envelope, and sealed it.
   2. Jesus said to Peter, "What is that to thee? Follow thou Me."

C. Write the correct pronouns. After each one, write *S, PN, DO, IO,* or *OP* to tell whether it is a subject, predicate nominative, direct object, indirect object, or object of a preposition.
   1. The people and (he, him) followed Jesus.
   2. (Who, Whom) was Bartimaeus calling?
   3. To (who, whom) was Jesus speaking?
   4. The man (who, whom) had been blind was (he, him).
   5. Jesus healed Bartimaeus and (he, him).
   6. Jesus had compassion on the people and (he, him).
   7. (We, Us) girls sang a new song together.
   8. Brother John taught (we, us) boys the song too.
   9. They sang it to (we, us) older women.
   10. Mary brought Mother and (I, me) those flowers.
   11. The students (who, whom) had a bird in their classroom made a report.
   12. The teacher to (who, whom) I spoke did not know his name.
   13. The person (who, whom) we told was glad to know.
   14. The person (who, whom) lost the parakeet identified the bird.

D. Write the correct words in parentheses.
   1. (Its, It's) time to go to (their, they're) house.
   2. (Your, You're) drawing of a squirrel is good except that (its, it's) tail is too long.
   3. As for (its, it's) ears, (their, they're) not even (there, they're).

E. Write *adj.* or *pron.* to tell how each underlined word is used. If the word is an adjective, write the word it modifies.
   1. <u>That</u> snail climbed right up the side of the glass.
   2. <u>This</u> is not a poisonous kind.
   3. <u>Some</u> ocean-dwelling snails are poisonous, but <u>most</u> of them are harmless.
   4. A <u>few</u> are as small as a pinhead.
   5. <u>Each</u> carries his little house with him.
   6. <u>His</u> is in <u>her</u> aquarium.
   7. <u>Which</u> kind of snail is two feet long?
   8. <u>Who</u> wrote that there are over eighty thousand varieties of snails?

F. Write the correct words in parentheses. When you write a verb, also write the subject that it agrees with.
1. One of the students (is, are) not here.
2. Few (has, have) brought (his, their) lunches.
3. Each of the girls (is, are) bringing (her, their) own.
4. None of the boys (is, are) ready yet.
5. None of the glue (was, were) spilled.
6. Both of us (has, have) a new pen.

G. Write whether each underlined pronoun is *interrogative* or *relative*. Write the antecedent of each relative pronoun.
1. <u>Who</u> saw the strange bird first?
2. The boy <u>who</u> saw the strange bird first told the teacher.
3. <u>Whose</u> is it?
4. The girl <u>whose</u> parrot came along to school may come to my desk.
5. The bird <u>which</u> has a yellow head is a cockatiel.

H. Rewrite the following letter, correcting the errors and improving the body.

361 mobile drive
Montgomery Al 36108
january 1 20—

public inquiries
national park service
washington, DC 20013

gentlemen;

    My name is melinda neville. My class will soon be studying the state of Alaska. We studied Alabama last week. I like studying geography a lot. I would appreciate information on the state parks of Alaska that would help us in our study.

sincerely

melinda neville

Chapter Seven

Using Correct Capitalization and Punctuation

Writing Stories

Capital
letters and punctuation
marks help us to better read
what others have
written.

One jot or one tittle shall in no wise pass . . . till all be fulfilled.

Matthew 5:18

73. Using Capital Letters

You already know the main rules for capitalizing words and abbreviations. They are listed below.

1. *Capitalize the first word of every sentence.* This includes the first word in a direct quotation.

2. *Capitalize the first word in every line of poetry.*

Diligence
<u>D</u>o each task with diligence,
    <u>W</u>hether large or small;
<u>W</u>hat seems insignificant
    <u>M</u>ay be best of all.
—Ada L. Wine

3. *Capitalize every personal name.* Also capitalize initials used with the names of persons.

A. W. Tozer   C. B. White   Alice M. Long

4. *Capitalize a title that is part of a name.*

Aunt Martha   Grandpa Weaver
Uncle Alvin   Brother John

When a noun is used as a title *before* a name, it is usually capitalized because it is considered part of the name. If the same noun comes *after* a name, it is not capitalized because it is not part of the name.

Will <u>Governor Smith</u> reduce taxes?
Will <u>Nolan Smith</u>, the new <u>governor</u>, reduce taxes?

We all admire the wisdom of <u>King Solomon</u>.
<u>Solomon</u> was the wisest <u>king</u> of Israel.

5. *Capitalize a title when it is used alone as a name.* One common example is the use of a title such as *father, mother,* or *uncle* in direct address. But when these titles are used after articles, possessive pronouns, or other limiting adjectives, they are not usually capitalized.

When can I leave the hospital, <u>Doctor</u>?
    (used in direct address)
He asked the <u>doctor</u> an important question.
    (used after an article)

Charles asked <u>Mother</u> where his lunch was. (used as a name)
His <u>mother</u> visited school yesterday.
    (used after a possessive pronoun)

When you are not sure whether to capitalize a title, try substituting a name for the title. You should capitalize the title only if you can replace it with a personal name.

My (Mother, mother) helped me with the work.
    Think: My <u>Sara</u> helped me with the work.
               (incorrect; use *mother*)

I believe (Mother, mother) can do it for me.
    Think: I believe <u>Sara</u> can do it for me.
               (correct; use *Mother*)

6. *Capitalize* I *and* O *when they are used as words.*

    Forever will <u>I</u> praise Thee, <u>O</u> my Lord!

7. *Use proper capitalization in the heading, the greeting, the closing, and the signature of a letter.* In the heading, this includes all proper nouns, such as the name of the street, the city, the state, and the month. In the greeting and the closing, you must capitalize the first word. The signature is your name, which of course must be capitalized.

115 Maple Street
Altoona, PA 16601
April 19, 20—

Dear Amy,   Sincerely yours,
My dear sister,   Yours truly,

- Capitalize the first word of every sentence, the first word in a direct quotation, and the first word in every line of poetry.

- Capitalize every personal name and any initial or title.

- Capitalize a title used as a name.

- Capitalize *I* and *O* when they are written as words.

- Use proper capitalization in the address, the date, the greeting, the closing, and the signature of a letter.

Class Practice

Tell which words need to be capitalized.

1. a horse can't pull while kicking;
   this fact i merely mention;
   and he can't kick while pulling—
   which is my chief contention.

2. "but thou, o Lord, art a shield for me; my glory, and the lifter up of mine head" (Psalm 3:3).

3. aunt martha read an interesting poem to us, written by h. w. longfellow.

4. thomas jefferson, a former president, once wrote to john adams, "i cannot live without books."

5. my mother read the verse from job that says, "with the ancient is wisdom; and in length of days is understanding."

6. do you know when queen elizabeth I ruled in england?

7.

54 birch road
alma, ne 68920
july 17, 20—

dear sister rose,
    thank you for being my teacher this past year. i appreciate all you have done for me. i hope you have a refreshing summer vacation.

with warm regards,
jean

Written Exercises

Copy the following sentences, stanza, and letter parts, using correct capitalization. Underline all the letters you capitalize.

1. hear me when i call, o God of my righteousness.

2. j. g. saxe wrote a poem about six blind men and an elephant.

3. my brother repeated the words that jesus said: "ask, and it shall be given you; seek, and ye shall find; knock, and it shall be opened unto you."

4. I think grandma martin has gone to see a. b. smith, her doctor.

5. tell me, father, where I can find the hammer.

6. we read that king solomon received much cedar wood from hiram, king of tyre.

7.   **being kind**
try to practice being kind;
then most surely you will find
someone who is very near
needing comfort, help, or cheer.
—Ada L. Wine

8.
117 main street
holland, mi 49424
may 4, 20—

dear gerald,

in 1 Peter 5:7 we read, "he careth for you."

we had an interesting school trip on may 1. you should have been along, gerald! The teachers, sister phoebe martin and brother ivan lapp, took us to a historic coal mine. it was cold in the mine, and water dripped on our heads from time to time. we saw where miners used to dig coal out of the ground, and how different tunnels branched off the main tunnel. at one place the mine had even caved in, but the part we were in is checked daily for safety. When our guide, mr. n. snowden, turned all the lights off, we could see how pitch-dark it really is under the ground!

come and see us sometime soon.

your friend,
mervin l. white

Review Exercises

For each group of pronouns, write the letter of the kind that it is. [61–69]

a. personal—nominative case
b. personal—objective case
c. personal—possessive case
d. personal—archaic

e. demonstrative
f. indefinite
g. interrogative
h. relative

1. thou, thee, thy, thine
2. me, you, him, her, it, us, them
3. this, that, these, those
4. anyone, somebody, few, all, many
5. I, you, he, she, it, we, they
6. who, whom, whose, which, that
7. my, your, his, her, ours, theirs
8. who, whom, whose, which, what

74. Capitalizing Proper Nouns and Proper Adjectives

Every proper noun must be capitalized. A proper noun names a particular person, place, or thing. Review the following rules of capitalization.

1. *Capitalize a noun or pronoun that refers to God.*

> In the beginning was the <u>Word</u>.
> The <u>Father</u>, the <u>Son</u>, and the <u>Holy Spirit</u> are all present in Luke 3:22.
> When <u>He</u> calls me, I will answer <u>Him</u>.

When the King James Bible was written, there were no rules for capitalizing pronouns referring to God. So when we copy directly from the Bible, we usually write pronouns for God in small letters. (Verses quoted from the Bible are in quotation marks and usually have the reference added.) In all other writing, we capitalize the pronouns that refer to God.

Bible verse:
> "Casting all your care upon him; for he careth for you" (1 Peter 5:7).

Other writing:
> We should cast our cares on Him because He cares for us.

2. *Capitalize the names of the days of the week and the months of the year. Do not capitalize the names of the seasons.*

Sunday	January	spring
Monday	February	summer
Thursday	June	fall (autumn)
Saturday	October	winter

> The second <u>Wednesday</u> of <u>August</u> was the warmest day of the <u>summer</u>.
> On <u>Friday</u>, <u>September</u> 23, <u>autumn</u> arrived.

3. *Capitalize the first and last words and all important words in the title of a book, newspaper, magazine, song, story, or poem. Do not capitalize the articles a, an, and the; the conjunctions and, but, and or; or a preposition with fewer than four letters, unless it is the first or last word in the title.*

Title of a book:
Home Fires at the Foot of the Rockies

Title of a magazine:
Nature Friend

Title of a song:
"Dare to Be a Daniel"
    (*Be* has only two letters, but it is a verb.)

Title of a story:
"The Family Across the Road"
    (*Across* is a preposition, but it has six letters.)

Title of a poem:
"The Blind Men and the Elephant"

4. *Capitalize a common noun that is part of a proper noun.* Many place names include words like *street, river, lake,* and *mountain.* These words are part of the name and should be capitalized.

Pennsylvania Avenue	Little Bighorn River
Empire State Building	Black Horse Road
Allegheny Mountain	Grant Christian School

Words like *school, hill, street, creek, lake,* and *mountain* are not capitalized when they are not part of a name.

We visited <u>Little Mountain School</u> beside the <u>Red River</u>.
The <u>school</u> is on a little <u>mountain</u> beside a <u>river</u>.

5. *Capitalize an abbreviation made from a proper noun or used with a proper noun.* Use a dictionary if you are not sure whether an abbreviation should be capitalized.

<u>Ill.</u> (for Illinois)	<u>Dr.</u> Richard Calhoun
<u>Mrs.</u> Smith	Adam Martin, <u>Jr.</u>

6. *Capitalize a proper adjective, which is formed from a proper noun.*

Proper Noun	Proper Adjective
America	American
Rome	Roman
France	French
Poland	Polish
China	Chinese
Texas	Texan
Canada	Canadian

When a proper adjective comes just before a common noun, the common noun is usually *not* capitalized.

French toast   Roman soldier
Canadian friend   American car

- Capitalize a noun or pronoun that refers to God.

- Capitalize the names of the days of the week and the months of the year, but not the names of the seasons.

- Capitalize the first and last words and all important words in the title of a book, newspaper, magazine, song, story, or poem.

- Capitalize a common noun that is part of a proper noun.

- Capitalize an abbreviation made from a proper noun or used with a proper noun.

- Capitalize a proper adjective, which is formed from a proper noun.

Class Practice

Tell which words need capital letters.

1. if jesus came to your house
       to spend a day or two,
   if he came unexpectedly,
       i wonder what you'd do.

   i know you'd give your nicest room
       to such an honored Guest,
   and all the food you'd serve to him
       would be the very best.
                              —Author unknown

2. the snow is like a blanket that
       god spreads across the land
   where wheat and oats and barley sleep,
       awaiting spring's command.

3. in australia, winter begins in may and ends in october.
4. the summer months in australia are from november to april.

5. in a book about australia called *the land down under,* i read about the red desert.

6. the first day of the week is always sunday, and the second day is monday.

7. the antarctic peninsula points toward the tip of south america.

8. the great dividing range is the largest mountain range of australia.

9. mr. richard byrd flew over antarctica and made many maps of it.

10. captain james cook claimed australia for great britain.

11. roald amundsen was a norwegian who led a group of explorers to the South Pole.

12. an english explorer named robert f. scott went to antarctica at the same time.

13. the chinese were probably the first to use coal for heating.

14. david went the second mile for a roman soldier.

Written Exercises

A. Copy the following stanzas and titles, using correct capitalization. Underline each letter that you capitalize.

1. sometimes i walk in the shadow,
        sometimes in the sunlight clear;
    but whether in gloom or brightness,
        the lord is very near.
                        —Anonymous

2.   **god's care**
    the grasses are clothed
    and the ravens are fed
        from his store;
    but you, who are loved
    and guarded and led,
        how much more

    will he clothe and feed you and give you his care?
    then leave it with him; he has everywhere
        ample store.
                        —Anonymous

B. Write correctly each word that should be capitalized but is not.

1. in antarctica the sun drops a little lower in the sky every autumn day.
2. finally, in winter, the sun does not shine at all.
3. during summer the sun never sets, but shines day and night.
4. from november to april, the warmest temperature in summer is about 32 degrees Fahrenheit.
5. mr. andrew uses the english language at home, the spanish language at work, and the french language with his mother.
6. mr. and mrs. martin took jonathan and adam, jr., to see the empire state building.
7. black horse road runs along the black creek for several miles.
8. our italian friend, dr. savant, lives on cherry avenue in the city of baltimore.
9. point barrow is the northernmost point of alaska and the united states.
10. the mont blanc tunnel runs under mont blanc, the highest mountain in the alps, for almost eight miles.

C. Write a proper adjective for each proper noun. Use a dictionary if you need help.

1. England	3. Germany	5. France
2. Italy	4. Poland	6. Switzerland

D. Write each of the following in abbreviated form.

1. Wednesday	3. February	5. California
2. Sunday	4. Doctor Brown	6. Allan, Junior

Review Exercises

Write the correct verbs. [48–52]

1. The little ants (drug, dragged) crumbs of food several times their size to their nest.
2. One ant almost (drownded, drowned) when it fell into a puddle of water.
3. The red ants (attacked, attackted) the intruding black ants.
4. The huge soap bubbles (raised, rose) high into the air before they (busted, burst).
5. (May, Can) I (set, sit) this vase on your windowsill?

75. The Three Parts of a Story

In Chapter 1 you learned that every story tells about a problem to be solved. That problem is the *conflict* in the story. In this chapter you will learn more about writing an effective story.

A story can be divided into three main parts: the *beginning,* the *middle,* and the *ending.* Each of these parts must be well written to make a good story.

The Beginning

The beginning of a story should arouse the reader's interest. It should make him want to find out what the rest of the story is about. The beginning must tell who, when, where, what, and why in order to keep the reader's interest.

You tell *who* by introducing the characters of your story. The first character you mention should be the *main character*—the one on whom the story centers. If any other character is mentioned, the story should show how he is related to the main character.

When and *where* a story takes place is known as the *setting.* Do not give details that are not important to the story. For instance, do not give an exact time or date unless it is significant to the story. But give enough details so that the reader can understand when and where the story took place. Study the following examples of statements that help to show the settings of different stories.

When:
> By 10:00 that morning, the ground was covered with snow.
> The hazy clouds could not keep the August sun from pouring its heat upon us.

Where:
> The playground at Shady Glen School was too quiet for comfort.
> The Millers' back yard, with its grape arbor, orchard trees, and woodpile, was the perfect place for hide-and-seek.

The problem or conflict in a story tells *what* the story is about. This problem is not fully explained in the beginning of the story. But the beginning should give a hint of the conflict so that the reader will want to find out more.

Finally, the *why* of a story is the author's reason for writing it. The author does not usually tell directly what lesson he wants to teach.

Rather, he uses the story to *show* the lesson. The beginning of the story often gives a hint of what the lesson will be.

The beginning of a story gives only the information that is needed to understand the story. In the short stories that you will write, this will generally be only one or two paragraphs.

Read the following two story beginnings. How many ways can you see that the first one is better than the second?

> Linford donned his coat quickly and hurried outside for recess. "Oh, I forgot to sharpen my pencils!" exclaimed Linford. "I'd better go in right away, or I won't have any pencils to use." As Linford stepped into the classroom, he saw Daniel standing beside the teacher's desk, looking at a book. Surely it could not be . . . but yes, it was the sixth grade math teacher's manual.
>
> "P-please, Linford," Daniel stammered, "don't tell Brother James."
>
> Linford was surprised. "Why, I never thought Daniel would do something like this." His mind was whirling as he sharpened his pencils.
>
>   *   *   *   *   *
>
> Daniel glanced at the clock. It was 9:50 A.M. on Wednesday morning one winter day. "Oh, no," he thought, "only ten minutes left. I'll never finish this math on time."
>
> When Brother James dismissed them, all the boys except Daniel hurried out for recess.
>
> "Oh, I forgot to sharpen my pencils!" exclaimed Linford. "I'd better go in right away, or I won't have any pencils to use." His grandmother had just given him some new pencils.
>
> "Hurry back out!" called Mark. "We'll need your help." Daniel and Linford were good players, and Mark hated to lose two good players off his team.
>
> As Linford stepped inside, he saw Daniel looking at the sixth grade math teacher's manual.
>
> Linford was surprised. "Why, I never thought Daniel would do something like this."

The first story begins with Linford, the main character. But the second story introduces two other characters before it gets to Linford. The first story gives the setting in a natural way; the second one gives too many details that are not important to the story. The first story gives better hints to the conflict and purpose of the story.

The Middle

The middle of a story is its main part. Here we live with the main character as he deals with his conflict, and we read on anxiously to discover how he will overcome his problem. Every story must show conflict in order to hold the reader's attention.

Just as you face different kinds of problems in real life, stories show different kinds of conflict. The three main kinds of conflict are described below.

1. *The main character may be in conflict with another person.* The story of Joseph being sold by his brothers has this kind of conflict. In a story about a disobedient child, the child is in conflict with his parents.

2. *The main character may be in conflict with his circumstances.* A child faces this kind of conflict when his plans for a hike are spoiled because of rain. So does a child who suffers from sickness or an accident.

3. *The main character may be in conflict with his own conscience.* For example, a person may be tempted to lie or cheat. Whenever a person knows what is right but finds it hard to do right, he is facing this kind of conflict.

The conflict in a story does not need to be something great or unusual. Simple, everyday happenings have conflict in them too. Do not think you must write about a boy being chased by wolves or a girl being tempted to steal hundreds of dollars. Something as simple as a child trying to overcome a bad habit can result in a great struggle. You have likely discovered that yourself.

Near the end of the story, the conflict rises to its highest point of intensity. The main character comes face to face with his problem, and he either overcomes it in victory or goes down in defeat. This is called the *climax* of the story.

The Ending

The ending of a story tells what happened after the climax. Since the conflict is over, the reader is satisfied and there is not much action left to write about. So the ending should be short and to the point.

Do not end a story by stating the lesson that you intend to teach. The lesson should be clear from the story itself. If it is not clear, you will not impress anyone by tacking the lesson onto the end!

Read the following sets of paragraphs. Both show the climax and ending of a story. Which one is better?

> When Linford went back out to play, all the enjoyment seemed to have gone out of the game. "Should I tell Brother James?" he thought. "What if Daniel doesn't like me anymore?"
>
> Finally Linford decided to ask Father what to do.
>
> When Linford related to Father what had taken place, he said, "And I just don't know if I should tell Brother James."
>
> His father told him to tell the teacher.
>
> Linford told the teacher early the next morning. The teacher thanked Linford for telling.
>
> We should always ask our parents for advice. We should be honest and tell the teacher even though it means telling on a close friend. The teacher can take measures to correct it. Also we will have a lighter heart when we do what we know is right.
>
>   *   *   *   *   *
>
> Linford did not know what to do. Should he tell, or shouldn't he? Finally Linford decided to talk with his father about it. After Linford related the story, he said, "And I just don't know if I should tell Brother James. Would I be a tattletale then?"
>
> "No, you would not be a tattletale, Linford," Father said thoughtfully. "It's very important that you tell Brother James something like this so that he can take care of the problem."
>
> Linford told the teacher early the next morning when Brother James was alone in the classroom.
>
> "Thank you for telling me," Brother James said. "I appreciate your honesty in this, even though Daniel is your close friend."
>
> Linford left the room with a lighter heart, satisfied that he had done right.

The second set is better because it *shows* rather than tells the lesson of the story. Father and the teacher give the lesson in conversation with Linford. The second story also has a better conclusion. Linford leaves with a happy heart because he knows he has done what is right.

- A good story has three main parts: the beginning, the middle, and the ending.

- The beginning of a story should arouse the reader's interest by introducing the main character or characters, by describing the setting briefly, and by hinting at the conflict and purpose of the story.

- The middle of a story should describe the conflict and lead to a climax.

- The ending of a story should conclude the story. It should be short and to the point.

Class Practice

A. Tell which story beginning is better, and why.

1.   "Be careful!" Mother called as Gerald stumbled sleepily. "Help me get the little children to bed," she said.

Marie unlocked the door and snapped on the light. "Gerald, come back! You're making muddy tracks all over the floor!" she wailed.

"Oh, we must clear out this smoke!" Mother hurried to open the windows. Soon it was very cold in the house.

In the basement, little wisps of smoke curled from every joint of the stovepipe and seeped out around the edges of the stove door.

2.   "Marie, help me get the little children to bed," said Mother as Father braked to a stop in front of the house late one cold winter night.

Marie unlocked the door and snapped on the kitchen light. "Whew, it's smoky in here!" she exclaimed.

"Oh, we must clear out this smoke!" Mother hurried to open the windows. She opened the basement door and coughed as smoke swirled around her.

Downstairs Mother found Father leaning over the woodstove. Little wisps of smoke curled from every joint of the stovepipe and seeped out around the edges of the stove door.

B. Identify which of the three kinds of conflict is shown in each of these.

1.   When Linford went back out to play, all the enjoyment seemed to have gone out of the game. "Should I tell Brother James?" he thought. "What if Daniel doesn't like me anymore?"

2.   "What shall we do?" Marie coughed. Her eyes watered, and she was shivering. Tears threatened to spill over.

"It looks like everything is covered with smoke," Mother said helplessly.

"This is going to be more of a job than we can handle ourselves," Father decided. "We'll all go to bed, as best we can, and in the morning we'll get some help."

The next morning Father called Brother Elvin, the deacon of their church. "You'll need help," Brother Elvin agreed. "I'll take care of it."

The first carload of helpers arrived before they had finished breakfast.

C. Tell which ending is better, and why.

1.   Mrs. Ruftin, a neighbor, wanted to hear the whole story. "It must be nice to have friends who will pitch in and help you like this," she said.

The house hummed with activity. Mother met Father in the hallway. "I hardly know what to do," she said, throwing up her hands. "They're doing it all!"

2.   Mrs. Ruftin, a neighbor, wanted to hear the whole story. "It must be nice to have friends who will pitch in and help you like this," she said.

Mother agreed heartily. "It's a real blessing to have Christian friends who help bear our burdens."

Marie was no longer tempted to feel frustrated and discouraged. In her heart she thanked the Lord for helping them in this time of need.

Written Exercises

Choose an idea for a story to write in a later lesson. Write brief notes to answer the following questions. Be sure to save your notes for use in Lesson 82.

1. Who is the main character of your story?

2. Are there any other characters? If so, write who they are and how they are related to the main character.
3. When and where does your story take place?
4. What is the conflict in your story—the main problem to be solved?
5. What lesson will your story teach?

Review Exercises

Write the answers. [63, 67]
1. Name the five parts of a friendly letter.
2. Name the extra part in a business letter.
3. Give two reasons for writing friendly letters.

---

76. End Punctuation

Punctuation marks help us to read what others have written. How would you like to get a letter from a friend written this way?

> DEAR FRIEND HOW ARE YOU TODAY TRULY THE MERCIES OF THE LORD ARE NEW EVERY MORNING ARE THEY NOT WE PLAN TO COME THROUGH YOUR TOWN THE FIRST TUESDAY OF NEXT MONTH MAY WE LODGE AT YOUR HOUSE THAT EVENING PLEASE LET US KNOW SINCERELY HANS

Long ago, writing was harder to read because there were no special rules for punctuation. Writers used whatever marks they chose, and printers used whatever marks they had in their typecases. The ancient Greeks used semicolons for question marks.

In the 1400s and 1500s, people began to follow rules for punctuation so that writing could be understood more easily. Learn the rules of correct punctuation well so that your writing is simple to read.

1. *Use a period after a declarative or an imperative sentence.*

> Ships have been built for hundreds of years.
> Come and see the pictures of ships in these books.

2. *Use a question mark after an interrogative sentence.*

> Which Indians used the birch bark canoe?
> Who first used sails on their ships?

3. *Use an exclamation point after an exclamatory sentence or a strong interjection.*

   Oh! What a large ship that is!

   What! Do you mean sailors could not tell where they were?

4. *Use a period after each initial that is part of a name.*

   Mrs. L. A. Johnson   Dr. Ronald M. Towers

5. *Use periods after most abbreviations.* An abbreviation is a short form that stands for one or more longer words.

   a. Many names of measures can be abbreviated.

inch—in.	teaspoon—tsp.	second—sec.
foot—ft.	tablespoon—tbsp.	minute—min.
yard—yd.	cup—c.	hour—hr.
mile—mi.	pint—pt.	week—wk.
peck—pk.	quart—qt.	month—mo.
bushel—bu.	gallon—gal.	year—yr.
dozen—doz.		

   b. The names of the months of the year and the days of the week can be abbreviated.

January—Jan.	September—Sept.
April—Apr.	October—Oct.
August—Aug.	November—Nov.
Sunday—Sun.	Tuesday—Tues.
Monday—Mon.	Wednesday—Wed.

   c. Some abbreviations come from foreign words.

   A.M. from Latin *ante meridiem* (before midday)

   P.M. from Latin *post meridiem* (after midday)

   A.D. from Latin *anno Domini* (in the year of the Lord; that is, after Christ's birth)

   (B.C. stands for the English phrase "before Christ.")

   etc. from Latin *et cetera* (and the rest)

   lb. from Latin *libra* (pound)

   oz. from Italian *onza* (ounce)

6. *Use no periods with some abbreviations for well-known phrases or for the names of certain organizations.*

> KJV—King James Version
> WW II—World War II
> UN—United Nations
> POW—prisoner of war
> TVA—Tennessee Valley Authority
> UPS—United Parcel Service
> IRS—Internal Revenue Service
> FBI—Federal Bureau of Investigation

7. *For state names in addresses, use the two-letter abbreviations developed by the postal service to be used with Zip Codes.* These are printed with all capital letters and no end punctuation. See the list at the end of Lesson 63. (Remember that the mailing address on an envelope should be printed in all capital letters.)

> BETHLEHEM PA 18016   NORFOLK NE 68701

8. *Most abbreviations should not be used in general writing, such as letters, stories, and reports.* But they may be used in note-taking, or in school lessons, such as English and math.

A few standard abbreviations may be used in all writing.

a. Abbreviations used with proper nouns. (Note that the title *Miss* is not an abbreviation. Also note that if an abbreviation comes at the end of a sentence, only one period is needed.)

> Mr.—Mister   Sr.—Senior
> Mrs.—Mistress   Jr.—Junior
> Dr.—Doctor

The visitor was Clarence Miller, Jr.

b. Abbreviations used in writing a time or date.

> A.M.   P.M.   B.C.   A.D.

Use your dictionary for reference. Check it when you are not sure about the form of an abbreviation.

- Use a period after a declarative or an imperative sentence, a question mark after an interrogative sentence, and an exclamation point after an exclamatory sentence or a strong interjection.

- Use a period after each initial that is part of a name.

- Use a period after most abbreviations.

- Use no period with some abbreviations for well-known phrases or for the names of certain organizations.

- For state names in addresses, use the two-letter abbreviations developed by the postal service to be used with Zip Codes.

- Most abbreviations should not be used in general writing, such as letters, stories, and reports.

Class Practice

A. Tell how to divide each group of words into sentences with proper capitalization and end punctuation.
   1. Do you hear that robin how cheerfully he sings we should sing too
   2. What an enormous tree that is what kind is it find it in the field guide

B. Give the meaning of each abbreviation.

1. in.	4. mi.	7. KJV
2. pk.	5. mo.	8. NY
3. yd.	6. Wed.	9. A.M.

C. Tell whether each abbreviation may be used in general writing.

1. A.M.	4. lb.	7. Jr.
2. Mrs.	5. KJV	8. Aug.
3. oz.	6. B.C.	

Written Exercises

A. Divide each group of words into sentences with proper capitalization and end punctuation.
   1. See how fast he runs is something chasing him well what a dog
   2. Was that thunder hurry and get the clothes in here comes the rain
   3. I can hear the breakers can you hear them roar what a tremendous noise they make the ocean is four miles away

B. Copy these sentences, and add the missing periods, question marks, and exclamation points.
   1. Weren't the Jews taken captive to Babylon about 500 BC
   2. The Roman Empire fell about AD 500
   3. Be here by 1:00 PM to meet Mr and Mrs Homer
   4. How seriously wrong I was

C. Write the postal service abbreviations for the following states.

1. Virginia	3. Pennsylvania	5. Maryland
2. Illinois	4. Ohio	6. Texas

D. Write the correct abbreviations for these words.

1. teaspoon	5. second	9. before midday
2. cup	6. bushel	10. in the year of the Lord
3. inch	7. month	11. pound
4. peck	8. September	12. World War I

E. Write one of each of the four types of sentences, using the correct end punctuation. Include one strong interjection in one of your sentences.

Review Exercises

Correct the run-on errors as indicated. [14]

1. Use end punctuation and capital letters.

   butterflies' scales come in many colors yellow, brown, black, and red colors are made by pigments in the scales shimmering colors like gold, silver, and shiny green or blue are made by light reflecting off the surface of the scales

2. Use commas and suitable conjunctions.
   a. My brother caught a little catfish he gave it to me.
   b. I had waited a long time I had caught no fish.
   c. I will put this little fish on my hook then I can pretend I caught a fish.

3. Use semicolons.
   a. Suddenly my pole gave a tremendous jerk my brother had to help me hold it.
   b. On my line was the biggest catfish we had ever seen it had swallowed the little one!

77. Direct Quotations

Sometimes in writing we want to repeat the exact words of a speaker or writer. The exact words of a speaker or writer are a *direct quotation.* The other words in the sentence are called *explanatory words.* In the following sentence, the explanatory words are underlined.

"Where do you live?" <u>Eunice inquired</u>.

Direct quotations can be written in different ways. The quoted words may come first in a sentence, or they may come last. Direct quotations are put at different places in sentences for variety.

<u>"Oh, look at this!"</u> called Robert. (quotation first)
Robert called, <u>"Oh, look at this!"</u> (quotation last)

Use the following rules to write a sentence in which the direct quotation comes first.

1. *Place quotation marks around the quoted words.*
2. *Begin the quotation with a capital letter.*

"<u>W</u>e haven't started yet," Andy admitted.

3. *Place the correct punctuation at the end of the quoted words.* Use a comma after a statement or command, a question mark after a question, and an exclamation point after an exclamation. The mark at the end of the quoted words comes *before* the ending quotation marks.

"My father works here<u>,</u>" said Nathan. (statement)
"Bake a cake<u>,</u>" Mother directed. (command)
"Will you help us<u>?</u>" they asked. (question)
"That was a mountain lion<u>!</u>" shouted Darvin. (exclamation)

4. *Put a period after the explanatory words at the end of the sentence.* This is done because the whole sentence is usually a statement, even though the direct quotation may be a question or an exclamation.

"Could we wait on your porch?" asked the children<u>.</u>
"I never saw a mountain lion around here before!" exclaimed
Allen<u>.</u>

Use the following rules to write a sentence in which the direct quotation comes last.

1. *Place quotation marks around the quoted words.*
2. *Begin the first word with a capital letter,* since it is the beginning of the sentence. *Also begin the direct quotation with a capital letter.* This is done because the speaker's words are a sentence within a longer sentence.

> <u>I</u>n his report Andrew said, "<u>A</u> jackrabbit can leap over ten times its body length in one jump."

3. *Place a comma at the end of the explanatory words.* Be sure to place this comma *before* the beginning quotation marks.

> He added<u>,</u> <u>"</u>A person who is good at jumping can jump only about five times his own length."

4. *At the end of the quotation, place a period, a question mark, or an exclamation point, depending on whether the quotation tells, asks, or exclaims.* The mark at the end of the quoted words comes *before* the ending quotation marks.

> Andrew continued, "A flea, by comparison, can jump 350 times its body length<u>!"</u>
> He also said, "An elephant can't jump at all<u>."</u>
> Then he added, "But why would an elephant need to jump<u>?"</u>

- A direct quotation is enclosed in quotation marks, and a comma usually separates it from the explanatory words.

- A direct quotation begins with a capital letter because the speaker's words are a sentence within a longer sentence.

- Other punctuation marks usually come before quotation marks.

Class Practice

Each sentence below has two mistakes. Tell how to correct the mistakes.

1. Karen said, "oh, look, this book says some ants can lift about fifty times their own weight.
2. Samuel exclaimed, "that's about like a person lifting four tons"!
3. "it also says an ant can carry the weight a long way, Karen continued.

4. "How much weight can one person lift," Roy asked?
5. "A person can lift as much as his own weight," but even that is difficult for many men", Kevin answered.

Written Exercises

Copy each sentence, and add the correct punctuation and capital letters.

1. rise up and walk said Peter
2. Jesus said I am the Good Shepherd
3. if I go away, I will come again He told them
4. Lord, how can we know the way asked Thomas
5. he asked them have ye any meat
6. the teacher asked how many know the answer
7. help the little ones Mother told us
8. my home is far away said the stranger
9. Ray asked is it true that the fastest animal is the cheetah
10. Jay answered yes, a cheetah can run seventy miles per hour
11. a cheetah can go from standing still to forty-five miles per hour in only two seconds said Joshua
12. he added but a cheetah cannot keep up his speed for a long distance
13. Ronald said an antelope or a gazelle doesn't tire nearly as quickly
14. the pronghorn antelope can maintain a speed of sixty miles per hour he continued
15. Brother Martin said God gave these animals the special abilities of speed and endurance to outrun the cheetah
16. he continued God also gave the cheetah the ability of extra speed so that he can catch his food
17. so if an antelope or a gazelle sees the cheetah in time, he can escape Ray concluded
18. Brother Martin said that is right

Review Exercises

A. Copy the underlined pronouns. Identify each one by writing *P* for personal, *D* for demonstrative, *ID* for indefinite, *IR* for interrogative, or *R* for relative. [61–69]
1. Was it <u>they</u> <u>who</u> called <u>us</u>?
2. <u>My</u> sister gave <u>that</u> to <u>me</u>.
3. <u>Everyone</u> seems to like <u>it</u>.
4. <u>Who</u> brought <u>him</u> the papers?

B. Write correctly each word that is not capitalized but should be. [20, 73, 74]

1. christian miller arrived in philadelphia in 1737, having sailed from rotterdam in the netherlands to america for religious freedom.

2. (a) the lord is my Shepherd, i shall not want;
   (b) he maketh me down to lie
   (c) in pastures green, he leadeth me
   (d) the quiet waters by.
   (e) his yoke is easy, his burden is light,
   (f) i've found it so, i've found it so;
   (g) he leadeth me by day and by night,
   (h) where living waters flow.

—Author unknown

---

78. Direct and Indirect Quotations

When we tell what a speaker has said or a writer has written, we are using a *quotation*. It may be a *direct quotation* or an *indirect quotation*.

A direct quotation repeats the exact words of a speaker or writer.

Jesus said, "Blessed are the pure in heart: for they shall see God."
Solomon wrote, "A wise man will hear, and will increase learning."

An indirect quotation tells what a person said, without repeating his exact words.

Jesus said that the pure in heart are blessed, for they shall see God.

Solomon wrote that a wise man will hear and will increase learning.

Here are the four main differences between direct and indirect quotations.

1. Quotation marks are used with a direct quotation, but not with an indirect quotation.

"The fence needs to be painted," said Father. (direct quotation)
Father said that the fence needs to be painted. (indirect quotation)

2. The word *that* often comes before an indirect quotation.

> Doris said to us, "My mother is coming to school today."
> Doris told us <u>that</u> her mother is coming to school today.

3. Some pronouns may be different in an indirect quotation.

> The boys suggested, "<u>We</u> can do the work for <u>you</u>."
> The boys suggested that <u>they</u> could do the work for <u>us</u>.

4. Some verb forms may be different in an indirect quotation.

> "<u>Are</u> the birds cold in wet weather?" asked Timothy.
> Timothy asked if the birds <u>were</u> cold in wet weather.
> "We <u>will</u> soon be there!" exclaimed Doris.
> Doris exclaimed that they <u>would</u> soon be there.

- A direct quotation repeats the exact words of a speaker or writer. An indirect quotation tells what a speaker said, without repeating his exact words.

- When a direct quotation is changed to an indirect quotation, the quotation marks are removed, the word *that* may be added, and some pronouns and verb forms may change.

Class Practice

A. Tell whether each sentence has a *direct quotation,* an *indirect quotation,* or *no quotation* at all. (All quotation marks have been omitted.)
   1. I have filled all the boxes, Amos announced.
   2. Amos announced that he had filled all the boxes.
   3. Amos carried the boxes to the van.
   4. At breakfast Donna said that today is the shortest day of the year.
   5. Barbara said that the thermometer showed 20°.
   6. The thermometer shows 20°, said Barbara.

B. Read each direct quotation as an indirect quotation.
   1. Jonathan said, "It is twelve o'clock already!"
   2. "I should make pies today," said Rosene.
   3. Mother said to Aunt Mary, "I haven't seen you for a long time!"

C. Read each indirect quotation as a direct quotation.
1. Lloyd said that he was sure it would be very useful.
2. Mervin asked them if they could stay for supper.
3. Mark exclaimed that he had never before seen such a playful goat.

Written Exercises

A. Write *direct* or *indirect* to tell what kind of quotation is found in each sentence. (All quotation marks have been omitted.)
1. Come quickly, Donald, called Peter.
2. I'll be right there, Donald answered.
3. Donald said that he would be right there.
4. Daniel said that the cows were out.
5. Mark said, Let's chase them all back in.
6. Daniel said that they should tie the gate shut the next time.
7. Janelle said that she would like to go skating.
8. No, you shouldn't, because the ice is too thin, Father said.

B. Write each sentence, changing the indirect quotation to a direct quotation.
1. Charlotte said that she found this sweater lying in the lane.
2. Harold told us that we may sit here awhile.

C. Write each sentence, changing the direct quotation to an indirect quotation.
1. My sister said, "I saw the new lambs in the pasture."
2. "You must water the strawberries," Henry told us.

Review Exercises

A. Copy the verb or verb phrase in each sentence. If there is a word that receives the action, also copy that word. [55]
1. The recipe for this apple pie was invented in the 1800s.
2. My aunt wrote the recipe for us.
3. Jonathan had come in the morning.
4. The bell has already rung.
5. The trumpets were blown before each assembly.
6. The priests always blew the trumpets.

B. After each answer in Part A, write *transitive* or *not transitive* to label the verb. [55]

79. Dialogue in a Story

Dialogue in a story is written conversation. Dialogue helps to make a story more interesting. It helps the reader to "see" the action, and it makes the characters seem more real. Compare the two story beginnings below. Which one makes the characters seem more real?

Kathy couldn't wait to tell her friend Brenda the news she had just gotten from her cousin. She told Brenda that Smithville School had lice. Brenda was so surprised that her mouth dropped open.

*   *   *   *   *

"Oh, Brenda," Kathy burst out the moment the two of them got together at school. "I got a letter from my cousin yesterday. Guess what they have at Smithville School?"

"Is it a gerbil?" Brenda guessed.

"Oh, no, nothing like that," Kathy groaned. "Lice," she hissed. Brenda's mouth dropped open, and she was speechless.

The second beginning is better because it *shows* the action by using dialogue instead of just telling what happened. As we hear the characters talking to each other, the story and the characters seem to come alive.

In dialogue, be careful to put quotation marks only where they belong. If a speaker says several sentences together, do not put quotation marks around every sentence. Put them only at the beginning and end of the whole quotation. The words that simply tell the story should not be inside quotation marks. In the example below, the direct quotation is in italics.

"*I'm glad I don't go to that school,*" Kathy declared. "*Just thinking about lice is enough to get me scratching. It would be absolutely horrifying to have lice, with the treatments and all!*"

The door opened, and more students arrived.

Begin a new paragraph in your story each time you begin a new topic. (See the last sentence in the example above.) Also begin a new paragraph each time a different person begins to speak. Notice how this second rule is observed in the following paragraphs.

"Good morning, Elsie," Brenda greeted her classmate.

"Good morning," Elsie returned, and then she broke into a wide yawn.

"Did you get to bed late?" Kathy teased.

"Yes, we did," Elsie replied with a smile. "My father just started a week of revival meetings at Smithville."

Do not use only the word *said* in the explanatory words. There are other words that give more meaning to the story. The previous conversation would be less interesting if it used only *said*.

"Good morning, Elsie," Brenda <u>said</u> to her classmate.

"Good morning," <u>said</u> Elsie, and then she broke into a wide yawn.

"Did you get to bed late?" Kathy <u>said</u>.

"Yes, we did," Elsie <u>said</u> with a smile. "My father just started a week of revival meetings at Smithville."

You cannot use a different explanatory word in every sentence. *Said* is often the best word to use. But you should use other words when they add meaning. Try to use some of the following when they fit well in your stories.

asked	whispered	declared	continued
called	exclaimed	asserted	suggested
added	shouted	demanded	countered
stated	complained	insisted	admonished

Keep the dialogue natural. That is, write conversation in the way people actually talk. Two things especially will help to make your conversations sound natural. One is *contractions,* and the other is *incomplete sentences.* It is true that neither of these should be used in formal writing, such as a report. But in the dialogue of a story, these are fully acceptable because this is the way people actually speak. Notice how the contractions and incomplete sentences make the following dialogue sound true to life.

"Oh, Mother, Kathy <u>doesn't</u> seem to like me anymore," Elsie shared that evening as they were doing the dishes.

"Why, what makes you think that?" asked Mother.

"<u>The look on her face.</u> Several times today I noticed her looking at me as grimly as if <u>she'd</u> lost her last friend," Elsie began. "When I smiled at her, she <u>didn't</u> smile back."

"<u>Didn't she?</u> Well, maybe she was having an especially hard time with her lessons," Mother suggested helpfully.

"<u>Maybe,</u>" Elsie said doubtfully. "But Kathy has never treated me like this before."

"Make sure you do your part to be friendly, but <u>don't</u> be overbearing in it," Mother advised.

When you use dialogue, the sentences should vary in length. Natural conversation has some long sentences and some short ones. Do not write quotations that are too long, because they do not sound natural.

Another way to have variety in dialogue is to use different kinds of quotations. Begin some sentences with explanatory words and some with direct quotations.

Finally, have the characters in your story speak according to their age level. Their language should sound natural for themselves, but they should not use slang, poor grammar, or other unsuitable expressions.

- Use dialogue in a story to make the story more interesting.

- Begin a new paragraph every time a different person begins to speak.

- Keep conversation natural.

Class Practice

A. Tell where the quotation marks and paragraph divisions should be.

Do I have to go to school this morning? Kathy pleaded with her mother. I have a headache. Just a headache doesn't seem like a good-enough reason to stay at home, Kathy's mother answered. Take a Tylenol tablet, and see if you feel better soon. Tylenol probably won't help it, Kathy grumbled while she braided her hair. Is something else the matter? Mother eyed her daughter closely. It's those lice! Kathy burst into tears. I'm just sure Elsie got them at Smithville on Sunday. Next thing I'll have them too!

B. Tell how to improve the following dialogue so that it sounds more natural and has better variety.

"Kathy, Kathy, I had no idea you were so upset about this. Getting head lice would not be the worst thing that could happen," Mother said.

"What could be worse!" said Kathy.

"Losing Elsie as a friend would be worse. In Proverbs it says that a brother offended is harder to be won than a strong city," Mother said to Kathy. "I am sure Elsie's family will do what they can to avoid getting lice. But it will take more than head lice to keep Elsie's father from doing his duty as a minister at Smithville. I would not be surprised if Elsie has detected your attitude," Mother said.

Several moments passed in silence. "She probably has detected it. I will have to apologize to Elsie for the way I have been acting," Kathy said.

"That sounds better. We are not wishing for lice, but if we get them, we can be treated for them just as others have been," Mother said with a smile.

Written Exercises

A. Rewrite this dialogue, using correct punctuation and paragraph division.

Juanita said Since school started, I hardly have time to read my book anymore. I know agreed Noreen. I wish there'd be some way of getting more time to read. Don't you think we could read a little bit right now before we go to sleep? asked Juanita. So a few evenings passed, and each night the girls read a little longer. I'm afraid Mother will see that the light is on in here Juanita worried one evening. Maybe we shouldn't be reading. But we don't need to go to bed so early reasoned Noreen. We deserve a little time to read. I guess you're right Juanita agreed slowly. All at once a floorboard creaked in the hall. The books closed instantly, and the light switch snapped off. We're caught Noreen whispered. It's ten o'clock! breathed Juanita. The door opened, and Mother appeared. What's going on in here? she wondered. The next morning Father called Noreen and Juanita to his study. You were being disobedient as well as acting a lie he said. After the punishment each girl said I'm sorry. I won't do it again. I'm sure you won't Father told them. We're expecting you to do better after this.

B. Rewrite this dialogue, making it more natural and using more variety.

"How was school today?" asked Mother.

"Oh, school wasn't too bad today," said Beth. "You see, it's this way. It seems the girls do not care to be with me anymore. I cannot understand it."

Mother asked, "Are you remembering to follow the verse which says that a man who has friends must show himself friendly? I think you should try being more friendly to the girls."

"I guess you are right, Mother. I need to try harder to be friendly," said Beth.

"Oh, Mother, it worked!" said Beth the next day. "I had a much better time with my friends today. I am so glad for the advice you gave me."

Review Exercises

A. Write the number of the paragraph below that has better *unity*. [16]

1. The aardvark is a strange creature. *Aardvark* comes from the Dutch expression for "earth pig." Many Dutch settlers moved to South Africa long ago, taking their language with them. The aardvark is more like an anteater than a pig. It eats ants like an anteater. The giant anteater lives in damp tropical forests and grassy plains of Central and South America. With its claws, the aardvark rips open the nests of ants and termites. Anteaters also tear open ant nests and eat the insects.

2. The aardvark is a strange creature. It is about the size of a hog, and it has thick, gray-brown hair. It has long ears like a rabbit's and sharp claws like a raccoon's. The word *aardvark* means "earth pig." Dutch settlers in Africa gave it that name because it has a snout like a pig's and it digs burrows in the earth. But the aardvark is more like an anteater than a pig. With its claws, it rips open the nests of ants and termites. Then it uses its long, sticky tongue to catch and eat the insects.

B. Write the number of the paragraph that has better *coherence*. [16, 17]

1. The Panama Canal is the only canal in the world that connects two oceans. In 1882 a French company began digging the canal, but they ran into such great problems that they gave up. One of the problems was diseases spread by mosquitoes. Because of malaria and yellow fever, twenty thousand workers died. Then a man named William C. Gorgas took measures to control the mosquitoes that carried these diseases. Working with several other people, he greatly reduced the number of deaths caused by malaria and yellow fever. Finally in 1907, President Roosevelt appointed a company to continue digging the canal. The Panama Canal was finished in 1914.

2.   The Panama Canal is the only canal in the world that connects two oceans. In 1907 President Roosevelt appointed a company to dig the canal. A French company had begun digging the canal in 1882, but they ran into problems. Many workers became sick with malaria and yellow fever. A man named William C. Gorgas worked to wipe out the mosquitoes that carried the diseases. He greatly reduced the number of deaths caused by these diseases. But twenty thousand French workers had died. This caused the French to give up. The Panama Canal was finished in 1914.

---

80. Divided Quotations

Some direct quotations are divided. The explanatory words separate the quotation into two parts.

> "Did you know," <u>asked Martin,</u> "that birds have been used to send messages?"
>
> "Long ago," <u>he continued,</u> "the Chinese used homing pigeons to carry mail."

Some divided quotations are made of only one sentence. Others are made of two sentences.

One sentence:

> "This was also done more recently," said Martin, "when the French in Paris used pigeons in the 1870s."

Two sentences:

> "This was also done more recently," said Martin. "The French in Paris used pigeons in the 1870s."

Use the following steps to punctuate and capitalize divided quotations.

1. *Find the quoted words, and put quotation marks around them.* In the following sentence, the quoted words are underlined.

> "<u>An army surrounded Paris,</u>" said Martin, "<u>and the people could not travel in or out.</u>"

2. *Use a capital letter at the beginning of the direct quotation.* In a divided quotation, the beginning of the direct quotation is at the same place as the beginning of the sentence that contains it.

> "The Frenchmen outside Paris used homing pigeons," continued Martin, "to send letters into the city."

3. *Decide whether the quoted words make one or two sentences.* If the words on either side of the explanatory words cannot stand alone, the quotation is made of only one sentence. If each set of quoted words can stand alone, the quotation is made of two sentences.

One sentence:

> "Messages were put into small canisters," said Martin, "and were attached to the pigeons." (The underlined words cannot stand alone as a sentence.)

Two sentences:

> "Messages were put into small canisters," said Martin. "They were attached to the pigeons." (Each set of quoted words can stand alone as a sentence.)

4. *If the divided quotation is made of only one sentence, continue with the following steps.*
   a. Use commas to separate the explanatory words from the quotation. Remember that commas come *before* quotation marks.

   > "Thirty thousand letters could be placed in each canister," explained Martin, "because the Frenchmen first reduced the letters by photography."

   b. Add the needed end punctuation. Remember that end marks come *before* quotation marks.

   > "The Frenchmen were determined," said Martin, "to get the messages through."

   c. Begin the second part of the divided quotation with a small letter, unless of course the first word is capitalized for some other reason.

   > "The same letters were sent with thirty-five different pigeons," said Martin, "so that each message would be sure to get through."

"If the pigeons get through," thought a French boy, "I might get a letter today."

5. *If the divided quotation is made of two sentences, continue with the following steps.*
   a. Include the explanatory words with the first sentence.

   "The print of the letters was too tiny to read," <u>said Galen</u>. "The postmen of Paris had to project the letters on screens and copy them by hand."

   b. Place a period after the explanatory words. (The first sentence is punctuated like a sentence with the direct quotation coming first.)

   "In this way, mail was delivered to homes in the city," said Arlen<u>.</u> "It was called the pigeon post!"

   c. Begin the second sentence with a capital letter, and use the correct punctuation at the end.

   "In this way, mail was delivered to homes in the city," said Arlen. "<u>I</u>t was called the pigeon post<u>!</u>"

- In a sentence with a divided quotation, each part of the quotation is enclosed in quotation marks.

- The second part of a divided quotation usually does not begin with a capital letter unless it begins a new sentence or is capitalized for another reason.

Class Practice
Tell how to correct the mistakes in the following sentences.
1. "As soon as you arrive," Mother instructed, "Call and tell us."
2. "Why do we see so many bees?" asked Sharon, "when we eat outside."
3. "The insects you see, replied Robert, are probably yellow jackets."
4. "Yellow jackets like sweet foods" continued Robert "like you probably have on your picnics."
5. "That is not a bee" exclaimed Mark. "it's a hummingbird."
6. "Several years ago we put up a feeder," said Mother, "the hummingbirds have come back each summer."

Written Exercises

Copy these sentences, and add the correct capitalization and punctuation.

1. did you know asked John that Jupiter is about thirteen hundred times as large as the earth
2. if you could drive to the sun Galen wondered how long would it take to get there in a car
3. at fifty-five miles per hour said Robert it would take about 190 years to reach the sun
4. after all Robert added the sun is 93 million miles away
5. it's good that the sun is so far away said Galen if it were too close, we would burn up
6. I'm glad the sun is not too far away either added Robert everything would freeze then
7. because God knows exactly what we need Brother Joel added the distance is just right
8. on Saturn said Thomas winds blow about four times faster than the fastest winds ever clocked on earth
9. on that huge planet said Brother Joel winds blow up to eleven hundred miles per hour
10. did you say asked Grace that the Milky Way is a galaxy
11. do you mean Grace wondered that the white band of light is really a galaxy of millions of stars
12. do you know how the Milky Way got its name asked Brother Joel people long ago thought the white light from the thousands of stars looked like a stream of spilled milk
13. our word *galaxy* comes from the Greek word for milk said Robert isn't that interesting
14. God has created all these wonders said Brother Joel what a mighty God He is

Review Exercises

In these sentences, the main verbs are underlined twice and the receivers of their action are underlined once. Write whether each receiver is a *subject* or a *direct object,* and whether the verb is in the *active* or the *passive* voice. [55]

1. Why do dogs <u>bury</u> <u>bones</u>?
2. God <u>taught</u> <u>them</u> to save leftover food.
3. Often, however, buried <u>bones</u> are <u>forgotten</u> by well-fed dogs.

4. How much leftover <u>food</u> in your refrigerator is eventually <u>forgotten</u>?

5. When <u>cats</u> are <u>fed</u> too well, they may not <u>catch</u> many <u>mice</u>.

Challenge Exercises

Copy the following poem, and add the missing capitalization and punctuation. This poem contains many direct quotations that tell how people in some other countries greet each other.

how do you do?

how can you friend? the swedish say.
  the dutch, how do you fare
how do you have yourself today
  has quite a polish air.

in italy, how do you stand?
  will greet you every hour;
in turkey, when one takes your hand
  be under god's great power

how do you carry you is heard
  when frenchmen so inquire,
while egypt's friendly greeting word
  is how do you perspire?

thin may thy shadow never grow,
  the persian wish is true;
his arab cousin, bowing low,
  says praise god! how are you

but cutest of them all is when
  two chinese meet, for thrice
they shake their own two hands and then
  ask have you eaten rice

—H. Bedford Jones

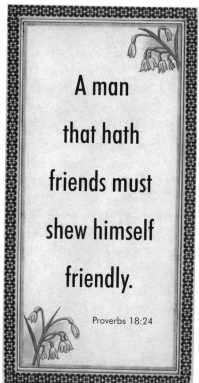

A man
that hath
friends must
shew himself
friendly.

Proverbs 18:24

81. Commas in a Series

Commas are among the most commonly used punctuation marks. Do commas make a difference? Read the following sentences.

> What can you make with ice cream and milk?
> What can you make with ice, cream, and milk?

Commas do make a difference! They completely change the meaning of the sentences above. Learn the following rules for using commas.

1. *Words in a series are separated by commas.* (A series is a list of several items in a row.) Words in a series may be nouns, verbs, or some other part of speech.

> The New England States are Maine, Vermont, New Hampshire, Massachusetts, Connecticut, and Rhode Island.
> The girls washed, swept, dusted, and painted all day.

2. *Phrases in a series are separated by commas.*

> There were books on the table, on the floor, and on the shelf.
> During the Great Depression, many people ate beans and potatoes for breakfast, for dinner, and for supper.

3. *Two or more descriptive adjectives modifying the same noun are often separated by commas.* Notice the use of commas in the following examples. Observe that no comma is placed after the last adjective, just before the noun that is modified.

> A dark, threatening sky developed as the day went on.
> The apples were red, shiny, and expensive.
> The roaring, tumbling, splashing water plunged over the falls.

But how can you tell when to use commas between the adjectives? First, remember that commas are used only after descriptive adjectives (those that tell *what kind of*). Articles (*a, an, the*) and adjectives that tell *which, whose,* and *how many* are limiting adjectives. These limiting adjectives are not followed by commas.

Correct:
> Gerald has a large, black, friendly dog.
> *Large, black,* and *friendly* are all descriptive adjectives.

Incorrect:
> John's, five, little puppies are growing rapidly.
> *John's* and *five* are limiting adjectives.

Second, if the adjectives are descriptive adjectives, try placing the word *and* between them. If it sounds right to use *and,* separate the adjectives with a comma. If it sounds odd, do not use a comma. Use this test to decide whether the underlined adjectives in these sentences should be separated by commas.

I nearly dropped the <u>big clumsy</u> package.
   Think: *Big and clumsy package* sounds right. Use a comma.
   Write: I nearly dropped the big, clumsy package.

The <u>kind old</u> gentleman held the door open for my mother.
   Think: *Kind and old gentleman* sounds odd. Do not use a comma.
   Write: The kind old gentleman held the door open for my mother.

Three <u>pleasant cheerful young</u> men were distributing Gospel tracts.
   Think: *Pleasant and cheerful men* sounds right; use a comma. *Cheerful and young men* sounds odd; do not use a comma.
   Write: Three pleasant, cheerful young men were distributing Gospel tracts.

Finally, remember that a comma indicates a pause. Do you pause between the adjectives as you read the sentence? If so, you should probably place a comma between them. Notice how this is true as you read the examples above.

It is not always easy to tell whether a comma is needed. But as you think carefully and gain practice, you will find that it becomes easier to decide.

- Words or phrases in a series are separated by commas.

- Two or more descriptive adjectives modifying the same noun are often separated by commas. A comma should be placed between two adjectives if they are descriptive adjectives, if it sounds right to use *and* between them, and if there is a pause between them in reading.

Class Practice

A. Read these sentences, saying *comma* at each place where a comma is needed. Try saying *and* for all the commas after adjectives.

1. Boots shoes slippers and sandals are all made of leather.
2. There were geese in the grass on the rocks and on the water of the lake.
3. Did you ever see such sparkling white snow?
4. Sarah uses this thick warm quilt in the wintertime.
5. We pumped water from an old hand pump.

B. Tell which commas are not needed in the following sentences.

1. Many, other, little boats were on the lake.
2. Bananas, oranges, and mangoes, are tropical fruits.
3. We bought a large, intelligent, German, shepherd dog.
4. Jesus entered the small, fishing boat, sat down, and began to teach.

Written Exercises

A. Copy each word that needs a comma after it, and add the missing comma. (Commas are not needed in all the sentences.)

1. The rabbit nibbled at the clover looked up and hopped away.
2. The boys were selling cabbage squash carrots and beans.
3. Our older boys dug raked trimmed and planted.
4. On the shelf you will find books tablets pencils and erasers.
5. The little boy observed listened and learned much.
6. They have a friendly Old English sheepdog.
7. The cinnamon graham crackers are tasty.
8. They passed out tracts in front of the store along the sidewalk and on the street corners.
9. Abraham Isaac and Jacob are called the patriarchs.
10. Peter James and John went up the mountain with Christ.
11. A poor unselfish widow cast her last two mites into the treasury.
12. Jesus visited Galilee Samaria Judea and Decapolis.
13. The small fragile boat was tossed on the angry stormy sea.
14. Jesus quickly changed the stormy raging sea to a calm peaceful place.

B. Write sentences of your own with the following kinds of series.

1. a series of nouns
2. a series of verbs
3. a series of phrases
4. a series of adjectives modifying the same noun

Review Exercises

Diagram the skeletons of the following sentences. Also diagram the direct objects, indirect objects, and predicate nominatives. [38–42]

1. Was it they in that car?
2. My brother told me in the morning.
3. Gerald gave John the book, and John passed it on to Nathan.
4. Here is an interesting story.

---

82. Writing a Story: First Draft

In order to write a good story, you must plan your story well. Use an orderly method, and proceed step by step from start to finish. The following points will help you.

Step 1: *Get the conflict clear in your mind.* What is the problem that must be solved? You will find it helpful to write a sentence or two briefly stating what the conflict will be.

Example:

> A boy hears about different accidents and wonders how people can make such foolish mistakes. Then he makes a foolish mistake himself and learns a lesson from it.

Step 2: *Decide who will be the main character.* What kind of person is he or she? What kind of people are the other characters in the story?

Example:

Main character: Daniel, who seems quite sure of himself
Other characters: Rhonda, Daniel's sister
Allen, a neighbor
Daniel's Christian father

Step 3: *Write a good beginning for the story.* You will need to introduce the main character and show the setting right at the beginning. (This is the *who, when,* and *where.*) You will also need to introduce the conflict and give a hint of your purpose. (This is the *what* and *why*.) Notice how these things are done in the story beginning below.

> "Good-bye!" Daniel called to his friends, Evan and Mark, as he and his sister got off the school van.
>
> "Good-bye!" they returned as the van started on its way again.
>
> "Did you hear about Greg's accident?" Daniel asked Rhonda as they walked in the lane together.
>
> "Yes, I did," Rhonda answered. "It's too bad. It sounds as though he'll have to miss several weeks of school with his broken arm and leg. I feel sorry for him."
>
> "I don't really," Daniel said. "That was a dumb thing to do. I would have known better than to jump off that limb. Why, it must be ten feet off the ground, and there are rocks under the tree. He just got what he asked for."

Step 4: *Write the middle part of the story.* Show how the happenings build up and lead to the "highest point," or climax.

> That evening Father and Daniel were working in the shop when Allen, a neighbor, stopped in for a few minutes. "Did you hear about Leroy Fannin's accident?" he asked. "He was out last night on his bicycle. It got dark before he arrived home, and the lights on his bicycle weren't working. A car hit him from behind, and now Leroy is in the hospital with serious head injuries," Allen informed them.
>
> "Why are some people so careless?" Daniel asked Father when Allen had left. "Anyone should know better than to be out on the road after dark without lights."
>
> "We don't always know why, Daniel," Father answered. "It certainly is unwise to be out on the road on a bicycle after dark without lights. But maybe Leroy didn't realize that his lights weren't working until it got dark. He probably did need to get home."
>
> Daniel shrugged. "Maybe," he said, but he did not sound convinced.
>
> Several days later Daniel's family was butchering, and Daniel was using the meat grinder. "Something seems to be wrong here," he thought. "It must be plugged up." Without thinking, Daniel put his hand down into the grinder to try to unplug it.

"Oh-h-h! Ou-ouch!" Daniel cried. He pulled his hand quickly out of the grinder, but it was too late. Blood flowed from deep gashes in two of his fingers and from several cuts in his other fingers.

Father acted quickly, getting cold, wet cloths to wrap around Daniel's hand. Soon they were on their way to the hospital. A sober Daniel entered the emergency room, where a doctor stitched his mangled fingers.

Step 5: *Write a good ending for the story.* Bring the story to a close quickly after the climax is reached. Be sure to *show* rather than *tell* the lesson of the story.

"The Lord may be using this to teach you a lesson," Father said kindly. "I have heard you several times lately exclaiming about other people's foolish mistakes and declaring that you would never do such a thing. Let's be careful not to judge others when they make mistakes. And let's realize that God can use even our mistakes for a good purpose if we have right attitudes about them."

Daniel nodded. "This is a painful lesson," he said, "and I'm sure my fingers will be a reminder for a long time not to judge others unkindly for the mistakes they make."

Step 6: *Write an interesting title for the story.* It is usually better to decide on a title after the story is written, although a good idea for a title may come to you sooner. A title should be short, rarely over five words. It should be interesting and catchy so that the reader will want to find out what the story is about. But a title should not tell too much, and it must never give away the outcome of the story.

Good: Just Foolish?
Poor: Daniel Makes a Foolish Mistake (tells too much)

Good: The Big Smoke
Poor: When the House Was Full of Smoke (too long; tells too much)

Good: Should I Tell?
Poor: Telling Was the Right Thing (gives away the outcome)

In Lessons 56 and 57, you learned that reports are usually written in two drafts. The same is true of stories. The first draft is the rough, unpolished form, and the second draft is the story in its final form.

When you write the first draft of a story, leave every other line blank so that you can mark changes later. Write in complete sentences, but do not lose too much time in trying to make everything exactly right. Concentrate rather on getting the basic story on paper. You can make improvements later as you revise your story and write the second draft.

- To write a story, use the following steps.
    1. Get the conflict clear in your mind.
    2. Decide who will be the main character.
    3. Write a good beginning for the story.
    4. Write the middle part of the story.
    5. Write a good ending for the story.
    6. Write an interesting title for the story.

Class Practice

Give the answers.
1. What is meant by conflict in a story? What is a good way of getting the conflict clear in your mind?
2. What five questions must you answer when you write a story?
3. What term refers to the "highest point" in a story?
4. What two things must you remember about the ending of a story?
5. Describe a good story title. What must a title *not* do?

Written Exercises

Use your story notes from Lesson 75 to write the first draft of a story. Follow the steps taught in this lesson.

Review Exercises

Write *true* or *false* for each sentence.
1. A paragraph has unity when all the sentences in the paragraph tell about the topic given in the topic sentence.
2. If a topic sentence is good, few details are needed to develop it.
3. The details should show that the topic sentence is true.
4. Giving convincing details, using examples and illustrations, and using comparison or contrast are some good ways to develop paragraphs.

5. A paragraph that is developed by contrast shows differences between two persons, places, things, or ideas.

6. When using comparison or contrast, you must list all the points about one thing before you mention any points about the second thing.

---

83. Commas That Set Off Words

Commas help us when we read. They also help us to write clearly. In this lesson you will study several more ways that commas are used in sentences.

1. *Use commas to set off an appositive.* An appositive is a noun coming after another noun or a pronoun to explain it more fully. Sometimes the appositive includes modifiers. The appositives in these sentences are underlined.

> Our first president, <u>George Washington,</u> was from Virginia.
> The opossum, <u>a marsupial,</u> has a pouch in which to carry her young.
> The coyote, <u>an expert at surviving and adapting,</u> continues to spread its range into new territories.

2. *Use commas to set off a noun of direct address.* A noun of direct address names the person to whom one is speaking. Sometimes a noun of direct address includes modifiers.

> I want you to know, <u>Vernon,</u> that the job is still available.
> Your answer, <u>my friend,</u> has greatly encouraged me.

When a noun of direct address comes at the beginning or end of a sentence, only one comma is needed.

> Lynn, did you see that it is snowing?
> It probably won't snow very much, Mark.

3. *Use commas to set off a parenthetical element.* Parenthetical elements are words that interrupt the main thought of a sentence. You can easily pick out a parenthetical element. It stands out as an inserted thought, and it is not needed to make the sentence complete.

You have all learned, <u>I suppose,</u> that the building has been sold.

We shall try, <u>of course,</u> to find a new meeting place soon.

It is much easier, <u>you know,</u> to tear down than to build up.

This whole matter, <u>I am sure,</u> can easily be explained.

Appositives, nouns of direct address, and parenthetical elements are alike in that they are not needed for a sentence to make sense. These words and phrases are not needed to *prevent* confusion, but they can easily *cause* confusion if they are not set off with commas. The following sentences show that commas can indeed make a great difference.

Please help my friend because the need is great.

Friend is a direct object.

Please help, my friend, because the need is great.

Friend is a noun of direct address.

- Use commas to set off appositives, nouns of direct address, and parenthetical elements from the rest of a sentence.

Class Practice

A. Identify each item within commas as an *appositive,* a *noun of direct address,* or a *parenthetical element.*
  1. The second man, Noah Weaver, has always been a good worker.
  2. I shall not forget, Shirley, how kind you have been.
  3. He will come, I expect, sometime after dark.
  4. Other boys and girls, you must recognize, are much less fortunate.
  5. I want to visit your farm, Uncle Reynold, as soon as I have time.
  6. My kitten, a gift from our neighbor, has black-and-white fur.

B. Tell whether each sentence has an *appositive,* a *noun of direct address,* or *neither.*
  1. Aunt Susan, our neighbor will be glad to help.
  2. Aunt Susan, our neighbor, will be glad to help.
  3. Please call Grandmother when you get home.
  4. Please call, Grandmother, when you get home.

C. Read these sentences, saying *comma* at each place where a comma is needed.

1. During the summer of course the stream always dries up.
2. In six months my friend you will see a remarkable change.
3. Emil a native of Poland speaks several Slavic languages.
4. The large tree an old Norway maple completely blocked the front window.
5. Wait here Paul until the rain stops.
6. Flies and mosquitoes annoying pests to us are serious threats in many countries.

Written Exercises

A. Copy each word that should have a comma after it, and add the missing comma.

1. Lillian who invented pretzels?
2. They were given as treats to Italian children several hundred years ago Marlin.
3. In fact they were first called *pretiola,* which means "little rewards."
4. Soon of course the name changed to *pretzel.*
5. Howard my cousin works in a pretzel bakery.
6. Soft pretzels in fact were invented before hard ones.
7. Who invented hard pretzels Doreen?
8. The baker's helper a young German boy fell asleep while watching some pretzels bake.
9. The baker as you can guess was not very happy about that.
10. He was ready to throw out all those pretzels Maria.
11. Then he saw his helpers eating the pretzels even though they were hard as if they liked them.
12. The baker it is said passed them out to people in the street.
13. Hard pretzels surprisingly enough were well liked; and soon customers were asking for them.
14. The first commercial pretzel baker in America Julius Sturgis made and sold them in Lititz, Pennsylvania, in 1861.

B. Write whether each sentence has an *appositive,* a *noun of direct address,* or *neither.*

1. We tried to call, Father, but the line was busy each time.
2. We tried to call Father, but the line was busy each time.
3. Brother Charles, my teacher, would like to meet you.
4. Brother Charles, my teacher would like to meet you.

C. Write sentences of your own as described below. Use commas correctly.

1. A sentence using *Brother Henry* as an appositive.
2. A sentence using *it is clear* as a parenthetical element.
3. A sentence using *neighbor* as a noun of direct address.
4. A sentence using *I'm sure* as a parenthetical element.

Review Exercises

Write the correct words. [62, 64]

1. The woman invited Elisha and (he, him).
2. (She, Her) and her husband built (he, him) a room.
3. Elisha and (he, him) went to visit the prophets at Gilgal.
4. Elisha's servant prepared food for the prophets and (they, them).
5. Poisonous gourds were found in the food; Elisha and (they, them) might die!
6. "Throw in some meal," Elisha said to (they, them).
7. (We, Us) prophets of Gilgal want you to go with (we, us) to Jordan.
8. Elisha, please go with (we, us) your servants to build a house for (we, us) prophets.

84. More Practice With Commas

When we are speaking, the tone of our voice helps to explain what we mean. But in writing we cannot use our voice to make the meaning clear. We use punctuation marks for this purpose. A comma represents a slight pause and a change in voice pitch. In this lesson you will study some more rules for using commas.

1. *Use a comma before the conjunction in a compound sentence.*

He was in a hurry, but he did the work well.

Remember, a compound sentence has a skeleton on each side of the conjunction. A simple sentence may have a compound subject or a compound predicate, but it has only one skeleton. Do not place a comma between a subject and a verb. Do not place a comma before a conjunction if it joins only two subjects or two verbs.

Incorrect:

The boys, found the den of a bear.
The bear dug it out, and hibernated.
Jacob, and Tim looked, and listened.

Correct:

The boys found the den of a bear.
The bear dug it out and hibernated.
Jacob and Tim looked and listened.

2. *Use commas correctly in letters and addresses.* In the heading of
   a letter, use a comma to separate the route number from the box
   number, the city from the state, and the day from the year. Use
   a comma after the greeting and after the closing. Do not place a
   comma between a house number and a street name or between
   a state name and a Zip Code.

   Incorrect:

   315, State Street
   Zanesville OH, 43701

   Correct:

   315 State Street
   Zanesville, OH 43701

   Remember that on an envelope, the postal service wants the
   receiver's address printed with all capital letters and with no
   punctuation.

   315 STATE STREET
   ZANESVILLE OH 43701

3. *Use a comma after* yes *or* no *and after a mild interjection like*
   oh *or* well *when these words come at the beginning of a sentence.*
   Remember that interjections are words that show strong feeling
   and are not related to the rest of the sentence.

   No, we have never heard such an explanation before.
   Well, I suppose it could be possible.

   Remember that a strong interjection is followed by an exclamation point and that the following words begin a new sentence.

   Well! How could I have forgotten to add the salt?
   Indeed! We never said such a thing!

4. *When an adverb phrase comes before the subject of a sentence, it is usually followed by a comma.*

> In the evening, the snow began falling fast.
> During the snowstorm, the villagers heard the wolves howling.

- A comma is used before the conjunction in a compound sentence.

- Commas are used in letters and addresses.

- A comma is used after *yes* or *no* and after a mild interjection like *oh* or *well* when these words come at the beginning of a sentence.

- When an adverb phrase comes before the subject of a sentence, it is usually followed by a comma.

Class Practice

Read these sentences and letter parts, saying *comma* at each place where a comma is needed.

1. Peas and carrots taste good and they are nutritious as well.
2. Yes I heard it too.
3. 234 Cartwright Road
   Sweet Valley PA 18656
   September 13 20—
4. Dear Marvin
5. Sincerely
   Richard
6. Late in the afternoon the men returned with their families.
7. Across the river we could see the deer.
8. Oh it was a lovely scene!

Written Exercises

A. Copy these letter parts, and add the missing commas.
   1. 115 Vista Lane
      Collingdale PA 19023
      Sept. 4 20—

2. Route 4 Box 250
   Fayette UT 84630
   June 3 20—

3. Dear Joan

4. Your friend
   Judith

B. Copy each word that should have a comma after it, and add the missing comma.
   1. Righteousness exalteth a nation but sin is a reproach to any people.
   2. For some animals' protection God has given them the ability to hibernate.
   3. Oh the boys think they heard a bear snoring out in the woods.
   4. Well why would a bear snore while it is hibernating?
   5. During hibernation bears are in a very deep sleep.
   6. Yes the warm weather could have roused it enough to snore.
   7. Deep inside the den they saw a whimpering cub.
   8. In April the mother bear left the den.

C. Write two compound sentences of your own, using commas correctly.

Review Exercises

A. Write whether the underlined verbs are *linking* verbs or *action* verbs. [44]
   1. A dog <u>is</u> more than a good pet.
   2. Some dogs <u>are trained</u> to find certain things.
   3. They <u>smell</u> nests of termites in old buildings.
   4. Some dogs <u>sniff</u> out illegal drugs that people try to smuggle into the United States.
   5. If a suitcase <u>smells</u> suspicious, the traveler must stop.
   6. The collie <u>has been used</u> for many years to herd sheep.
   7. Your collie <u>looks</u> handsome since you brushed his coat.
   8. This German shepherd and the night watchman <u>look</u> for trouble in the museum at night.

B. Copy each word that should be followed by a comma, and add the missing comma. [81, 83]

1. That dog a black Labrador retriever picks up things his handicapped owner has dropped.
2. Dogs work in homes in museums in airports in meadows in the woods on city streets and in many other places.
3. The dachshund in fact was used long ago in Germany to help chase badgers out of their burrows.
4. The Saint Bernard is a large friendly brown dog that helps to rescue lost people in the Alps.
5. Her pet likes to eat crispy brown graham crackers.

---

85. Writing a Story: Second Draft

You should usually not try to write the first and second drafts of a story all at one time. As with a report, it is better to lay aside the first draft at least until the next day and then come back to it. In this way you will have a fresh view of your work, and you will be better able to make improvements.

In Lesson 82 you studied the six steps for writing the first draft of a story. They are shown here.

Step 1: *Get the conflict clear in your mind.*
Step 2: *Decide who will be the main character.*
Step 3: *Write a good beginning for the story.*
Step 4: *Write the middle part of the story.*
Step 5: *Write a good ending for the story.*
Step 6: *Write an interesting title for the story.*

To write the second draft of your story, follow steps 7 and 8.

Step 7: *Proofread and improve the first draft of the story.* Use the following questions in checking the first draft of your story.

a. *Are the important facts introduced promptly?*

> **Poor:** (setting and main character not clear)
> "Good-bye!" called Ellen and Mark as they waved to their friends.

"Good-bye!" replied Rhonda and Daniel as they started walking in the lane.

"Did you hear about Greg's accident?" Rhonda asked Daniel.

Good:

"Good-bye!" Daniel called to his friends, Evan and Mark, as he and his sister got out of the school van.

"Good-bye!" they returned as the van started on its way again.

"Did you hear about Greg's accident?" Daniel asked Rhonda as they walked in the lane together.

b. *Is the conflict clear? Do events build up to a climax in a natural, logical way?*

Poor: (unrelated problem brought in)

That evening Father and Daniel were working together in the shop. Daniel was trying to put a roof on his birdhouse, but things were not going well for him. "Why can't I make these nails go in straight?" he asked.

Father came over for a look. "Your wood has quite a few knots," he observed. "It helps if you put a bit of soap on the tip of the nail. Then make sure you hit the nail squarely each time as you hammer it in."

Later Allen, a neighbor, stopped in for a few minutes. "Did you hear about Leroy Fannin's accident?" he asked. "He was out last night on his bicycle...."

Good:

That evening Father and Daniel were working in the shop when Allen, a neighbor, stopped in for a few minutes. "Did you hear about Leroy Fannin's accident?" he asked. "He was out last night on his bicycle. It got dark before he arrived home, and the lights on his bicycle weren't working. A car hit him from behind, and now Leroy is in the hospital with serious head injuries," Allen informed them.

"Why are some people so careless?" Daniel asked Father when Allen had left. "Anyone should know better than to be out on the road after dark without lights."

c. *Is the dialogue natural?*

Poor: (all complete sentences and no contractions)

"We do not always know why such things happen, Daniel," Father answered. "It certainly is unwise to be out on the road on a bicycle after dark without lights. But maybe Leroy did not realize that his lights were not working until it got dark. He probably did need to get home."

Daniel shrugged. "Maybe that is how it was," he said, but he did not sound convinced.

Good:

"We don't always know why, Daniel," Father answered. "It certainly is unwise to be out on the road on a bicycle after dark without lights. But maybe Leroy didn't realize that his lights weren't working until it got dark. He probably did need to get home."

Daniel shrugged. "Maybe," he said, but he did not sound convinced.

d. *Does the story end promptly after the climax? Does the ending show the purpose of the story, rather than telling it?*

Poor: (lesson told rather than shown)

The Lord used this experience to teach Daniel a lesson. He learned not to be critical of others when they make mistakes. He also learned that God can use even a mistake for a good purpose. It was a painful lesson; but for a long time afterward, Daniel's fingers were a good reminder that he must not judge others unkindly.

Good:

"The Lord may be using this to teach you a lesson," Father said kindly. "I have heard you several times lately exclaiming about other people's foolish mistakes, and declaring that you would never do such a thing. Let's be careful not to judge others when they make mistakes. And let's realize that God can use even our mistakes for a good purpose if we have right attitudes about them."

Daniel nodded. "This is a painful lesson," he said, "and I'm sure my fingers will be a reminder for a long time not to judge others unkindly for the mistakes they make."

e. *Did you use correct grammar, punctuation, and spelling?*

"Did you hear about Gregs accident," Daniel asked Rhonda
as they walk in the lane together?
        ed

Soon they were on there way to the hospital. A sober
                their

Daniel entered the emerjency room, where a doctor stiched
                         g   t

his mangled fingers.

Mark your corrections and improvements in the blank lines you left between the lines of your story. Change and reword sentences until you are satisfied that the story is as good as you can possibly make it.

Step 8: *Write the story in its final form.* Include the improvements that you marked. Do not leave blank lines in this second draft. Use neat penmanship, and leave good margins. Keep the left margin straight and the right margin as straight as possible.

- To write a story, use the following steps.
    1. Get the conflict clear in your mind.
    2. Decide who will be the main character.
    3. Write a good beginning for the story.
    4. Write the middle part of the story.
    5. Write a good ending for the story.
    6. Write an interesting title for the story.
    7. Proofread and improve the story.
    8. Write the story in its final form.

Class Practice

Do the following exercises with the paragraphs.

1. Tell how to improve this story opening.

"I don't know what is the matter with Mary Ann," Ruth thought. "She just ignores me. And today wasn't the first time!"

Ruth saw Father watching her in the rearview mirror, and she quickly sat up straight. Father, she well knew, had little time for long faces and dismal hearts. Sooner or later he would find out what was wrong!

2. Find one error in grammar, two errors in punctuation, and four errors in spelling.

The next day Ruth came huffishly into the kitchen. "Mother, when I went past Mary Anns house, I seen her picking cherries and I called to her, but she totaly ignored me!" In fact, her skirt gave a little flounce as if she had purposely turned the other way. I can't believe anyone could be so unfreindly!"

"Maybe she didn't hear you," Mother consoled with a smile. "Give her the benifit of the doubt. Or maybe it was even someone else."

"I know it was Mary Ann, because I recogized her old school dress," Ruth said, "even though I couldn't see her very well in the branches."

3. Tell how to improve this dialogue.

Several days later Mother came into the kitchen with a bag of groceries. "Ruth," she said, "Mary Ann was still up in that cherry tree, and she did not wave at me either when I waved. At first I did not know what to think of that. But then I realized it was only a dress hanging in the tree, probably to scare the birds." Mother laughed heartily, and Ruth also joined in.

"Ruth," Mother said after a while, "I think probably most of your suspicions about Mary Ann are empty. They are probably about as weightless as that dress without any body in it!"

4. Tell how to improve this story ending.

"Oh, Mother," said Ruth after prayer meeting, "I told Mary Ann how we called and waved to her dress in the cherry tree, and how we couldn't understand why she didn't respond. We both had to laugh. She seemed like herself tonight. In fact, she had thought I was ignoring her, and she couldn't figure out why!"

Ruth was happy as she sat in the van. It always makes us happy when right attitudes are restored. We need to remember that wrong attitudes are often based on empty imaginations.

Written Exercises

A. Proofread the first draft of the story that you began writing in Lesson 82. Mark the changes that should be made. Keep your corrected first draft for your teacher to see.

B. Write the second draft of your story, making the changes you marked.

---

86. Apostrophes

The apostrophe (') has two main uses. It is used in possessive forms and in contractions.

Possessive Forms

You have already learned much about possessive forms. Remember that a possessive noun or pronoun tells *whose*. A possessive form is used as an adjective when it comes before a noun.

1. The possessive case of most singular nouns is formed by adding *'s*. This includes most singular nouns that end with *s*.

Harold's book	the waitress's pencil
the cat's paws	Charles's brother
a day's wages	the octopus's arms

For a singular noun ending with a *zus* sound, the possessive form would be awkward to pronounce if *'s* were added. Therefore, the possessive form is made by adding only an apostrophe.

Moses' sister   Jesus' words

2. If a plural noun ends with *-s*, the possessive case is formed by adding only an apostrophe. If a plural noun does not end with -

is added.

my two sisters' friends
the four farmers' animals
the children's pets
our geese's feathers
the mice's nest

Study the possessive forms on this chart.

Singular	Singular Possessive	Plural	Plural Possessive
woman	woman's	women	women's
baby	baby's	babies	babies'
waitress	waitress's	waitresses	waitresses'
child	child's	children	children's

3. Apostrophes are not used to make the plural forms of nouns.

Incorrect:
The <u>waitress's</u> served the cherry <u>pie's</u> to the <u>lady's</u>.

Correct:
The <u>waitresses</u> served the cherry <u>pies</u> to the <u>ladies</u>.

However, apostrophes are used to make the plural forms of letters, digits, signs, and symbols.

4's   T's $'s   ?'s

Frank's *F*'<u>s</u> look like *7*'<u>s</u>, and his *r*'<u>s</u> look like *i*'<u>s</u>.

4. Apostrophes are used to make the possessive forms of indefinite pronouns that end with *one* or *body*. But they are not used to make the possessive forms of personal pronouns.

someone's	hers (*not* her's)
nobody's	ours (*not* our's)
everyone's	theirs (*not* their's)
anybody's	

Contractions

1. An apostrophe shows where one or more letters have been omitted in a contraction.

can't (can not)	I'll (I shall *or* I will)
don't (do not)	he'd (he had *or* he would)
we're (we are)	let's (let us)
they've (they have)	there's (there is)

2. Contractions must not be confused with possessive pronouns.

Contractions	Possessive Pronouns	
you're (you are)	your (belonging to you)	<u>your</u> book
they're (they are)	their (belonging to them)	<u>their</u> car
it's (it is *or* it has)	its (belonging to it)	<u>its</u> food
who's (who is)	whose (belonging to whom)	<u>whose</u> box

- Apostrophes are used to make possessive forms and contractions.

- Apostrophes are also used to make the plural forms of numbers, letters, signs, and symbols.

Class Practice

A. In the following sentences, tell where possessive forms could be used. Write the possessive forms on the chalkboard.
1. The servant of Abraham was sent to find a wife for Isaac.
2. The sister of Moses was Miriam.
3. The sisters of my mother are coming today.
4. I like the eggs of brown chickens best.
5. The teacher answered the questions of the children.
6. The coat of someone was left out on the playground.

B. Tell how to spell the missing words. Give an original sentence for each possessive word you spelled.

Singular	Singular Possessive	Plural	Plural Possessive
1. deer	———	———	———
2. wolf	———	———	———

C. Find the words that have mistakes in the use of apostrophes, and tell how to spell them correctly.
1. I found my pencil's beside Marthas seat.
2. Arent you're book's on anybodys desk?
3. Ive found them; theyre on the library shelves'.
4. I dont know why I put them they're.
5. Its good to have helpful friend's when your confused.

Written Exercises

A. Copy and complete the chart.

Singular	Singular Possessive	Plural	Plural Possessive
1. pet	_____	_____	_____
2. puppy	_____	_____	_____
3. sheep	_____	_____	_____

B. Rewrite these phrases, using possessive forms.
1. a track of a bear
2. the milk of several goats
3. problems of people
4. the love of Jesus
5. the gloves of somebody
6. the instructions for the waitresses

C. Write contractions for the following words.

1. I am	4. does not	7. was not
2. it is	5. they have	8. she will
3. we shall	6. he has	

D. Write the plural form of each item.

2   j $ #   5

E. Find the words that have mistakes in the use of apostrophes, and write those words correctly.
1. Alexs teacher couldnt make out several pupils *p*s and *q*s.
2. Theyre using Mothers scissors, but she wont care if theres a good reason.
3. Many people havent heard Jesus words of life.
4. Someones sweater was left outside; is it her's?
5. You're *d*s and *t*s shouldnt have loop's in them.
6. Octopus's have eight arm's, and squid's have ten.

Review Exercises

A. Write the simple subject of each sentence. Then write the correct word in parentheses, making sure it agrees with the word you wrote. [66]
1. Each day one of the students (watch, watches) the fox den.
2. Every one of the girls (pack, packs) (her, their) own lunch.
3. Each of the girls (comb, combs) (her, their) own hair.

4. Now all of the cleaning (is, are) finished.
5. All of the boys (is, are) glad they didn't have to help wash dishes.
6. Few of the women (like, likes) to drive the tractor.
7. Many (know, knows) how though.
8. Nobody (keep, keeps) his lunch in the room.

B. Copy each sentence, using correct capitalization and punctuation. [77, 80]

1. did you ever have a pet skink asked sara
2. no what is a skink asked susan
3. stephen replied it is a kind of striped lizard with an orange throat
4. is it true asked samuel that skinks drop their tails sometimes to get away from enemies
5. yes and young skinks have blue tails answered sara
6. sara said our pets eat ants gnats spiders and small moths

---

87. Hyphens, Colons, and Semicolons

In this lesson you will learn about three more punctuation marks. They are the hyphen (-), the colon (:), and the semicolon (;).

Hyphens

1. *Hyphens are used in writing compound number words from twenty-one through ninety-nine.*

   fifty-eight
   ninety-seven
   three hundred forty-five

2. *Hyphens are used in many compound words,* especially adjectives. Use your dictionary to be sure.

brother-in-law	great-grandchild	twice-mentioned
sisters-in-law	self-discipline	air-conditioned
great-grandfather	self-sealing	air-cooled
great-aunt	self-addressed	green-eyed

   All compound words that end with *in-law* are written with hyphens. Hyphens are also used in all *great-* compounds that refer to relatives. All compound words that begin with *self-* are hyphenated.

3. *A hyphen is used when it is necessary to divide a word between syllables at the end of a line of writing.* The following sentence shows examples of this.

> Sometimes it may be neces-
> sary to divide a word into syl-
> lables at the end of a line.

A word should be divided at the end of a line only when necessary. When you must divide a word, remember the following rules. Always use a dictionary when you are not sure.

a. Do not divide a one-syllable word.

> *not* sto-rm *or* cre-am

b. Divide only between syllables.

> ex-am-ples   care-ful-ly

c. Do not divide a word in such a way that a single letter is left at the beginning or end of a line.

> *not* husk-y *or* studi-o   *not* a-bundance *or* o-val

4. *A hyphen shows a series of connected verses.* The hyphen means "through." A comma shows a break in a series of verses.

> Jesse recited Psalm 119:1–8.
> Our Sunday school class memorized Hebrews 11:1–13, 32–34, 39.

Colons

1. *A colon is used after the greeting of a business letter.*

> Dear Sir: Dear Mr. Jones: Gentlemen:

2. *A colon is used for writing a time with numbers.* The colon is placed between the hour and the minute.

> 3:30 P.M.   9:22 in the evening   6:05 A.M.

3. *A colon is used to write Scripture references.* The colon is placed between the chapter and the verse.

> John 3:16   Colossians 3:12–16

Semicolons

1. *A semicolon is used between clauses in a compound sentence when no conjunction is used.* You know that a comma is not strong enough to hold two clauses together.

   Incorrect:
   >It had happened often before, this time it was more serious.
   >
   >The lawyer asked Jesus a question, he learned more than he had expected.

   Correct:
   >It had happened often before; this time it was more serious.
   >
   >The lawyer asked Jesus a question; he learned more than he had expected.

2. *A semicolon is also used between clauses in a compound sentence that does have a conjunction if commas are already used within one or more of the clauses.*

   >Esau begged, pleaded, and wept; but it was to no avail.
   >
   >If we stop, they'll want us to stay for dinner, I'm sure; and we don't have time for that.

   Ordinarily, a comma and a conjunction are enough to join the clauses. But when commas are used between smaller units (words or phrases), semicolons are used between larger units (clauses).

- The hyphen is used in many compound words.

- The hyphen is used when it is necessary to divide a word between syllables at the end of a line.

- The colon is used after the greeting of a business letter, between the hour and the minute when a time is written with numbers, and between the chapter and the verse in a Bible reference.

- The semicolon is used to join clauses in a compound sentence when no conjunction is used. It is also used to join clauses in a compound sentence when a comma is already used within one or more of the clauses.

Class Practice

A. Tell where these words may be divided between syllables at the end of a line of writing.

1. amidships
2. meaty
3. oversleep
4. ecliptic
5. oiliness
6. apothecary

B. Tell where hyphens, colons, and semicolons are needed in the following sentences.

1. He said that he had twenty two great uncles and great aunts.
2. She didn't list the sisters in law she said she didn't have time.
3. His brother in law sent a self addressed envelope with the order.
4. My great aunt recited Psalm 103 1 12 without a mistake.
5. In the family reunion, forty eight people gathered at 189 Wal nut Street at 1 00 P.M.
6. My aunt brought celery, carrots, and cheese and her sister in law brought fruit.

Written Exercises

A. Write each word, using hyphens to show where it could be divided between syllables at the end of a line of writing. (Insert no hyphen if the word should not be divided.) Use a dictionary for help.

1. amendment
2. many
3. electrician
4. identification
5. realm
6. fascination

B. Copy these sentences, and add the missing hyphens, colons, and semicolons.

1. Twenty three great grandchildren sang for their great grandfather at 1 30 in the afternoon.
2. At my brother in law's self service station, he had one hun dred seventy two customers in one day.
3. Every morning at 9 00, we recited Philippians 4 1 8.
4. He didn't recognize his sister in law he hadn't seen her for twenty four years.
5. His brothers in law are John, David, and Jonas and his sisters in law are Doreen and Mary.

C. Use numerals and abbreviations to write each time.

>   **Example:**   Half past five in the morning
>   **Answer:**   5:30 A.M.

1. Thirteen minutes after nine in the evening
2. Thirty minutes before noon
3. A quarter to ten at night
4. Two minutes after midnight

D. Write two correct greetings for business letters.

E. Write two of your favorite Bible verses, with correct chapter and verse references.

Review Exercises

Copy each verb or verb phrase, and write whether its tense is *present, past, future, present perfect, past perfect,* or *future perfect.* [32–36]

1. At birth, a blue whale weighs about three tons.
2. The goose's eggs have hatched.
3. She chased away any intruder.
4. She had honked a warning in plenty of time.
5. We will stay away from the nest.
6. Before winter, the goslings will have flown south.

---

88. Chapter 7 Review

Class Practice

A. Give the meaning of each abbreviation.

1. Jan.	3. gal.	5. KJV	7. A.M.
2. oz.	4. min.	6. FBI	8. A.D.

B. Say *yes* or *no* to tell whether the following abbreviations may be used in general writing, such as letters, stories, and reports.

1. Mr.	3. Jr.	5. etc.
2. lb.	4. Aug.	6. B.C.

C. Give the postal service abbreviations for these states.

1. New Mexico	3. New York
2. Michigan	4. Minnesota

D. Identify each item set off by commas as an *appositive,* a *noun of direct address,* or a *parenthetical element.*
1. Some turtles, strangely enough, live to be over one hundred years old.
2. Barbara, did you know it takes a bullfrog tadpole three years to change into an adult?
3. Guppies, little South American fish, are easy to raise, Barbara.
4. They don't fight or get sick easily, I am told.
5. Corydoras, a certain type of catfish, are good for keeping the gravel in an aquarium clean.

E. Tell which commas are not needed in the following sentences.
1. The sea horse is a, small, mysterious, sea, creature.
2. Two, antique, cuckoo clocks, struck the hour.
3. Three, tall, eager young men stood ready to work.

F. Tell whether each sentence has a *direct quotation,* an *indirect quotation,* or *no quotation.* (All quotation marks have been omitted.)
1. I have some pet cormorants said Hugo.
2. Hugo said that his pets help him to fish!
3. The Japanese fasten collars to the necks of these birds so that they don't swallow the fish they catch.
4. These birds said Hugo help us to make a living.

G. Change each sentence so that it has an indirect quotation.
1. "We are raising an orphan kangaroo," said Eric.
2. "Whenever the joey wants her mother's pouch, she crawls into the sack we hung from the back fence," he said.
3. Eric said, "We will use electric heating pads to keep the sack warm during cold weather."

H. Change each sentence so that it has a direct quotation.
1. Eric said that he was sure their pet kangaroo would soon be ready to join other kangaroos in the wild.
2. Eric said that she eats grasses and low shrubs.
3. He said that kangaroos are natives of his country, Australia.

I. Tell how to spell the missing words.

Singular	Singular Possessive	Plural	Plural Possessive
1. camel	————	————	————
2. guppy	————	————	————
3. goose	————	————	————

J. On the chalkboard, write a phrase with a possessive form for each item below.
1. antlers of a moose
2. dish of the cats
3. tracks of the geese
4. bone of the dog

Written Exercises

A. Write correctly each word that should be capitalized.

1. **the bumblebee**
i watched a striped bumblebee
    spin off into the air
when he was finished with his lunch
    among the clover fair.

god gives him nectar sweet to drink;
    he gives me milk and bread.
he gives his creatures what they need,
    and by him we are fed!
    —Edith Witmer

2. "o lord, to thee will i cry" (joel 1:19).
3. in the spring of 1896, henry ford tried out his first horseless carriage.
4. on june 16, 1903, the ford motor company began production of this sturdy, inexpensive american car.
5. the museum at greenfield village has several buildings about famous people, including president a. lincoln, noah webster, and the wright brothers.
6. the book *the times, the man, and the company* is about henry ford.
7. in 1922 some men from dearborn, michigan, wanted henry ford to run for president of the united states.
8. his father was william ford, and his mother was mary litogot.
9. father said, "please give this to mother."
10. mr. john b. chapman was the teacher at miller school, a small school in springwells township, michigan.

B. Copy this paragraph, adding the missing punctuation and capital letters.

john deere was an american inventor he was born in 1804 in rutland vermont he was an excellent blacksmith after losing two shops by fire, he moved west in grand detour illinois he invented a steel plow that farmers badly needed soon he started a factory to make them it was the beginning of one of the largest farm equipment factories in the united states

C. Copy each sentence or letter part, and add the missing capital letters and punctuation marks.
   1. 616 n johnson street   dear friend
      detroit mi 48216   sincerely yours
      jan 10 1893
   2. mr and mrs taylors address is 867 south third street, springfield il 62703
   3. who was the teacher of the apostle paul asked brother john
   4. jason replied it was gamaliel
   5. where in the Bible asked brother john can you read about this
   6. it is written in acts 22:3 said gerald this verse also tells where paul was born

D. Write the correct abbreviations for these words. Use a dictionary if you are not sure.
   1. tablespoon   5. hour   9. after midday
   2. quart   6. year   10. before Christ
   3. foot   7. week   11. ounce
   4. gallon   8. October   12. King James Version

E. Copy each word that needs a comma after it, and add the missing comma.
   1. The Ford Company the Chrysler Corporation and the General Motors Corporation in fact are leading car manufacturers in the United States.
   2. Designing the product getting raw materials making the product and selling the product Mark are four main steps in manufacturing.
   3. Well the Chrysler Corporation was a leader in some modern well-liked ideas like front-wheel drive Larry.
   4. Yes more than one company has manufactured automobiles over the years but the competition has given customers better products for less money.
   5. In the 1870s Alexander Graham Bell invented the telephone.
   6. After many demonstrations of his invention people finally became interested in the new instrument.

F. Write contractions for the following words.
   1. they are   3. it is   5. we are
   2. who is   4. I am   6. they have

G. Find the words that have mistakes in the use of apostrophes, and write them correctly.
1. Jasons brother read Jesus word's from Matthew 5 to us.
2. The ladies purses are found on the second floor of Andys store.
3. Someones paper had 5s that looked like Ss.

H. Copy each word, and place a hyphen between the syllables that could be divided at the end of a line of writing.
1. abating
2. periphery
3. iguana
4. immediately

I. Find each word that should have a hyphen or should be followed by a colon or semicolon. Write that word, and add the missing punctuation.
1. When my great grandfather was twenty one years old, he came here from Germany.
2. Sarah Jane's sister in law ordered thirty six self sealing envelopes.
3. At 9 30 we recited 2 Corinthians 6 14 18.
4. Dear Sir
   Please send me some information on your heavy-duty wagons a self addressed envelope is enclosed.

   Sincerely,
   Robert Martin
5. Michael broke his leg he missed his step and fell out of a tree.
6. Mark, John, and Justin went to see him and Glen, Gerald, and Daryl sent cards.

J. Rewrite this dialogue, adding necessary punctuation and dividing paragraphs properly.

One day a young man came to where Jesus was teaching. Good Master, he asked, what shall I do to inherit eternal life? You know the commandments Jesus replied. Do not commit adultery. Do not kill. Do not steal. Do not lie. And honor your father and your mother. The young man answered I have always done all these things, ever since I was a boy. Jesus loved the young man very much. One thing remains for you to do He told him. Sell all your possessions; and come, follow Me. The young man said nothing and went sadly away. He was rich with many possessions.

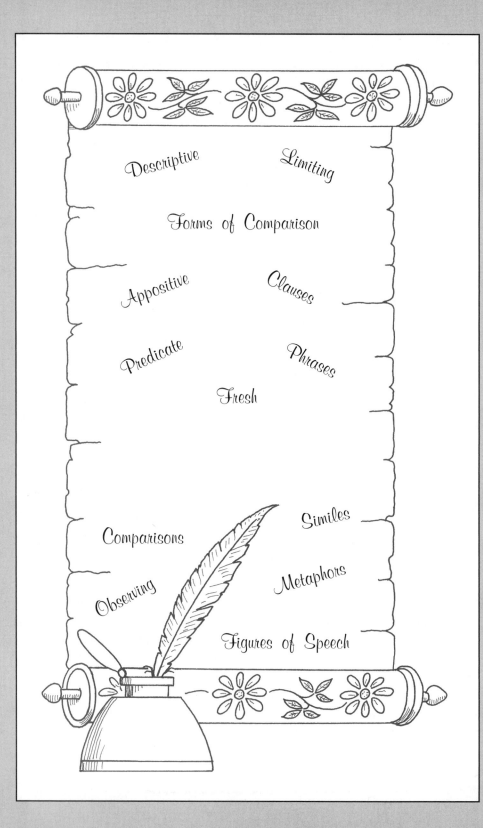

Chapter Eight

Working With Adjectives

Writing Descriptions

An
adjective is a
word that modifies a noun
or pronoun.

He hath made every thing beautiful in his time.

Ecclesiastes 3:11

Adjectives

Limiting Adjectives

Which
Articles:
   a, an, the
Demonstrative pronouns:
   this, that,
   these, those
Ordinal Numbers:
   first, second,
   tenth, fiftieth
Interrogative and Relative Pronouns:
   which, whose, what

Whose
Possessive Nouns:
   boy's, lady's,
   Paul's, Mary's,
   bird's, men's
Possessive Pronouns:
   my, our, its,
   your, his,
   her, their

How Many
Cardinal Numbers:
   two, seven,
   twelve, ninety
Indefinite Pronouns:
   few, several,
   some, many

Descriptive Adjectives

What Kind of
Color:
   red, green,
   brown, pink
Size:
   tiny, huge,
   high, long
Shape:
   round, oval,
   square, oblong
Taste:
   bitter, salty,
   spicy, sweet
Sound:
   harsh, musical,
   shrill, loud
Touch:
   rough, sharp,
   cold, soft
Traits:
   kind, thoughtful,
   lazy, angry
Others:
   late, swift,
   Scottish, French

Adjectives are words that describe, or modify, nouns and pronouns.

89. Adjectives

Adjectives are words that modify, or describe, nouns and pronouns. They tell *which, whose, how many,* and *what kind of.*

Adjectives can be placed in two general classes: *limiting adjectives* and *descriptive adjectives.* Limiting adjectives tell *which, whose,* and *how many.* They limit the meaning of nouns and pronouns in certain ways. There are several kinds of limiting adjectives.

1. The articles *a, an,* and *the* are limiting adjectives.

2. Demonstrative pronouns can be used as limiting adjectives to tell *which.*

   this   that   these   those

3. Ordinal numbers are used as limiting adjectives to tell *which. Ordinal* numbers show the *order* of things.

   third   sixth   twelfth

4. Some interrogative and relative pronouns can be used as limiting adjectives.

   which   whose   what

5. Possessive nouns are often used as limiting adjectives to tell *whose.*

   Harold's   boy's

6. Possessive pronouns are often used as limiting adjectives to tell *whose.*

   somebody's   my   their

7. Cardinal numbers are used as limiting adjectives to tell *how many. Cardinal* numbers are numbers like those on flash *cards.*

   two   seven   ten

8. Indefinite pronouns can be used as limiting adjectives to tell *how many.*

   many   several   few   every   other

Descriptive adjectives tell *what kind of.* There are hundreds of descriptive adjectives. Here are some of them listed in groups.

color: blue, orange, copper, green
size: small, tiny, huge, wide
shape: round, square, oval, triangular
taste: sour, spicy, sweet, salty
sound: harsh, shrill, quiet, harmonious
touch: rough, cold, soft, fuzzy
traits: kind, considerate, lazy, stubborn

Some descriptive adjectives are made from nouns by adding adjective suffixes. Here are some examples. Can you give the nouns from which they are formed?

-ish: babyish, foolish, selfish, feverish
-like: childlike, lifelike, cloudlike, Godlike
-ic: historic, angelic, volcanic, Icelandic
-en: woolen, earthen, wooden, silken

Nouns are often used before other nouns as descriptive adjectives.

<u>farm</u> animals   <u>shade</u> trees   <u>hand</u> soap   <u>garden</u> soil

Sometimes an adjective looks like a verb.

God made the <u>leaping</u> frogs and the <u>flying</u> birds.
Mother's garden is full of brightly <u>colored</u> flowers.

Leaping and *flying* are verb forms. But in the first example above, they describe *frogs* and *birds.* So they are used as adjectives. *Colored* is also a verb form. But in the second example, it describes *flowers.* So *colored* is an adjective in that sentence.

How can you tell whether a word is an adjective or another part of speech? You can tell by the way the word is used in a sentence. Whenever a word modifies a noun or pronoun by telling *which, whose, how many, or what kind of,* it is an adjective.

- An adjective modifies a noun or pronoun.

- A limiting adjective tells *which, whose,* or *how many.*

- A descriptive adjective tells *what kind of.*

Class Practice

A. The seven colors of the rainbow are red, orange, yellow, green, blue, indigo, and violet. Name five other colors.

B. Find the adjectives in these sentences. Tell whether each one is *limiting* or *descriptive*.
   1. Bullfrogs hide in the cool mud at the bottom of the pond.
   2. Out on the grassy bank, the plump bullfrog whips out his long tongue and snaps up a juicy insect.
   3. Pointy or round, huge or tiny, speckled or plain, and green, blue, white, or brown eggs are found among the nine thousand different kinds of eggs that birds lay.

C. Tell whether each underlined word is an *adjective* or a *pronoun*. If it is an adjective, tell which word it modifies.
   1. This is mine; that book is yours.
   2. Several were found on that shelf.
   3. Many people have read them.

Written Exercises

A. Copy all the adjectives in these sentences. Include the nouns and pronouns used as descriptive adjectives. Underline the limiting adjectives.
   1. Common, ordinary insects are interesting creatures.
   2. These insects live in our yards and vegetable gardens.
   3. Some tiny insects hide in the tender, growing tips of young plants.
   4. Other insects feed only in dark, shady areas.
   5. Many brilliant butterflies flit about in the bright sunshine.
   6. The huge beetles of tropical lands may have a length of six inches.

B. Write *adj.* or *pron.* for each underlined word. If it is an adjective, write the word it modifies.
   1. Our pony is three years older than his.
   2. That one is two years old.
   3. His is younger than mine.
   4. Their house is near ours.

C. List the eight kinds of limiting adjectives, and give two examples of each.

D. List all the personal pronouns that can be used as adjectives.

E. Write the definitions of cardinal and ordinal numbers, and write the first five of each.

Review Exercises

A. Write the three principal parts of each verb. Use *have* with the past participle. [30, 31]

1. attack	3. speak	5. forget
2. buy	4. wear	

B. Copy these sentences, and label each word with one of the abbreviations shown.

noun—n.	verb—v.
pronoun—pron.	adjective—adj.

1. Grandmother gave me these two ripe peaches.
2. Six fluffy, yellow chicks hatched.

---

90. Predicate Adjectives

You have learned that adjectives are words that modify nouns and pronouns. They usually come just before the nouns they modify. However, an adjective may also come after a linking verb and modify the subject of the sentence. This is a *predicate adjective.*

The air was <u>cold</u>.
The apple pie tasted <u>delicious</u>.

In the first example above, the adjective *cold* comes after the linking verb *was* and modifies the subject *air*. We know that *cold* modifies *air* because it is sensible to say *cold air*. In the second example, *delicious* comes after the linking verb *tasted* and modifies the subject *pie*. We know that *delicious* modifies *pie* because it is sensible to say *delicious pie*.

Review the list of linking verbs. Be sure you know them by memory.

Forms of *be:*
am, is, are, was, were, be, been, being

Verbs of sense:
taste, feel, smell, sound, look, appear

Other linking verbs:
grow, seem, stay, become, remain

To find a predicate adjective in a sentence, first find the verb. If it is not a linking verb, your work is finished. There is no predicate adjective in the sentence.

If the verb can be a linking verb, see if it is followed by an adjective that modifies the subject. (Say the adjective before the subject to see if that makes sense.) If the adjective modifies the subject, it is a predicate adjective.

> We <u>finished</u> our work.
>> *Finished* cannot be a linking verb. There can be no predicate adjective.

> The cat's dish <u>was</u> <u>empty</u>.
>> *Was* can be a linking verb, and it is followed by the adjective *empty*. *Empty* modifies the subject because it is sensible to say *empty dish*. So *empty* is a predicate adjective.

> These ripe bananas <u>feel</u> <u>soft</u>.
>> *Feel* can be a linking verb, and it is followed by the adjective *soft*. *Soft* modifies the subject because it is sensible to say *soft bananas*. So *soft* is a predicate adjective.

An adjective in the predicate does not always modify the subject. It may modify a direct object, a predicate nominative, or some other word. Such an adjective is not a predicate adjective. It is a predicate adjective only if it modifies the subject.

> These are <u>soft</u> bananas.
>> *Soft* modifies the predicate nominative *bananas*. There is no predicate adjective in this sentence.

Some linking verbs may be used as either linking verbs or action verbs. How can you tell the difference? There are three tests that you can use.

Test 1: *Is the subject performing any action?* If so, the verb is an action verb and not a linking verb.

> We <u>smelled</u> the tulips.
>> (subject performs action; action verb)
> The tulips <u>smelled</u> fragrant.
>> (subject performs no action; linking verb)

Test 2: *Can the verb be replaced by a form of* be? If the sentence still makes sense, the verb is a linking verb.

>The painters <u>appeared</u> tired.
>>(*The painters were tired* is sensible; linking verb.)

>The painters <u>appeared</u> today.
>>(*The painters were today* is not sensible; action verb.)

Test 3: *Is the verb followed by an adjective that modifies the subject?* If so, the adjective is a predicate adjective and the verb is a linking verb.

>The man <u>stayed</u> calm.
>>(*Calm man* is sensible; *calm* is a predicate adjective; *stayed* is a linking verb.)

>The man <u>stayed</u> there.
>>(*There man* is not sensible; no predicate adjective; no linking verb.)

A sentence can have more than one adjective in the predicate that modifies the subject. Such a sentence has a compound predicate adjective.

>Loren looked <u>happy</u> and <u>surprised</u>.

Remember that the main verb is the last word in a verb phrase. A form of *be* is a linking verb only if it is the main verb. Otherwise, it is a helping verb.

>The little house <u>has been</u> vacant.
>>*Been* is a linking verb followed by the predicate adjective *vacant*.

>The little house <u>has been standing</u> there for many years.
>>*Been* is a helping verb, not a linking verb.

- A predicate adjective follows a linking verb and modifies the subject of a sentence.

Class Practice

A. Find each adjective, and tell whether it is a *predicate* adjective or some *other* adjective.
   1. The problems on this page are easy.
   2. The tornado damage may be severe.
   3. This cardboard is tough.
   4. The children were happy with their new sandbox.
   5. The tired hikers were cold and hungry.
   6. The grass grew tall and straight.

B. Tell whether each underlined word is an *action* verb or a *linking* verb. If it is a linking verb, also give any predicate adjective.
   1. The water <u>looked</u> cold and deep.
   2. We <u>looked</u> at the new books.
   3. The flower soon <u>appeared</u> wilted.
   4. The lost dog <u>appeared</u> suddenly.
   5. Jonathan <u>became</u> David's friend.
   6. Jonathan <u>became</u> upset because of Saul's words.

Written Exercises

A. Copy all the adjectives in these sentences. Write *P* after each predicate adjective.
   1. We soon became tired.
   2. The dogs on the front lawn sounded noisy.
   3. All children should be kind.
   4. The old building appeared large.
   5. In this dim room, the cloth looks gray.
   6. The little girl looked frightened and unhappy.
   7. That water should taste cold and fresh.
   8. Are you willing and obedient?
   9. The old, dark prison cell felt cold.
   10. The giants were great and strong.

B. Write *A* or *L* to tell whether each underlined verb is action or linking. Copy all the predicate adjectives.
   1. The poplar trees <u>grew</u> quickly.
   2. The poplar trees <u>grew</u> large.
   3. Did you <u>look</u> at the bananas?
   4. Those bananas <u>look</u> green.
   5. We <u>tasted</u> the bean soup.

6. The soup <u>tasted</u> spicy.
7. I <u>smelled</u> freshly baked cookies.
8. The room <u>smelled</u> fresh and clean.
9. Jason <u>felt</u> happy with his new bike.
10. Jason <u>felt</u> the smooth paint.

Review Exercises

Copy only the sentences that have direct quotations, and add the missing capital letters and punctuation marks. [77–80]

1. When did you get these peaches asked Sarah.
2. This morning said Mother on my way to the bank.
3. Mother said that we should not eat too many of the peaches.
4. Brian exclaimed they taste better than any I ever had before.
5. Do you like these peaches, which are very firm?

---

91. Diagraming Adjectives, and Using Appositive Adjectives

Adjectives usually come before the nouns they modify. Such an adjective may modify a subject, a direct object, an indirect object, the object of a preposition, or a predicate nominative.

> The <u>ancient</u>, <u>run-down</u> shed gave <u>the</u> <u>black</u> cat <u>a</u> <u>hiding</u> place.
> One of <u>those</u> <u>three</u> calves is <u>Susan's</u> calf.

In the first example above, *The, ancient,* and *run-down* modify the subject *shed; the* and *black* modify the indirect object *cat;* and *a* and *hiding* modify the direct object *place.* In the second example, *those* and *three* modify *calves,* the object of a preposition; and *Susan's* modifies *calf,* a predicate nominative. All these adjectives are diagramed on slanted lines beneath the nouns they modify.

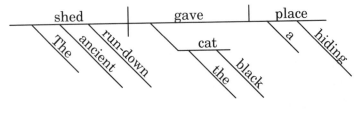

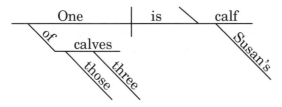

Adjectives may be put in other places in a sentence. For example, an adjective may follow a linking verb and modify the subject. Then it is a predicate adjective.

>The pie was <u>tasty</u>.
>The fruit punch was <u>cold</u>, <u>sweet</u>, and <u>delicious</u>.

Predicate adjectives are diagramed in the same way as predicate nominatives. A slanted line shows that the adjective in the predicate modifies the subject. If the predicate adjective is compound, the fork comes *after* the slanted line.

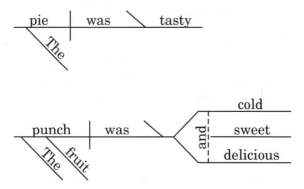

These are the two most common positions of an adjective: before the noun it modifies, and after a linking verb as a predicate adjective. But adjectives in these positions often receive little emphasis. For greater emphasis and better sentence variety, adjectives may also be placed directly after the nouns they modify. Such adjectives are in the *appositive* position. Appositive adjectives usually come in pairs joined by *and*.

>Our dog, <u>keen</u> and <u>alert</u>, spotted the small animal.
>**Compare:** Our keen, alert dog spotted the small animal.
>(Adjectives receive less emphasis.)

Appositive adjectives are set off by commas. A comma is placed just before the first adjective and right after the second adjective.

Adjectives in the appositive position are diagramed below the noun they modify, the same as other adjectives. The conjunction *and* is placed on a dotted line between the two adjectives.

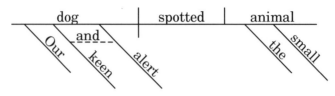

- An adjective usually comes before the noun it modifies, and it is diagramed on a slanted line beneath that noun.

- A predicate adjective follows a linking verb and modifies the subject. It is diagramed on the base line after the verb, with a slanted line between the verb and the predicate adjective.

- Appositive adjectives directly follow the noun they modify. These adjectives usually come in pairs, and they are set off by commas. Appositive adjectives are diagramed on slanted lines beneath the noun they modify, with the conjunction on a dotted line between them.

Class Practice

A. Change each sentence by placing two adjectives in the appositive position. Tell where commas are needed.
1. The large, white snowman had melted in the sun.
2. The fresh, cold water quenched our thirst.
3. Joseph's new, colorful coat was a gift from his father.

B. Diagram these sentences on the chalkboard. You need not diagram the words in italics.
1. Dates, delicious and nourishing, are fruits *of a palm tree.*
2. The afternoon treat, creamy and cold, tasted delicious.
3. The gander is that large goose *under the maple tree.*

C. Read each underlined adjective. Tell whether it comes *before* the noun it modifies, whether it is a *predicate* adjective, or whether it is an *appositive* adjective.
1. A bird, plump and brown, crouched under the evergreen bush.
2. Its eyes were beady and red.

Written Exercises

A. Rewrite each sentence, placing two adjectives in the appositive position. Use commas where they are needed.
1. The small, green fruit turns yellow as it ripens.
2. The tasty, nutritious treat was dates with peanut butter.
3. The Good Samaritan's deed showed pure, sincere love.

B. Copy each underlined adjective. After it, write *B* if it comes before the noun it modifies, *P* if it is a predicate adjective, or *A* if it is an appositive adjective.
1. The trees, well-tended and healthy, produce much fruit.
2. These dates, firm and chewy, taste sweet.
3. The farmer's frightened pigs ruined his new garden.
4. The old fence seemed weak at many places.

C. Diagram these sentences. Do not diagram the words in italics.
1. My dear younger sister drew me a pretty birthday card.
2. The morning sky grew dark and cloudy.
3. We watched the swans, calm and tranquil, *on the pond.*
4. A sudden, furious storm blew *over the plains.*
5. The poor dog, cringing and shivering, could *hardly* stay *on his feet.*

Review Exercises

Diagram these sentences.
1. She is a thoughtful girl.
2. Roses may be red or yellow.
3. Count the peacocks and the swans.
4. The potter made a bowl, but it broke.
5. Did you see that beautiful painting?

92. Using Fresh Adjectives

Adjectives should add meaning and interest to sentences. However, many adjectives fail to do this because they are overused or misused. Here are some examples of overused, worn-out adjectives: *nice, big, great, real, awful,* and *funny.* There are adjectives with fresher, more vivid meanings that make writing clearer and more interesting. Study the following chart.

Overused Adjectives	More Meaningful Adjectives
awful:	dreadful, frightful, shocking, terrifying, horrible, alarming
bad:	harmful, unhealthy, hateful, faulty, evil, ungodly, painful, wrong
big:	huge, mountainous, impressive, bulky, enormous, important, massive
funny:	amusing, humorous, witty, absurd, laughable (Do not write *funny* when you mean *strange* or *unusual.*)
good:	helpful, excellent, profitable, valuable, useful, interesting
great:	huge, heavy, widespread, abundant, deep, extensive, strong, high (Do not write *great* when you mean *wonderful* or *excellent.*)
nice:	pleasant, agreeable, enjoyable, friendly, attractive, appealing
real:	actual, definite, certain, true, genuine, sure (Do not write *real* when you mean *severe* or *extreme.*)

It adds little meaning to call everything *great, real, awful,* or *nice* (or even *awful nice!*). Choose adjectives that describe your meaning more clearly. Learn to use adjectives that have fresh, vivid meanings. But where can you get them?

Most of your vocabulary comes from what you read. If you do not read, you will not have a rich vocabulary. Pay attention to reading. Textbooks, readers, library books, and periodicals are good places to learn new words. Learn to use the words you are studying in vocabulary and spelling lessons. Notice the many words and phrases that capture your attention.

Do the same when you are listening to others speak. Notice what words they use to express themselves.

Develop the dictionary habit. Find the meanings of new words you meet. Synonym dictionaries are especially helpful.

Learn synonyms and antonyms. Synonyms are words with much the same meaning, such as *wonderful* and *marvelous*. Antonyms are words with opposite meanings, such as *common* and *unique*. Do not stop with learning just one synonym or antonym for a word; learn several if you can.

Try to choose the most suitable adjectives when you speak or write. You should be able to use more adjectives than *great, real, awful,* and *nice.*

- Adjectives with fresh, vivid meanings help to make writing clear and interesting. Textbooks, readers, library books, periodicals, and dictionaries are good helps for learning new words.

- Studying synonyms and antonyms will help to increase one's vocabulary.

Class Practice

A. Replace the underlined words with adjectives that are more descriptive. You may use words from the chart in the lesson.
   1. My wallet is made of <u>real</u> leather.
   2. The apples in that basket are <u>bad</u>.
   3. The drinking water here is <u>bad</u>.
   4. This is a <u>good</u> book on gardening.
   5. The tablet and pen set was a <u>good</u> gift.
   6. I made an <u>awful</u> mistake.

B. Give some synonyms and some antonyms for each adjective.
   1. smooth   2. fast

C. Supply fresh, descriptive adjectives to modify these nouns.

Example: children
Answer: noisy, merry, active, energetic, curious, helpful, playful

1. house
2. friend

Written Exercises

A. For each underlined word, write two adjectives that are more descriptive. You may use words from the chart in the lesson.
1. Ronald told some <u>funny</u> stories about his dog.
2. Eating applesauce on cereal seems <u>funny</u> to me.
3. The <u>big</u> stuffed mattresses were hard to move.
4. It looked like a <u>big</u> pile of dishes.
5. The teachers had a <u>big</u> problem to solve.
6. Her grandmother has a <u>nice</u> set of old china.
7. We had a <u>nice</u> school trip.
8. Mary is a <u>nice</u> lady.

B. Write the words that are more descriptive.
1. Yesterday was a (nice, sunny) day.
2. We had (a great, an enjoyable) time playing outside.
3. Last year on this date we had a (severe, real) snowstorm.
4. Sometimes the wind made (funny, strange) wailing sounds.
5. The storm left a (huge, big) drift right in front of our house.
6. We had (a difficult, an awful) time getting out of our driveway.
7. A (good, helpful) neighbor brought his tractor and opened our drive.

C. Write a synonym and an antonym for each of these adjectives. Be sure your answers are also adjectives.
1. curious   4. new
2. pleasant   5. sad
3. excited   6. enough

Review Exercises

Rewrite each expression, using a possessive form. [26]
1. the cart of the oxen   4. the pen of the calves
2. the tail of the ox   5. the game of the boys
3. the ears of the donkey   6. the book of my mother

Challenge Exercises

Supply five meaningful adjectives to modify each of these nouns.

1. table
2. toad
3. forest
4. squirrel

---

93. Writing Descriptions: Observing With Your Five Senses

In a description, a writer describes something he has seen, heard, or felt. A good description helps others to experience what the writer has experienced. Study the following paragraph.

> The old cabin drooped in the midmorning sun, heedless of our rare visit. The ancient roof, blackened by sun and rain, still reached from one gable to the other, but it sagged feebly in the center. Its wooden shingles wore a shabby growth of green moss like a patched coat. Much glass had disappeared from the windows, although some remained. A spider had patched one empty place with her flimsy web. The door still hung on one hinge, ready to fall flat in the next fresh breeze or from the push of any schoolboy. The stone walls still stood, but here and there the frost and wind had torn out the plaster from between the stones, leaving cracks large enough to put one's finger into. Close against one wall grew a few gorgeous orange poppies. If they felt sad or lonely, they did not show it. They smiled back at the sun as brilliantly as any poppies would do anywhere.

The paragraph above does not tell a story. It does not show a problem to be solved, nor does it include dialogue. It simply describes a scene.

If writing is to describe well, it must paint colorful pictures in the mind of the reader. A good writer of description must be observant. He depends mostly on his sight, but he also tells what he has heard, tasted, felt, or smelled.

How can you write about sounds? You might describe the noise of a city street—rumbling trucks, honking horns, and screeching brakes. The sounds of animals on a farm may be squealing pigs, quacking ducks, or bleating sheep. Perhaps you are describing geese that are migrating. Does their excited honking sound like fifty people at a family reunion all talking at once?

In some cases you may describe how something tastes, smells, or feels. What flavors of candy did Aunt Mary make? Did the piece you sampled taste sweet, spicy, or tart? Did a sweet aroma come from the kitchen, or did it smell as if something had burned? A newly sanded board might feel smooth, while the bark on a tree might feel rough and scratchy. Be sure your five senses are alert as you create the picture. Use vivid, precise words that tell about colors, sounds, shapes, smells, sizes, and flavors.

The description of a cabin uses exact nouns and descriptive verbs. For example, it says *spider* and *poppies,* not just *bug, creature,* or *flowers.* It uses descriptive verbs like *sagged, drooped, torn, patched,* and *disappeared.*

Notice the difference in the following sentences.

Too vague and general:
> The <u>man</u> <u>arose</u> and <u>went</u> to the <u>barn</u> because his <u>animals</u> were <u>making</u> a lot of <u>noise</u>.

Much more descriptive:
> The <u>farmer</u> <u>hopped</u> out of bed and <u>raced</u> to the <u>barn</u> because his <u>pigs</u> were <u>squealing</u>, his <u>calves</u> were <u>bawling</u>, and his <u>turkeys</u> were <u>gobbling</u> in alarm.

The description of a cabin uses fresh, meaningful adjectives. Study the following lists. The first list shows examples from the description above. The second list shows less descriptive ways of writing the same thing.

More Descriptive	**Less Descriptive**
ancient roof	very old roof
shabby growth of green moss	green stuff
flimsy web	very weak web
fresh breeze	little wind
gorgeous poppies	nice flowers
large cracks	big holes

Remember not to use adjectives like *big, nice,* and *good* when you could use more exact words like *huge, pleasant, valuable, strong,* and *useful.* Use descriptive adjectives with nouns. For example, do not just say *the horse, the pig,* or *the grass* when you could say the *hardworking horse,* the *friendly old horse,* the *greedy little pig,* the *lush green grass,* or the *parched brown grass.*

A description should be arranged in a logical order. Notice the order in the following example, which describes an elephant. It begins with his trunk and ends with his tail.

Do you know what an elephant looks like? His nose, called a trunk, looks like a large rubber hose hanging from his upper jaw. The tusks at the base of his trunk are like two ivory spears pointing forward, ready to fight any troublemaker. His ears look like huge fans, which he flaps to keep himself cool. The distance from the ground to the top of his back is about the same as from his trunk to his tail. He may be nine or ten feet tall. His back is broad and flat, a perfect place to sit for a ride. His legs, as thick as the trunk of a tree, are supported by round, flat feet. His tail is like a thin rope about three and one-half feet long. An elephant's tail is quite small compared to the rest of his body.

The order used in descriptions is called *spatial order,* or the order of space. Details may be given from top to bottom, from left to right, from front to back, from outside to inside, from near to far, or in the reverse order of any of these. The *kind* of order is not as important as having a *definite* order. Do not be haphazard in description—for example, first describing the trunk of an elephant, then his feet, then his tail, then his tusks, and then his back. Decide what order you will use, and stick to it.

- A good description paints colorful pictures in the mind of the reader.

- A good description uses exact nouns, verbs, and adjectives.

- A good description uses spatial order.

Class Practice

A. Give more exact nouns for the underlined words.

1. The hungry boy could hardly wait to eat the <u>good</u> <u>food</u> that he saw on the table.

2. <u>Certain toys</u> in the toy department caught the <u>child's</u> interest.
3. He described the <u>scenery</u> of Guatemala to us.

B. From the list, choose several suitable verbs that are more exact than the verb *went* in each sentence.

slithered	crashed	ambled	plodded
scuttled	sneaked	trotted	charged
crawled	pranced	squirmed	wriggled
stumbled	darted	waddled	scurried

1. The contented brown cow went down the path.
2. The fat old duck went toward the pond.
3. The surprised beetle went into the crack.
4. A shiny, brown-spotted snake went across the rock.
5. The hungry cat went through the tall grass.
6. The friendly white pony went up to the fence.

Written Exercises

A. Write three exact nouns or adjectives that could be used to replace each underlined word.
1. Eugene especially enjoyed watching the playful <u>animals</u> at the zoo.
2. Sister Mary read an <u>interesting</u> book to the class.
3. From the window of the hospital, we watched many <u>vehicles</u> jostling in the busy street below.

B. Write a more exact verb from the list for each underlined verb.

squirmed	soared	sailed	crawled
scurried	wallowed	slithered	bounded
floated	crashed	wriggled	glided
charged	rolled	hopped	

1. A wary rabbit <u>ran</u> across the lawn.
2. A frightened mouse <u>ran</u> under the cupboard.
3. The angry steer <u>went</u> through the fence.
4. A little pink worm <u>moved</u> through the mud.
5. A red-tailed hawk <u>flew</u> over the meadow.
6. The beautiful white swan <u>swam</u> across the water.
7. Two fat hogs <u>were</u> in the mudhole.

C. Write a descriptive paragraph for one of the following. (About one hundred words.)

1. a storm
2. a woodland scene
3. a waterfall
4. a giraffe

5. inside a busy shop
6. inside a barn at milking time
7. a playground during recess
8. a kitchen on baking day

Review Exercises

Write the number of the better set of directions. Be ready to tell in class why it is better. [8, 17]

1.   It is not hard to make a new friend if you follow a few simple steps. Introduce yourself to a friend. Of course you must look for a friend first. He may be the stranger who has come to your church. Give him your name and ask for his name. Show an interest in him by asking polite questions. Sooner or later you may hit upon a subject that is interesting to both of you, and you will not find it hard to talk. He may know someone that you know. Ask him about his church and school. Before you know it, you will have made a new friend. Perhaps you know someone with the same last name as his. Ask polite questions about his family. Early in the conversation, make him feel welcome by assuring him that you are glad to meet him.

2.   It is not hard to make a new friend if you follow a few simple steps. First, look for a friend. He may be the stranger who has come to your church. Second, introduce yourself to him. Give him your name and ask for his name. Then make him feel welcome by assuring him that you are glad to meet him. Show an interest in him by asking polite questions. Perhaps you know someone with the same last name as his. Or he may know someone that you know. Ask him about his church and school. Ask polite questions about his family. Sooner or later you may hit upon a subject that is interesting to both of you, and you will not find it hard to talk. Before you know it, you will have made a new friend.

94. Forms of Comparison for Adjectives

God is *great*. He is *greater* than the angels. He is the *greatest* Being of all, for He alone is God.

Most descriptive adjectives have three forms, or degrees, of comparison. In the paragraph above, the adjective *great* is used in all three degrees. *Great* is the *positive degree*. It describes without making a comparison. *Greater,* the *comparative degree,* compares God's greatness with the greatness of angels. *Greatest,* the *superlative degree,* compares His power with the power of all other beings. *Greatest* tells us that God is above all other beings in greatness.

The *positive degree* is the simplest form of an adjective. It is used to describe only one thing. It is not used to compare.

kind	hot	tiny
late	quiet	

The *comparative degree* is used to compare only two things. The comparative degree of one-syllable adjectives and a few two-syllable adjectives is made by adding *-er.* If necessary, double the final consonant or change the *y* to *i* before adding *-er.*

kinder	hotter	tinier
later	quieter	

The *superlative degree* is used to compare more than two things. The superlative degree of one-syllable adjectives and a few two-syllable adjectives is made by adding *-est.* Again, it may be necessary to double the final consonant or change a final *y* to *i* before adding *-est.*

kindest	hottest	tiniest
latest	quietest	

Study the following chart.

Positive	Comparative	Superlative
smooth	smoother	smoothest
glad	gladder	gladdest
busy	busier	busiest

For most adjectives with two or more syllables, the comparative and superlative forms are made by using the words *more* and *most* with the positive degree. This is done because words like *beautifuller* and *frightfullest* would be awkward to pronounce.

Positive	Comparative	Superlative
wonderful	more wonderful	most wonderful
pleasant	more pleasant	most pleasant
durable	more durable	most durable

One common error when making comparisons is to use the superlative degree when only two things are compared.

Incorrect: Of the two boys, Harold is <u>oldest</u> but Henry is <u>tallest</u>.
Correct: Of the two boys, Harold is <u>older</u> but Henry is <u>taller</u>.

Another error is to use *more* and *most* with the *-er* and *-est* endings to form the comparative and superlative degrees.

Incorrect: Laurel is the <u>more faster</u> worker of the two girls.
Correct: Laurel is the <u>faster</u> worker of the two girls.

Incorrect:
Wednesday was the <u>most pleasantest</u> day of the whole week.
Correct:
Wednesday was the <u>most pleasant</u> day of the whole week.

A few common adjectives have irregular forms.

Positive	Comparative	Superlative
good	better	best
well	better	best
bad	worse	worst
ill	worse	worst
far	farther	farthest
much	more	most
many	more	most
little	less	least

Littler and *littlest* are also correct forms. *Littler* and *littlest* refer to size. *Less* and *least* refer to an amount.

The <u>littlest</u> puppy was sold for the <u>least</u> money.

Use a dictionary whenever you are not sure how to form the comparative and superlative degrees. In most dictionaries, if no forms of comparison are shown, they are formed in the usual way. Add *-er* or *-est* if the adjective has one syllable, and use *more* or *most* if the adjective has two or more syllables.

- The positive degree of adjectives is used to describe without comparing.

- The comparative degree is used to compare two things. It is formed by adding -er or by using the word *more*.

- The superlative degree is used to compare more than two things. It is formed by adding -est or by using the word *most*.

- Do not use the superlative degree when only two things are compared. Do not use *more* and *most* with the -er and -est endings.

- Check a dictionary if you are not sure how to form the comparative and superlative degrees of an adjective.

Class Practice

A. Give the comparative and superlative forms of the descriptive adjectives in these sentences.
1. This tree is tall.
2. The little kitten is mine.
3. Irises are delicate flowers.
4. Father's chair is comfortable.
5. Good shoes cost much.
6. The old man raised some large pumpkins.

B. Tell what is wrong in each sentence. Read the sentences correctly.
1. These are the most smallest seeds I have ever seen.
2. James and William are both fast, but William is fastest.
3. Peas are the most early vegetable that we plant.
4. Of the two dogs, Scott is largest and strongest.
5. It was the terriblest sight I ever saw.
6. Alice is usually carefuller than Irene.

Written Exercises

A. Write the correct form of each word in parentheses.
1. We had (little) rain at school than we had at home.
2. Our north field has (many) rocks, but our south field has even (many) rocks.

3. Of all the hurricanes in 1992, Hurricane Andrew was the (bad) one.
4. The teacher gave (small) assignments on Bible school nights than on other nights.
5. He is the (tall) twelve-year-old I ever saw!
6. She has a soft voice, but it is (loud) than this at recess.
7. The weather today is (pleasant) than yesterday.
8. The painting of the autumn scene is (beautiful) than the painting of the winter scene.
9. Of the two girls, Maria is the (good) cook.
10. Of the twins, Ronald is (tall).
11. The people of Berea were (noble) than the people of Thessalonica because they put (much) effort into searching the Scriptures.
12. The Word of God is (precious) than silver or gold.

B. Write the positive, comparative, and superlative degrees of these adjectives. Give two sets of answers for number 7.

1. generous	4. rapid	7. little
2. dark	5. bad	8. marvelous
3. far	6. careful	

C. Choose any two adjectives in Part B, and use all three forms in sentences of your own. Underline the words you use. (You should underline six words altogether.)

Review Exercises

Copy and capitalize correctly. [20, 73, 74]

1.   **thanksgiving prayer**
   we thank thee for the morning light,
   for rest and shelter of the night,
   for health and food, for love and friends,
   for everything thy goodness sends.
                        —Author unknown

2. one wednesday in march, i read the poem "o god, our help in ages past," by isaac watts, to my class at lake view school.
3. do you know any poems written by the english poet elizabeth b. browning?
4. Next spring i hope to see mount st. helens in washington.

95. Prepositional Phrases as Adjectives

You have met many single words that are used as adjectives. A *prepositional phrase* can also be used as an adjective. Use the following steps to find a prepositional phrase in a sentence.

1. *Find the preposition.* Most prepositions are small, simple words like the ones listed below.

at	from	near	over	up
by	in	of	to	with
for	like	on	under	

For more prepositions, see the chart on page 508.

2. *Find the object of the preposition.* This is done by saying the preposition and asking *whom* or *what.* The object is always a noun or pronoun.

3. *The prepositional phrase includes all the words from the preposition to its object.* Any words in between are adjectives that modify the object. Not all phrases have adjectives.

> You may come <u>with me</u>.
> We went <u>to a large grocery store</u>.

Not all prepositional phrases are used as adjectives. Some act as adverbs. Compare the following sentences.

> The boy <u>in the car</u> is Thomas. (adjective telling *which* boy)
> The boy sat <u>in the car</u>. (adverb telling *where* he sat)

If a prepositional phrase is used as an adjective, it is called an *adjective phrase.* You can recognize an adjective phrase in three ways.

1. *An adjective phrase always modifies a noun or pronoun.*

> The giant <u>of Gath</u> saw someone <u>with a sling</u>.
> The phrase *of Gath* modifies the noun *giant.*
> The phrase *with a sling* modifies the pronoun *someone.*

2. *An adjective phrase usually tells* which *or* what kind of *about the word it modifies.*

> The boy <u>with red hair</u> is a visitor <u>from another country</u>.
> *Which* boy is a visitor? The phrase *with red hair* modifies the noun *boy* by telling *which.*

What kind of visitor is he? The phrase *from another country* modifies the noun *visitor* by telling *what kind of.*

3. *An adjective phrase must come right after the word it modifies.*

The book <u>on the desk</u> is a gift <u>for my little sister</u>.

The phrase *on the desk* comes right after *book* and tells *which.*

The phrase *for my little sister* comes right after *gift* and tells *what kind of.*

An adjective phrase is diagramed beneath the noun or pronoun that it modifies. The preposition is diagramed on a slanted line, and its object goes on a horizontal line connected to it. Any adjectives go on slanted lines below the object of the preposition.

An adjective phrase can modify a subject, a direct object, an indirect object, a predicate nominative, or the object of a preposition. Study the following examples.

Adjective phrase modifying a subject:

The pictures <u>of the snowcapped mountains</u> are beautiful.

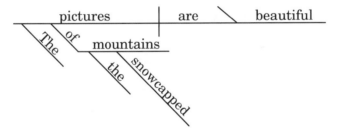

Adjective phrase modifying a direct object:

My white cat was watching the little birds <u>on the sunny lawn</u>.

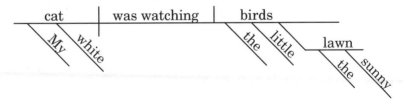

Adjective phrase modifying an indirect object:
Jonathan gave the son <u>of Jesse</u> his sword.

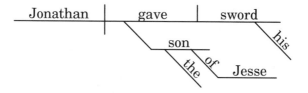

Adjective phrase modifying a predicate nominative:
France is a country <u>in Europe</u>.

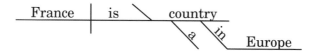

Adjective phrase modifying the object of a preposition:
Saul came from the smallest tribe <u>of Israel</u>.

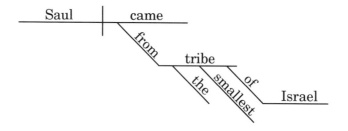

In the last example above, the prepositional phrase *from the smallest tribe* modifies the verb *came.* So this is an adverb phrase, not an adjective phrase. But the phrase *of Israel* modifies the noun *tribe,* so it is an adjective phrase.

- A prepositional phrase may be used as an adjective.

- A prepositional phrase includes a preposition, its object, and any adjectives that modify the object.

- An adjective phrase modifies a noun or pronoun.

Class Practice

A. Read each adjective phrase. Tell which noun it modifies.
1. That black spot in the sky is a flock of birds.
2. Grandfather gave the boys a bag of nuts on Monday.
3. Noah built an ark of gopher wood.
4. The grass in our yard looked greener after the rain.
5. The manager gave the foreman of the crew some instructions about the work.
6. The little birds in the nest in this tree are robins.
7. The boy with the coat of many colors was Joseph.
8. Hezekiah showed the visitors from Babylon his house of treasures.

B. Diagram sentences 1–5 of Part A at the chalkboard. You do not need to diagram adverb phrases.

C. Use these prepositional phrases as adjectives in sentences of your own. Be sure each one comes after a noun and tells *which* or *what kind of.*
1. by the shallow pool
2. with blue shutters

Written Exercises

A. Copy each adjective phrase, and write the noun it modifies.
1. The bridge over the creek was built by the men from the village.
2. That picture on the desk shows a bird with long yellow legs.
3. The dogs in the back yard would not be quiet last night.
4. One letter from my brother had news about the fierce storm in the West.
5. The man in the garden is my uncle.
6. This is a book about some tornadoes in Indiana.
7. Our song leader was a man from the valley across the mountain.
8. Eve was the mother of all living.
9. The disciples spoke the Word of God with boldness.
10. The second king of Israel was the son of Jesse.
11. We had heavy rains on the second day of school.
12. A stamp belongs in the upper right corner of an envelope.

B. Diagram these sentences, including the prepositional phrases.
1. Grandpa told us a story about his childhood days.
2. The book with the blue cover is a collection of interesting poems.
3. The first book on this shelf is a guide on birds.
4. Six large crates of bananas were unloaded.
5. Antarctica is the continent at the South Pole.
6. The booklet at the left end of the shelf is a guide on insects.

C. Use these prepositional phrases as adjectives in sentences of your own. Be sure each one comes after a noun and tells *which* or *what kind of.*
1. with brown braids
2. with pink icing
3. beside the dusty road
4. across the river

Review Exercises

Write the correct verbs. [47–52]
1. I might have (drowned, drownded) when I was accidentally (drug, dragged) into the water, but my brother had (taught, learned) me how to swim.
2. The weather balloon (raised, rose) high into the air before it (burst, busted).
3. (Let, Leave) me help you (lay, lie) those shelf papers in place.
4. Brian often (tug, tagged) along with us, and we (let, left) him help us.
5. We went away and (let, left) the dog in the barn, and he (laid, lay) down in the straw.
6. (Can, May) I help you (set, sit) the glasses on the table?
7. Father (raised, rose) the lawn mower blade a little.
8. The wolf that had (attacked, attackted) the sheep has (laid, lain) in his den all day.
9. Since Jeremy has been ill, he either (sets, sits) in the easy chair or (lays, lies) in bed.
10. Grandfather (laid, lay) down his book and listened with interest to my little brother's amusing story.

96. Writing Descriptions: Using Comparisons

You have learned that a description is different from a story. A description does not have conflict or dialogue. Its purpose is to help the reader "see" what the writer has seen. A good description uses exact nouns, descriptive verbs, and fresh adjectives to paint colorful pictures in the mind of the reader. It is arranged in *spatial order,* or the order of space.

Using clear, exact words is not the only way to describe something. Another way is to describe by using comparisons. The sun may be described as setting in the western sky *like a huge orange ball.* We could say that a person was as excited *as a mother bird whose babies are out of the nest* or as uncomfortable *as a wet chicken.* We may say that a boy ran *like a scared rabbit* or worked *like a beaver.*

When we compare two things that really are not alike, and we use the word *like* or *as,* we are using a *simile* (sim′·ə·lē). A simile uses the word *like* or *as* to make an imaginative comparison. The Bible uses many similes. Study the following examples.

> "All flesh is <u>as grass</u>" (1 Peter 1:24).
> "The kingdom of heaven is <u>like to a grain of mustard seed</u>" (Matthew 13:31).
> "And he shall be <u>like a tree planted by the rivers of water</u>" (Psalm 1:3).

A *metaphor* is much like a simile, but it does not use *like* or *as.* A metaphor usually includes a form of *be: am, is, are, was,* or *were.* The following comparisons are metaphors. See how the first one is different from the simile in the paragraph above.

> The sun in the western sky <u>was a huge orange ball</u>.
> The stone walls <u>were soldiers standing erect and impressive</u>.

The comparison in a metaphor is not actually stated, but implied or understood. To say that a mountain *is an old man hovering over the village* or that the trees *were soldiers standing in straight rows* is to use a metaphor. The Bible contains many metaphors, as illustrated by the following examples.

> "The tongue <u>is a fire</u>" (James 3:6).
> "Ye <u>are the light of the world</u>" (Matthew 5:14).
> "Jesus said unto them, I <u>am the bread of life</u>" (John 6:35).

Study the following paragraphs. The second one is much more descriptive because it uses a variety of exact nouns, verbs, and adjectives. It also uses some similes and metaphors.

A kind of fish that can fly lives in some oceans. Other sea animals may cause him to come up out of the water. How does he do it? First, he goes very fast under the water and starts moving up until he gets to the top. Then he goes a short way, he moves his tail, and he rises into the air. He uses his fins like wings by making them go apart, and he uses his tail to go right or left. He can stay in the air for a good while, and he can go a good distance before he comes down again. Then, by moving his tail, he can go right up again! Sometimes a flying fish goes into a boat. Then a person may have him for a meal because all flying fish are good to eat.

*   *   *   *   *

In warm oceans live several species of fish that can fly like model airplanes. Underwater enemies probably cause these fish to propel themselves out of the water. How does a flying fish fly? First, on an underwater runway, he swims upward faster and faster. When he reaches the surface, he skims along for a short distance. Finally with a flip of his powerful tail, he glides into the air. There he spreads his strong fins, which act as the wings of an airplane. His tail is the rudder that turns him to the right or left. His glistening scales shimmer in the sunlight for about one minute; he may travel one hundred fifty to one thousand feet before he hits the surface again. Then with another flip of his tail, he may go for a second cruise! The wind sometimes carries him high above the water. Once in a while, the flight of a flying fish ends on the deck of a boat. Then he may become a fine breakfast for some hungry sailor! All species of flying fish make tasty meals.

Both similes and metaphors are *figures of speech*. Both are imaginative comparisons between things that are really not similar. Not every comparison is a figure of speech. If you say that Charles ran as swiftly as Anthony, that is simply a comparison; it is not a simile.

• Comparisons help to make descriptions meaningful. A simile compares two unlike things by using the word *like* or *as*. A metaphor compares two unlike things by saying one thing is another thing.

Class Practice

A. Read the following paragraph. Pick out the descriptive nouns, verbs, and adjectives. Find the similes and the metaphors.

The grassy knoll lay just twenty feet from the peaceful stream, where small trout were breaking through the surface to catch unwary insects. Close by, but out of sight, sat a toad. He was a musician, singing for anyone who cared to listen. A trio of young maple trees was a canopy, shading half the knoll. Beside the stream, a margin of gravel and sand recorded that deer, raccoons, and various birds had been there earlier for a drink. A large black bird, like a guardian soldier, complained nervously that we had advanced too close to his nest. Already the sun was like a blazing torch, flooding us with strong heat and dazzling brightness.

B. Find each figure of speech in these sentences, and tell whether it is a *simile* or a *metaphor*.
   1. The men worked like machines, their arms and legs moving in unison.
   2. The duck led her little ones carefully over the grass like a school-teacher on a field trip.
   3. The pile of cornhusks was a testimony to the hard work of the morning.
   4. His Bible was his constant companion.
   5. Her heart leaped within her like a terrified animal.

C. Complete the following similes and metaphors with ideas of your own.
   1. He seemed to be as strong as ...
   2. The shop was as cluttered as ...
   3. He runs like ...
   4. Wise words are ...
   5. Kind and pleasant words are ...
   6. Words of an unkind talebearer are ...

D. Tell how you would use spatial order to describe the following things.
   1. an old barn
   2. a garden
   3. a large jet plane
   4. a small town

Written Exercises

A. Write whether each proverb contains a *simile* or a *metaphor.*
1. A merry heart doeth good like a medicine.
2. The righteous shall flourish as a branch.
3. The fear of the Lord is a fountain of life.
4. Counsel in the heart of a man is like deep water.
5. Children's children are the crown of old men.
6. The way of the slothful man is as an hedge of thorns.

B. Complete each sentence with a simile or metaphor of your own.
1. The mosquitoes buzzed around us like ...
2. The lone large tree looked like a ...
3. The Bible is a ...
4. The welcome news was like ...
5. The wind was howling like ...

C. Describe one of these things in a paragraph of about one hundred words. Use at least one simile and one metaphor in your paragraph.

1. an old barn	7. a stray cat or dog
2. a mountain	8. a large jet plane
3. a garden	9. any big animal
4. a small town	10. a disorderly bedroom
5. a building site	11. a new snowfall
6. a brisk October night	12. a dismal swamp

Review Exercises

These sentences review making an outline from notes. Write whether each one is *true* or *false.* [53]
1. The first step is to identify the main ideas in your notes.
2. The main ideas from all the reference sources should be grouped together.
3. The main ideas on your outline should be in the same order as you find them in your notes.
4. All the details in your notes should be included on your outline.
5. A good outline helps to give you a sense of direction for writing your report.

97. Adjective Clauses

In Chapter 1 you learned that a clause is a group of words with a subject and a verb. In Chapter 6 you studied relative clauses, which are introduced by relative pronouns (*who, whom, whose, which, that*). The following sentences contain relative clauses in parentheses. In each sentence, the relative pronoun is in italics, the subject is underlined once, and the verb is underlined twice.

> Jesus welcomed the children (*who* came to Him).
> The man (*whose* son was sick) believed Jesus' words and returned home.
> The table (*that* we bought) looks like a sturdy one.

Relative clauses are also called *adjective clauses* because they modify nouns and pronouns. An adjective clause usually tells *which* or *what kind of.* In the following sentences, the underlined nouns are modified by the adjective clauses in parentheses.

> The table (that we bought) looks like a sturdy one.
> My uncle is the man (who sold it to us).
> We talked with the girl (whom you met in the hospital).

You know that an adjective phrase must come immediately after the word it modifies. The same is true of an adjective clause.

> **Correct:**   The man who was born blind could now see.
> **Incorrect:** The man could now see who was born blind.

The second sentence is incorrect because the adjective clause is misplaced. The clause should come right after *man* because that is the word it modifies. Otherwise, the sentence is confusing. It sounds as if the man could see which person was born blind!

An adjective clause can modify a subject, an object, or a predicate nominative. It is not hard to tell which word it modifies because the clause comes right after that word. Study the following examples.

> **Adjective clause modifying a subject:**
> The tree (that Zacchaeus climbed) was a sycamore tree.

> **Adjective clause modifying a direct object:**
> Zacchaeus returned the money (that he had wrongfully taken).

Adjective clause modifying an indirect object:

Jesus showed <u>Zacchaeus</u> (who was a publican) His great love.

Adjective clause modifying the object of a preposition:

Zacchaeus came down from the sycamore <u>tree</u> (which he had climbed).

Adjective clause modifying a predicate nominative:

Zacchaeus was a short <u>man</u> (who climbed a tree).

An adjective clause is called a *dependent clause* because it depends on the rest of the sentence for its meaning. A dependent clause does not make sense if it stands alone as a simple sentence. A clause that does make sense by itself is called an *independent clause.* Study the following example.

A bat swooped after the <u>rock</u> (that Dan had thrown).

Independent clause:

A bat swooped after the rock. (sensible by itself)

Dependent clause:

That Dan had thrown. (not sensible by itself)

You have learned about simple and compound sentences. A sentence with only one clause is a *simple sentence,* and a sentence with two independent clauses is a *compound sentence.* If a sentence has one independent clause and one dependent clause, it is a *complex sentence.* The examples below compare simple, compound, and complex sentences.

Simple sentence:

<u>You</u> <u>should</u> not <u>get</u> too close to a bat.

Compound sentence:

Bats' <u>teeth</u> <u>are</u> sharp, and some <u>bats</u> <u>carry</u> rabies.

Complex sentence:

The <u>bat</u> (that <u>we</u> <u>took</u> to school) <u>had</u> a wing span of twelve inches.

The independent clause in a complex sentence can also be called the *main clause.* A main clause can stand alone as a simple sentence.

- A noun or pronoun may be modified by an adjective clause. An adjective clause is also called a relative clause because it begins with a relative pronoun (*who, whom, whose, which, that*).

- An adjective clause comes directly after the word it modifies.

- A sentence with an adjective clause is a *complex sentence*. A complex sentence contains one *independent clause* (main clause) and one *dependent clause*.

Class Practice

A. First read the dependent clause in each sentence. Then read only the independent (main) clause, and notice that it makes sense by itself.

1. A message from God came to Jonah, who was a prophet.
2. Nineveh, which was a wicked city, was in danger of God's judgment.
3. Jonah tried to flee to Tarshish, which was a faraway place.
4. The prophet was swallowed by a great fish that God had prepared.
5. The people to whom Jonah preached believed his message and repented.
6. Afterward Jonah learned an important lesson from a plant that God caused to grow.

B. Change each underlined word to a relative pronoun, and combine the two clauses into a complex sentence.

Example: I called the dog. <u>It</u> was lying in the lane.
Answer: I called the dog that was lying in the lane.

1. The man came to the door. <u>His</u> car was out of gasoline.
2. Father bought the black calves. He had admired <u>them</u> for some time.
3. The people ate supper at our house. <u>They</u> had visited our school.
4. The boys put on the shirts. My sister had ironed <u>them</u>.

Written Exercises

A. Copy each adjective clause. Draw one line under the subject and two lines under the verb, and circle the relative pronoun. (Sometimes you will underline and circle the same word.)
1. Disciples who worshiped the Lord were found in many cities.
2. They believed the Word of God, which was preached to them.
3. Some Christians whom Peter visited were at Lydda.
4. Lydda, which was near the Great Sea, was the home of Aeneas.
5. Peter healed Aeneas, who had palsy.
6. He was a man who had been sick eight years.
7. The power that healed him came from God.
8. Many people who saw Aeneas turned to the Lord.

B. Change each underlined word to a relative pronoun. Then combine the two clauses into a complex sentence as in Class Practice, Part B.
1. The book is ruined. It was left out in the rain.
2. Frank Meese wrote us a letter. We met him last winter.
3. The answers are not correct. You wrote them on your paper.
4. The woman seemed very grateful. We had helped her.

Review Exercises

Write the correct pronouns. [61–64]
1. (He, Him) and his three friends decided they would not eat the king's meat.
2. Daniel said to the officer, "Please do not force (we, us) to eat the king's meat."
3. For ten days the officer gave (they, them) the food they had requested.
4. At the end of the ten days, Daniel and (they, them) looked healthier than the others.
5. Soon (he, him) and (they, them) were found to be ten times better than the wisest men in Nebuchadnezzar's kingdom.
6. (We, Us) boys will do what is right no matter how hard it may seem.
7. The wisest man was (he, him).
8. The Lord spoke to (he, him) in a dream.

98. Diagraming Adjective Clauses

An adjective clause is a relative clause that modifies a noun or pronoun. Such a clause is diagramed below the main clause. A broken line connects the relative pronoun to its antecedent, which is the word that the clause modifies. No word is written on the connecting line; for the relative pronoun is the connecting word, and it also has a function within the relative clause.

I chose the game (that my aunt bought in the toy department).

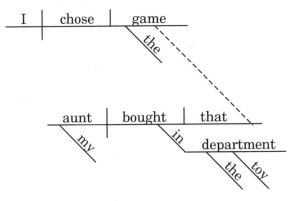

Adjective clauses can modify subjects, objects, or predicate nominatives. Study the following examples.

Adjective clause modifying a subject:

Saul (who had persecuted Christians) was converted.

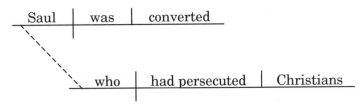

Adjective clause modifying a direct object:
The apostles feared the man (who had persecuted them).

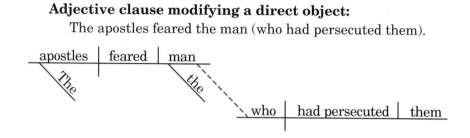

Adjective clause modifying a predicate nominative:
Barnabas was the man (who reassured them).

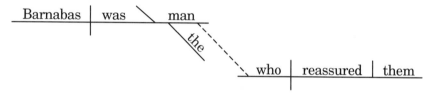

Relative pronouns may have different functions in relative clauses. They may be used as subjects, objects, predicate nominatives, or modifiers.

Subjects: who, which, that (nominative case)
Objects: whom, which, that (objective case)
Modifier: whose (possessive case)

Relative pronoun used as a subject:
This is the man <u>who</u> preached the Gospel boldly.

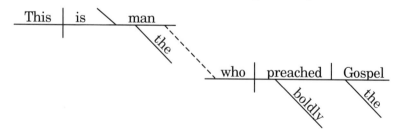

Relative pronoun used as a direct object:

This is the man <u>whom</u> the Lord stopped.

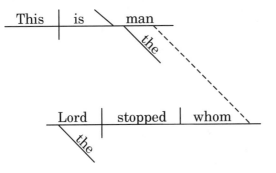

Relative pronoun used as a predicate nominative:

He was not the same man <u>that</u> he had been before.

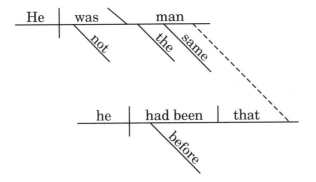

Relative pronoun used as a modifier:

He was a man <u>whose</u> heart had been changed.

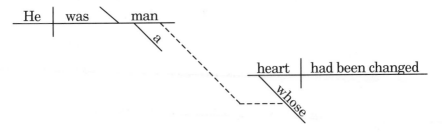

- An adjective clause is diagramed below the main clause. A broken line connects the relative pronoun to its antecedent, which is the word that the clause modifies.

Class Practice

Diagram the following sentences at the chalkboard.
1. Ananias helped Saul, who was blind.
2. Ananias, who trusted God, encouraged Saul.
3. Saul, who had been a persecutor, became a Christian.
4. Saul was preaching Jesus, whose followers he had joined.
5. The people who heard Saul were amazed.

Written Exercises

Diagram the following sentences. You do not need to diagram the underlined words.
1. Jewish rulers who were angry <u>with Saul</u> placed guards <u>at the city gates</u>.
2. His friends found a basket that was large <u>enough to hold a man</u>.
3. Saul was the man whom the apostles feared.
4. Barnabas was the one who brought Saul <u>to the apostles</u>.
5. The man whose former violence had frightened them was received <u>gladly</u>.
6. <u>In Jerusalem</u> Saul <u>boldly</u> preached Jesus, whom he was serving.
7. The Grecians who hated Saul were plotting <u>against him</u>.
8. <u>Then</u> Saul, who was a native of Tarsus, returned <u>to his home town</u>.
9. The Christians who had been persecuted <u>now</u> had rest.
10. Saul became a man whom the Lord used <u>mightily</u>.

Review Exercises

Copy these sentences, and add the missing commas, apostrophes, hyphens, colons, and semicolons. [81–87]
1. Marie bought them at a self service stand for ninety five cents.
2. The sessions begin at 9 00 A.M. and 2 00 P.M.
3. We memorized Psalm 119 1 8.
4. June made raisin cookies chocolate drops and pinwheels and Lisa made rolls doughnuts and bread.

5. All of Junes cookies were sold before lunch and most of Lisas bread was gone by evening.

6. Isnt her address Route 2 Box 114 Allentown Pennsylvania?

Challenge Exercises

Diagram the following sentences. They include adjective clauses that modify indirect objects and objects of prepositions.

Examples:

The king issued the command to Haman, who had made the suggestion.

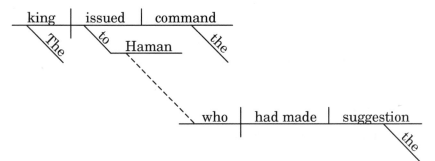

Haman gave Mordecai, whom he despised, a great honor.

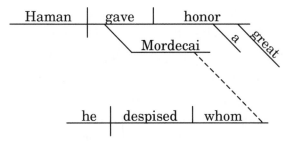

1. Esther made her request to Ahasuerus, who was greatly astonished.

2. The king gave Haman, who had plotted against the Jews, the punishment that he deserved.

3. Ahasuerus gave Mordecai, who had saved his life, Haman's position.

4. The king gave Haman's house to Esther, who was the queen.

---

99. Chapter 8 Review

Class Practice

A. Give the definition of an adjective.

B. Tell whether each underlined word is an *adjective* or a *pronoun*. If it is an adjective, tell which word it modifies.
   1. We had <u>our</u> test yesterday.
   2. <u>That</u> was not a hard test.
   3. <u>This</u> question is about the planets.
   4. <u>Theirs</u> lasted about a half hour.

C. Replace the underlined words with more descriptive adjectives.
   1. Many deep-sea fish look <u>funny</u>.
   2. Raising produce is a <u>good</u> work.
   3. Aunt Mary usually makes <u>good</u> meals.
   4. We found some <u>real</u> bargains at the sale.

D. Give the comparative and superlative degrees of these adjectives.
   1. glad   3. ill   5. much
   2. late   4. pleasant   6. good

E. Tell which of the following paragraphs is a description. Discuss the descriptive words it uses.

   1.   Popcorn is easy to raise. To plant it, make rows in loose, rich soil and drop the popcorn kernels three at a place, about six inches apart. Keep the young plants well hoed. Popcorn ears are ready to pick when the husk is dry. After they are picked, let them dry until the kernels shell off easily. Then they are ready to pop.

   2.   Oily black smoke poured upward into the bright blue sky. From under the eaves, orange-red flames darted out eagerly, like angry serpents' tongues. The roaring fire was a savage, snarling giant. Weird, crackling explosions erupted from deep inside the old mill, which shivered and trembled in its agony. Far off in the village, the siren began to scream the alarm—hurry! hurry!

Written Exercises

A. Copy all the descriptive adjectives. Write *P* after each predicate adjective and *A* after each appositive adjective.
1. The hottest, swiftest planet is Mercury.
2. Of all the planets, Venus is the brightest.
3. Jupiter, large and bright, orbits the sun once every twelve years.
4. Saturn with its huge rings appears beautiful.

B. Write the correct form of each word in parentheses.
1. Uranus is a (large) planet, but Saturn is (large) than Uranus.
2. Jupiter is the (large) of the nine planets.
3. Of Uranus and Neptune, Neptune is (far) away from the sun.
4. Of all the planets, Pluto is usually the (far) away from the sun.
5. Sometimes Pluto is (close) to the sun than Neptune is.
6. Rigel and Betelgeuse are (bright) stars in the constellation of Orion, but Betelgeuse is the (bright) of the two.
7. Of all the stars, Sirius is the (bright).

Saturn

PhotoDisc by Getty Images

C. Copy each adjective phrase. After it, write the noun it modifies.
1. Jacob gave Joseph a coat of many colors.
2. Joseph's brothers tended large flocks of sheep.
3. Soon a caravan of camels and merchants came along.

D. Copy each adjective clause, and underline the relative pronoun.
1. The brothers were jealous of the boy who had a coat of many colors.
2. The dreams which God sent to Joseph had a special meaning.
3. The dreams that made the brothers angry came true in Egypt.
4. The boy whom they hated became a leader in Egypt.
5. The brothers who had sold Joseph repented of their wickedness.

E. Diagram these sentences.
1. The Word of the Lord is pure.
2. Praise the Lord who created all things.
3. The Lord is merciful and gracious.
4. The moon, large and bright, is the ruler of the night.
5. The soft, silvery moonlight brightens the dark night.

F. Write a more descriptive verb to replace *looked* or *looked at* in each sentence.

| gazed | peered | viewed | spied |
| stared | inspected | scanned | beheld |

1. Moses sent twelve men, who <u>looked</u> on the land of Canaan for forty days.
2. If anyone <u>looked at</u> the serpent of brass, he lived.
3. Moses <u>looked at</u> the land of Canaan from a mountaintop.
4. John <u>looked</u> into the empty sepulcher.
5. When Jesus ascended, the disciples stood and <u>looked</u> toward heaven.

————————————

Phrases

Forms of Comparison

Complex Sentences

Clauses

Poetry

Rhyme   Rhythm

Figures of Speech

Chapter Nine
Working With Adverbs
Studying Poetry

An
adverb is a
word that modifies a verb,
an adjective, or another
adverb.

Oh that men would praise the LORD for his goodness,
and for his wonderful works to the children of men!

Psalm 107:15

100. Poetry

There are two main types of literature: *prose* and *poetry*. Prose is written in sentences and paragraphs. Stories, reports, and descriptions are three examples of prose.

Poetry is writing put into a special form that is pleasing to hear. Poetry is not written in sentences and paragraphs, but in lines and stanzas. Each line of a poem begins with a capital letter. Study the following example.

Who Hath a Book

Who hath a book
    Has friends at hand,
And gold and gear
    At his command;
And rich estates,
    If he but look,
Are held by him
    Who hath a book.

Who hath a book
    Has but to read,
And he may be
    A king, indeed;
His kingdom is
    His inglenook—
All this is his
    Who hath a book.
    —Wilbur D. Nesbit

Most poems make use of *rhyme*. Rhyming words have endings that sound alike, such as *right—might, sing—bring,* and *fine—combine.* In the poem above, every other line rhymes: *hand—command; look—book; read—indeed;* and *inglenook—book.*

Most poems also make use of *rhythm*. Rhythm is a regular pattern of accented and unaccented syllables, with a certain number of syllables in each line. In the poem above, each line has four syllables. The first and third syllables are unaccented, and the second and fourth syllables are accented.

⌣ ′ ⌣ ′
Who hath a book

⌣ ′ ⌣ ′
Has friends at hand,

Rhythm and rhyme work together to produce a certain feeling or mood. The even rhythm of this poem helps to give a feeling of study and thoughtfulness. The short lines add a feeling of happiness or thankfulness.

Poetry usually has more meaning packed into a few words than prose does. Poetry is rich and concentrated. The reader needs to meditate on the words to extract all their meaning and beauty. For example, the poem above says, "Who hath a book has friends at hand." What does this mean? As we read a good story, we live with the characters and share their struggles and their joys. We get to know them so well that they seem like familiar friends. We learn many things from the people in good stories, just as we learn many helpful things from being with good friends.

The poem also says that a person with a book has "gold and gear at his command." How might this be true? Many books have information that is as valuable as gold. If a book explains how to do something, it is as useful as gear (tools or equipment). The poem gives many other hints like this that stir our thinking.

Poetry makes special use of descriptive words and figurative language to stir the reader's imagination. Consider these lines: "And he may be a king, indeed; / His kingdom is his inglenook." Of course, having a book does not actually make the reader a king. What is meant by this figure of speech? If a person reads about a king, he identifies with the king and "rules" with him. Also, an inglenook (reading corner) with a wealth of good books is like a kingdom with a wealth of natural riches— all there for the reader to enjoy. These figures of speech are metaphors. Various kinds of figures of speech may be used in a poem.

Poetry is easier to memorize than prose. A poem can be set to music and sung with a group. The special beauty of poetry can affect our feelings and leave deep, meaningful impressions on us.

- Poetry is a special kind of writing arranged in lines and stanzas. Each line begins with a capital letter.

- Most poetry makes use of rhythm and rhyme.

- Good poetry is rich with meaningful, descriptive words and figurative language.

Class Practice

Read the poem below, and do these exercises.

1. Which lines rhyme in each stanza?
2. a. How many syllables are in lines 1, 3, 5, and 7?
   b. How many syllables are in lines 2, 4, 6, and 8?
3. Does each line begin with an accented syllable or an unaccented one?
4. What feelings does this poem give you?
5. This poem describes things according to some of the five senses.
   a. Tell which words describe things you can see.
   b. Tell which phrases describe things you can hear; things you can smell; something you can feel.
6. Find the phrase that speaks of a plant as doing something a person could do. What feeling does this phrase add to the poem?
7. The poet wrote, "I lost them yesterday" and "I cast them all away." What is the difference between *losing* one's worries and *casting* them away?
8. Why is it that "ill thoughts die and good are born" out in the fields?

Out in the Fields With God

The little cares that fretted me,
    I lost them yesterday,
Among the fields, above the sea,
    Among the winds at play;
Among the lowing of the herds,
    The rustling of the trees,
Among the singing of the birds,
    The humming of the bees.

The fears of what may come to pass,
    I cast them all away,
Among the clover-scented grass,
    Among the new-mown hay;
Among the husking of the corn,
    Where drowsy posies nod,
Where ill thoughts die and good are born—
    Out in the fields with God.

—Elizabeth Browning

Written Exercises

A. Read the poem below, and do these exercises.
1. Which words in this poem rhyme? Write them in pairs.
2. a. How many syllables are in the first line of the poem?
   b. How many syllables are in the second line?
   c. Does the whole poem follow this pattern in the number of syllables per line?
3. What feeling does this poem give to you?
4. In your own words, tell the main lesson of this poem.

Mr. Meant-To

Mr. Meant-To has a comrade,
And his name is Didn't-Do;
Have you ever chanced to meet them?
Did they ever call on you?

These two fellows live together
In the house of Never-Win,
And I'm told that it is shadowed
By the cloud of Might-Have-Been.

—Anonymous

B. Find a poem that you enjoy, and be prepared to read it in class. Your appreciation for this poem should help to prepare you for writing your own poem later in this chapter.

Review Exercises

Answer the following questions. [75, 79]
1. What are the three main parts of a story?
2. Which part of a story should describe the story conflict?
3. Which part should arouse the reader's interest?
4. Which part should conclude the story?
5. What is another term for conversation in a story?
6. In written conversation, when should you begin a new paragraph?

Adverbs

Adverbs modify verbs, adjectives, and other adverbs.

How	When	Where	To What Degree
well	now	here	very
loudly	yesterday	there	almost
cheerfully	later	in	unusually
fast	soon	out	moderately
silently	usually	away	so
how	when	where	too
briefly	often	around	surely
softly	then	outside	rather
			quite
			partly

101. Adverbs

Adverbs are words that modify verbs, adjectives, and other adverbs. To remember the definition of adverbs, think of this statement: "Adverbs add to verbs." In this lesson you will study adverbs that modify verbs, and in the next lesson you will study adverbs that modify adjectives and adverbs.

Adverbs tell *how, when, where,* and *to what degree.*

> They read the Bible stories <u>eagerly</u>.
> (*Eagerly* tells *how* they read.)

> Will you come <u>tomorrow</u>?
> (*Tomorrow* tells *when* you will come.)

> We climbed steadily <u>upward</u>.
> (*Upward* tells *where* we climbed.)

Many adverbs end with *-ly*. They are formed by adding *-ly* to adjectives.

quiet—quietly   former—formerly
hasty—hastily   exceeding—exceedingly

The words *not, never, ever, almost, always, hardly, scarcely,* and *seldom* are always adverbs. These adverbs may come between the parts of a verb phrase. But they are not part of the verb phrase; they only modify it.

The cat <u>can</u> **never** <u>climb</u> down easily.
The car <u>had</u> **almost** <u>hit</u> a pole.

The words *how, when, where,* and *why* are also adverbs. These words ask *how, when, where,* and *why* rather than telling. When you answer questions beginning with these adverbs, you often use other adverbs.

<u>How</u> does he write?   He writes <u>well</u>.
<u>When</u> will they come?   They will come <u>tomorrow</u>.
<u>Where</u> are the children?   They are <u>here</u>.

If an adverb modifies a verb, it may be found at different places in a sentence. It may come just before or after the verb. It may come at the beginning of a sentence or at the end. The adverbs in the following sentences are in italics. The verbs they modify are underlined twice.

Harold *always* <u>sits</u> there.
The mower <u>works</u> *better now.*
Tomorrow we <u>shall work</u> *harder.*
Overhead, the wind <u>howled</u> *fiercely.*

An adverb is diagramed on a slanted line beneath the verb it modifies. This is true no matter where the adverb is in the sentence. In a sentence with *cannot,* the word *not* is an adverb and must be diagramed separately. If there is a contraction ending with *n't,* the *n't* is changed to *not* and diagramed separately.

Quietly the children entered the room.

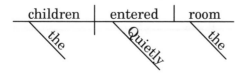

I already saw a robin.

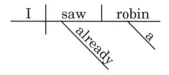

I cannot hear you well.
I can't hear you well.

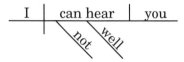

- Adverbs modify verbs, adjectives, and other adverbs. They tell *how, when, where,* and *to what degree.*

- Many adverbs end with *-ly.*

- The words *not, never, ever, almost, always, hardly, scarcely,* and *seldom* are adverbs that may interrupt a verb phrase.

- An adverb may be found at different places in a sentence.

Class Practice

A. Tell which words are adverbs. Tell whether they tell *how, when,* or *where.* (Negative words like *not* and *hardly* tell *how.* *Never* tells *when.*)
1. Come back here again soon.
2. We should always live peaceably.
3. We could not go anywhere.
4. Eagerly the children came inside.
5. The healed man had never walked before.
6. Then I could scarcely see.
7. How are new pencils made?

B. Read each sentence, putting the underlined adverb at the beginning of the sentence. Notice that it still modifies the verb.
1. The robin swallowed the worm <u>hungrily</u>.
2. The wild geese were honking <u>loudly</u>.
3. We went to the zoo <u>yesterday</u>.

C. Diagram the following sentences on the chalkboard.
1. I can't find my pen today.
2. The lost pen must surely be somewhere nearby.
3. Where should we work now?

Written Exercises

A. Copy each adverb, and write whether it tells *how, when,* or *where.* (Negative words like *not* and *hardly* tell *how. Never* tells *when.*)
1. Father carefully carried the burning rags outside.
2. We cannot find them anywhere.
3. The Lord will never leave us nor forsake us.
4. Afterward, the men earnestly discussed the matter.
5. Soon we shall be writing faster and better.
6. The settlers originally built the dam here.
7. Promptly, the old dog faithfully followed along.
8. A lazy person seldom works willingly.
9. Immediately the wind pulled the kite upward.
10. Finally the train moved forward again.
11. We could hardly finish the job sooner.

B. Diagram these sentences.
1. Later we shall carefully consider the results.
2. An owl was hooting mournfully nearby.
3. We cannot go there tomorrow.
4. The man patiently waited awhile.
5. I barely saw it there.
6. Why did you leave early?

C. Write four adverbs that tell how students should do their lessons.

D. Write four adverbs that tell when we do our lessons.

Review Exercises

Diagram the following sentences.
1. Do you always give the kittens table scraps?
2. See these lovely, small white snowdrops here!

3. Rosa's favorite flowers are rhododendrons.

4. The flowers which we saw there yesterday were primroses and zinnias.

---

102. Adverbs of Degree

You know that "adverbs add to verbs." Adverbs can also modify adjectives and other adverbs. When they are used in this way, they are called *adverbs of degree* because they usually tell *to what degree*. These adverbs include words like *very, so, too, rather, quite, surely, partly, unusually,* and *extremely.*

> Wilbur tore the package open <u>too</u> hastily.
>> *Hastily* modifies *tore* by telling *how. Too* modifies *hastily* by telling *to what degree* Wilbur acted hastily.

> The barrel was <u>practically</u> empty.
>> *Empty* is a predicate adjective modifying *barrel. Practically* tells *to what degree* the barrel was empty.

An adverb of degree comes just before the word it modifies. So whenever you find two modifiers together, you must decide which word each one modifies. You can tell by saying each modifier with the word you think it may modify, and asking, "Is this sensible? Is it what the sentence really means?"

> Plants in the tundra grow <u>incredibly slowly</u>.
>> **Think:** Grow incredibly? No; *incredibly* does not modify *grow.*
>>
>> Grow slowly? Yes; *slowly* is an adverb modifying the verb *grow.*
>>
>> Incredibly slowly? Yes; *incredibly* is an adverb modifying *slowly.*

> Several <u>especially large</u> peaches had ripened.
>> **Think:** Especially peaches? No; *especially* does not modify *peaches.*
>>
>> Large peaches? Yes; *large* is an adjective modifying the noun *peaches.*
>>
>> Especially large? Yes; *especially* is an adverb modifying *large.*

Father explained the reason, and we understood <u>fully then</u>.

Think: Understood fully? Yes; *fully* is an adverb modifying the verb *understood*.

Fully then? No; *fully* does not modify *then*.

Understood then? Yes; *then* is an adverb modifying *understood*.

Both adverbs modify the verb. There is no adverb modifying an adjective or another adverb.

Good writers use adverbs of degree sparingly, for these adverbs usually add little meaning to a sentence. This is especially true of adverbs like *very, really, surely,* and *awfully.* You will usually do better if you choose specific nouns, verbs, and adjectives to say exactly what you mean.

Poor: The rich man lived in an <u>awfully big house</u>.
Better: The rich man lived in a <u>mansion</u>.

Poor: Grandmother made a <u>really good</u> dinner.
Better: Grandmother made a <u>delicious</u> dinner.

Poor: The boys <u>ran very fast</u> to Father's truck.
Better: The boys <u>raced</u> to Father's truck.

- Adverbs of degree modify adjectives and other adverbs. They tell *to what degree*.

- Good writers use adverbs of degree sparingly.

Class Practice

A. Find each adverb of degree, tell which word it modifies, and tell what part of speech the modified word is.
   1. In 1967, an unusually long train traveled about 150 miles in West Virginia.
   2. Moving at twelve miles per hour, the five hundred coal cars and six engines traveled quite slowly.
   3. It took twenty minutes for that very long train to pass by.
   4. A person could count the cars rather easily.
   5. A train that takes so much time to pass has too many cars!

B. Give an adverb of degree for the blank. How many different ones can you think of?

The wind was ——— cold.

C. Replace the underlined words with more effective ones. Choose from the list below.

immaculate	dashed	rushed	rudely
spotless	scurried	surged	neatly
continually	sped	carelessly	frequently
thoroughly			

1. Loren and Mark <u>ran very fast</u> to the bus.
2. Joseph did his job <u>really badly</u>.
3. He did it <u>quite well</u> after Mother helped him.
4. The floor was <u>surely clean</u>.
5. Janelle visits her grandmother <u>quite often</u>.

Written Exercises

A. Copy each adverb of degree and the word it modifies.
1. Royal Gorge is spanned by an extremely high suspension bridge.
2. The Verrazano-Narrows bridge in New York is sixty feet longer than the very famous Golden Gate Bridge in San Francisco.
3. In winter, Alaskan seals swim amazingly far to warmer seas.
4. The unusually long round trip is about six thousand miles.
5. A Persian poet named Firdausi once wrote a poem with an extremely large number of verses.
6. The Persian sultan quite generously offered one gold piece for every verse that Firdausi wrote.
7. In thirty-five years, the very ambitious poet wrote sixty thousand verses.
8. His poem filled 2,084 pages in nine rather heavy books.
9. This exceptionally long poem, "Book of Kings," was a complete history of Persia.
10. The poet was quite unhappy when the sultan sent him sixty thousand pieces of silver instead of the more valuable gold pieces.
11. He was so upset that he quite foolishly gave away all the silver pieces.
12. Too many people are like this man; they depend almost entirely on earthly things to bring them happiness.

B. Write an adverb of degree for each blank. Do not use *very, really, surely,* or *awfully.*
1. The work went —— fast.
2. The road seemed —— long.
3. He spoke —— calmly.

C. Write a more effective word from the list to replace each underlined phrase.

pleasant	bulky	worn-out
friendly	immense	briskly
towering	antique	speedy
gigantic		

1. The <u>very big</u> skyscrapers in Malaysia became the world's tallest buildings in 1998.
2. The <u>very old</u> table sold for several hundred dollars.
3. Every morning we walked <u>very fast</u> to school.
4. Mrs. Rogers is a <u>very nice</u> old lady, and I like to visit her.
5. We had a <u>very fast</u> ride on the electric train.

Review Exercises

Copy the three sentences with direct quotations. Use correct capitalization and punctuation. [77–80]
1. how can a dog help a blind person asked mark
2. charles said that a dog is trained before it is given to a blind person
3. susan said the blind person must then be trained to work with the dog
4. each dog said jonathan learns to obey several simple commands
5. some of the commands are *forward, left, right, stop,* and *sit*

---

103. Diagraming Adverbs of Degree

Adverbs that modify adjectives or other adverbs are called adverbs of degree. An adverb of degree is diagramed beneath the word it modifies. But before you diagram a modifier, remember to say it with the other word to be sure it makes sense. Study the following examples.

Adverb of degree modifying an adjective, which modifies a subject:

A partly finished sketch was found.

> **Think:** Partly sketch? No; *partly* does not modify *sketch*.
>
> Finished sketch? Yes; *finished* modifies *sketch*.
>
> Partly finished? Yes; *partly* modifies *finished*.

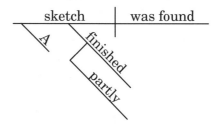

Adverb of degree modifying an adjective, which modifies a direct object:

Grandfather brought an unusually large watermelon.

> **Think:** Unusually watermelon? No; *unusually* does not modify *watermelon*.
>
> Large watermelon? Yes; *large* modifies *watermelon*.
>
> Unusually large? Yes; *unusually* modifies *large*.

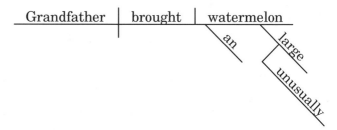

Adverb of degree modifying an adjective, which modifies a predicate nominative:

Your uncle is a rather tall man.

> **Think:** Uncle is man? Yes; *man* is a predicate nominative.
>
> Rather man? No; *rather* does not modify *man*.
>
> Tall man? Yes; *tall* modifies *man*.
>
> Rather tall? Yes; *rather* modifies *tall*.

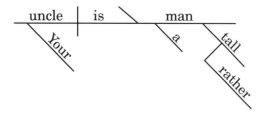

Adverb of degree modifying a predicate adjective:

Beth is feeling quite well again.

Think: Beth is well? Yes; *well* is a predicate adjective.

Feeling quite? No; *quite* does not modify the verb.

Quite well? Yes; *quite* modifies *well*.

Well again? This sounds reasonable, but *again* can also be moved to another place in the sentence: *Beth is again feeling quite well.*

So *again* must be a modifier of the verb.

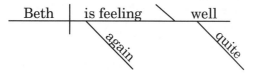

Adverb of degree modifying another adverb:

The peaches will ripen very soon.

Think: Will ripen very? No; *very* does not modify *will ripen*.

Will ripen soon? Yes; *soon* modifies *will ripen*.

Very soon? Yes; *very* modifies *soon*.

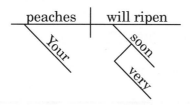

> • An adverb of degree is diagramed beneath the word it modifies.

Class Practice

Diagram these sentences at the chalkboard.

1. It is raining unusually fast now.
2. The old lantern was not very bright.
3. That star has a somewhat bluish color.
4. The remarkably short usher cordially greeted the visitors.
5. The little kittens became skilled mousers incredibly soon.

Written Exercises

A. Copy each adverb of degree and the word it modifies.

1. Yesterday it rained unusually hard.
2. Solomon was a very rich man.
3. He was exceedingly wise, but he acted quite foolishly.
4. It is rather uncertain whether Solomon repented.
5. Gerald can write especially well.
6. It is extremely cold at the South Pole.
7. These partly cooked hamburgers are too raw.
8. Why did you take them off so soon?
9. The roses are surely beautiful this year.
10. Only later, Charles grew seriously interested.

B. Diagram these sentences.

1. Too many chickens are dying.
2. How can Joel figure so accurately?
3. The telephone rang almost immediately.
4. A skyscraper is a very tall building.
5. We are almost there now.
6. It is quite cool today.
7. A rather tall tree blew over.
8. The boys left too soon.

Review Exercises

Write the kind of pronoun that each underlined word is: *personal, demonstrative, indefinite, interrogative,* or *relative.* Also write *archaic* for the archaic pronoun. [61–69]

1. <u>What</u> kind of dog is it?

2. <u>That</u> is a German shepherd.
3. The trainers are Mr. May and <u>he</u>.
4. <u>Both</u> are training dogs to help blind people.
5. The person <u>whom</u> you saw was blind from birth.
6. <u>Thou</u> shalt not put a stumbling block before the blind.

---

104. Rhythm in Poetry

Most poems have a regular pattern of accented and unaccented syllables. This is called rhythm. Different patterns of rhythm give different feelings or moods to poetry. Read the following lines. What feeling does the rhythm help to produce?

> Father, in my life's young morning,
> May Thy Word direct my way;
> Let me heed each gracious warning,
> Lest my feet should go astray.

In the poem above, each line begins with an accented syllable and alternates between one accented and one unaccented syllable. This pattern often gives a serious mood to a poem. Notice how the rhythm pattern is well suited to the lines above.

The accented syllables are the most important syllables in the pattern of rhythm. They are used to divide lines of poetry into units called feet. A *foot* of poetry contains one accented syllable and the unaccented syllables associated with it. Usually each line of poetry has the same number of syllables, or at least the lines follow a pattern in the number of syllables they have.

Accents in poetry usually follow the natural pattern of speech. One-syllable words are arranged so that the most important words are accented, and multisyllable words are arranged so that the accents fall on syllables normally accented. Study the four patterns of poetry and the examples given on the next page.

The first rhythm pattern below is the *iambic* (ī·am′·bik) pattern. The iambic foot has one *unaccented* syllable followed by one *accented* syllable. This pattern is the most common one used in our language. Its light, cheerful rhythm is well suited to poems with a theme of joy or beauty. Study the following lines.

> ˘ ′ ˘ ′ ˘ ′ ˘ ′
> I wandered lonely as a cloud
> ˘ ′ ˘ ′ ˘ ′ ˘ ′
> That floats on high o'er vales and hills
> ˘ ′ ˘ ′ ˘ ′ ˘ ′
> When all at once I saw a crowd—
> ˘ ′ ˘ ′ ˘ ′ ˘ ′
> A host of golden daffodils.
> —William Wordsworth

The second rhythm pattern is the *trochaic* (trō·kā′·ik) pattern. The trochaic foot has one *accented* syllable followed by one *unaccented* syllable. (Iambic and trochaic patterns are opposite.) Trochaic rhythm is the pattern used in the first example of poetry in the lesson. This pattern is well suited to deep thoughts and sober words. It is also suited to feelings of earnestness and enthusiasm.

> ′ ˘ ′ ˘ ′ ˘ ′ ˘
> Courage, brother! Do not stumble,
> ′ ˘ ′ ˘ ′ ˘ ′
> Though thy path be dark as night;
> ′ ˘ ′ ˘ ′ ˘ ′ ˘
> There's a star to guide the humble—
> ′ ˘ ′ ˘ ′ ˘ ′
> Trust in God and do the right.

In the third pattern, each foot has two *unaccented* syllables followed by one *accented* syllable. This pattern gives the lines a light, flowing style.

> ˘ ˘ ′ ˘ ˘ ′ ˘ ˘ ′
> There's a land that is fairer than day,
> ˘ ˘ ′ ˘ ˘ ′ ˘ ˘ ′
> And by faith we can see it afar;
> ˘ ˘ ′ ˘ ˘ ′ ˘ ˘ ′
> For the Father waits over the way
> ˘ ˘ ′ ˘ ˘ ′ ˘ ˘ ′
> To prepare us a dwelling place there.

In the fourth pattern, each foot has one *accented* syllable followed by two *unaccented* syllables. (The third and fourth patterns are opposite.) The fourth pattern is well suited to a poem with a happy, delightful mood.

/ ᵕ ᵕ / ᵕ ᵕ / ᵕ ᵕ /
I am so glad that our Father in heav'n
/ ᵕ ᵕ / ᵕ ᵕ / ᵕ ᵕ /
Tells of His love in the Book He has giv'n;
/ ᵕ ᵕ / ᵕ ᵕ / ᵕ ᵕ /
Wonderful things in the Bible I see,
/ ᵕ ᵕ / ᵕ ᵕ / ᵕ ᵕ /
This is the dearest, that Jesus loves me.

A good poet makes careful use of rhythm to produce just the right mood for the message of his poem.

- Different patterns of rhythm give different feelings or moods to poetry.

- In the iambic pattern, each foot has one unaccented syllable followed by one accented syllable.

- In the trochaic pattern, each foot has one accented syllable followed by one unaccented syllable.

- In the third rhythm pattern, each foot has two unaccented syllables followed by one accented syllable.

- In the fourth rhythm pattern, each foot has one accented syllable followed by two unaccented syllables.

Class Practice

A. Tell what pattern of rhythm is used in each poem.

1. **What Bird Am I?**
Largest of earth's birds am I,
I have wings but cannot fly;
To escape I run with speed,
Sometimes swifter than a steed.

2. **What Bird Am I?**
I am an early riser,
My call is loud and clear;
When Jesus was on trial,
I must have been quite near.

3.   **What Bird Am I?**
Harmless and gentle, the symbol of peace,
Used by the poor for their firstborn's release;
Jesus once said that His servants should be
Wise as the serpents and harmless as we.

4.   **With Your Might**
If you do with your might what your hand finds to do,
You will find work a pleasure and soon you'll be through;
If you murmur and whine and find ways to delay,
Not a thing will get done and you'll spoil the whole day.

B. On the chalkboard, mark the rhythm pattern of each line. Then tell which line fits best for the last line of each poem.

1.   **A Snowfall**
When I awoke this morning,
    The sun was very bright.
I hurried to the window,
    Unconscious of the sight
That held my breath in rapture—

    _____
                                —Velma Orcutt

a. How white was everything in sight.
b. The secret of the night.
c. Snow had fallen in the night.

2.   **Diligence**
Do each task with diligence,
    Whether large or small;
What seems insignificant

    _____

a. May be the best job of all.
b. The best job may be of all.
c. May be best of all.

Written Exercises

A. Write the letter of the line that fits best for the last line of each stanza. Then copy the first line of the stanza, and mark the rhythm pattern.

1. There dwelt a miller, hale and bold,
       Beside the River Dee;
   He wrought and sang from morn till night,

   _____

   a. No other man as blithe as he.
   b. No lark more blithe than he.
   c. No one was as blithe as he.

2. Toiling through the changing seasons
       In the sunshine and the rain,
   Earnest prayer and faithful labor

   _____

   a. Yield a harvest of golden grain.
   b. Provide a wealth of golden grain.
   c. Yield a wealth of golden grain.

3. God gives the milk, but not the pail.
   God gives the wood, but not the nail.
   God gives the fish, but not the hook.
   God gives the food, but not the cook.
   He gives each one a task to do,

   _____

   a. And then the rest is up to you.
   b. All of the rest is dependent on you.
   c. All the rest is up to you.

4. One honest John Thompkins, a hedger and ditcher,
   Although he was poor, did not wish to be richer;
   For all such vain wishes in him were prevented

   _____

   a. Because he was always contented.
   b. He had a habit of being contented.
   c. By means of the habit of being contented.

B. Name the rhythm pattern of each pair of lines (*iambic* or *trochaic*). Then write a line of your own to match that rhythm. Your line does not have to rhyme with the lines that are given. (This practice will be helpful when you write an original poem later in this chapter.)

1. God sent sparkling snow last night,
   Clean and spotless, pure and white . . .

2. My mother is so kind and true,
   She loves to help in all I do . . .

3. Spring is here, with March winds blowing,
   Bluebirds singing, flowers growing . . .

Review Exercises

Copy one wrong word in each sentence, and write the correct word beside it. [33]

1. Some outlines must have titles.
2. The main topics of an outline are marked with Arabic numerals.
3. Subtopics are marked with small letters.
4. Points are marked with Roman numerals.
5. A comma is placed after each numeral or capital letter that marks a division on the outline.
6. Each division of an outline should have at least three parts.

---

105. Forms of Comparison for Adverbs

Adverbs have three degrees of comparison, the same as adjectives. They are the positive degree, the comparative degree, and the superlative degree.

Positive	Comparative	Superlative
fast	faster	fastest
swiftly	more swiftly	most swiftly

The positive degree shows no comparison. The comparative degree is used to compare *two* actions. The superlative degree is used to compare *more than two* actions.

For some short adverbs, the comparative and superlative degrees are formed by adding -er and -est.

Positive	Comparative	Superlative
deep	deeper	deepest
late	later	latest
high	higher	highest

But many adverbs end with -ly. For this reason, more and most are used to form the comparative and superlative degrees of most adverbs. The suffixes -er and -est are not used with many adverbs because words like slowlier and carefulliest would sound awkward. Check a dictionary if you are not sure whether -er and -est may be added.

Positive	Comparative	Superlative
slowly	more slowly	most slowly
carefully	more carefully	most carefully
easily	more easily	most easily
loudly	more loudly	most loudly

Exceptions:

early	earlier	earliest
lively	livelier	liveliest

Be careful to use the correct degree of comparison. Use the comparative degree for comparing two actions. Use the superlative degree for comparing more than two actions.

Incorrect: Of the two machines, this one runs <u>most slowly</u>.
Correct: Of the two machines, this one runs <u>more slowly</u>.

Incorrect: Roger runs the <u>fastest</u> of my two brothers.
Correct: Roger runs the <u>faster</u> of my two brothers.

Do not add -er to an adverb and also use more with it, or add -est and also use most with it.

Incorrect: Brian went <u>more farther</u> than Marcus did.
Correct: Brian went <u>farther</u> than Marcus did.

Some adverbs have irregular forms of comparison. Check a dictionary if you are not sure how to form the comparative and superlative degrees of an adverb.

Positive	Comparative	Superlative
well	better	best
badly	worse	worst
ill	worse	worst
little	less	least
much	more	most
far	farther	farthest

Some words in the list above can be used as adjectives or adverbs. Their use in a sentence determines what part of speech they are.

- The positive degree of adverbs expresses no comparison.

- The comparative degree is used to compare two actions. It is formed by adding -er or by using the word *more*.

- The superlative degree is used to compare more than two actions. It is formed by adding -est or by using the word *most*.

- Do not use the superlative degree when only two actions are compared. Do not use *more* and *most* with the -er and -est endings.

- Check a dictionary if you are not sure how to form the comparative and superlative degrees of an adverb.

Class Practice

A. Give the comparative and superlative degrees of these adverbs.
1. swiftly   3. soon   5. happily
2. well   4. slowly   6. high

B. Tell how to correct the following sentences. Practice reading each one correctly.
1. Of the twins, Marjorie works fastest.
2. This pony walks slowlier than that one.
3. She sings more softlier than her sister.
4. The smallest boy talked the most loudliest of all.
5. Brenda spoke the politeliest of all the girls.
6. This cake pan should be floured the most lightly of the two.
7. Which bakes most quickly, an oatmeal cake or a carrot cake?
8. The peanut butter cookies baked the quickliest of all.

Written Exercises

A. Write the three degrees of comparison for each adverb.

1. warmly	5. ill	9. abundantly	13. perfectly
2. much	6. often	10. interestingly	14. little
3. hard	7. well	11. naturally	15. tenderly
4. softly	8. far	12. smoothly	16. richly

B. Write the correct form of each word in parentheses.
1. Read it (clearly) this time than you did the first time.
2. Lisa reads (well) this year than last year.
3. Joseph writes the (well) of all the pupils in his class.
4. Ronald worked (hard) than Robert, but Robert worked the (thoroughly) of the two.
5. Father worked the (hard) and (fast) of them all.
6. Mother can sew (swiftly) than the girls can.
7. The sinful woman loved Jesus (much) than Simon did.
8. Instead of calling (quietly) than before, Bartimaeus called even (loudly).

C. Write the correct words in parentheses.
1. Thistles grow (quicklier, more quickly) than garden vegetables.
2. Alma worked (neatlier, more neatly) than Sarah, even though Sarah worked (longer, more long).
3. Of all the boys in our class, David can jump the (higher, highest).
4. The rain started (sooner, more sooner) than we expected.
5. My arm hurt (terriblier, more terribly) than anything else I can remember.
6. Who picked strawberries (faster, fastest), June or Robin?
7. The Good Samaritan acted (neighborlier, more neighborly) than the priest or the Levite.
8. Peter and John ran toward Jesus' tomb, but John ran (faster, more faster).

Review Exercises

Copy the adjective clause in each sentence. After it, write the word the clause modifies, and put parentheses around it. [97]

Example: Many of the choices that Lot made were wrong.
Answer: that Lot made (choices)

1. The visitors whom Abraham entertained were angels.

2. The city that they came to visit was Sodom.
3. The woman who turned into a pillar of salt was Lot's wife.
4. The man whom the angels saved was Lot.
5. The little city to which Lot fled was Zoar.

---

106. Using *Good, Well,* and Negative Words

The words *good* and *well* are easily confused. *Good* is an adjective that modifies a noun or pronoun. Do not use it to modify a verb.

Correct: The farmer has a <u>good</u> horse.
Good modifies *horse.*

Incorrect: The horse works <u>good</u>.
The adjective *good* cannot modify the verb *works.*

Good may be used as a predicate adjective. Remember that a predicate adjective follows a linking verb and modifies the subject of a sentence.

Mother's apple pies are always <u>good</u>. (good pies)
The stories in this book are <u>good</u>. (good stories)

Well is usually an adverb that tells *how* something is done. *Well* can also mean "healthy," and then it is an adjective. But *good* must not be used as an adjective to mean "healthy."

Correct: The wire held <u>well</u>.
Well tells *how* the wire held.

Correct: Marcia is <u>well</u> again.
Well is a predicate adjective that means "healthy."

Incorrect: Grandmother has not been <u>good</u> ever since she had the flu.
Good must not be used to mean "healthy."

Negative words mean "not" or "almost not." Usually they change a sentence so that it has an opposite meaning. These are some common negative words.

no	never	neither	barely
not	nobody	nowhere	hardly
none	nothing		scarcely

Most negative words are adverbs or adjectives. A few, such as *none* and *nobody,* are pronouns. Some negative words are contractions formed by joining verbs with *not.*

| isn't | haven't | couldn't | can't | won't |

The contraction *ain't* is not a standard English word. Do not use it.

Do not use a *double negative.* That is, do not use two negative words to express one negative thought.

Incorrect: He <u>couldn't</u> find <u>no</u> eraser.
Correct: He <u>couldn't</u> find any eraser.
Correct: He could find <u>no</u> eraser.

Words like the following are not negative words. They may be used with negative words to express negative thoughts.

| ever | anything | something |
| any | someone | |

Often there are two ways to correct a sentence with a double negative. Study the examples below; the negative words are underlined.

Incorrect: I <u>hardly</u> <u>never</u> go.
Correct: I <u>hardly</u> ever go.
Correct: I <u>never</u> go.

Incorrect: He <u>didn't</u> see <u>nothing</u>.
Correct: He <u>didn't</u> see anything.
Correct: He saw <u>nothing</u>.

- *Good* is always an adjective.

- *Well* is usually an adverb that tells *how.* It is also an adjective that means "healthy."

- Use only one negative word to express a negative thought.

Class Practice

A. Find the mistakes in the following sentences. Practice reading each sentence correctly.
   1. The oranges didn't look well, but they tasted sweet.
   2. Harvey works slowly, but he does his work good.
   3. Titus was pale and didn't feel good.
   4. The children sang good during the program at the old people's home.
   5. My grades were well on my last two tests.

B. Correct each sentence in two ways.
   1. We never take no money with us.
   2. Thomas has hardly no potatoes to sell.
   3. The baler doesn't scarcely work.
   4. She doesn't have no brothers.

C. Read each sentence correctly. Use *barely, hardly,* or *scarcely* as the negative words.
   1. I can't hardly hear him.
   2. The boys barely never wash the dishes.
   3. Hardly no snow fell in the valley.
   4. There's not scarcely enough for everyone.

Written Exercises

A. Write the correct words in parentheses.
   1. Cynthia is only in first grade, but she reads (good, well).
   2. Aunt Fanny's pies are very (good, well).
   3. Please clean your room (good, well).
   4. Did your mother pack a (good, well) lunch for you?
   5. Joel wrote a (good, well) story.
   6. Grandmother is resting because she doesn't feel (good, well).
   7. Your grades on these papers are (good, well).
   8. A soft feather bed feels (good, well).

B. Rewrite each sentence correctly.
   1. I haven't never seen a submarine.
   2. He didn't know none of the answers.
   3. I haven't seen nobody at their house all day.
   4. We don't need no more paper now.

5. We couldn't find the books nowhere.
6. We don't need nothing more to eat.
7. Nobody knew none of the answers.
8. I haven't had none of those papers.

C. Write each sentence correctly. Use *barely, hardly,* or *scarcely* as the negative words.
1. I can't scarcely see those small letters.
2. We can't hardly concentrate with so much noise.
3. We couldn't barely get our work finished on time.
4. I can't hardly wait until tomorrow.

Review Exercises

Write the correct form of each word in parentheses. [94, 105]
1. Of the two paintings, I like this one (well).
2. The tractor we have now is (powerful) than the one we had before.
3. God told Moses not to come (close) to the burning bush.
4. Moses went to Pharaoh, but Pharaoh made the people work (hard) than before.
5. In one plague, Egypt suffered the (bad) hailstorm in its history.

---

107. Prepositional Phrases as Adverbs

A *prepositional phrase* may be used to modify a verb. When it does this, it is an *adverb phrase.* A prepositional phrase includes a preposition, its object, and any adjectives that modify the object. Study the following example.

preposition   object
↓   ↓
Jesus went <u>up the mountain</u> and prayed.

Up the mountain is a prepositional phrase used as an adverb. It tells *where* Jesus went.

Review the common prepositions listed below. For more prepositions, see the chart on page 508.

across	behind	in	to
after	down	near	under
around	for	on	up
before	from	over	with

Review the following steps to find a prepositional phrase in a sentence.

1. *Find the preposition.*
2. *Find the object of the preposition.* This is done by saying the preposition and asking *whom* or *what.* The object is always a noun or pronoun.
3. *The prepositional phrase includes all the words from the preposition to its object.* Any words in between are adjectives that modify the object. Not all phrases have adjectives.

An adverb phrase may tell *how, when, where, why,* or *to what degree.* Like other adverbs, it may be found at different places in a sentence. It may come right after the verb, or it may be found at the beginning or end of the sentence.

Ronald came <u>on his bicycle</u>. (how)
<u>In the evening</u> Ronald came. (when)
Ronald came <u>to my house</u> after supper. (where)
Ronald came <u>for a tool</u>. (why)

Adverb phrases may also modify adjectives or other adverbs. When they do this, they usually tell *how.*

Store the cabbage separately <u>from the apples</u>.
   From the apples modifies the adverb *separately* by telling *how* to store the apples separately.

The sand was pure white <u>like fresh snow</u>.
   Like fresh snow modifies the adjective *white* by telling *how* white the sand was.

An adverb phrase is diagramed beneath the word it modifies.

Adverb phrase modifying a verb:

The sun shone brightly <u>in the afternoon</u>.

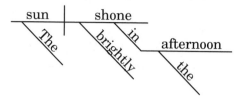

Adverb phrase modifying a predicate adjective:

The tree was full <u>of ripe peaches</u>.

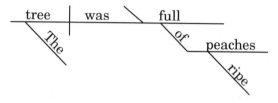

Adverb phrase modifying an adverb:

I will see you later <u>in the day</u>.

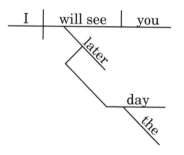

Sentence with several adverb phrases modifying the verb:

<u>On our trip</u>, we took pictures <u>in each state</u> <u>with our little camera</u>.

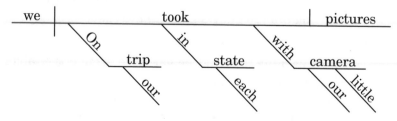

- A prepositional phrase may be used as an adverb.

- A prepositional phrase includes a preposition, its object, and any adjectives that modify the object.

- An adverb phrase modifies a verb, an adjective, or another adverb.

Class Practice

A. Read each adverb phrase. Tell which word it modifies, and what it tells about that word.
1. Trust in the Lord with all thine heart.
2. The ship will soon leave on a long voyage.
3. With a thud the book fell to the floor.
4. Nectarines are similar to peaches.
5. The weather was cold earlier in the month.
6. During the storm, a limb fell to the ground with a crash.

B. On the chalkboard, diagram the sentences in Part A.

Written Exercises

A. Copy each adverb phrase, and the verb, adjective, or adverb that it modifies.
1. After the storm, the boys floated around the pasture in a rowboat.
2. The rain was not noticed by the busy children.
3. We will move later in the year.
4. This bitter medicine is good for you.
5. In the afternoon the sun shone brightly.
6. I will look for Calicut on the map.
7. The baker baked the pies in an oven.
8. Mother made candy on the stovetop.
9. In our back yard we roasted hot dogs over a fire.
10. Did you put too many eggs into the cake?

B. Diagram these sentences.
1. In the evening the children gathered around the table.
2. My niece is afraid of dogs.
3. The workers became more tired by the minute.
4. After the Flood the ark rested on Mount Ararat.

Mount Ararat

Corel

5. You should get up earlier in the morning.
6. By evening the wind was roaring across the island at a high speed.

C. Write three sentences using prepositional phrases that tell *how,* *when,* and *where.*

Review Exercises

Diagram these sentences.

1. Clouds give us rain and shade.
2. Sometimes clouds trap heat that would otherwise escape from the earth.
3. Stratus clouds often bring rain or some other form of precipitation.
4. Those fluffy white clouds look especially beautiful.

---

108. Rhyme in Poetry

In many poems, the last word of one line rhymes with the last word of another line. These rhyming words add much to the beauty of good poetry. There are many different patterns of rhyme. In one common pattern, line 2 rhymes with line 4, line 6 rhymes with line 8, and so on. In another pattern, lines 1 and 2 rhyme, and lines 3 and 4 rhyme. In a third pattern, lines 1 and 3 rhyme, and lines 2 and 4 rhyme. These are just a few of the many patterns that are used.

Study the different rhyming patterns shown below. The rhyming pattern is shown by using a different small letter for each set of rhyming words.

Faithfulness

Though a task may seem quite small,	a
Hardly worth your time at all,	a
Do it promptly, do it well;	b
Who is watching, none can tell.	b
Faithfulness in little things	c
Sure promotion with it brings.	c

What Bird Am I?

I often nest in buildings,	a
Against an eave or wall;	b
I come in early springtime	c
And leave again in fall.	b

Speak the Truth

Speak the truth!	a
Speak it boldly, never fear;	b
Speak it so that all may hear;	b
In the end it shall appear	b
Truth is best in age and youth.	a
Speak the truth.	a
Speak the truth!	a
Truth is beautiful and brave,	c
Strong to bless and strong to save;	c
Falsehood is a cowardly knave;	c
From it turn thy steps in youth—	a
Follow truth.	a

—Anonymous

Here are some rules for writing good rhymes in poetry.

1. The vowel sounds of the rhyming words or syllables must be the same.

Rhyming words: good—would (*but not* good—food)
teeth—sheath (*but not* teeth—death)

2. The last consonant sound of the rhyming syllables must be the same.

Rhyming words: let—get (*but not* let—step)
soar—store (*but not* soar—cord)

3. The beginning consonant sounds of the rhyming syllables must be different.

Rhyming words: night—light (*but not* night—knight)
morn—borne (*but not* morn—mourn)

Words like *night—knight* are homophones, not rhyming words.

Poetry is usually recognized by its rhyme, but this does not mean that all poetry rhymes. One example is Bible poetry, which is found in Job, Psalms, and Proverbs. Bible poetry does not have rhyme, but it is poetic in other ways.

Bible poetry can be written in lines and stanzas. It is full of descriptive words and rich meaning. Often two lines are similar, with the second line repeating the first one but using different words. Study the following lines from Psalm 119:103.

How sweet are thy words unto my taste!
Yea, sweeter than honey to my mouth!

These lines are beautifully descriptive. They rhyme in thought rather than sound. For this reason, Bible poems are true poetry in any language.

- The use of rhyme adds beauty to a poem.

- Rhyme is the matching of sounds at the ends of words or lines.

- Bible poetry is full of descriptive words and is rich in meaning.

Class Practice

A. Give letters to tell which lines rhyme in the poems below. Follow the pattern in the lesson.

1.   **The Old Lamp**

A lamp once hung in an ancient town,
    At the corner of a street,
Where the wind was keen, and the way was dark,
    And the rain would often beat;
And all night long, its light would shine
    To guide the travelers' feet.

The lamp was rough and plain and old,
    And the storm had beaten it sore;
'Twas not a thing one would care to show,
    Whate'er it had been before,
But no one thought what the lantern was,
    'Twas the light that, within, it bore.

—Anonymous

2.   **What We Give Away**

Love that is hoarded molds at last
    Until we know some day,
The only thing we ever have
    Is what we give away.

And kindness that is never used
    But hidden all alone
Will slowly harden till it is
    As hard as any stone.

It is the things we always hold
    That we will lose some day;
The only things we ever keep
    Are what we give away.

—Author unknown

B. Look up Psalm 103. Discuss some of the descriptive words and phrases in the first few verses of this Bible poetry.

C. Look up Proverbs 4:1–4. Pick out the pairs of lines with similar thoughts in this Bible poetry.

Written Exercises

A. Study the following poem, and write which rhyming pattern is used in the first stanza: *aabb, abab,* or *abcb.* Then copy all the pairs of rhyming words.

I Saw God Wash the World

I saw God wash the world last night
    With His sweet shower on high;
And then when morning came, I saw
    Him hang it out to dry.

He washed each tiny blade of grass
    And every trembling tree;
He flung His showers against the hills
    And swept the billowy sea.

The white rose is a cleaner white,
    The red rose is more red,
Since God washed every fragrant face
    And put them all to bed.

There's not a bird, there's not a bee,
    That wings along the way,
But is a cleaner bird and bee
    Than it was yesterday.

I saw God wash the world last night;
    Ah, would He had washed me
As clean of all my dust and dirt
    As that old white birch tree!

            —William L. Stidger

B. Copy Psalm 23:1–3 in lines as in a poem. Write each verse in two lines, and begin each line with a capital letter. Follow the pattern shown below for Psalm 24:1, 2.

> The earth is the Lord's, and the fulness thereof;
> The world, and they that dwell therein.
> For he hath founded it upon the seas,
> And established it upon the floods.

C. Write a good rhyming word to fit in each blank.

The Fountain

1. Into the sunshine,
     Full of the light,
   Leaping and flashing
     From morn till ———!

2. Into the moonlight,
     Whiter than snow,
   Waving so flowerlike
     When the winds ———!

3. Into the starlight,
     Rushing in spray,
   Happy at midnight,
     Happy by ———!

4. Ever in motion,
     Blithesome and ———,
   Still climbing heavenward,
     Never aweary.

5. Full of a nature
     Nothing can tame,
   Changed every moment,
     Ever the ———;

6. Glorious fountain!
     Let my heart be
   Fresh, cheerful, constant,
     Upward like ———!

—James Russell Lowell

D. Choose a topic for writing a poem, and make a list of ideas that you might include in it. Here are some suggested topics.
   1. Describe a winter scene just after a fresh snow.
   2. Describe some of the kind things your mother does for you.
   3. Describe your pet dog, kitten, or goldfish.
   4. Describe the beauties of springtime.
   5. Describe a thrilling bicycle ride down a steep hill.

Review Exercises

Choose and write the best answers. [93, 96]
   1. A description usually (tells, does not tell) a story.
   2. A description usually tells about a (scene, happening).
   3. The sense of (sight, hearing) is used most in descriptions.
   4. The word (*building, house*) is a more exact noun.

5. The word (*ran, raced*) is a more exact verb.
6. The word (*wise, good*) is a more descriptive adjective.
7. The order of (time, space, importance) should be used in descriptions.
8. A (simile, metaphor) compares two unlike things by using the word *like* or *as.*

---

109. Distinguishing Adverbs and Adjectives

How can you tell the difference between adverbs and adjectives? There are two tests that you can use.

The first test is to see what part of speech the word modifies. An adjective always modifies a noun or pronoun. An adverb always modifies a verb, an adjective, or another adverb.

> This engine starts <u>hard</u>.
> > *Hard* modifies *starts,* which is a verb. So *hard* is an adverb.

> This factory makes <u>hard</u> candy.
> > *Hard* modifies *candy,* which is a noun. So *hard* is an adjective.

> This soil is <u>hard</u> and <u>dry</u>.
> > *Hard* and *dry* follow the linking verb *is* and modify the subject *soil. Hard* and *dry* are predicate adjectives.

A second test is to see what question the modifier answers. Adjectives tell *which, whose, how many,* and *what kind of.* Adverbs tell *how, when, where, why,* and *to what degree.*

> This engine starts <u>hard</u>.
> > *Hard* tells *how* the engine starts, so *hard* is an adverb.

> This factory makes <u>hard</u> candy.
> > *Hard* tells *what kind of* candy, so *hard* is an adjective.

> This soil is <u>hard</u> and <u>dry</u>.
> > *Hard* and *dry* tell *what kind of* soil, so *hard* and *dry* are predicate adjectives.

Remember that adverbs of degree modify adjectives or other adverbs. Test each modifier separately to see what part of speech it is.

> Louann took the kettle <u>off</u> <u>too</u> <u>soon</u>.
>> *Off* modifies the verb *took* by telling *where. Off* is an adverb.
>>
>> *Too* modifies the adverb *soon* by telling *to what degree. Too* is an adverb.
>>
>> *Soon* modifies the verb *took* by telling *when. Soon* is an adverb.

> He is an <u>especially</u> <u>courteous</u> <u>young</u> man.
>> *Especially* modifies the adjective *courteous* by telling *to what degree. Especially* is an adverb.
>>
>> *Courteous* modifies the predicate nominative *man* by telling *what kind of. Courteous* is an adjective.
>>
>> *Young* modifies the predicate nominative *man* by telling *what kind of. Young* is an adjective.

Many adverbs end with *-ly.* However, not all words that end with *-ly* are adverbs. Some *-ly* words tell *what kind of.* Study the following words that are often used as adjectives.

lonely	lovely	costly	brotherly
lowly	orderly	friendly	neighborly

How can you tell whether a word ending with *-ly* is an adjective or an adverb? Use the same two tests: See what part of speech the word modifies, and notice what question it answers.

> The lady seemed <u>kindly</u> in her actions.
>> *Kindly* modifies the noun *lady* by telling *what kind of.* It is a predicate adjective. (*Seemed* is a linking verb because it can be replaced by a form of *be:* The lady *was* kindly in her actions.)

> She spoke <u>kindly</u> to us.
>> *Kindly* modifies the verb *spoke* by telling *how,* so it is an adverb.

A prepositional phrase is either an adjective phrase or an adverb phrase. How can you tell the difference? Again, use the same two tests.

That letter <u>on my desk</u> came today.

> The phrase *on my desk* modifies the noun *letter* by telling *which*. So *on my desk* is an adjective phrase.

I found a letter <u>on my desk</u>.

> The phrase *on my desk* modifies the verb *found* by telling *where*. So *on my desk* is an adverb phrase.

The position of a phrase within a sentence is another clue for deciding what kind of phrase it is. An adjective phrase must come *immediately after* the noun or pronoun that it modifies.

Adjective phrases:

> The paper <u>on the desk</u> is mine.
> John fed the calves <u>in the barn</u>.

An adverb phrase may be found almost anywhere in a sentence. It can often be moved to a different place without changing the meaning. Of course, if a prepositional phrase is at the beginning of a sentence, it must be an adverb phrase.

Adverb phrases:

> The boys worked <u>with all their might</u> yesterday.
> The boys worked yesterday <u>with all their might</u>.

> We visited awhile <u>after church</u>.
> <u>After church</u> we visited awhile.

The following sentence has an adverb phrase and an adjective phrase. Study this sentence and its diagram.

<u>For devotions</u> we read the parable <u>of the sower</u>.

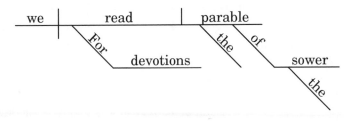

An adjective phrase may modify the object of a prepositional phrase just before it. Study the following sentence and its diagram.

Fish live <u>beneath the surface</u> <u>of the water</u>.

Beneath the surface modifies *live* by telling *where* fish live. So it is an adverb phrase.

Of the water modifies *surface* by telling *what kind of* surface. So it is an adjective phrase.

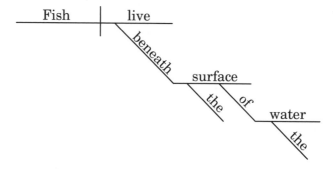

In the example above, you may think *beneath the surface* and *of the water* are both adverb phrases because both follow the verb. But the two tests show that the first is an adverb phrase and the second is an adjective phrase.

- One way to distinguish an adverb from an adjective is to see what part of speech the word or phrase modifies. An adjective modifies a noun or pronoun, but an adverb modifies a verb, an adjective, or another adverb.

- Another way to distinguish an adverb from an adjective is to see what question the word or phrase answers. An adjective tells *which, whose, how many,* or *what kind of;* but an adverb tells *how, when, where, why,* or *to what degree.*

- An additional way to distinguish an adverb phrase from an adjective phrase is to check the position of the phrase in a sentence. An adjective phrase comes directly after the noun or pronoun that it modifies, but an adverb phrase may be found almost anywhere in a sentence.

Class Practice

Look at each underlined word or phrase. Tell which word or words it modifies and what question it answers. Then tell whether it is used as an *adverb* or an *adjective*.

1. A jet is <u>fast</u>.
2. The bus came <u>late</u> again.
3. Sylvia can draw <u>well</u>.
4. Christians should practice <u>brotherly</u> kindness.
5. If you want to be known as a <u>friendly</u> person, you must act <u>friendly</u>.
6. We have not seen our cousins <u>from Alabama</u> <u>since last winter</u>.
7. Will we pay the toll <u>at the other side</u> <u>of the bridge</u>?
8. Get some water <u>at the faucet</u> <u>in the kitchen</u>.
9. How many verses <u>from the Bible</u> can you quote <u>by memory</u>?
10. <u>On the way home</u> we talked and sang.
11. The boy <u>in the wheelchair</u> can walk <u>with crutches</u>.
12. My grandfather walked <u>to school</u> <u>in his boyhood</u>.

Written Exercises

Write *adj.* or *adv.* to identify each underlined word or phrase.

1. The travelers walked <u>hurriedly</u>.
2. The <u>fresh</u> concrete soon became <u>hard</u>.
3. The farmers <u>of those days</u> worked <u>hard</u>.
4. That island is <u>almost</u> completely covered <u>with water</u>.
5. The crops are growing <u>well</u>.
6. The <u>old</u> car still runs <u>well</u>.
7. She has been feeling <u>quite</u> <u>well</u>.
8. A <u>beautiful</u> rainbow arched <u>across the sky</u>.
9. The Word <u>of God</u> will stand <u>forever</u>.
10. Your bouquet is <u>lovely</u>.
11. Such a trip would be <u>rather</u> <u>costly</u>.
12. The children <u>in the printer's shop</u> saw some huge rolls <u>of paper</u>.
13. <u>In the springtime</u> the shearers cut the thick fleece <u>off the sheep</u>.
14. The <u>old</u> people <u>in the nursing home</u> thanked us for coming.
15. Coal miners <u>of past days</u> worked <u>in dark and dangerous surroundings</u>.
16. Some coal lies <u>too</u> <u>deep</u> for surface mining.

Review Exercises

Match the names of the sentence parts to the descriptions.

subject   direct object   predicate nominative
predicate indirect object predicate adjective

1. It tells *to whom or what* or *for whom or what* the action of the verb is done.
2. It follows a linking verb and renames the subject.
3. It receives the action of a transitive verb.
4. It tells *who* or *what* the sentence is about.
5. It follows a linking verb and modifies the subject.
6. It tells what the subject does or is.

---

110. Adverb Clauses

You know that a word or a phrase can be used as an adverb to tell *how, when, where,* or *why.* A *clause* can also be used as an adverb. Remember that a clause is any group of words with a subject and a predicate. In the following sentences, the underlined words are adverbs that tell *when.*

> Snow was falling <u>yesterday</u>. (single-word adverb)
> Snow was falling <u>on Monday</u>. (adverb phrase)
> Snow was falling <u>before we reached home</u>. (adverb clause)

Adverb clauses can answer questions other than *how, when, where, why,* and *to what degree.* They can also tell *how long, how much, in spite of what, under what condition,* and other things.

> Daniel was delivered <u>because he trusted in God</u>.
> (modifies *was delivered* by telling *why*)

> We shall be rewarded <u>if we are faithful</u>.
> (modifies *shall be rewarded* by telling *under what condition*)

An adjective clause begins with a relative pronoun and modifies a noun or a pronoun. But an adverb clause begins with a *subordinating conjunction,* and it modifies a verb, an adjective, or another adverb. Here are some common subordinating conjunctions.

after	before	until
although	if	when
as	since	where
because	unless	while

An adverb clause is a *dependent clause,* the same as an adjective clause. It cannot stand alone as a complete sentence. It depends on a *main clause* (an independent clause) for its meaning.

Dependent clause:

If <u>we</u> <u>are</u> faithful. (cannot stand alone)

Main, or independent, clause: <u>We</u> <u>shall be rewarded</u>.

A sentence that contains a dependent clause and an independent clause is a *complex sentence.* The dependent clause may be an adverb clause or an adjective clause.

We shall study <u>when recess is over</u>. (adverb clause)
The boy <u>whom you saw</u> is my brother. (adjective clause)

To find an adverb clause in a sentence, look for a clause that begins with a subordinating conjunction. It may come before or after the main clause.

The fluffy snowflake quickly melted <u>after it fell on my hand</u>.
<u>After it fell on my hand</u>, the fluffy snowflake quickly melted.

An adverb clause is set off by a comma when it comes before the main clause. Notice how this is done in the sentence above.

- An adverb clause is a clause that modifies a verb, an adjective, or an adverb. Adverb clauses may tell *how, when, where, why,* and *to what degree,* as well as *how long, how much, in spite of what, under what condition,* and other things.

- An adverb clause begins with a subordinating conjunction, such as *after, although, as, because, before, if, since, unless, until, when, where,* and *while.*

- A sentence with an adverb clause is a complex sentence.

- An adverb clause may be found before or after the main clause in a sentence.

Class Practice

A. First read the adverb clause in each sentence. Then read the main clause.

1. The old stairs creaked as we went up.
2. The disciples felt sad because Jesus would leave them soon.
3. Although dark clouds covered the sky, we received no rain.
4. Leave the pan on the stove until the water boils.
5. Things do not always happen as we had planned.
6. Do not rejoice when your enemy falls.

B. Read the adverb clauses in Part A again. Tell which words they modify, and what questions they answer.

C. Use these adverb clauses in sentences of your own. Begin the second sentence with the adverb clause, and write it correctly on the chalkboard.

1. where the catfish were biting   2. unless we fix it soon

Written Exercises

A. Copy each adverb clause, and underline the subordinating conjunction.

Example: As we drove through Wyoming, we saw some buffaloes.
Answer: <u>As</u> we drove through Wyoming

1. I have not seen Uncle Wilbur's since they moved to Illinois.
2. Put all these tools away where they belong.
3. Because you have carelessly damaged the book, you must pay for it.
4. The girls washed the windows until they sparkled.
5. If a horse is not thirsty, it will not drink much water.
6. The wash dries faster when a breeze is blowing.

B. Copy each adverb clause. Also copy the verb or verb phrase that each clause modifies.

Example: King Nebuchadnezzar was startled when he saw four
              men in the furnace.
Answer: when he saw four men in the furnace, was startled

1. Daniel was serving Nebuchadnezzar when the king had a frightening dream.
2. The king told his dream when Daniel came.

3. After Daniel was silent for a long time, he explained the dream.
4. As Nebuchadnezzar was boasting one day, a voice spoke from heaven.
5. The people drove Nebuchadnezzar from the palace because he acted like an animal.
6. After Nebuchadnezzar had his right mind again, he honored the King of heaven.

C. Write complex sentences of your own, using these dependent clauses. Begin sentences 1 and 2 with the adverb clause, and sentences 3 and 4 with the main clause.
   1. before anyone could stop him
   2. if you do not know the answer
   3. because we were late
   4. although I had not seen it

Review Exercises

A. Write the correct words in parentheses. [106]
   1. Marilyn can write (good, well).
   2. Jonathan is feeling quite (good, well) again.
   3. This book about foxes is (good, well).
   4. We had not seen (none, any) of the girls.
   5. We hadn't seen (none, any) of the boys either.
   6. I (can, can't) hardly see where we are going.

B. Write the correct word for each sentence. Also write whether that word is a *direct object,* an *indirect object,* a *predicate nominative,* or a *predicate adjective.* [64, 106]
   1. Mother gave (we, us) girls the directions.
   2. Sarah brought (she, her) to us.
   3. The song leader is (he, him).
   4. This pie tastes (good, well).
   5. Father told (we, us) boys the story.

111. Diagraming Adverb Clauses

You know how to diagram a single word used as an adverb. It is placed on a slanted line beneath the word it modifies.

The visitors arrived late.

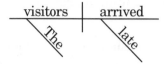

An adverb phrase is also diagramed beneath the word it modifies.

The visitors arrived after midnight.

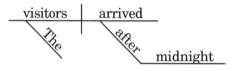

Likewise, an adverb clause is diagramed beneath the word it modifies. A broken line is drawn from the word (usually the verb) that the clause modifies, to the verb in the adverb clause. The subordinating conjunction is placed on the broken line.

The visitors arrived after the clock struck twelve.

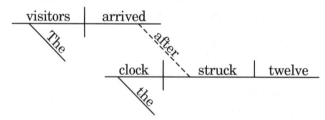

The last diagram above shows how the main clause and the adverb clause are related. The main clause contains the main thought of the sentence, and the adverb clause modifies the verb in the main clause by telling *when*.

When you diagram a sentence with an adverb clause, you must recognize which part of the sentence is the main clause and which part is the adverb clause. Look for a subordinating conjunction, such as *after,* *although, as, because, before, if, since, unless, until, when, where,* and *while.* Then find the rest of the adverb clause, being sure it includes a subject and a verb. Diagram the main clause first, and then diagram the adverb clause as shown in the lesson.

- An adverb clause is diagramed beneath the main clause. The subordinating conjunction is written on the broken line that connects the modified word in the main clause to the verb in the adverb clause.

Class Practice

Diagram these sentences on the chalkboard.
1. After Sandra ate her breakfast, she gathered the eggs.
2. Tonight we will work until the sun sets.
3. We saw you before you saw us.
4. When you come, she will be ready.

Written Exercises

A. Copy each adverb clause, and underline the subordinating conjunction. Also copy the word or phrase that the adverb clause modifies.
1. God gave Abraham a son as He had promised.
2. If You had been here, Lazarus would not have died.
3. While the farmer slept, an enemy sowed weed seeds in his field.
4. Before the lamp of God went out, Samuel lay down to sleep.
5. He ran to Eli several times because he heard a voice.
6. After Samuel went back again, the Lord called him.
7. In those days the word of the Lord was precious because the Lord did not frequently speak to anyone.
8. Wherever Jesus leads, we will follow.

B. Diagram these sentences.
1. We traveled slowly because it was very foggy.
2. The children sang because they were happy.
3. He asked for money when he saw Peter and John.

4. The lame man was healed when Peter lifted him up.
5. Many people believed in Jesus after this happened.
6. When Jesus spoke, the leprosy departed from the man.

Review Exercises

A. Write the plural form of each word. [22, 23]

1. key	6. alto
2. town	7. hero
3. bus	8. gentleman
4. leaf	9. tooth
5. safe	10. child

B. Write the better words in parentheses. [23]
1. Measles (is, are) a disease that can cause serious harm.
2. Leon's new trousers (is, are) dark blue.
3. Where (is, are) the scissors?

C. Diagram these sentences, which have adjective clauses. [98]
1. The bird book, which Father gave me, was helpful.
2. Mother served the ice cream that Grandmother brought.
3. The people who helped us live in Dalton.

---

112. The Special Language of Poetry

Good poetry often uses figures of speech. You studied similes and metaphors in Lesson 96. Poems also contain similes, metaphors, and other figures of speech.

A simile is a figure of speech comparing two things that are not really alike, with the use of *like* or *as*. The similes in the following poems are underlined.

Words
Words are <u>like kites</u>—
    We send them away
On the wing of the air
    When we speak or we pray.

Words fly away
    For good or for ill,
But we can't pull them in,
    Like kites, at our will.

Winter Blanket

The snow is <u>like a blanket</u> that
    God spreads across the land,
Where wheat and oats and barley sleep,
    Awaiting spring's command.

The first poem shows a comparison between words and kites: both words and kites go flying through the air. It also shows a contrast: we can pull kites back in, but we cannot do that with words. The second poem compares snow to a blanket that is spread across the land while crops "sleep" under it. These comparisons are so fitting that we can easily understand what the poems mean.

A metaphor is much like a simile, but the word *like* or *as* is not used. The metaphors in the following poems are underlined.

I Am Jesus' Little Lamb

<u>I am Jesus' little lamb,</u>
Ever glad at heart I am;
For my Shepherd gently guides me,
Knows my need, and well provides me,
Loves me every day the same,
Even calls me by my name.
                —Henrietta Louisa von Hayn

Thy Word Have I Hid in My Heart

<u>Thy Word is a lamp</u> to my feet,
<u>A light</u> to my path alway;
To guide and to save me from sin,
And show me the heavenly way.
                —Ernest O. Sellers

Be on Guard
Guard well your thoughts,
For they are seeds
For lovely blooms
Or ugly weeds.

Guard well your words,
For they have power
To cheer and bless
Or wound and mar.

"I am Jesus' little lamb" because He tenderly cares for me. "Thy Word is a lamp" because it shows us the right way to go. "Thoughts are seeds" because they grow into words and deeds. Again, the comparisons are well suited to the thoughts in the poems.

In another figure of speech, the characteristics of a person or animal are applied to an inanimate object (neither person nor animal). This is called *personification*. Study the following lines from the poem "Columbus."

They sailed. They sailed. Then spake the mate:
"This mad sea shows his teeth tonight;
He curls his lips, he lies in wait,
With lifted teeth as if to bite;
Brave Admiral, say but one good word.
What shall we say when hope is gone?"
The words leaped like a leaping sword:
"Sail on! sail on! sail on! and on!"

—Joaquin Miller

These lines speak of the mad sea showing his teeth, curling his lips, and lying in wait as if to bite. Of course, the sea never actually does these things. It does not even have teeth or lips. But if one imagines the raging sea to be a vicious animal, the personification is truly fitting.

A poet often uses words that suggest the sounds of what they refer to. For example, the word *smooth* is a smooth-sounding word. The word *purr* sounds like the noise made by a contented kitten, and *pitter, patter* sounds like raindrops on a windowpane. Study the underlined examples in the following stanzas.

The Barnyard Chorus

The cows are singing bass notes
    As they raise their heads and <u>moo</u>,
The hens are <u>clucking</u> alto to their brood;
The mourning doves sing tenor
    With a harmonizing <u>coo</u>,
The pigs <u>squeal</u> high soprano for some food.

What a racket, what a <u>babble</u>,
    As the turkeys add their <u>gabble</u>,
The gander <u>honks</u>, the mule starts to <u>bray</u>;
Then the rooster adds his <u>crowing</u>,
    So I think that I'll be going,
And listen to their music—far away!

—Viola Jacobson Berg

From *Pathways for the Poet*, copyright 1977
Reprinted by permission of Baker Book House
Company

The Waters of Lodore

And <u>rushing</u> and <u>flushing</u> and <u>brushing</u> and <u>gushing</u>,
And <u>flapping</u> and <u>rapping</u> and <u>clapping</u> and <u>slapping</u>,
And <u>thumping</u> and <u>plumping</u> and <u>bumping</u> and <u>jumping</u>,
And <u>dashing</u> and <u>flashing</u> and <u>splashing</u> and <u>clashing</u>;
And so never ending, but always descending,
Sounds and motions forever and ever are blending,
All at once and all o'er, with a mighty <u>uproar</u>:
And this way, the water comes down at Lodore.

—Robert Southey

In the first example above, many words are so much like animal sounds that we can almost hear the clamor of a barnyard. The second example has many words that suggest the sound of rushing water, and this helps us to "hear" the roaring waterfall.

The sound of words can make poetry beautiful in other ways. You have already studied rhyme, in which words with the same ending sound are placed close together. Words with the same *beginning sound* can also be placed close together to make poetry sound pleasing. Notice how this is done in the example below.

Light After Darkness

Light after darkness, gain after loss,
Strength after weakness, <u>crown</u> after <u>cross</u>,
Sweet after bitter, hope after fears,
Home after wandering, praise after tears.

<u>Sheaves</u> after <u>sowing</u>, <u>sun</u> after rain,
Sight after mystery, <u>peace</u> after <u>pain</u>;
Joy after sorrow, calm after blast,
Rest after weariness, sweet rest at last.

Near after distant, <u>gleam</u> after <u>gloom</u>,
<u>Love</u> after <u>loneliness</u>, <u>life</u> after tomb;
<u>After</u> long <u>agony</u>, rapture of bliss;
Right was the pathway leading to this!
—Frances R. Havergal

Words with similar beginning sounds may have similar meanings, such as *<u>b</u>lessing and <u>b</u>liss* or *<u>p</u>eace and <u>p</u>leasure*. They may have opposite meanings, such as *<u>c</u>rown after <u>c</u>ross, <u>p</u>eace after <u>p</u>ain,* and several other examples in the poem above. The words may not be related at all, such as *<u>a</u>fter long <u>a</u>gony*. In any case, words with similar beginning sounds add to the beauty and appeal of poetry.

- Good poetry has many figures of speech.
  a. A simile compares two unlike things by using *like* or *as*.
  b. A metaphor makes a comparison without using *like* or *as*.
  c. Personification applies the characteristics of a person or an animal to an inanimate object.

- Various methods are used to give poetry a pleasing sound.
  a. Words are used that suggest the sounds they describe.
  b. Several words beginning with the same sound are placed close together.

Class Practice

Tell what figures of speech are used in the poetry below. Tell how the sound of the words makes the lines pleasing to hear.

1. Amidst the storm they sang,
       And the stars heard, and the sea;
   And the sounding aisles of the dim woods rang
       To the anthem of the free.

2. Thy Word is like a garden, Lord,
   With flowers bright and fair;
                                    —Edwin Hodder

3. The Lord is my Shepherd, I shall not want;
       He maketh me down to lie
   In pastures green, He leadeth me
       The quiet waters by.

4. **Drop a Pebble in the Water**
   Drop a pebble in the water,
       Just a splash, and it is gone;
   But there's half-a-hundred ripples,
       Circling on and on and on,
   Spreading, spreading from the center,
       Flowing on out to the sea;
   And there is no way of telling
       Where the end is going to be.

   Drop a word of cheer and kindness,
       Just a flash and it is gone;
   But there's half-a-hundred ripples
       Circling on and on and on,
   Bearing hope and joy and comfort
       On each splashing, dashing wave
   Till you wouldn't believe the volume
       Of the one kind word you gave.
                                    —Author unknown

Written Exercises

A. Write whether each line contains an example of a *metaphor,* a *simile,* or *personification.*
   1. Clouds like floating shadows
   2. When spring was in her youth

3. The blue sky is the temple's arch
4. The ocean looketh up to heaven
5. Blessings like a shower of gold
6. The sands of time are diamond sparks

B. Copy the words with similar beginning sounds that help to make each stanza pleasing to the ear.

1. **The Valley of Silence**

I walk down the valley of silence,
    Down the dim, voiceless valley alone;
And I hear not the fall of a footstep
    Around me—save God's and my own,
And the hush of my heart is as holy
    As hovers where angels have flown.

2. **The Lark**

O'er fell and fountain sheen,
O'er moor and mountain green,
O'er the red banner that blazons the day,
    Over the cloudlet dim,
    Over the rainbow's rim,
Musical jewel, soar, singing away!

C. Finish the similes and metaphors.
1. The boys were as noisy as ———.
2. As quick as ———, the deer disappeared.
3. The tall tree stood like ———.
4. Her words were smoother than ———, but deceit was in her heart.
5. The pleasant little girl was a ———, and her friendly brother was a ———.
6. Words are ———.

D. Write an original poem of at least eight lines. Use your notes from Lesson 108. Your poem should include at least one figure of speech and one of the methods that make poetry pleasing to hear, as introduced in this lesson.

Review Exercises

Find one mistake in each numbered line. If it is an error of capitalization, write the word correctly. If it is an error of punctuation, write the word before the error and add the correct punctuation. [63]

1.   Route 1, box 3310
2.   Newark DE 19702
3.   april 5, 20—
4. Dear Brent
5.   I am so sorry to hear that you broke your leg. we are praying
6. that you will be better soon. Im hoping to see you back in school
7. before long
8.   Sincerely
9.   mark

        *   *   *   *   *

10.   855 East King st.
11.   Newville, pa 17241
12.   July 10 20—

13. Crafts Especially For Boys
14. 504 Crescent Ave
15. Eugene, Or 97401

16. Dear Sirs,

17.   I am interested in the book *Building bluebird Houses.*
18. please send me information on how I can order it.

19.   Sincerely:

20.   John bowens

---

113. Simple, Compound, and Complex Sentences

Sentences may be simple, compound, or complex, according to their structure. How can you tell which is which? One help is to use sentence formulas as you studied earlier. S stands for the subject, V stands for the verb, and + stands for a conjunction.

1. *A simple sentence has only one skeleton.*

Some <u>planets</u> | <u>shine</u> brightly in the night sky.
S | V = simple sentence

A simple sentence may have a compound subject or a compound verb, but it is still a simple sentence.

The <u>sun</u> | <u>rises</u> and <u>sets</u> faithfully every day. (compound verb)
S | V + V = simple sentence

<u>Mercury</u> and <u>Venus</u> | <u>are</u> closest to the sun. (compound subject)
S + S | V = simple sentence

2. *A compound sentence has two skeletons joined by a conjunction.*

<u>Mars</u> | <u>reflects</u> a reddish color, **and** <u>Jupiter</u> | <u>shows</u> bands of red, yellow, and brown on its surface.
S | V + S | V = compound sentence

3. *A complex sentence has two skeletons joined by a conjunction.*

A five-mile-deep <u>canyon</u> | <u>was discovered</u> on Mars **after** <u>satellites</u> | <u>took</u> pictures there.
S | V + S | V = complex sentence

The formulas for compound and complex sentences are the same. How can you tell the difference between them? The main way is to see what kind of conjunction is used to join the two clauses.

1. *The two clauses of a compound sentence are joined by a* coordinating conjunction.

Coordinating conjunctions:

and	but	or	for	nor	yet

Mars reflects a reddish color, <u>and</u> Jupiter shows bands of red, yellow, and brown on its surface. (compound sentence)

Jupiter is beautiful, <u>but</u> it would not be a good place to live. (compound sentence)

2. *The two clauses of a complex sentence are joined by a* subordinating conjunction *or a* relative pronoun.

Subordinating conjunctions: (used to introduce adverb clauses)

after	because	since	when
although	before	unless	where
as	if	until	while

A five-mile-deep canyon was discovered on Mars <u>after</u> satellites took pictures there. (complex sentence with adverb clause)

<u>Before</u> close-up pictures were taken, scientists knew little about the surface of Mars. (complex sentence with adverb clause)

Relative pronouns: (used to introduce adjective clauses)

who   whom   whose   which   that

Venus is the planet <u>that</u> shines brightly as an evening or a morning star.
(complex sentence with adjective clause)

We should praise God, <u>who</u> made the beautiful, fascinating planets for His glory.
(complex sentence with adjective clause)

Another way to tell the difference between a compound and a complex sentence is to study the clauses of each sentence.

1. *A compound sentence is made of two independent clauses.* Remember that an independent clause makes sense by itself. Either clause in a compound sentence can stand alone as a complete sentence.

   Compound sentence:
   Mars reflects a reddish color, and Jupiter shows bands of red, yellow, and brown on its surface.

   Clauses standing alone:
   Mars reflects a reddish color. (complete sentence)

   And Jupiter shows bands of red, yellow, and brown on its surface. (complete sentence; *and* is a transitional word)

2. *A complex sentence is made of one independent clause and one dependent clause.* The independent clause is a complete sentence by itself, but the dependent clause is not.

   Complex sentences:
   A five-mile-deep canyon was discovered on Mars after satellites took pictures there.
   Mars has polar caps that appear white from the earth.

Clauses standing alone:

A five-mile-deep canyon was discovered on Mars.
(complete)

After satellites took pictures there.
(not complete; *after* is not a transitional word)

Mars has polar caps. (complete)

That appear white from the earth. (not complete)

- A simple sentence has only one skeleton. A compound or complex sentence has two skeletons joined by a conjunction.

- The two clauses of a compound sentence are joined by a coordinating conjunction. The two clauses of a complex sentence are joined by a subordinating conjunction or a relative pronoun.

- A compound sentence is made of two independent clauses. A complex sentence is made of one independent clause and one dependent clause.

Class Practice

A. Tell whether each underlined word is a *coordinating conjunction,* a *subordinating conjunction,* or a *relative pronoun.*
  1. Ostriches cannot fly, <u>but</u> they can run very fast.
  2. This is one mother bird <u>that</u> uses solar energy to incubate her eggs.
  3. The ostrich does sit on her eggs <u>when</u> the sun does not shine.
  4. Young ostriches are hard to spot <u>because</u> the color of their feathers matches the desert sand.

B. Tell whether each underlined clause is *dependent* or *independent.* If it is dependent, tell whether it is an *adjective clause* or an *adverb clause.*
  1. A young ostrich lies very still <u>when an enemy comes near</u>.
  2. When blowing desert sands partly cover a motionless ostrich, <u>he may appear to be hiding his head in the sand</u>.
  3. <u>The ostrich closes his eyes</u> so that an enemy cannot easily spot him.
  4. The special instincts <u>that God gave the ostrich</u> help it.

C. Tell whether each sentence is *simple, compound,* or *complex.*
1. A mother ostrich is not really deserting her chicks when she runs away from them.
2. She is leading the enemy away from her hidden chicks.
3. The ostrich has no understanding of her own, but God has given her special instincts.

D. On the chalkboard, write the formulas for the sentences in Part C.

Written Exercises

A. Write whether each underlined clause is *dependent* or *independent.* If it is dependent, write whether it is an adjective clause (*adj.*) or an adverb clause (*adv.*).
1. The children of Israel cried to the Lord <u>when the Midianites came against them</u>.
2. <u>Gideon was threshing wheat by the winepress</u> when the angel of the Lord came to him.
3. God wanted to use Gideon for greater work <u>because Gideon was already working faithfully</u>.
4. Twenty-two thousand men <u>who were fearful</u> returned home.

B. Write whether each underlined word is a *coordinating conjunction,* a *subordinating conjunction,* or a *relative pronoun.*
1. The earth around the fleece was dry, <u>but</u> Gideon wrung a bowlful of water out of the fleece.
2. Gideon knew that God would save Israel <u>because</u> the fleece was dry on the second morning.
3. On the second day, the ground <u>that</u> was around the fleece was wet with dew.
4. Gideon was ready to go <u>after</u> he knew that God would be with him.

C. Write whether each sentence is *simple, compound,* or *complex.*
1. The Lord gave another special sign to Gideon.
2. Gideon asked his servant to go with him, and they crept to the edge of the Midianite camp.
3. A Midianite was telling his dream when Gideon came near.
4. In his dream a cake of barley bread tumbled into the camp of the Midianites, and the rolling cake overturned one of the tents.
5. Another soldier explained the meaning of the dream.
6. Gideon worshiped the Lord after he heard the interpretation.

7. He divided his three hundred men into three groups, and then he stationed them around the Midianite camp.
8. Gideon and his men blew the trumpets, broke the pitchers, and raised a battle cry.

Review Exercises

Diagram the following sentences.

1. When Gideon's men blew the trumpets, the Midianites were greatly frightened.
2. The whole host cried out and fled in panic.
3. God helped Gideon because Gideon obeyed God.

---

114. Chapter 9 Review

Class Practice

A. Give the definition of an adverb.

B. Give the three degrees of comparison for each modifier.

1. fast	4. little	7. well	9. easily
2. swiftly	5. early	8. far	10. ill
3. late	6. lively		

C. For each underlined phrase, give a word or phrase that is more effective.
1. The teacher is reading a <u>really good</u> book to us.
2. The weather was <u>really awful</u> yesterday.
3. My grandmother was <u>very bad</u> again yesterday.
4. We saw an <u>awfully hot</u> fire last night.
5. That car went <u>very fast</u> past our house.

D. Tell whether each underlined word, phrase, or clause is used as an *adverb* or an *adjective*. Also tell which word each one modifies, and what question the modifier answers.
1. We wanted to make handprints in the new concrete, but it was already <u>hard</u>.
2. The crank on the old car turned <u>hard</u>.
3. Jennifer is a <u>friendly</u> girl.
4. The book <u>on the table</u> is for you.

5. I put the book about ships <u>on the living room table</u>.
6. Sister Janice tacks a box of tissues on the side <u>of her desk</u>.
7. The tissues <u>that she put on the table</u> are for everyone.
8. Several students became curious <u>when Sister Jane placed a box on the table</u>.

E. Read the poem below, and do these exercises.
1. Find the similes in the poem.
2. Find one metaphor.
3. Find some words that are close together, which begin with the same sound.
4. Find one example of personification.
5. Find some words that imitate the sounds they describe.

The Village Blacksmith

Under a spreading chestnut tree
    The village smithy stands;
The smith, a mighty man is he,
    With large and sinewy hands,
And the muscles of his brawny arms
    Are strong as iron bands.

His hair is crisp and black and long,
    His face is like the tan;
His brow is wet with honest sweat,
    He earns whate'er he can,
And looks the whole world in the face,
    For he owes not any man.

Week in, week out, from morn till night,
    You can hear his bellows blow;
You can hear him swing his heavy sledge
    With measured beat and slow,
Like a sexton ringing the village bell
    When the evening sun is low.

And children coming home from school
    Look in at the open door;
They love to see the flaming forge,
    And hear the bellows roar,
And catch the burning sparks that fly
    Like chaff from a threshing floor.

Toiling, rejoicing, sorrowing,
    Onward through life he goes;
Each morning sees some task begun,
    Each evening sees it close;
Something attempted, something done,
    Has earned a night's repose.

Thanks, thanks to thee, my worthy friend,
    For the lesson thou hast taught!
Thus at the flaming forge of life
    Our fortunes must be wrought;
Thus on its sounding anvil shaped
    Each burning deed and thought!

—Henry W. Longfellow

Written Exercises

A. Copy all the adverbs. Write whether each one tells *how, when, where,* or *to what degree.*

1. We are happiest when we work cheerfully.
2. I usually sweep the floors first.
3. The tide rose unusually high there yesterday.
4. Does she speak Spanish well?
5. We have not often met here.

B. Copy each adverb of degree. After it, write the word that it modifies.
   1. This manual on repairing small engines is surely helpful.
   2. After James studied the rules of good penmanship, he learned to write quite well.
   3. Before he studied, he felt that writing neatly was too difficult.
   4. We arrived at our friends' house rather early.
   5. Mother said that she had brought too many doughnuts.

C. Write the correct forms in parentheses.
   1. Of the two cars, this one runs (more, most) quietly.
   2. On our school hike this year, we hiked (more farther, farther) than we did last year.
   3. We hiked (farthest, fartherest) of all two years ago.
   4. Today we arrived at school (more early, earlier) than yesterday.
   5. The horse walked (more slowly, slowlier) yesterday.
   6. Grandfather seems (more well, better) this week than last week.
   7. I like to read Janet's stories; she writes (good, well).
   8. Marilyn is a (good, well) seamstress.
   9. It is (good, well) that you are here on time.
   10. I couldn't see (anything, nothing) on the shelves.
   11. I didn't hear (any, no) birds singing in the woods.
   12. Carolyn said she hadn't (ever, never) seen such a tall giraffe before.

D. Write each sentence correctly, using *barely, hardly,* and *scarcely.*
   1. Brian couldn't hardly see that sign.
   2. We hadn't barely made it on time.
   3. I couldn't scarcely see anything through his telescope.

E. Copy each adverb clause, and underline the subordinating conjunction. Also copy the word or phrase that each clause modifies.
   1. Jacob grieved because Joseph had disappeared.
   2. The brothers were afraid when Joseph spoke roughly to them.
   3. They feared even more after Joseph revealed his identity.
   4. Although the brothers had acted wickedly, God was caring for them.
   5. After Joseph tested his brothers, he assured them of his forgiveness.

F. Diagram these sentences.
1. Soon the water of our creek rose quite high.
2. It rose over the banks of the creek.
3. The wheat field was flooded after it had rained for several hours.
4. The sheaves in that field are rather wet.
5. After the storm passed, the men went out to the wheat field.

G. Copy the first line of each poem, and mark the rhythm pattern. Then write the correct words for numbers 5 and 6.

1.
Swans
These fair birds when full-grown are a beautiful sight,
They have long necks and feathers of pure, sparkling white;
Though quite often on ponds or in gardens they're seen,
They are listed with those whom God's Word calls unclean.

2. ### Who Has Seen the Wind?
Who has seen the wind?
    Neither I nor you.
But when the leaves hang trembling,
    The wind is passing through.

Who has seen the wind?
    Neither you nor I.
But when the trees bow down their heads,
    The wind is passing by.
            —Christina G. Rossetti

3. ### The Sparrow
My relatives are numerous,
    We're found most ev'rywhere;
But God the Father feeds us all
    And keeps us in His care.

4. ### The Eagle
High on the crags of the mountain I nest,
For I fly far without stopping to rest;
Swift is my flight and my wings are so strong,
On my broad back I can carry my young.
Sometimes this picture is used to compare
How our great God for His children doth care.

5. The rhythm pattern in number 2 is (iambic, trochaic).
6. The rhythm pattern in number 3 is (iambic, trochaic).

H. Write the pairs of rhyming words in the poems of Part G.

———————————————

Prepositions

Objects

Phrases

Conjunctions

Coordinating

Correlative

Interjections

Subordinating

Introductions

Conversations

Courtesy

Chapter Ten

Using Prepositions, Conjunctions, and Interjections

Communicating Orally

A preposition is a connecting word that begins a prepositional phrase.
A conjunction is a word that joins words, phrases, or clauses.
An interjection is a word that expresses strong feeling.

Sound speech, that cannot be condemned.

Titus 2:8

Common Prepositions

aboard	before	except	off	under
about	behind	for	on	underneath
above	below	from	over	until
across	beneath	in	past	unto
after	beside	inside	since	up
against	between	into	through	upon
along	beyond	like	throughout	with
among	by	near	to	within
around	down	of	toward	without
at	during			

115. Prepositions

A *preposition* is a connecting word that begins a *prepositional phrase.* It shows the relationship between its *object* and some other word in the sentence.

preposition   object
  ↓   ↓

A bird flew <u>over the lake</u>.

(*Over* shows the relationship between *flew* and *lake.*)

Most prepositions are simple, basic words. Study the chart above. You do not need to memorize the list, but you should become thoroughly familiar with the common prepositions. Many words in the list may also be used as adverbs or conjunctions. But a preposition always begins a phrase, and it always has an object.

There are other prepositions that are not on the list. You can easily recognize those if you are familiar with the most common prepositions. A dictionary will tell you whether a word can be used as a preposition.

A preposition is always the first word of a prepositional phrase. A prepositional phrase includes the preposition, its object, and any adjectives that modify the object. The object of a preposition is the noun or pronoun at the end of the phrase. Here is another sentence with a prepositional phrase.

preposition adjectives object
↓   ↓   ↓   ↓

Joseph told Pharaoh the meaning <u>of his two dreams</u>.

Use the following steps to find a prepositional phrase in a sentence.

1. *Find the preposition.*
2. *Find the object of the preposition by saying the preposition and asking* whom *or* what. The answer is the object; it is always a noun or pronoun.
3. *The prepositional phrase includes all the words from the preposition to its object.* Any words in between are adjectives that modify the object. Not all prepositional phrases have adjectives.

Use these steps to find the prepositional phrase in this sentence.

Sing unto the Lord a new song.
Think: 1. The preposition is *unto.*
2. Unto *whom*? The object is *Lord.*
3. The prepositional phrase is *unto the Lord.*

Prepositional phrases can be used as adjectives to modify nouns and pronouns. An adjective phrase comes immediately after the noun that it modifies.

The flowers <u>along the road</u> are poppies. (modifies *flowers*)
Finally we reached the top <u>of the hill</u>. (modifies *top*)

Prepositional phrases can be used as adverbs to modify verbs, adjectives, and other adverbs. Adverb phrases tell *how, when, where, why,* and *to what degree.* An adverb phrase may be found at various places in a sentence.

The visitors arrived yesterday <u>before noon</u>.
The visitors arrived <u>before noon</u> yesterday.
<u>Before noon</u> yesterday, the visitors arrived.
(In every sentence, *before noon* tells *when* the visitors arrived.)

A prepositional phrase is diagramed beneath the word it modifies. The preposition is written on a slanted line, and its object goes on a horizontal line connected to it. Any adjectives go on slanted lines below the object of the preposition.

Sing unto the Lord a new song.

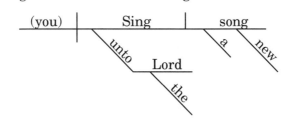

If a prepositional phrase has a compound object, the objects are diagramed on a fork.

We looked for strawberries and raspberries.

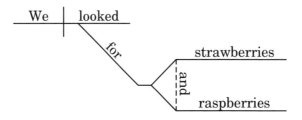

The object of a preposition cannot be the subject of a sentence. Make sure you choose the right word for the subject when it is followed by a prepositional phrase.

A bag (of juicy oranges) was (on the table).

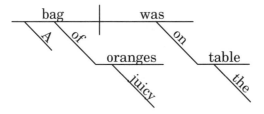

Sometimes more than one phrase modifies the same word.

Several trees fell across the road during the storm.

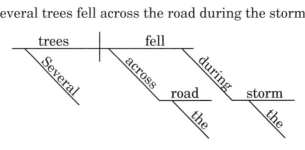

Sometimes a prepositional phrase modifies the object of another preposition. Study the following sentence.

The sun was shining <u>through a crack</u> <u>in the wall</u>.

In the sentence above, the two phrases work together to tell *where*. *Through a crack* is an adverb phrase. *In the wall* is an adjective phrase that tells *which* about the noun *crack*. The second phrase does not directly modify the verb, for the sun was not shining *in the wall*!

Because *in the wall* modifies *crack*, it is diagramed below that word. It is not placed directly below the verb.

The sun was shining through a crack in the wall.

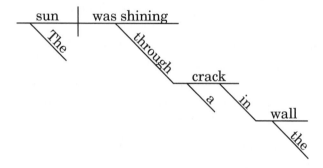

Do not confuse prepositions and adverbs. A preposition begins a phrase, but an adverb stands alone. Compare the following sentences and their diagrams.

We were inside.

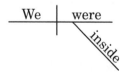

We were inside the barn.

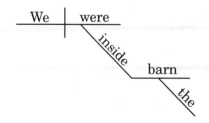

- A preposition is a connecting word that begins a prepositional phrase. The object of a preposition is a noun or pronoun.

- A prepositional phrase may be used as an adjective to modify a noun or pronoun.

- A prepositional phrase may be used as an adverb to modify a verb, an adjective, or another adverb.

Class Practice

A. Read each prepositional phrase. Tell what kind of phrase it is, and which word it modifies.
1. My cousins from Illinois arrived after midnight.
2. At first Uncle Ben's lived across the river.
3. Brother John calmly read from the book in his hands.
4. James was working on the window near the chimney.
5. We received several letters from Aunt Mary since last month.

B. Write the prepositional phrases from numbers 1–3 in Part A on the chalkboard. Underline each preposition, and put parentheses around each object.

C. Diagram the following sentences on the chalkboard.
1. The weasel lined its den with dry grass for the winter.
2. These flowers are for Grandfather and Grandmother.
3. The first book on the shelf was about ships.
4. The chipmunk in the back yard has dived into its hole.

Written Exercises

A. Copy the prepositional phrases. Write whether each one is an *adjective* or an *adverb*.
1. A journey of forty days was before them.
2. By the end of June, we had finished.
3. Lot beheld all the plain of Jordan.
4. We memorized from the books of Psalms and Proverbs.
5. Philip went down to the city of Samaria.
6. The angel of the Lord sent him toward the south.
7. A man of Ethiopia was reading from Isaiah.

8. In the days of King Josiah, God spoke to Jeremiah.
9. Jesus taught with authority.
10. God is with us.

B. Diagram the following sentences.
1. The wise men rejoiced with exceeding joy.
2. John prepared the way for Christ.
3. At the Jordan, he baptized the people.
4. Jesus came into Galilee.
5. Beside the Sea of Galilee, He taught the people.
6. The angel of the Lord descended from heaven.

C. Write two original sentences in which the simple subjects are modified by prepositional phrases. Then write two original sentences in which the verbs are modified by prepositional phrases.

Review Exercises

Copy each sentence, and add the missing punctuation marks. [77–87]
1. Raccoons eat young grass shoots earthworms frogs salamanders turtles fish and insects in the spring and they eat strawberries cherries blackberries and wild grapes in the summer and fall.
2. One of their favorite foods is corn they especially like the kernels that are almost ripe.
3. The raccoons break down the cornstalks by climbing them and they usually taste a few bites from every ear.
4. Theyre also especially fond of sugar cane sweet potatoes peanuts and buckwheat.
5. We found thirty three ruined cornstalks in my great uncles garden this morning.
6. Proverbs 12 10 is a verse about being kind to animals.
7. Sister Lois said Finish memorizing Exodus 20 1 17 by Monday.

116. Using Prepositions Correctly

It is easy to make mistakes in using certain prepositions, especially if they are similar in spelling or meaning. A dictionary is helpful in learning the actual meanings and uses of troublesome prepositions. But most people need study and practice to use them correctly. Learn the following rules for the proper use of prepositions.

1. *In* refers to location. *Into* refers to movement from one location to another.

   Incorrect: The mother cat climbed <u>in</u> the box with her kittens.

   Correct: The mother cat climbed <u>into</u> the box with her kittens.

   Correct: The mother cat was <u>in</u> the box with her kittens.

2. *Except* is a preposition that means "not including." *Accept* is a verb that means "to receive."

   Incorrect: Everyone is here <u>accept</u> Jean.

   Correct: Everyone is here <u>except</u> Jean.

   Correct: I will gladly <u>accept</u> your advice.

3. *Between* refers to only two objects. *Among* refers to more than two.

   Incorrect: The village was hidden <u>between</u> many hills.

   Correct: The village was hidden <u>among</u> many hills.

   Correct: The village was located <u>between</u> the mountain and the lake.

4. *Beside* means "by the side of." *Besides* means "in addition to."

   Correct: Come and sit <u>beside</u> me.

   Correct: Two girls, <u>besides</u> Carol, went along.

5. Do not use *at* or *on* when you mean *to*. We do not talk *at* people or listen *on* them; we talk *to* them and listen *to* them.

   Incorrect: I was talking <u>at</u> my neighbor.

   Correct: I was talking <u>to</u> my neighbor.

   Incorrect: You should listen <u>on</u> your older sister.

   Correct: You should listen <u>to</u> your older sister.

6. Do not use the preposition *of* for the verb *have*. Do not say *could of, should of, would of,* and *must of* for *could have, should have, would have,* and *must have.*

   Incorrect: It must <u>of</u> rained during the night.

   Correct: It must <u>have</u> rained during the night.

7. Do not say *different than*. Say *different from*.

> **Incorrect:** This is <u>different than</u> that one.
> **Correct:**   This is <u>different from</u> that one.

8. Do not say *in back of* for *behind*.

> **Incorrect:** We went <u>in back of</u> the house.
> **Correct:**   We went <u>behind</u> the house.

Do not use unnecessary prepositions. Study the following examples.
1. Do not use *of* with *off, inside,* or *outside*.

> **Incorrect:** Some calves are outside <u>of</u> their pen.
> **Correct:**   Some calves are outside their pen.

> **Incorrect:** Try to keep them off <u>of</u> the lawn.
> **Correct:**   Try to keep them off the lawn.

2. Do not use *at* or *to* with *where*.

> **Incorrect:** Where did you buy that shovel <u>at</u>?
> **Correct:**   Where did you buy that shovel?

> **Incorrect:** Where are we going <u>to</u> for dinner?
> **Correct:**   Where are we going for dinner?

3. Do not use *with* after *over.*

> **Incorrect:** The meeting was soon <u>over with</u>.
> **Correct:**   The meeting was soon <u>over</u>.

A preposition usually comes before its object. But sometimes the object comes before the preposition. This is especially common with the pronouns *what, whom, which,* and *that.*

> <u>What</u> were you talking <u>about</u>?
> This is the shovel <u>which</u> I was digging <u>with</u>.

These sentences can often be reworded, with the words in their normal positions. Compare these sentences with the ones above.

> <u>About what</u> were you talking?
> This is the shovel <u>with which</u> I was digging.

As you can see, it is not always wrong to have a preposition at the end of a sentence. Sometimes the preposition is needed because the meaning is not complete without it. Compare the following sentences with the previous ones. The meaning of each one is incomplete because a needed preposition is missing.

Incomplete: What were you talking?
Incomplete: This is the shovel which I was digging.

- When prepositions are similar in spelling or meaning, be careful to use the correct one.

- Do not use *of* for *have*. Do not use unnecessary prepositions.

- A sentence may end with a preposition if it is needed to complete the meaning.

Class Practice

Read these sentences correctly. Sometimes you simply need to leave words out. Not all the sentences contain mistakes.

1. Where will the visitors stay at tonight?
2. We are all here accept Charles.
3. We would of seen them go if we could of been there on time.
4. The money was divided between the four brothers.
5. Where are all the children running to?
6. Gerald fell off of the wagon and got hurt.
7. Rover is different than the other dog we had.
8. He has sneaked in the house again.
9. This is the machine that she sewed the purses with.
10. When he talks at you, you should listen on him.
11. After the test was over with, we played ball in back of the school.
12. Please put the bicycles inside of the barn.
13. She must of wanted to sit besides her mother.
14. Whom are you traveling with?

Written Exercises

Write the headings *Mistakes* and *Corrections.* Under *Mistakes,* write the words that should be omitted or changed in the sentences. Beside the wrong words, write any corrected words under *Corrections.* (Some sentences have only words that should be omitted. They will not have words under *Corrections.*)

Examples: a. Where did you get that drink at?
             b. Jerry sat among Samuel and me.

Answers: **Mistakes**   **Corrections**
             a. at
             b. among   between

1. Divide the candy among you two girls.
2. All the frogs accept one jumped off of the bank and in the water.
3. After the lesson was over with, we took a quiz.
4. John fell off of the roof; he should of been more careful.
5. The children hid between all the trees in back of the house.
6. Does anyone know where Richard is at now?
7. This pretty picture came off of a calendar.
8. Ruth went in Boaz's field to gather grain among all the other reapers.
9. This secret is only among you and me.
10. You should listen on your teacher.
11. James came in the house and sat down besides the stove.
12. Come to the telephone; your brother wants to talk at you.
13. Everyone accept Jane was there before.
14. The place where we went to is hundreds of miles away.
15. I hope my friend sits here besides me.
16. The car was parked in back of a large tree.
17. This test is different than the other one we had.
18. I'll be glad when it is over with.
19. The children sat between the many flowers in the grass.
20. Where are you staying at?

Review Exercises

Copy each adverb clause, and underline the subordinating conjunction. Also copy the verb that the clause modifies. [110]

Example: Lot fled from Sodom before the Lord destroyed the city.
Answer: before the Lord destroyed the city, fled

1. Lot was taken captive when Sodom was defeated.
2. Although Lot had taken the best land, Abraham rescued him.
3. Melchizedek met Abraham after he had defeated the kings.
4. Abraham would not accept the spoils when the king of Sodom offered them to him.

117. Making an Introduction

An introduction helps people who are strangers to get acquainted. Knowing how to introduce people will help you to make friends more easily. The Bible says, "A man that hath friends must shew himself friendly" (Proverbs 18:24). It also says, "Be ye kind one to another" (Ephesians 4:32).

Introducing people that you know can be enjoyable if you follow the rules. There are six main rules for making introductions.

1. To introduce a younger person and an older person, say the older person's name first.

   "Father, this is my friend Roy."
   "Roy, this is my father."

2. To introduce a man and a woman or a boy and a girl of about the same age, say the woman's or girl's name first.

   "Sister Hannah, this is Brother John."
   "Brother John, this is Sister Hannah."

3. To introduce two boys, two girls, two men, or two women of about the same age, say either name first.

   "James, this is my cousin Mark Weaver."
   "Mark, this is my friend James Martin."

4. To introduce anyone to your mother, say "Mother" first.

   "Mother, meet my teacher, Sister Mary."
   "Sister Mary, this is my mother."

5. To introduce one person to a group, say the person's name first.

   "Mark, this is the sixth grade class."
   "This is my friend Mark Hoover from Missouri."

6. To introduce yourself to a stranger, say "Hello" and give your name. Sometimes you will be alone with another person whom you do not know. A good thing to do then is to walk up, smile, and say "Hello. My name is ——— ———. I don't think we have ever met before."

Speak names clearly when you make an introduction. Let your voice and manner show your pleasure in what you are doing. It is also a good idea to add a bit of information about the one whom you are introducing.

If possible, tell about something that you know both persons are interested in, to help them get started in conversation.

> "Laura, this is Carrie Martin. Carrie lived in Guatemala for three years, and she came back only two weeks ago."

When you are introduced to someone, it is a good idea to repeat his name at once. If you have heard it wrong, your mistake can be corrected right away. Repeating the name will also help you to remember it.

> "I'm glad to meet you, Carrie. Are you going back to Guatemala very soon?"

- Be courteous, respectful, and gracious when you make introductions.

- Say an older person's name before a younger person's.

- Say a woman's name before a man's.

- Say either name first when introducing two men, two women, two boys, or two girls of about the same age.

- Always say "Mother" first.

- When introducing one person to a group, say the person's name first.

- Introduce yourself to a stranger when no one else does it for you.

Class Practice

A. Tell which rule in the lesson applies to each introduction.
1. Hello. My name is Susan White. What is yours?
2. Jason, this is my Sunday school class.
3. Father, this is my friend Frank.
4. Donna, this is my cousin Darla.
5. Mother, this is Sister Mary, my teacher.

B. Tell whose name should be said first in the following introductions. Also tell what you might say in each case. You may use real names.
1. Your teacher who is a woman, and your uncle
2. Your mother and your Bible school teacher
3. Your brother and a boy who is his age
4. Yourself and a stranger

5. Your cousin and your classmates
6. Your younger brother and your Sunday school teacher

C. Make an introduction in class, using real names. You may get ideas from Part B.

Written Exercises

Write what you might say in the following introductions. You may use real names.

1. Your sister and a girl who is her age
2. Your teacher who is a man, and your aunt
3. Your cousin and your Bible school class
4. Your mother and a friend from school
5. Yourself and a stranger
6. Your grandfather and a neighbor man about your father's age

Review Exercises

A. Write the names of the two rhythm patterns you have studied. [104]

B. Read the poem below, and do these exercises. [104, 108, 112]
1. Copy the first line, mark the rhythm, and name the rhythm pattern.
2. Copy all the pairs of rhyming words.
3. Copy the simile in the first line.
4. Personification is used in this poem.
   a. What prepositional phrase describes the appearance of each wave?
   b. What are three verbs that tell what the waves did?

Twilight at Sea

The twilight hours, like birds, flew by,
    As lightly and as free;
Ten thousand stars were in the sky,
    Ten thousand on the sea;
For every wave, with dimpled face,
    That leaped upon the air,
Had caught a star in its embrace,
    And held it trembling there.
                    —Amelia Welby

118. Coordinating Conjunctions

A conjunction is a word that joins words, phrases, or clauses in a sentence. A conjunction is often called a *connector* because it connects various sentence parts.

A *coordinating conjunction* joins sentence parts of parallel structure. Words are joined to words, phrases to phrases, and clauses to clauses.

> Oranges **and** bananas were sold at the stand.
> (single words joined by *and*)

> The sparrow flew around the room **and** out the window.
> (phrases joined by *and*)

> I just had it yesterday, **but** now I cannot find it.
> (clauses joined by *but*)

When you use coordinating conjunctions, be careful to join only sentence parts that are parallel. Perhaps the most common mistake is to join words to phrases. Study the following examples.

> **Incorrect:** The dog ran around the room **and** outside.
> (phrase joined to word)
> **Correct:** The dog ran around the room **and** out the door.
> (phrase joined to phrase)
> **Correct:** The dog ran around the room, **and** then he ran outside. (clause joined to clause)

> **Incorrect:** A car slid across the road, into a guardrail, **and** hit a tree. (phrases joined to word)
> **Correct:** A car slid across the road, into a guardrail, **and** into a tree. (three parallel phrases)
> **Correct:** A car slid across the road and into a guardrail, **and** then it hit a tree. (phrase joined to phrase, and clause joined to clause)

The main coordinating conjunctions are *and, but, or, for, nor,* and *yet.* *So* can be used as a coordinating conjunction when it means *therefore.* Coordinating conjunctions can show various relationships, as shown below.

> **Continuation or addition:**
> Pennsylvania has beautiful rivers **and** mountains.
> Mary and Edith washed the dishes **and** swept the floors.
> Children should not talk back, **nor** should they pout.

Contrast:

David sinned, **but** he repented.

God warned Solomon, **yet** he fell into idolatry.

Choice or option:

I'm sure they were raccoons **or** opossums.

Go to the bus stop now, **or** you will be late.

Cause and effect:

We had recess inside, **for** it was raining.

It was raining, **so** we had recess inside.

A comma is placed before a conjunction that joins two independent clauses in a compound sentence.

Cover the plants carefully, or the frost will ruin them.

Correlative conjunctions are connecting words used in pairs.

either—or   neither—nor
both—and   not only—but also

Correlative conjunctions also join sentence parts of parallel structure, the same as coordinating conjunctions. Study the following examples.

We hoe **either** in the morning **or** in the evening.

Both Jesus **and** His disciples were Galileans.

Neither you **nor** I can fully understand God's great love.

Not only petroleum **but also** coal is scarce in some places.

When using *not only—but also,* as correlative conjunctions, be sure to include all the words in the pair. Do not omit the word *also.*

Incorrect: We had **not only** pie **but** cake for dessert.

Correct: We had **not only** pie **but also** cake for dessert.

Sometimes *or, either-or,* or *neither-nor* is used with two subjects, one singular and one plural. Then the verb should agree with the subject that is nearer to it.

Either the dog **or** the kittens were fed. (plural)

Either the kittens **or** the dog was fed. (singular)

Neither the door **nor** the windows are securely closed. (plural)

Neither the windows **nor** the door is securely closed. (singular)

- A conjunction is a word that joins words, phrases, or clauses in a sentence.

- A *coordinating conjunction* joins sentence parts of parallel structure. It must not be used to join a word to a phrase.

- *Correlative conjunctions* are connecting words used in pairs.

- Correlative conjunctions also join sentence parts of parallel structure.

Class Practice

A. Tell which words are conjunctions. Tell whether they join *words, phrases,* or *clauses.*
   1. A large tan-and-white cat was hunting in the meadow.
   2. The children raised corn in their garden and in the field.
   3. One cow stood on the road and bawled.
   4. Both the hired man and the boys chased her back in.
   5. Father will leave either in the morning or after lunch.
   6. We wanted to plant corn, but it rained.

B. Tell how to correct these sentences so that the parts joined are parallel.
   1. Our cousins will come today or in the morning.
   2. The shoes were not under the bed, the dresser, or in the closet.
   3. Be of good cheer and brave.
   4. Father is outside or in the basement.
   5. The ball flew across the yard, over the road, and hit the barn.

C. Tell how to correct the following sentences.
   1. We learned not only the capital but the shape of each state.
   2. Either the pills or the injection are helpful.
   3. Neither the mother nor her girls was helpless when it came to cooking.
   4. We found the recipe and made the dough but Mother baked the bread.
   5. The cats or the dog dig holes in the flower beds.

Written Exercises

A. Copy the conjunctions. Write whether they join *words*, *phrases*, or *clauses*.
1. Uncle David is a carpenter and farmer.
2. Mother bought new shoes for John, but they do not fit him.
3. This cake is for lunch or for supper.
4. Both you and I can use this.
5. We will shop either on Friday or on Saturday.
6. The deer looked at us for a little, but soon it ran into the woods.

B. Rewrite these sentences so that the parts joined are parallel.
1. They read loudly and in a distinct manner.
2. We usually pray in the morning, at noon, and evening.
3. The owl flew silently and with great swiftness.
4. We ran downhill and into the woods.
5. Swiftly and with skill, the nurse cleaned the boy's wounds.
6. We should be respectful to our teachers, our ministers, and respect our parents.

C. Rewrite the following sentences correctly.
1. Neither Father nor the boys has ever been there.
2. Either you boys or Susan were helping us.
3. Pick not only the beans but the peas.
4. We got three bushels of beans and they got four bushels of peas.
5. The storm brought not only rain but hail.
6. We gathered a bucket full of hailstones and Mother made ice cream.

Review Exercises

Diagram the following sentences.

1. Harold repaired the roof of the shed while Jacob painted the trim around the windows.
2. Yesterday we picked some pretty yellow daffodils for Grandmother and Grandfather.
3. The purple lilacs by the side of the house smell rich and sweet.
4. The boy who was here today is my cousin.

---

119. Subordinating Conjunctions

Conjunctions are in two main classes: *coordinating conjunctions* and *subordinating conjunctions*. Something that is subordinate is in a lower class, or it is dependent on something else. A subordinating conjunction introduces a dependent clause. A dependent clause cannot stand alone as a main clause can.

Subordinating conjunctions join clauses of *unequal* rank in a sentence. They do not join words or phrases, as coordinating conjunctions do. They are used only to join dependent clauses to independent clauses.

There are more subordinating conjunctions than coordinating conjunctions. Some common subordinating conjunctions are listed here.

after	if	until
although	since	when
as	than	where
because	though	while
before	unless	

Some words in the list above may also be used as adverbs or prepositions. They are subordinating conjunctions only when they connect two clauses.

Subordinating conjunctions introduce adverb clauses that tell *how, when, where,* or *why.*

Do unto others <u>as you would have them do to you</u>. (tells *how*)
<u>After I did the right thing</u>, I felt better. (tells *when*)
I will go <u>where you go</u>. (tells *where*)
<u>Since you are not ready</u>, we must go without you. (tells *why*)

Since an adverb clause functions as an adverb, the entire clause is diagramed as an adverb. It is placed on its own base line below the word it modifies.

After the hammer hit his thumb, he was more careful.

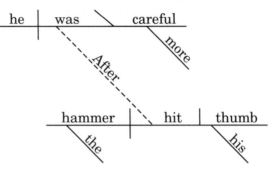

We could hardly see because it was very foggy.

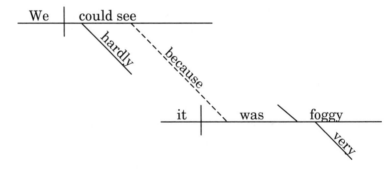

When *as* or *than* is used to state a comparison, it is followed by a clause rather than a single word. Consider this sentence. Which pronoun in parentheses is correct?

Elizabeth is not as tall as (I, me).

Since *as* is a conjunction in this sentence, it must be followed by a clause having a subject and a verb. But where is the verb? It is the word *am*. (The verb is not stated, but understood.) The sentence is really saying, *Elizabeth is not as tall as I am*. So the nominative case *I* must be used.

Consider the following sentence, which uses the conjunction *than*.

They came sooner than (we, us).

This sentence means, *They came sooner than <u>we came</u>.* So the nominative case *we* must be used.

- A *subordinating conjunction* joins clauses of *unequal* rank in a sentence. The clause it introduces in an adverb clause.

- When *as* or *than* is used to state a comparison, it is followed by a clause rather than a single word. If a pronoun follows *as* or *than*, it is the subject and must be in the nominative case.

Class Practice

A. Tell which words are subordinating conjunctions. Read the clause that each one introduces.
   1. While the boys waited, they studied their Bible lessons.
   2. He came before I did.
   3. Jesus departed to a mountain after He sent the multitude away.
   4. When the lame man saw Peter and John, he asked for money.
   5. A lamp shines more brightly than a candle does.

B. On the chalkboard, diagram sentences 1–4 in Part A.

C. Read each sentence, using the correct pronoun. Also tell what verb is understood.
   1. These trees are not as tall as (they, them).
   2. She can write more neatly than (I, me).
   3. Can you type as fast as (she, her)?
   4. Saul was not as brave as (he, him).
   5. God is wiser than (we, us).

Written Exercises

A. Copy the subordinating conjunctions in these sentences.
   1. When we plant a garden, we look forward to the harvest.
   2. The motor stopped because the electricity went off.
   3. Since we oiled the sewing machine, it works fine.
   4. Venus travels around the sun faster than Mars does.
   5. Unless we work faster, we will not finish on time.
   6. We should bale the hay after it is dry.
   7. If it rains, the hay will be ruined.
   8. When the mailman comes, he might bring us a letter.

B. Diagram these sentences.
1. These apples should be picked when they are ripe.
2. While we were waiting, he was studying.
3. Farmers rode their machines as the horses pulled them.
4. The fields were very dry before the rain came.
5. Because his leg was broken, the boy walked with crutches.

C. Choose a fitting subordinating conjunction for each short blank, and supply a main clause of your own for the long blank. Write the whole sentence.
1. ―――― Marcus looked up from his work, ―――――――.
2. ―――― I realized what was happening, ―――――――.
3. ―――― the rain stopped, ―――――――.

D. Write the correct pronoun for each sentence. Also write the verb that is understood, and put parentheses around it.

> **Examples:** a. He can work faster than (I, me).
> b. We did not arrive as soon as (they, them).
> **Answers:** a. I (can work)
> b. they (arrived)

1. Our parents have more experience than (we, us).
2. Did you miss as many days of school as (I, me)?
3. John declared that Jesus was greater than (he, him).
4. I cannot sew as well as (she, her).
5. We were later than (they, them).

Review Exercises

A. These sentences contain adjective clauses, which are introduced by relative pronouns rather than subordinating conjunctions. Copy each adjective clause, and underline the relative pronoun. [97]
1. He is the man whom Father saw.
2. My brother sold the chairs that he sanded.
3. They came from the lady whose house Father remodeled.
4. The dog that barked the loudest ran away first.
5. Andrew read the short note, which the teacher left on his desk.
6. Dr. Alvin L. Punt, who teaches at Smith College, has experimented with plant diseases.
7. John telephoned the man whose wallet he had found.
8. Only those who have a license may drive on the road.

B. Write the correct words in parentheses.

1. Most of the girls (know, knows) their verses.
2. None of the milk (is, are) sour.
3. Most of the children usually (choose, chooses) the colorful posters.
4. No one (bring, brings) (his, their) lunch anymore.
5. None of the boys (is, are) ready yet.
6. Many of the children (walk, walks) to our school.
7. Cousin Ann sews very (good, well).
8. Aunt Sarah surely makes (good, well) candy.
9. Mark doesn't feel (good, well).
10. I haven't told (nobody, anybody) the secret.
11. Gerald and Ben don't have (none, any) at all.
12. I hardly had (no, any) time to finish.

---

120. Avoiding Misplaced Phrases and Clauses

When phrases and clauses are used as modifiers, they may be put at various places in a sentence. But you must be careful, or you may put them in the wrong place—with absurd or confusing results. Be sure that your sentences say what you mean for them to say.

An adjective phrase must be placed immediately after the noun or pronoun that it modifies.

Misplaced: The car ran into a post <u>without brakes</u>.
Correct: The car <u>without brakes</u> ran into a post.

Misplaced: Sister Anna brought a book for the boy <u>in a paper bag</u>.
Correct: Sister Anna brought a book <u>in a paper bag</u> for the boy.

An adjective clause must also be placed immediately after the noun or pronoun that it modifies.

Misplaced: The tree house is in that tree <u>which the boys built</u>.
Correct: The tree house <u>which the boys built</u> is in that tree.

Misplaced: He sold the table to his uncle <u>that he just made</u>.
Correct: He sold the table <u>that he just made</u> to his uncle.
Correct: He sold his uncle the table <u>that he just made</u>.

In the last sentence above, notice that the phrase *to his uncle* is changed to an indirect object. This is another useful way to correct some sentences with misplaced modifiers.

An adverb phrase may come immediately after the word it modifies, but it may also be found at other places in a sentence. Always be sure it is in a place where it clearly modifies the word you intend.

I received a package <u>from my grandmother</u> <u>in the mailbox</u>.

Both *from my grandmother* and *in the mailbox* are adverb phrases that modify *received*. But the second phrase could seem like an adjective phrase that tells which grandmother. Surely your grandmother was not in the mailbox! And if the phrases are exchanged, the sentence seems to say that the mailbox was from your grandmother.

I received a package <u>in the mailbox</u> <u>from my grandmother</u>.

The best and clearest way is to put one phrase at the beginning of the sentence.

<u>In the mailbox</u> I received a package <u>from my grandmother</u>.

Here are several more sentences with misplaced adverb phrases.

Misplaced: I saw the children playing softball <u>through the window</u>.
Correct: <u>Through the window</u> I saw the children playing softball.

Misplaced: I read about the earthquake that destroyed many homes <u>in our church paper</u>.
Correct: I read <u>in our church paper</u> about the earthquake that destroyed many homes.

Do not place an adverb phrase between two verbs when it could logically modify either one.

Mother said <u>on Wednesday</u> she would pack my lunch.

Does this sentence mean that Mother *said* something on Wednesday, or that she *would pack* something on Wednesday? It could mean either. Compare the following, corrected sentences.

On <u>Wednesday</u> Mother said she would pack my lunch.
Mother said she would pack my lunch <u>on Wednesday</u>.

- An adjective phrase or clause must be placed immediately after the noun or pronoun that it modifies.

- An adverb phrase must be put in a place where it clearly modifies the word intended.

Class Practice

Decide where the misplaced phrases or clauses belong. Read each sentence correctly.

1. The train stopped and let the people off with two steam locomotives.
2. She sent her granddaughter a card that had measles.
3. The girl went to the doctor with severe headaches.
4. School was closed because of the storm by the principal.
5. We watched the geese flying south through our binoculars.
6. The man bought several dozen ears of corn with a gold watch.
7. Martha wrote a letter while she traveled on a piece of notebook paper.
8. In the clothes basket I saw the wet laundry and hung it up.
9. My teacher said on Monday she would give the test.
10. Mother said on my birthday we would have a picnic.
11. The auctioneer sold the chair to the wealthy lady that was two hundred years old.
12. That chocolate cake was baked by Nancy which was so delicious.
13. We helped the Martins to clean the house on Railroad Avenue that they had recently bought.
14. We bought a new table from the carpenter with a hardwood top.

Written Exercises

Rewrite these sentences, putting the misplaced phrases or clauses where they belong.

1. John wrote a note while he waited on a piece of scrap paper.
2. I saw the dessert that Mother had made in the refrigerator.
3. My uncle told me on my birthday he would take us to the zoo.
4. The boy came slowly down the stairs with a broken leg.

5. Brother Daniel told us about pioneers who used oxen in history class.
6. The motorist was fined for violating a traffic law by the judge.
7. The teacher read us a story about some missionaries from the church papers.
8. The boy found a blacksnake that was wearing a straw hat.
9. Sarah passed chips to her friends on paper plates.
10. He shot the bear just before it reached him with his gun.
11. Janice saw a fisherman catch a huge trout from her bicycle.
12. That man is the father of the baby girl in the black suit.
13. Father said on Wednesday he wanted to begin planting.
14. Grandmother said on my birthday she would send me a book.
15. Gerald bought a whistle at the department store that cost four dollars.
16. She gave a can of juice to each student that weighed sixteen ounces.
17. The museum bought a book from the antique man that was three hundred years old.
18. A motorist stopped me who wanted directions.

Review Exercises

A. Write *yes* or *no* to tell whether each underlined verb is transitive. If it is transitive, write its direct object. [38]
  1. Hornets <u>chew</u> wood to make the paper for their nests.
  2. Strangely enough, the paper nest <u>is</u> waterproof!
  3. Honeybees <u>lose</u> their stingers, but hornets do not.
  4. That hornet's nest <u>looks</u> unusually big.
  5. A hornet <u>stings</u> sooner than a wasp or a bee.
  6. A hornet is the farmer's friend because it <u>eats</u> harmful insects.

B. Write whether each sentence is in the active or passive voice. [55]
  1. She was stung by a hornet.
  2. A hornet does inject a venom into the wound.
  3. The venom causes a very painful sting.
  4. That large nest was built by hornets.
  5. Each nest is used only one summer.

C. Copy and capitalize correctly. [73, 74]
  1. barbara said, "every wednesday in the fall and winter, i go to see my spanish teacher, miss viola n. monteroso, who lives in millersville, pennsylvania."

2.   **to remember**
find out what god would have you do,
    and do that little well;
for what is great and what is small,
    this only he can tell.

                  —Author unknown

121. Courtesy in Conversation

We all enjoy talking with our friends. We want to exchange news and express our opinions. We want to encourage each other to keep doing right. Even when we have nothing spectacular to say, we can still find something worthwhile to talk about!

We enjoy talking with some friends more than with others. One reason may be that they have such interesting things to say. But there may be another reason. Perhaps we enjoy talking with them because they *listen* so well!

One of the most important rules in good conversation is to listen carefully. The Bible says, "Let every man be swift to hear, slow to speak, slow to wrath" (James 1:19). By being more ready to listen than to speak, we will also follow the verse that says, "In honour preferring one another" (Romans 12:10).

When someone is talking to you, listen with interest and follow his train of thought. Do not just wait quietly until it is your turn to speak. Of course you would not interrupt another person who is talking, but that is not enough. You must take a real interest in what he is saying. How few of us do this really well!

Part of good listening is asking questions and talking about things that are of interest to others. This is not difficult because friends naturally share common interests. Guide the topic into areas where your friends feel at ease. Then you will learn more about them and their interests. Do not be selfish and talk only about yourself or the things that happen to you. And of course you must not boast about your own accomplishments. Learn to be interested in others, and take pleasure in their successes.

Another important rule is to speak kindly. One familiar Bible command is "Be ye kind" (Ephesians 4:32). Another command is "Speak not evil one of another" (James 4:11). Never speak *to* others or *about* others in a way that you would not want them to speak.

Do not be eager to criticize, correct, or contradict the things others say. That is like throwing dirt into the machinery! When you need to disagree with someone, be kind and considerate. Do not boldly challenge him or rudely contradict him, and do not get into an argument with him. You may say something like "Some people believe differently about that" or "Could it be that it is like this?" When you agree with what someone says, tell him so. Be positive about areas of agreement, and do not emphasize differences.

Use correct, clear English when you speak. Do not talk too rapidly or too loudly. Do not use pronouns without antecedents ("They say...") or other vague, general expressions ("Everyone thinks ..."). Do not assume that people will know what you mean unless you express yourself clearly.

Courtesy in conversation is not based on keeping a set of rules. In fact, too much concern about "the proper rules" will make you uneasy and self-conscious (thinking mostly about yourself). But if you take a sincere interest in other people, your conversations with them will be truly enjoyable.

- The most important rules in good conversation are to listen carefully and to speak kindly.

- Ask polite questions, and show that you are interested in others.

- When you need to disagree, do it kindly.

- Use correct, clear English when you speak.

Class Practice

Answer these questions.

1. According to the lesson, what are the most important rules in conversation?
2. What are some things we should not do in conversation?
3. Why do we enjoy talking with some friends more than with others?
4. When you are speaking, what are some things that will make you hard to understand?

5. If there is someone in the group who has little to say, how might you encourage him to say more?

6. When someone is obviously wrong in what he is saying, what should you *not* do? What should you do?

Written Exercises

Write three polite questions that you might ask the following persons.

1. Your friend who just came back from visiting British Columbia.
2. Your friend who is in bed with a broken leg.
3. Your friend who has a new baby brother or sister.
4. A cousin your age who just moved to a new area and is visiting at your house.

Review Exercises

A. Write *true* or *false*. [50, 53]

1. When you take notes, you should use more than one reference source.
2. Knowing how to arrange notes in outline form will probably be valuable to you later in life.
3. Your outline should include main ideas from all your reference sources.
4. You should arrange the main ideas on your outline in the order you found them.
5. There is only one right way to arrange the order of your main ideas.
6. Your outline should include all the details that are in your notes.

B. Write the parts of speech described in these sentences.

1. It may be limiting or descriptive.
2. It modifies a verb, adjective, or adverb.
3. It takes the place of a noun.
4. It shows action or being.
5. It tells *which, whose, how many,* or *what kind of.*
6. It modifies a noun or pronoun.
7. It names a person, place, thing, or idea.
8. It is a connecting word that begins a phrase.
9. It may be an article (*a, an, the*).
10. It tells *how, when, where,* or *to what degree.*

C. Diagram the following sentences.
1. The sun is the nearest star.
2. The sun rotates on its axis.
3. Do not look at the sun without special protection for your eyes.
4. Some telescopes project the sun's image onto a screen.
5. Others have special sun filters.

---

122. Interjections

An *interjection* is a word that expresses strong feeling. It is not used as a subject, predicate, object, modifier, or any other sentence part. So we say that an interjection is not related to the rest of the sentence. It is an independent word.

An interjection usually comes at the beginning of a sentence. Some common interjections are listed below.

ah	ha	oh	well	whew
alas	ho	ouch	what	why

There are many interjections, but not all of them are proper to use. Words like *hello* and *good-bye* may be used as interjections in sentences. But it is not proper to use interjections that express anger or contempt. It is also improper to use interjections that are slang words or to use a common word as an interjection that has nothing to do with the normal meaning of the word. We should use only those interjections that are suitable for God's people.

The Bible uses several interjections. The words *lo* and *behold* are interjections used to call attention to something or to express wonder or surprise. *Amen* expresses agreement or approval. *Alas* shows sorrow, pity, or concern. The interjection *ah* is a synonym for *oh*. It expresses feelings such as astonishment, grief, or desire.

"Lo, I come to do thy will, O God" (Hebrews 10:9).
"Behold, he that keepeth Israel shall neither slumber nor sleep" (Psalm 121:4).
Gideon said, "Alas, O Lord God! for because I have seen an angel of the Lord face to face" (Judges 6:22).3

An interjection that is spoken with strong expression is followed by an exclamation point. The word after the interjection is capitalized as the first word of a new sentence.

> Ouch! Did I step on a nail?
> Hello! Come on in.

An interjection that is spoken mildly is followed by a comma. The word after the comma does not begin with a capital letter unless it is normally capitalized.

> Oh, it feels cool in the shade.
> Well, I don't know the answer yet.
> Say, did you see the clock?

Since an interjection is not related to the rest of the sentence, it is diagramed on a separate line.

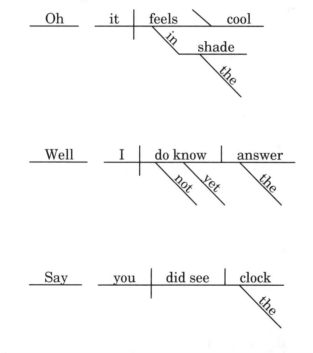

- An interjection is a word that expresses strong feeling. It is not used as a sentence part, but is an independent word.

- A strong interjection is followed by an exclamation point. A mild interjection is followed by a comma.

Class Practice

A. Read each interjection, and tell whether it should be followed by a *comma* or an *exclamation point*. Also tell whether the next word should begin with a *small letter* or a *capital letter.*
   1. Ouch my finger was in the way.
   2. Oh what a beautiful sunset that is.
   3. Well the job is finally completed.
   4. Hello do come in.

B. Diagram these sentences at the chalkboard.
   1. What! Haven't you finished yet?
   2. Why, there is your lost key!
   3. Alas! The axhead was borrowed.
   4. Behold, it is floating.

Written Exercises

A. Copy each interjection, and put a comma or an exclamation point after it. Write *yes* or *no* to tell whether the next word should be capitalized.
   1. Well it's time to leave for church.
   2. Whew it is windy tonight.
   3. Why this is a wonderful surprise!
   4. What this must be where the chickens are getting out.
   5. Oh look at that gurgling spring of water.
   6. Lo in her mouth was an olive leaf.
   7. Alas the great city of Babylon has been destroyed.

B. Diagram these sentences.
   1. Hello. My name is Jonathan.
   2. Say! Can you answer this question?
   3. Well, show me the problem.
   4. Ouch, this needle is sharp!
   5. Why, here is the book that I had lost.
   6. Lo, mine eye hath seen all this.

Review Exercises

A. Write the tense of each underlined verb or verb phrase. [32–36]

present	past	future
present perfect	past perfect	future perfect

1. I <u>see</u> a ruby-throated hummingbird on the clothesline.
2. I <u>saw</u> one sipping nectar from our trumpet vine yesterday.
3. I <u>have seen</u> several of them.
4. I <u>had</u> not <u>known</u> that they live in this area.
5. The Lord willing, we <u>shall see</u> you next Wednesday.
6. I am quite sure that <u>I shall have finished</u> before you return.

B. Rewrite each sentence, putting the misplaced phrase or clause where it belongs. [120]
1. The lonely old lady watched the happy children with sad eyes.
2. The car is in this garage that was wrecked.
3. My grandmother bought me the book at the bookstore that I wanted.
4. My mother said on Monday she hopes to bake pies.

C. Diagram these sentences. [111]
1. The garden looked greener after it had rained.
2. The bus had left before I got there.
3. When Christians pray, God hears them.
4. While they are yet speaking, I will hear.

---

123. Review of the Parts of Speech

There are eight parts of speech altogether: *noun* (n.), *pronoun* (pron.), *verb* (v.), *adjective* (adj.), *adverb* (adv.), *preposition* (prep.), *conjunction* (conj.), and *interjection* (interj.). Be sure you know their definitions and abbreviations.

A **noun** is a word that names a person, place, thing, or idea.

A **pronoun** is a word that takes the place of a noun.

A **verb** is a word that shows action or being.

An **adjective** is a word that modifies a noun or pronoun. A limiting adjective tells *which, whose,* or *how many.* A descriptive adjective tells *what kind of.* The articles *a, an,* and *the* are also adjectives.

An **adverb** is a word that modifies a verb, an adjective, or another adverb. It tells *how, when, where,* or *to what degree.*

A **preposition** is a connecting word that begins a prepositional phrase.

A **conjunction** is a word that joins words, phrases, or clauses.

An **interjection** is a word that expresses strong feeling.

The *parts of speech* are not always the same as the *parts of a sentence*. As a sentence part, a noun may be a subject, direct object, predicate nominative, indirect object, or object of a preposition. But as a part of speech, it is a noun no matter how it is used. The same is true of a pronoun.

There is less difference for the other parts of speech. For example, an adjective or an adverb is called the same whether we mean a sentence part or a part of speech. Compare the labels above the following sentences.

Sentence parts labeled:

v.   sub. adj.   d.o.   prep. adj.   o.p.

Hear ye the word of the Lord.

Parts of speech labeled:

v.   pron. adj.   n.   prep. adj.   n.

Hear ye the word of the Lord.

When you are told to label the parts of speech in a sentence, you should follow the second pattern shown above.

Generally, you can tell by looking at a word whether it is a noun or a verb or some other part of speech. But remember, the way a word is used in a sentence determines its part of speech. Sometimes you must think carefully to know for sure what part of speech a word is. Be especially careful in the following cases.

1. *Some words can be used as prepositions or adverbs.* A preposition always begins a phrase. An adverb stands alone. So you should say the word and ask *whom* or *what.* If there is no noun or pronoun to answer the question, the word must be an adverb.

> We went <u>down</u> in the morning.
> > **Think:** Down *what*? There is no noun or pronoun to answer the question. *Down* is an adverb.

> They went <u>down</u> the stairs.
> > **Think:** Down *what*? The answer is *stairs. Down* is a preposition.

2. *Sometimes a word that is normally a noun or pronoun is used as an adjective.* Be sure the word is not used as a modifier before you decide that it is a noun or a pronoun.

> That was a delicious <u>cherry</u>. (names a thing; noun)
> Mother made a delicious <u>cherry</u> pie. (modifies *pie;* adjective)
>
> <u>Each</u> child brings his own glove. (modifies *child*; adjective)
> <u>Each</u> brings his own glove. (stands alone; pronoun)

3. *Sometimes a word that is usually an adjective is used as a noun.*

> The <u>rich</u> and the <u>poor</u> meet together.
> A word to the <u>wise</u> is sufficient.

We normally expect the underlined words to be used as adjectives. However, in these sentences they do not modify other words. Rather, the words *rich, poor,* and *wise* all name people. So they are nouns in these sentences.

What is the best way to label the parts of speech in a sentence? Begin the same way you do when you diagram. First, find all the verbs and label them. Then find all the nouns and pronouns, and label them. Next, find all the adjectives and adverbs. Then look for prepositional phrases, and label the prepositions. Last of all, label the conjunctions and interjections.

- You should know the definitions and abbreviations of all the eight parts of speech.

- You cannot always tell what part of speech a word is just by looking at the word itself. The way the word is used in a sentence determines its part of speech.

Class Practice

A. Name the eight parts of speech, and write their abbreviations on the chalkboard.

B. Name the parts of speech described here.
1. It modifies a verb, adjective, or adverb.
2. It modifies a noun or pronoun.
3. It is a connecting word that begins a phrase.

4. It joins words, phrases, or clauses.
5. It expresses strong feeling.
6. It names a person, place, thing, or idea.
7. It can be limiting or descriptive.
8. It takes the place of a noun.
9. It shows action or being.
10. It may be an article (*a, an,* or *the*).
11. It tells *how, when, where,* or *to what degree.*
12. It tells *which, whose, how many,* or *what kind of.*

C. Tell whether each underlined word is a *preposition, adverb,* or a *conjunction.*
   1. <u>After</u> the crisis was <u>over</u>, we all came <u>back</u> <u>to</u> our seats <u>and</u> breathed a sigh of relief.
   2. <u>During</u> the night, the tree came <u>down</u> <u>across</u> the road.

D. Name the part of speech for each word.
   1. Well, bring your question here to me.
   2. The chocolate sundae, cold and creamy, tasted refreshing on that warm day.
   3. Jesus healed the blind and the lame.

Written Exercises

In all these exercises, you may use abbreviations for the parts of speech.

A. Write whether each underlined word is a *noun,* a *pronoun,* or an *adjective.*
   1. <u>His</u> <u>papers</u> are here. <u>Mine</u> are over there.
   2. <u>That</u> <u>boy</u> <u>who</u> is standing must be <u>your</u> <u>brother</u>.
   3. <u>Many</u> are called, but <u>few</u> are chosen.
   4. The <u>meek</u> shall inherit the <u>earth</u>.

B. Write whether each underlined word is a *preposition,* an *adverb,* or a *conjunction.*
   1. The lid came <u>off</u> <u>as</u> we drove <u>around</u> the corner.
   2. This is different <u>from</u> ours, <u>but</u> we like it anyway.
   3. The cows were <u>inside</u> the barn <u>before</u> the storm came <u>up</u>.
   4. Walter tore <u>up</u> his paper. (Be careful!)

C. Copy each sentence, and label the parts of speech.
   1. Whew! That was hard work.
   2. Well, either you or I must do it soon.

3. The red-and-orange butterfly flitted daintily from one fragrant flower to another.
4. Swiftly and skillfully, the blacksmith put a new shoe on the horse.
5. Jesus helped the sad, the sick, and the sinful.
6. We pray in the morning, at noon, and in the evening.
7. Today we shall wash, and tomorrow we shall iron.
8. This is the man whom you seek.

Review Exercises

Diagram these sentences.

1. A calculator is a small but useful machine.
2. The left margin should always be straight.
3. Some fruit from the basket was lying at the side of the road.
4. The deer were eating apples from the trees during the night.
5. After the storm, the rescuers helped the needy and the homeless.
6. Before the rain started, the boys closed their window.
7. We finally have a cherry tree that produces good fruit.
8. Heaven and earth shall pass away, but My words shall not pass away.
9. Every good gift and every perfect gift is from above, and cometh down from the Father of lights.
10. Parents, teachers, and ministers instruct us about God.

---

124. Chapter 10 Review

Class Practice

A. Give the definition of a preposition.

B. Read these sentences, correcting the errors.
1. I talked at the stranger that visited our class on Sunday.
2. I listened at what he said about his home and school.
3. All his cows were Holsteins accept one.
4. One Jersey cow stood among two Holsteins.
5. A new house is being built besides our house.
6. Their new porch is different than ours.
7. In back of the house is a garden.
8. Among the two houses is a large lawn.

9. Inside of this closet is an ironing board.
10. The treat was for the boys who helped outside of the house.
11. I should of brought more.
12. We gave a scrapbook to the sick girl with glossy white pages.
13. The boy lay on the bed with a broken leg all day long.
14. I received some fruit from my cousin in a basket.
15. The minister led the devotional at school from Guatemala.
16. Father said on Saturday we would go to the sale.
17. From the refrigerator I packed the basket with leftovers.
18. There was not only peach pie but cherry pie.
19. Either the two boys or the one girl clean the floors on Saturday.
20. Either Mary or the boys scrubs the tank every morning.
21. The book was about explorers that the teacher read aloud.
22. Yesterday I gave my report to my teacher that was several pages long.
23. Slowly and with care, the farmer backed the truck toward the loading ramp.
24. He unloaded the hogs, loaded some calves, and some goats.
25. The marble rolled down the steps, across the floor, and disappeared down the register.

C. Tell how the following introductions should be improved.
  1. Introducing yourself to a stranger:

> "Hello! What is your name?
> Where are you from?"

  2. Introducing your classmate to your father.

> "Samuel, this is my father."
> "Father, this is my classmate Samuel."

  3. Introducing your classmate to your cousin the same age.

> "Samuel, this is my cousin Raymond."
> "Raymond, this is my classmate Samuel."

D. Answer these questions.
  1. What are the most important rules in conversation?
  2. What are some things we should not do in conversation?
  3. If there is someone in the group who has little to say, how might you encourage him to say more?
  4. When someone is obviously wrong in what he is saying, what should you *not* do? What should you do?

Written Exercises

A. Copy each prepositional phrase. Underline the preposition, and put parentheses around the object of the preposition.
   1. Who came down to the river and saw the baby in the basket?
   2. What brave girl came from her hiding place and spoke to the princess?

B. Copy each dependent clause, and underline the subordinating conjunction that introduces it.
   1. Since the baby needed a nurse, the princess gave him to his mother.
   2. Moses' mother gave him back to the princess after several years had passed.
   3. Although Moses was raised in the king's palace, he chose to identify with the people of God.
   4. Moses led his people out of Egypt when he became a man.

C. Copy each sentence, and label the parts of speech.
   1. What! All the doughnuts that we made have been sold already.
   2. Mother had made dozens of doughnuts for the market, but they were sold before noon.
   3. In life we must accept the bad with the good.

D. Diagram the following sentences.
   1. The boy in first grade and the boy in third grade are brothers.
   2. Before they came here, they lived in New York.
   3. What! Is the man who spoke first your brother?
   4. Well, I hadn't seen him for a long time.

E. Write whose name should be said first in the following introductions.
   1. Your father and your classmate
   2. Your aunt and your teacher who is a man
   3. Your mother and your teacher who is a woman
   4. Your friend from another state and several friends from your Sunday school class
   5. Yourself and a stranger

Dictionary

Guide Words   Entry Words

Pronunciations

Word Families

Synonyms

Homophones

Antonyms

Bible Dictionary

Concordance

Word Order

Variety

Chapter Eleven

Studying Words

Using Sentence Variety

The
dictionary
helps us to use words
correctly.

A word fitly spoken is like apples of gold in pictures of silver.

Proverbs 25:11

125. Using the Dictionary

The dictionary is like a valuable servant. It quickly provides us with information on the pronunciations, spellings, and meanings of words. Learn to use this handy servant well.

The *entry words* in a dictionary are in boldface and are listed in alphabetical order. When entry words begin with the same letter, they are alphabetized by the second letter. *Element* comes before *erupt* because *el* comes before *er.* When the first two letters are alike, words are alphabetized by the third letter, and so forth. *Anchor* comes before *angry* because *anc* comes before *ang. Grope* comes before *group* because *grop* comes before *grou.*

Guide words at the top of the page show the first and last entry words on that page. The guide word at the left is the same as the first entry word on the page, and the guide word at the right is the same as the last word on the page. All the words on that page must come alphabetically between the guide words. See the sample dictionary page below.

Alberta   **audience**

Al ber ta (al bèr'tə), *n.* a province in western Canada.

al li ga tor (al'ə gā tər), *n.* 1. a large, thick-skinned reptile that looks much like a crocodile. 2. leather made from the skin of an alligator.

an nounce (ə nouns'), *v.* make known publicly; proclaim. **an nounced, an nounc ing. —an nounc'er** *n.*

an nounce ment (ə nouns' mənt), *n.* something made known publicly; a proclamation.

a pos tro phe (ə pos'trə fē), *n.* a punctuation mark (') used to show possession, to indicate omitted letters, or to form certain plurals: *dog's, we'll, 6's.*

ap pear (ə pir'), *v.* 1. come into view; become visible. 2. seem: *The corn appears to be growing well.* 3. come before a public audience; present oneself: *The governor is to appear in town next week.*

ap proach (ə prōch'), *v.* 1. move toward and come near to, in distance or time: *The plane approached the airport. We are approaching winter. —n.* 2. the act

of coming nearer: *the approach of spring.* 3. a way by which to reach (something); access: *The approach to the house was overgrown with weeds.* 4. method of dealing with a task or problems: *Your approach seems reasonable.*

ap prove (ə prüv'), *v.* 1. consider favorably; be pleased with. 2. agree to; consent to: *The board approved the plans.* **ap proved, ap prov ing.**

ar riv al (ə rī'vəl), *n.* 1. the act of arriving; the coming to a place: *the arrival of the visitors.* 2. a person or thing that arrives: *a bench for late arrivals.*

as sist (ə sist'), *v.* give help to; aid.

at tempt (ə tempt'), *v.* 1. put forth effort to accomplish; try; endeavor. *—n.* 2. an effort to accomplish; a trying.

at tic (at'ik), *n.* the story between the ceiling and the roof of a building.

au di ence (ô'dē əns), *n.* 1. a group of listeners. 2. a

After each entry word is a *phonetic spelling.* The phonetic spelling uses special symbols to show the correct pronunciation of the entry word. It shows the pronunciation of the word according to the pronunciation key.

The *pronunciation key* in the front of the dictionary shows the meaning of each pronunciation symbol. Many dictionaries also have a short pronunciation key at the bottom of each page. Each symbol in the pronunciation key stands for one particular speech sound.

Special symbols and diacritical marks are used in the pronunciation key because the English language has more sounds than letters. An upside-down *e* (ə) is called the *schwa* symbol. Diacritical marks include the bar or macron to show long vowels (such as ā), and one or two dots to show various other vowel sounds.

The phonetic spelling shows how the word is divided into syllables. Sometimes the syllable divisions in the entry word are different from the divisions in the phonetic spelling. This is because the entry word shows the *written* syllable divisions, but the phonetic spelling shows the *spoken* syllable divisions.

Written syllable divisions: morn·ing
Spoken syllable divisions: môr′·ning

Accent marks are used to show which syllables are stressed. Some words have a *primary* and a *secondary* accent. Usually a heavy accent mark shows that a syllable receives heavy stress. A lighter accent mark shows that a syllable receives medium stress. Unaccented syllables are not marked at all. Check your particular dictionary to see how it shows accent.

math′·ə·mat′·iks

If a word has more than one correct pronunciation, more than one pronunciation is shown. If only one syllable of a word has two correct pronunciations, the rest of the word may not be repeated in the second pronunciation. Study the following example.

garage (gə·räzh′, räj′)

You cannot always tell from the spelling how an English word should be pronounced. Do not just guess at the pronunciation of unfamiliar words that you meet in reading. Use your dictionary and find out for sure!

- *Entry words* in a dictionary are in boldface and are listed in alphabetical order.

- *Guide words* at the top of a dictionary page show the first and last entry words on that page.

- *Phonetic spellings* use special symbols to show the correct pronunciation of entry words.

Class Practice

A. Tell how you would pronounce these words. Your teacher may tell you to check the dictionary if you are wrong.

   1. aerie   2. draught   3. chaos   4. malefactor

B. Read each phonetic spelling, and tell how the word is actually spelled.

   1. līk   4. krēm   7. krīm
   2. lik   5. shō   8. shü
   3. nir′·sī′·tid   6. nē′·kap′   9. kwil′·ting

C. Tell whether each entry word would be found on a dictionary page with the guide words *object* and *old*.

   1. ocean   3. oily   5. olive
   2. obey   4. office   6. odd

Written Exercises

A. Make a single list with all these words in alphabetical order.

    scarf   scurry   scene   seal   scroll
    scrape   scour   scythe   scare   shuffle

B. Write *yes* or *no* to tell whether each entry word would be found on a dictionary page with the guide words *scoop* and *scuff*.

   1. scorn   4. scrape   7. scurry   10. scour
   2. scene   5. scythe   8. septic   11. seal
   3. scare   6. scroll   9. scotch   12. screw

C. Write these words in syllables as shown in the entry words. Then mark the primary and secondary accents as shown in the phonetic spellings.

   1. declarative   3. imperative   5. interrogative
   2. exclamatory   4. recognize   6. opportunity

D. Copy each word, and write the phonetic spelling after it. Include the syllable divisions and the accent marks.

   1. plateau   2. enumerate   3. symmetrical

Review Exercises

A. Rewrite each phrase, using a possessive form. [26]

   1. the paws of the raccoon
   2. the tails of the deer
   3. the antlers of the moose
   4. the food of the gulls
   5. the wings of the moth

B. Write the correct pronouns. [61–64]
1. Kendra and (she, her) were feeding bread crusts to the sea gulls.
2. (We, Us) girls picked up many colorful rocks.
3. Give (she, her) the one with white crystals.
4. Take Sandra and (they, them) to the big rocks.
5. These are for Grandmother and (he, him).
6. It was (they, them) at the door.

---

126. Spellings and Meanings in the Dictionary

The dictionary shows the correct spellings of words. If you cannot find a word in the dictionary, you probably do not know how to spell it. Think of other ways the word might be spelled, and keep looking. If you still cannot find it, you may need to ask someone to help you.

A few words have more than one correct spelling. If the alternate spellings are close together in alphabetical order, the more common spelling is used for the entry word and the other one is shown as an alternate spelling. See the entry for *fulfill* below. If the two spellings are not close together, each spelling is shown as a separate entry word, and the entry for the less common spelling refers you to the more common spelling. See the entry for *sceptic* below.

ful·fill or **ful·fil** (fŏŏl·fil′), *v.* To carry out, as a promise.

scep·tic (skep′·tik), *n.* Skeptic.

The dictionary shows irregular plural forms of nouns. It does not show plural forms for words such as *cup* and *glass,* because they are formed by simply adding *-s* or *-es.* But it does show irregular plural forms such as *calves* and *women.* To find an irregular plural form, look up the singular form of the word. The plural form is shown after the entry word, usually with the abbreviation *pl.*

calf (kaf), *n., pl.* **calves**

wom·an (wŏŏm′·ən), *n., pl.* **wom·en**

The dictionary also shows irregular verb forms. If only one past form is shown, the same spelling is used for the past form and the past participle. If two past forms are shown, the first is the past form and the second is the past participle.

bring (bring), *v.* **brought**

grow (grō), *v.* **grew, grown**

The dictionary shows irregular forms of comparison for adjectives and adverbs. If you look up *large,* you may not see *larger* and *largest,* because these are regular forms. But if you look up *ill,* you will also see *worse* and *worst* because these are irregular forms of comparison.

One of the main purposes of a dictionary is to give the meanings of words. If a word has more than one meaning, only one entry word is shown and the different meanings are given. The definitions are usually numbered. Read the definitions for the word *crane* in the illustration below.

crane (krān), *n.* 1. A tall wading bird. 2. A machine for moving heavy objects.

Can you find two cranes in this picture?

Sometimes two or more words come from different sources, but they happen to have the same spelling. Then they have separate entries because each one is actually a different word. See the examples below.

bark¹ (bärk), *n.* The tough outside covering of a tree.
   [from Scandinavian *börkr*]
bark² (bärk), *n.* The short, sharp cry of a dog.
   [from Old English *beorcan*]
bark³ (bärk), *n.* A kind of sailing ship.
   [from Italian *barca*]

A dictionary shows what part of speech a word is. Notice how this is done in the examples in this lesson. *Calf* and *woman* are nouns (*n.*), and *bring* and *grow* are verbs (*v.*).

Dictionaries also give *usage labels* to certain words. Four common labels are *informal, slang, dialectal,* and *archaic.* God has given us language for the purpose of sharing ideas with others. So it is important that we use words in such a way that others clearly understand what we mean.

Informal words are common in everyday use but are not proper in formal writing. They include expressions like *mike* for "microphone" and *elbow grease* for "hard physical effort."

Slang words were first used by people trying to invent clever new ways of saying things. They are not suitable for God's people to use, because many slang words have hidden evil meanings. Using *guy* for "person," *dough* for "money," and *chow* for "food" is slang and not proper English.

Dialectal words are used mainly by people living in certain areas. One example is the word *reckon,* whose standard meaning is "to consider or count." The dialectal meaning of *reckon* is "to suppose or guess." Other words with dialectal meanings are *poke,* meaning "sack," and *all,* meaning "all gone." We should avoid dialectal words in most writing because they may not be clear to the reader.

Archaic words are old words no longer in general use. They include words like *conversation* for "manner of life," *careful* for "anxious," and *chapman* for "merchant." We are especially interested in the archaic words used in the King James Bible.

- A dictionary shows the correct spellings and meanings of words.

- A dictionary shows what part of speech a word is.

- A dictionary gives usage labels to certain words.

Class Practice

A. Use a dictionary to find two different meanings for each word. Give the part of speech for each meaning.
   1. drill   3. right   5. steep
   2. fine   4. wrench   6. rung

B. Answer these questions. If the answer is *no,* tell what the underlined word means.
   1. Can a <u>staff</u> publish a paper?
   2. Can a person ride a <u>mount</u>?

3. Is <u>heartwood</u> shaped like a heart?
4. Can a <u>pointer</u> bark?
5. Can a <u>thunderbolt</u> hold two materials together?
6. Is <u>Phoebe</u> the name of a bird and a name for a girl?
7. Is any group of men a <u>council</u>?
8. Could a sack of feed fall <u>plump</u> beside you?

Written Exercises

A. Write the plural form of each word.
   1. policeman   2. handkerchief   3. secretary   4. zero

B. Write the present form, past form, and past participle of each verb.
   1. strive   2. dig   3. awake   4. forbid

C. Write the three forms of comparison for each adjective or adverb.
   1. early   2. good   3. much   4. far

D. Write the other correct spelling for each word.
   1. sizable   2. slue   3. counselor   4. pickax

E. Write the letter of the correct meaning for each underlined word in the sentences below. Choose from the meanings given. (You will not write all the letters.)

   a. Something that is heard.
   b. A long, wide body of water joining two larger bodies of water.
   c. To cause something to make a noise.
   d. To dive swiftly.
   e. Free from defect or disease.

   1. The priests <u>sounded</u> the trumpets.
   2. We should be thankful for <u>sound</u> minds.
   3. The whale <u>sounded</u> several times.
   4. We rowed across the <u>sound</u>.

   f. A class in school.
   g. A slope.
   h. To check and give a score to.
   i. To place in classes; sort.
   j. To make smooth and level.

   5. My teacher will <u>grade</u> the papers tomorrow.
   6. I am in the sixth <u>grade</u>.
   7. The workmen will <u>grade</u> the new road next week.
   8. Samuel was <u>grading</u> eggs all morning.

F. Write two different meanings for each word.
1. season   2. watch   3. switch

G. Write the part of speech for each underlined word, as it is used in that sentence. You may use abbreviations.
1. On Thursday we boarded the <u>train</u> at Sugarcreek.
2. <u>Train</u> up a child in the way he should go.
3. The queen of Sheba came to Jerusalem with a very great <u>train</u>.
4. Were you ever at the <u>train</u> museum?
5. What is the <u>charge</u> for crossing this bridge?
6. That hardware store <u>charges</u> high prices for tools.
7. When the ram <u>charged</u>, the boys clambered quickly up a tree.
8. Baby Jonathan is my special <u>charge</u> today.

Review Exercises

Copy the dependent clauses. Write whether each one is used as an adjective (*adj.*) or an adverb (*adv.*). Write which word the clause modifies. [97, 110]
1. The bird that you hear is a mockingbird.
2. He was still singing after we went to bed.
3. The boy who was parking cars is the janitor's son.
4. Before the meeting started, the parking lot was filled.
5. The boys could not go inside before they had finished their job.
6. The minister who spoke tonight was from Wisconsin.

---

127. Using a Bible Concordance and a Bible Dictionary

The Bible is the most important book we can study. But sometimes we need help in studying the Bible. We may want to know where a certain verse is found. Or we may need additional information to help us understand what a certain verse means. Two books that provide this kind of help are a Bible concordance and a Bible dictionary.

A *concordance* is useful for finding verses in the Bible that contain a certain word. You may have a concordance in the back of your Bible, but that is a very small, limited one. There are other concordances that are larger and more extensive. *Strong's Exhaustive Concordance* is a very good, complete concordance.

The entry words in a concordance are arranged in alphabetical order, as in a dictionary. Under each entry word are references showing where the word is found, and beside each reference is the phrase that contains the word. The references are listed in the order of the books of the Bible. If you want to find references only from the Book of Psalms, you would find the section with verses from Psalms.

Suppose you are making a scrapbook page for someone who is sick, and you want to find the reference for the verse "He careth for you." Which entry word should you find: *he, careth, for,* or *you*? Choose *careth,* the least common word in the verse, and look it up. There you will see several phrases from different references. The first is Deuteronomy 11:12: "which the Lord thy God *c* for." (The *c* stands for *careth.*) Keep looking until you find the phrase with the words you want. The reference you are looking for is 1 Peter 5:7.

Perhaps you want to find a longer verse like "Behold, what manner of love the Father hath bestowed upon us." Which word should you look up this time? You could find *behold, love,* and *Father,* but these are very common words in the Bible. You would probably need to go through many references before you found the right one. But if you look up *manner* or *bestowed,* you will find your verse much more easily because these words are less common. *Bestowed* has the fewest references of all, so you will find the verse most quickly if you look under *bestowed.* (The reference is 1 John 3:1.)

A *Bible dictionary* gives information about people, places, things, and customs of the Bible. Entry words are arranged in alphabetical order, as in a dictionary, and information is given about each item.

Perhaps you want to know if it ever snows in Jerusalem. You could look in a Bible dictionary for the information. Find the word *Jerusalem* as you would in a dictionary, using the guide words. Under *Jerusalem* are several subtitles. Look for one on weather or climate. There you will find that in the wintertime the lowest temperature is about 25 degrees. Sometimes as much as one foot of snow falls in Jerusalem, but it usually does not last long.

Or suppose you want to write a report about an animal of the Bible, such as the bear. So you look up *bear* in a Bible dictionary. There you may find a note that says, "See Animal Kingdom." So you turn to *A* and find the entry *Animal Kingdom.* The names of Bible animals are listed alphabetically under this entry word.

Bible concordances and Bible dictionaries are not perfect as the Bible is. We must carefully compare these reference books with the Bible itself because any other book may not always be accurate. However, these reference books will be a great help in studying the Bible if we use them wisely.

- A Bible concordance shows words from the Bible, along with references that contain those words.

- A Bible dictionary gives information about people, places, things, and customs of the Bible.

Class Practice

A. Use a concordance to find the reference for each verse.
1. When it is evening, ye say, It will be fair weather: for the sky is red.
2. As the clay is in the potter's hand, so are ye in mine hand.
3. Man looketh on the outward appearance, but the LORD looketh on the heart.
4. The effectual fervent prayer of a righteous man availeth much.
5. I will go before thee, and make the crooked places straight.
6. There is one God, and one mediator between God and men, the man Christ Jesus.

B. Do the following exercises.
1. Look up *train* in a concordance.
   a. How many references are given?
   b. Which books of the Bible contain this word?
2. Look up *train* in a Bible dictionary.
   a. What meanings does the word have?
   b. Does any meaning have the idea of a row of cars, as on a railroad?
3. Look up *bath* in a Bible dictionary.
   a. To what does the word refer?
   b. How does it compare with an English gallon?

Written Exercises

A. Write the reference for each verse, using a concordance.
1. The steps of a good man are ordered by the LORD: and he delighteth in his way.
2. Let every one of us please his neighbour for his good to edification.
3. Keep thy heart with all diligence; for out of it are the issues of life.

4. Watch ye, stand fast in the faith, quit you like men, be strong.
5. I have learned, in whatsoever state I am, therewith to be content.
6. Before they call, I will answer; and while they are yet speaking, I will hear.

B. Look up *hail* in a concordance.
   1. Write the reference for the following verse.

> "Hast thou entered into the treasures of the snow? or hast thou seen the treasures of the hail?"

   2. How many references from the Book of Psalms are given?
   3. How many different books of the Bible contain this word?

C. Look up *bees* in a Bible dictionary. Then do the following exercises.
   1. Write two references of verses that mention bees or honey.
   2. Write two interesting facts about bees in Palestine.

   Suggestions:
   Wild bees in Palestine
   Where wild bees make their homes
   How many bees are in Palestine today

   3. From the Book of Proverbs, give one caution about eating honey.

D. Read about one or more of the following subjects in a Bible dictionary, and write two interesting facts that you discover.

potter	threshing floor	Dead Sea
fishing	wine press	Bethlehem

Review Exercises

A. Write the three principal parts of each verb. Use *have* with the past participle. [31]
   1. ride   3. draw   5. begin
   2. send   4. come   6. put

B. Write the correct verbs. [47–52]
   1. When the dog (set, sat) on the sidewalk and would not move, it (raised, rose) a question in his master's mind.
   2. The dog had been (taught, learned) to protect his blind owner from danger.
   3. Some workmen had (digged, dug) a deep hole just the day before, and steam was (raising, rising) from it.

4. A water pipe had (burst, busted), but the workers had not (set, sat) barriers around it.

5. The faithful dog would not (let, leave) his master fall in to be (drowned, drownded).

6. The grateful owner patted the dog and (let, left) him have a juicy bone.

7. Later the dog (laid, lay) the chewed bone in the garden.

8. It has (laid, lain) there ever since.

9. The dog wanted to (let, leave) the house for a walk, but his master (laid, lay) down to rest awhile.

10. (Can, May) I pet your dog?

11. Please do not pet the dog while he is working, or you may be (attacked, attackted).

12. The dog (drug, dragged) his master home because he wanted a juicy bone.

13. The master decided that he must (learn, teach) the dog a lesson.

14. The dog should (have, of) obeyed his master's command.

Challenge Exercises

In *Strong's Concordance,* each Bible reference is followed by a number. By using that number, you can turn to the dictionaries in the back of the concordance and find the original Hebrew or Greek word used in that reference. (The Old Testament was written in Hebrew, and the New Testament in Greek.) The dictionaries give the root meanings of the Hebrew and Greek words.

1. In 1 Samuel 25:25, Abigail said, "Nabal is his name, and folly is with him." Why did she say that? (Find *Nabal* in the Hebrew dictionary.)

2. Find the Greek word that is translated *comfortless* in John 14:18. Which of the following English words comes from that Greek word?

    a. grief   b. orphan   c. forsake

3. Find the Greek word that is translated *offences* in Matthew 18:7. Which of the following English words comes from that Greek word?

    a. insult   b. confusion   c. scandal

4. When Jesus said "Verily, verily" (as in John 10:1), He used the word from which the English word ——— comes.

    a. solemn   b. amen   c. behold

128. Sentence Variety in Paragraphs

Good writers make careful use of sentence variety in their paragraphs. You have already studied declarative, interrogative, imperative, and exclamatory sentences, as well as simple, compound, and complex sentences. You have also studied different kinds of word order in sentences. So you should be well prepared to use sentence variety in paragraphs.

Study the sentences below. All four of them express admiration for a beautiful sunset. Notice how the same thought can be stated in the four different kinds of sentences.

> That sunset is beautiful. (declarative)
> Look at that beautiful sunset. (imperative)
> Have you ever seen such a beautiful sunset? (interrogative)
> What a beautiful sunset that is! (exclamatory)

The following sentences use the three different kinds of word order. Which one expresses the thought in the most interesting and forceful way?

> The lively heifers charged through the fence. (normal word order)
> Through the fence charged the lively heifers. (inverted word order)
> Through the fence the lively heifers charged. (mixed word order)

Normal word order makes statements in a plain, simple manner. That is why normal order is used most often. Inverted or mixed word order tends to catch the reader's attention more because it is different. When you write paragraphs, try to use an inverted or mixed sentence once in a while. This serves two purposes. First, it provides sentence variety. Second, it emphasizes the thought in that particular sentence.

Short sentences can sometimes be combined to make a compound sentence and thus add variety to a paragraph. In the following part of a paragraph, all the sentences are short and choppy. Notice how awkward this sounds.

> Henry threw the ball. David caught it. Then David began running toward the end of the playground. Robert ran after him. Soon David threw the ball back to Henry. . . .

The sentences are more readable if some of them are joined into compound sentences.

> Henry threw the ball, and David caught it. Then David began running toward the end of the playground. Robert ran after him, and David soon threw the ball back to Henry. . . .

Of course, not all short sentences should be combined to make them compound. Rather, you should combine sentences in a way that makes your writing flow smoothly and naturally.

Simple sentences can sometimes be changed to complex sentences by the use of adjective and adverb clauses.

> I ate three sandwiches. I was quite hungry.
> I ate three sandwiches because I was quite hungry.
>   (adverb clause)

> I ate three sandwiches. I enjoyed them very much.
> I ate three sandwiches, which I enjoyed very much.
>   (adjective clause)

Complex sentences are especially valuable because they clearly show the relationship between two ideas. Using complex sentences properly can be a complex problem! But with study and practice, you will be able to make these sentences a natural part of your writing. Soon you will find it hard to write without using complex sentences.

A paragraph should have some longer sentences and some shorter sentences. Of course, making some sentences compound or complex will automatically make some sentences longer. But short sentences are also needed for variety. Short sentences do not waste words. They get right to the point. Short sentences also sound more like natural conversation.

Read the two following paragraphs. Which one do you like better?

> Fossils are the remains of plants or animals that lived long ago. Most scientists agree that they were laid down by flood waters. Fossils are found all over the world. Many fossils of ocean animals have been found even on top of high mountains. They have been discovered on Mount Everest, the highest mountain in the world. They are convincing evidence of a worldwide flood. We know that the Bible account of Noah and the Flood is true, even without any special natural evidence. Fossils are an interesting evidence that God has given for us to observe.

*   *   *   *   *

What are fossils? They are the remains of plants or animals that lived long ago. How were fossils formed? Most scientists agree that they were laid down by flood waters. Fossils are found all over the world. Even on top of high mountains, many fossils of ocean animals have been found. They have been discovered on Mount Everest, the highest mountain in the world. Are they not convincing evidence of a worldwide flood? We know that the Bible account of Noah and the Flood is true, even without any special natural evidence. But fossils are an interesting evidence that God has given for us to observe.

Do you like the second paragraph better? Can you tell why? What kinds of sentence variety does it have?

Of course, sentence variety must be used carefully. We should usually avoid writing paragraphs in which all the sentences follow the same pattern. But neither should we write paragraphs filled with all kinds of unusual sentences. Variety is like spice. A little spice improves the flavor, but too much spice ruins the cake!

- Good writers make careful use of sentence variety in paragraphs.

- Declarative, interrogative, imperative, and exclamatory sentences can be used for variety in paragraphs.

- Normal, inverted, and mixed word order can be used for sentence variety.

- Simple, compound, and complex sentences can be used for sentence variety. This method also produces variety in the length of sentences.

Class Practice

A. The following paragraph contains only declarative sentences in normal word order. Tell how to improve the sentence variety in the following ways.

1. Change sentence *c* to mixed word order.
2. Change sentence *e* to an exclamatory sentence with inverted word order.
3. Tell which other sentence should be an exclamatory sentence.

^aThe sons of the prophets wanted to build a new house near the Jordan River. ^bThey asked Elisha the prophet to go with them. ^cThey cut down trees to make lumber for a new house at the Jordan. ^dOne of the servants was using a borrowed ax to fell a beam. ^eThe axhead flew into the river. ^fBut Elisha cut a stick and threw it into the water. ^gThe servant must have had a great surprise then. ^hThe iron axhead floated. ⁱElisha told him to take it out of the water, and he obeyed.

B. The following paragraph contains only simple sentences. Tell how to improve the sentence variety in the following ways.
1. Join sentences *a* and *b* into a complex sentence with an adjective clause.
2. Join sentences *d* and *e* into a complex sentence with an adverb clause. Begin with the transitional word *However.*
3. Join sentences *f* and *g* into a compound sentence.

^aMother thanked Brother Nathan. ^bHe had changed the tire. ^cThen she climbed in and started the engine. ^dShe put the car in gear. ^eIt did not move. ^fShe pressed the accelerator. ^gStill the car would not budge. ^hWhat could be the matter? ⁱSuddenly Mother realized that the emergency brake was on! ^jWith a sheepish smile, she released the brake and drove away.

Written Exercises

A. The paragraph below contains only declarative sentences. Improve the sentence variety in the following ways. (Write only the sentences that would be changed.)
1. Rewrite sentence *b* as an imperative sentence.
2. Rewrite sentence *c* as an interrogative sentence.
3. Rewrite sentence *g* as an exclamatory sentence.

^aA polar bear seems to like the cold. ^bYou should consider, for example, that he does not hurry to a warm cave as other bears do when cold weather comes. ^cYou may wonder how he stands the cold and wet. ^dGod has created the polar bear with layers of fat under his skin and with air spaces in his fur to keep him warm. ^eHis oily fur keeps him dry even when he swims under the icy water to hunt for his dinner. ^fHe has fur on the bottom of his feet to help him walk on ice without slipping. ^gIt is no wonder that the polar bear does not mind the cold.

B. The following paragraph contains many short, choppy sentences. Improve the sentence variety in the following ways. (Write the entire paragraph.)

1. Join sentences *a* and *b* into a complex sentence with an adverb clause. Move *long ago* to the beginning of the sentence.
2. Join sentences *c* and *d* into a compound sentence.
3. Join sentences *f* and *g* into a complex sentence with an adjective clause.
4. Move *immediately* to the beginning of sentence *h*.
5. Join sentences *i* and *j* into a complex sentence with an adverb clause. Begin the sentence with *when*.
6. Join sentences *k* and *l* into a compound sentence.
7. Join sentences *m* and *n* into a compound sentence. Move *soon* to the beginning of the sentence.
8. Rewrite sentence *o* as an exclamatory sentence, beginning with *how*.

> [a]An old man met a band of robbers long ago. [b]He was riding through the forests of Poland. [c]The robbers took all his valuables. [d]Then they asked if he had given them everything. [e]He said that he had. [f]But soon afterward he remembered some gold. [g]It was sewed in the hem of his robe. [h]He hurried back immediately and looked for the robbers. [i]He found them. [j]He told them that he had not been truthful. [k]He offered the gold to them. [l]They would not take it. [m]One robber soon went and brought back the old man's wallet. [n]Others brought back his horse and other valuables. [o]The man was very glad that he had been so honest.

Review Exercises

Write the correct phrase for each description. [21, 24, 27]

> developing by contrast
> developing by comparison
> developing with details
> developing with examples and illustrations

1. Paragraph development by showing similarities between two persons, places, things, or ideas.
2. Paragraph development by showing differences between two persons, places, things, or ideas.
3. Paragraph development by using an incident.

4. Paragraph development by giving a series of steps, such as showing the things to do in starting a stamp collection.

5. Paragraph development by describing American farm life in relation to European farm life.

---

129. Synonyms, Antonyms, and Homophones

The English language has a great variety of words. When you were only six years old, you probably knew three or four thousand English words already. However, as you continue to read, you recognize that there are many English words that you still need to learn. Your vocabulary grows mostly from speaking and reading, but you can help it to grow with word study. Learn pairs of synonyms and antonyms as an aid to vocabulary growth. Learn to distinguish between homophones to overcome one kind of spelling problem.

Synonyms are words with similar meanings. Two synonyms may be very close in meaning, but they never have exactly the same meaning. They cannot always be used in the same way. For example, *cheap* and *inexpensive* are synonyms. Which word would you use to describe something you want to sell? You might say, "Buy these; they are cheap." But *cheap* can mean "of poor quality." So if you are selling a well-made product, you should rather say, "Buy these; they are inexpensive."

Here are several more pairs of synonyms.

purpose—reason   drive—propel   enough—sufficient

Antonyms are words with opposite or nearly opposite meanings. Sometimes we can make a meaning clearer by using an antonym to tell what something is *not*. Some antonyms are words like *huge* and *tiny*. Other antonyms are formed by adding a prefix such as *un-* or *dis-* to a word. In this way we can form antonyms like *buckle—unbuckle* and *order—disorder*.

Here are several more pairs of antonyms.

arrive—depart   giant—dwarf   ordinary—special

True synonyms and antonyms are the same part of speech. Study the following examples.

Synonyms:

joy—gladness (nouns), *but not* rejoice (verb)
begin—start (verbs), *but not* first (adjective)
gentle—mild (adjectives), *but not* mildness (noun)

Antonyms:

joy—grief (nouns), *but not* grieve (verb)
begin—finish (verbs), *but not* last (adjective)
gentle—harsh (adjectives), *but not* roughness (noun)

Homophones are words that are pronounced alike, but their spellings and meanings are different. It takes care and thought to spell homophones correctly, but this is important so that you communicate the right idea.

The (rumors, roomers) usually come during the summer.
(*Rumors* usually come at any time of the year. Most likely the correct word is *roomers*.)

I'll go (by, buy) that store.
(Not many people can so easily *buy* a store. Most likely the correct word is *by*.)

Here are several more pairs of homophones.

ant—aunt	flee—flea	maze—maize
bin—been	guessed—guest	nay—neigh
cellar—seller	hour—our	oar—ore
die—dye	lane—lain	pale—pail

Some homophones come in sets of three or four.

air, heir, ere, e'er	heel, heal, he'll
burro, burrow, borough	I'll, isle, aisle
dew, do, due	meat, meet, mete
gnu, knew, new	right, write, rite, wright

In some sets of homophones, one word is a contraction. Be sure to use the correct word. Think of the words a contraction stands for when you use it.

your—you're (*You're* means "you are.")
its—it's (*It's* means "it is" or "it has.")

whose—who's (*Who's* means "who is" or "who has.")
aisle—isle—I'll (*I'll* means "I shall" or "I will.")
there—their—they're (*They're* means "they are.")

Use synonyms, antonyms, and homophones carefully. Check a dictionary when you are not sure of the spelling or meaning of a word.

- Synonyms are words with similar meanings.

- Antonyms are words with opposite meanings.

- Homophones are words that are pronounced alike, but their spellings and meanings are different.

Class Practice

A. Tell whether these pairs of words are *synonyms, antonyms,* or *homophones.*

1. unite—divide
2. rye—wry
3. region—area
4. sight—cite
5. convince—persuade
6. center—edge

B. Tell which words are incorrect. Tell how to spell each one correctly.
1. The break on my bicycle doesn't holed.
2. A bare usually has a short tale or none at all.
3. Last winter hour neighbors gave us slay rides.
4. Save that peace of construction paper; we don't want to waist it.
5. Harry tolled me that the bells were wringing because of a fire.

Written Exercises

A. Copy each word, and write the matching synonym.

1. brief   raise
2. dwelling   warped
3. bent   residence
4. consume   short
5. elevate   lowly
6. humble   devour

B. Copy each word, and write the matching antonym.

1. reckless   shorten
2. lengthen   sturdy
3. question   careful
4. frail   depart
5. simple   complex
6. arrive   answer

C. Write a homophone for each word.

1. blew   3. plane   5. steak
2. steel   4. wait   6. groan

D. Write whether the words in each pair are synonyms (*S*), antonyms (*A*), or homophones (*H*).

1. construct—build   5. eyelet—islet
2. clime—climb   6. shorten—abbreviate
3. pause—resume   7. rough—smooth
4. serious—sober   8. knead—need

E. Write the homophones that properly complete these sentences.

1. These (to, too, two) girls went (to, too, two) the city (to, too, two).
2. He made a (rye, wry) face.
3. The snow was (pact, packed) between the buildings.
4. Many people yield to the temptation of (pried, pride).
5. A full-grown (mail, male) lion has a (main, mane) around his neck.
6. The little boat moved by means of a large (sale, sail).
7. This (gored, gourd) is shaped like a (pair, pear).
8. How many inches have you (groan, grown) since last summer?

Review Exercises

A. Copy each sentence, and add the missing punctuation marks. [77–87]

1. In fact were taking twenty eight visitors to our great uncles house.
2. Yes Marie well sing for him and then well recite John 14 1 6 for him.
3. Soon after 12 00, theyll serve the meal.
4. Mother said, Martha will bring the bread butter and jelly and Marie will bring the potatoes meat and peas.
5. My great grandfather John Lane will be ninety four years old tomorrow.
6. In the early days a printer had to keep his *p*s and *q*s straight the *p*s could easily come out as *q*s.

B. Copy the incorrect words. If other words should be used instead, write the correct words beside them. [116]

1. My book is different than yours, accept for the first chapter.
2. After we are inside of the building, June will sit besides me.
3. The lawn mower is in back of the house.
4. The three bullfrogs on the bank leaped in the water.
5. Where is your book at?
6. After art class was over with, they shared the pictures between all the girls in the class.

---

130. Word Families

Have you ever met a stranger who guessed your last name before you even told him? Perhaps he said, "I can tell what family you belong to." The reason he could do this is that people in the same family are alike in many ways. They tend to look alike, and they have similar ways of talking and acting.

Words come in families too. If you become acquainted with several words in a *word family,* you can recognize other words in that family. With practice, you will sometimes be able to guess the meaning of a completely new word simply because you are acquainted with its "relatives."

People in the same family have the same last name. Words in the same family also have the same "last name." That is, they have the same *root* or basic word element. You can improve your vocabulary by studying words in groups according to their roots. If you know the meaning of a root, you can recognize more words in the same word family.

For example, the word *number* comes from the Latin root *numer,* which means "number." The following words have the same root, so they are in the same word family. How many of these words do you recognize?

numeral	numerable	innumerable	numerator
enumerate	numerical	numerous	numberless

The Latin root *vari* means "different." The following words are in the *vari* family. Can you see how they are related in meaning?

vary	variation	variable
various	variety	invariable

Roots may appear at different places in words. The root *graph* means "to write." Notice the various places where this root is found in the following words.

graphite   stenographer   photograph

Many words are formed by using prefixes and suffixes to change or add to the meanings of roots. If you know the meaning of the root and of the prefix or suffix, you can often tell the meaning of the word. For example, the root *port* means "to carry." The table below shows what happens when various prefixes are added to this root.

Prefix	New Word	New Meaning
ex- (out)	export	to carry out
im- (in)	import	to carry in
re- (back)	report	to carry back
de- (away)	deport	to carry away
trans- (across)	transport	to carry across

This chart shows what happens when suffixes are added to the root *port*.

Suffix	New Word	New Meaning
-able (able)	portable	able to be carried
-er (one who)	porter	one who carries
-age (act of)	portage	act of carrying

Sometimes both a prefix and a suffix are added to a root.

Prefix and Suffix	New Word	New Meaning
re- (back) -er (one who)	reporter	one who carries back
trans- (across) -ation (act of)	transportation	act of carrying across

Here are some members of another word family.

simple	simplify	simplification
simply	simplicity	simplistic

Simple is an adjective that means "having one part." The suffix *-ly* changes it to an adverb that means "in a simple way," and *-ify* changes it to a verb that means "to make simple." *Simplicity* is a noun that means "the state of being simple," and *simplification* is a different noun that means "the act of making simple." *Simplistic* is another adjective, but this word means "overly simple."

You can easily see that it is *simpler* to learn these six words together than to learn them one by one! A dictionary will introduce you to the individual "members" in a word family. It will give the part of speech for each word, along with its meaning. This will help you to avoid confusing "twins" like *simplicity* and *simplification,* which do not mean the same at all, even though both are nouns. You will learn all these things and more as you become acquainted with the whole family.

Exploring the meanings of roots, prefixes, and suffixes is a fascinating study. Do not miss the interesting discoveries that you can make by studying word families.

- A word family is a group of words with the same root. Prefixes and suffixes give different meanings to words in the same family.

- The study of word families will help to increase your vocabulary.

Class Practice

A. Give the root of each word family. Use a dictionary to find the meaning of the root, and also to find other words in that family.
1. hydrant, dehydrate, hydraulic, hydrophobia
2. endure, during, durable, durum
3. ire, irritate, irritable, irascible

B. Look up the following prefixes and suffixes in your dictionary. Tell what they mean, and give examples of words that have them.
1. dis-
2. pre-
3. mis-
4. -less
5. -er
6. -ish

C. Tell what the following words mean by the clues given.
1. The root *don* means "give," and the suffix *-or* means "one who."
   a. What does *donor* mean?
   b. How are the words *donate* and *donee* related?
   c. Two other forms of *don* are *dose* and *dote.* What is a dose?
   d. The prefix *anti-* means "against." What is an *antidote*?

2. The prefix *in-* means "in," the root *habit* means "dwell," and the suffix *-ant* means "one who."
   a. What is an inhabitant?
   b. What other words do you know that are related to *inhabitant*?

Written Exercises

A. Do these exercises with words from the same families. Check a dictionary to make sure your answers are correct.
   1. The root *cav* means "hollow."
      a. What word with this root names a large hollow space underground?
      b. The prefix *con-* means "with." The surface of a *concave* lens has (a hollow, an outward bulge).
      c. The suffix *-ity* means "condition of." If your tooth has a "condition of being hollow," it has a ———.
      d. The prefix *ex-* means "out." The suffix *-ate* means "to make." The suffix *-or* means "one who." If your father wants to call "one who makes a hollowed-out place," he will call an _____ cav _____.
   2. The root *circ* means "round" or "around."
      a. A *circle* is a ——— figure.
      b. A *circuit* is a trip or a line ——— something.
      c. The prefix *circum-* comes from the *circ* root. The root *spec* means "look." If a person is *circumspect,* he carefully does what?
      d. *Solar* means "of the sun." What is a *circumsolar* path?
      e. Find and write four more words that begin with *circu-* or *circum-*.

B. Write the correct word for each question by using the meanings given. You may use your dictionary.
   1. The root *geo* means "earth" or "land." Some words with this root are *geometry, geographer, geothermal,* and *geomagnetic.*
      a. The root *graph* means "to write." Which word means "one who writes about the earth"?
      b. Which word has to do with the earth's magnetism?
      c. The root *metr* means "measure." Which word names a branch of mathematics that deals with measures?
      d. Which word refers to heat from the earth?

2. The root *ped* means "foot." Some words with this root are *pedal, pedestrian, biped, centipede,* and *millipede.*

   a. The prefix *bi-* means "two." Which word names a creature with two feet?

   b. The prefix *centi-* means "hundred." Which word names a creature with a hundred feet? (It actually has from 15 to 170 pairs of legs.)

   c. The prefix *milli-* means "thousand." Which word names a creature that is supposed to have a thousand feet? (It actually has no more than 115 pairs of legs.)

   d. Which word names a lever or treadle that is operated by foot?

   e. Which word names a person traveling on foot?

C. Write original sentences using three new words that you learned by studying word families in this lesson.

Review Exercises

A. Copy the three sentences with direct quotations, and add the missing punctuation marks and capital letters. [77, 80]

1. On Sunday said Galen we saw fourteen deer in our garden
2. Yes and one buck was white Andrew exclaimed
3. Paul said it must have been an albino
4. Albino animals are born without the usual coloring in their skin.
5. My teacher said that a true albino is all white with pink eyes.

B. Write whether each underlined word is a *preposition,* a *conjunction,* or an *interjection.* You may use abbreviations. [115–122]

1. <u>What</u>! Did you see two hyenas <u>and</u> a leopard <u>in</u> the game park?
2. <u>Well</u>, four lions were running <u>after</u> a zebra, <u>but</u> it got away.

Challenge Exercises

For each word, write what part of speech it is. Then write three other words of that family, and name their parts of speech.

   1. respond   2. ample   3. reality

131. Chapter 11 Review

Class Practice

A. Look up the following words. Give several different meanings for each one. Tell what part of speech goes with each meaning.
1. bid   3. peep
2. pen   4. shy

B. Tell whether these pairs are *synonyms*, *antonyms*, or *homophones*.
1. nose—knows   3. exasperation—annoyance
2. aromatic—odorless   4. one—won

C. Tell which words are spelled incorrectly. Tell how to correct each one.
1. Jerry spoke in a courtious manor.
2. We sang in the hauls of the hospitel.
3. The right answer was guest by the last guessed.
4. Weal serve the desert for lunch.

D. Look up the following prefixes and suffixes in the dictionary. Tell what they mean, and give examples of words that begin with each prefix.
1. dis-   3. -ment
2. re-   4. -ous

E. Answer these questions about reference books.
1. What reference book would you use to find where in the Bible the following sentence is found? Which word would you look up?

    "But ask now the beasts, and they shall teach thee."

2. What reference book would you use to find how many men named James are mentioned in the New Testament, and what each one did?

3. What reference book would you use to find where Bethel was located?

F. Tell how to improve the sentence variety in the following paragraphs.
1. The sentences in the following paragraph are all in normal word order. Tell how to change sentence *b* to mixed word order, and sentence *d* to inverted word order.

*a*The sense of touch is a wonderful gift from God. *b*You can tell if an object is hot or cold, hard or soft, rough or smooth, wet or dry, by touching it. *c*If you put your fingers against your throat and sing, you can feel the quiver of your vibrating vocal cords. *d*You receive a pleasant sensation when you stroke the fur of a cat. *e*If you prick yourself with a pin, you feel pain. *f*You know how hard to grip a paper cup because you can feel the pressure of your fingers against it. *g*The sense of touch helps us in many ways.

—Lester Showalter

2. The following paragraph contains all simple sentences. Tell how to join each pair of underlined sentences into a compound or complex sentence.

The mink is a brown, furry animal with pointed ears and bright eyes. <u>He looks appealing. He is a fierce hunter.</u> He finds much of his food like crayfish, frogs, and minnows in the water. On land he finds mice, muskrats, rabbits, and snakes to eat. <u>He has a bad reputation among farmers. He sometimes steals chickens from them.</u>

3. The following paragraph contains all declarative sentences. Tell how to change the paragraph so that it has at least one interrogative sentence, one imperative sentence, and one exclamatory sentence.

*a*It was a topsy-turvy Saturday. *b*First of all, my alarm clock didn't ring and I overslept. *c*I awoke to hear Mother telling me to get up immediately. *d*"The chimney is clogged, and the wood stove is smoking!" she said. *e*You can imagine how I hurried then. *f*I wondered what would happen next. *g*Soon Father had extinguished the fire in the stove, but not before the whole house was full of white, choking smoke. *h*Instead of doing what we had planned that day, Mother and I washed bedding, curtains, and clothes until the lines were full and we were tired out. *i*I am glad that not every day is like that one.

Written Exercises

A. For each entry word, write *yes* or *no* to tell whether you would find it on a dictionary page with the guide words *Joab* and *Jonah*.
   1. John
   3. Joash
   5. Johanan
   2. Jezreel
   4. Jordan
   6. Joel

B. Divide these words into syllables, and mark the accents.
   1. solidify
   2. facility
   3. intertwine

C. Copy each word, and write the phonetic spelling beside it. Include the accent marks.
   1. photographic
   3. misdemeanor
   2. competent
   4. liquefaction

D. Write the plural form of each word.
   1. ratio
   4. medley
   2. proof
   5. novelty
   3. spoonful
   6. radius

E. Write the forms of comparison for these adjectives and adverbs.
   1. many
   3. bad
   2. hardy
   4. energetic

F. Write the other correct spelling for each word.
   1. jailor
   2. helixes

G. Write the part of speech that each underlined word is. Use a dictionary if you need help.
   1. There is a small <u>spring</u> in the woods behind our house.
   2. These plants <u>spring</u> from seeds blown here by the wind.
   3. This is a <u>spring</u> flower; it blooms in early May.
   4. The ninety-year-old lady is still quite <u>spry</u>.

H. Write the root of each word family. Then write another word with that root.
   1. thermal, thermometer, thermograph
   2. vitamin, vitality, revitalize
   3. vision, supervision, visualize, visible

I. Rewrite one of the paragraphs in Part F of Class Practice, making the suggested improvements.

132. Final Review

Class Practice

A. Name the part of speech described.
   1. It modifies a verb, adjective, or adverb.
   2. It modifies a noun or pronoun.
   3. It is a connecting word that begins a phrase.
   4. It joins words, phrases, or clauses.
   5. It expresses strong feeling.
   6. It names a person, place, thing, or idea.
   7. It can be limiting or descriptive.
   8. It takes the place of a noun.
   9. It shows action or being.
   10. It may be an article (*a, an, the*).
   11. It tells *how, when, where,* or *to what degree.*
   12. It tells *which, whose, how many,* or *what kind of.*

B. Say the verbs in each group.
   1. The twenty-three helping verbs.
   2. The most common linking verbs.
   3. Verbs of sense used as linking verbs.
   4. Other linking verbs.

C. Say the three principal parts of each verb.
   1. bring   4. raise
   2. come   5. set
   3. reach   6. tear

D. Say each verb in the tense shown in parentheses.
   1. freeze (simple past)   4. buy (future perfect)
   2. keep (present perfect)   5. dig (simple present)
   3. list (simple future)   6. begin (past perfect)

E. Tell whether each sentence is *declarative, interrogative, imperative,* or *exclamatory.* Also tell whether it is *simple, compound,* or *complex.* (All punctuation has been omitted.)
   1. Who came to Bethany after Lazarus died
   2. Roll away the stone
   3. Jesus called Lazarus and he came forth
   4. What a great miracle that was

F. Name the kind of pronouns in each set. Choose from this list.

>   demonstrative   personal—nominative case
>   indefinite   personal—objective case
>   interrogative   personal—possessive case
>   relative

1. this, that, these, those
2. I, you, he, she, it, we, they
3. my, mine, your, yours, his, her, hers, its, our, ours, their, theirs
4. some, any, none, all, most, each, either, one, nobody, anyone, any-
    body, both, few, several, many
5. who, whom, whose, which, what
6. me, you, him, her, it, us, them
7. who, whom, whose, which, that

G. Give the correct words.
1. A good description is developed by (chronological order, spatial
    order, the order of importance).
2. The three main parts of a story include all the following except
    (the beginning, the conflict, the middle, the ending).
3. The title of a story should *not* (be short, be interesting, give away
    the outcome, arouse the reader's curiosity).
4. The extra part of a business letter is the (heading, inside address,
    greeting, body, closing, signature).
5. Paragraphs can be developed in all the following ways except
    (by using details, by using examples and illustrations, by using
    comparison or contrast, by using rhyme and rhythm).
6. "For pleasures are like poppies spread,
    You seize the flower, its bloom is shed."

    a. These lines follow the (iambic: ˘ ′ ˘ ′, trochaic: ′ ˘ ′ ˘)
        rhythm pattern.
    b. The figure of speech in the first line is (a simile, a metaphor,
        personification).
    c. One thing that makes the lines sound appealing is (words
        with similar beginning sounds, words that suggest the sounds
        they refer to).

Written Exercises

A. Write the parts of speech for the underlined words.
1. Myron <u>and</u> John will be choosing the new songs <u>tomorrow</u>.

2. Will the <u>service</u> be held <u>in</u> the morning?
3. <u>Oh</u>, the singing <u>sounded</u> beautiful!
4. <u>We</u> sang several <u>new</u> songs.

B. Identify the underlined words as follows: direct object (*DO*), indirect object (*IO*), object of a preposition (*OP*), predicate nominative (*PN*), predicate adjective (*PA*), or appositive adjective (*AA*).
   1. Paul and Barnabas were <u>missionaries</u> in the early days.
   2. They preached the <u>Gospel</u> at every opportunity.
   3. Many of the Gentiles were quite <u>ignorant</u>.
   4. The apostles taught <u>them</u> the truth.
   5. Paul, bold and <u>courageous</u>, was not afraid of suffering.
   6. Please read the story to <u>me</u>.

C. Write whether each group of words is a sentence (*S*), a fragment (*F*), or a run-on error (*R*).
   1. Long ago my great-grandmother washed with a washboard.
   2. Finally bought her a washing machine.
   3. She was quite pleased now she no longer had to scrub by hand.
   4. The children were helping to wash.
   5. By turning a great wheel by hand.

D. Write *yes* or *no* to tell whether the underlined words should be capitalized.
   1. on a <u>sunday</u> morning
   2. one day last <u>spring</u>
   3. with <u>uncle</u> James
   4. this Sunbeam <u>mixer</u>
   5. David, the <u>king</u> of Israel
   6. Jesus and <u>his</u> disciples
   7. the song "Abide <u>with</u> Me"
   8. an interesting <u>scottish</u> custom

E. Write the best words for these sentences.
   1. Several (boy's, boys') projects are finished.
   2. The first (minister's, ministers') topic was on loving others.
   3. Show kindness to the one (who, whom) asks you to go one mile by going with him two miles.
   4. Did the man (who, whom) you helped seem surprised by your kindness?
   5. The horse (who, that) had run away was caught by my brother.
   6. The (chair's rungs, rungs of the chair) were broken.
   7. (This, This here) job looks endless.
   8. (Them, Those) girls worked determinedly.
   9. It was (we, us) children who finished the job.
   10. It must have been John and (they, them).

11. Mother and (she, her) cleaned the rooms.
12. Brother Andrew took Paul and (they, them) to church.
13. (It's, Its) time to give the kitten (it's, its) milk.
14. (They're, Their) mother was waiting for them.
15. He (could, couldn't) scarcely see to drive down the mountain.
16. We didn't have (no, any) visitors at church.
17. My pet kitten is (laying, lying) on the rug.
18. Please (raise, rise) the window a bit.
19. Because of the dry weather, the price of corn will (raise, rise).
20. The boys usually (set, sit) with their fathers in church services.
21. Father (let, left) me help with the plowing.
22. Please (let, leave) the dolls at home.
23. My brother (taught, learned) me how to beat time for this song.
24. (Can, May) we please see your pictures?
25. Of the two girls, Judith is (taller, tallest).
26. This is the (baddest, worst) storm we've had this summer.
27. This snail crawls (more slowly, slowlier) than I imagined it would.
28. The frogs jumped (off, off of) the bank and (in, into) the water.
29. You should (except, accept) a gift graciously.
30. Please divide the cookies evenly (between, among) the two of you.
31. No one was there (beside, besides) the Owen family.
32. I want to talk (to, at) Aunt Miriam before she leaves.
33. I should (of, have) brought my grandfather along to see you.
34. These peaches taste different (from, than) the peaches on the other tree.
35. The peach orchard is (in back of, behind) the house.
36. Where is the new (shovel, shovel at)?
37. I saw it just (outside, outside of) the door.
38. We can hardly wait until this job is (over, over with).
39. What were you (talking, talking about)?
40. The evening was (nice, pleasant) and cool.

F. Write the subjects, and then write the correct words in parentheses.
1. None of the children (was, were) idle.
2. Both of the girls (wash, washes) dishes.
3. Some of the mothers (prepare, prepares) fruit for the meeting.

    4. Elizabeth and Lois (don't, doesn't) have paring knives.

    5. Father or Mother (sharpen, sharpens) the knives.

    6. There (was, were) several dull knives already.

    7. (Here's, Here are) the sharpeners.

    8. Henry (don't, doesn't) go to that school.

G. Write the word that receives the action of each verb. Then write whether the voice of the verb is *active* or *passive*.

    1. A widow was helped by Elijah.

    2. Elijah raised her son to life.

    3. Elijah was protected by God.

    4. God sent ravens to feed Elijah.

H. Copy each underlined item, and add the punctuation mark that should be used after it.

    1. <u>Yes</u> a package has arrived for <u>Joan</u> my sister.

    2. Janice, Sandra, and June helped Miss <u>Taylor</u> but Dawn, Louise, and Kristen helped <u>Mrs</u> Smith.

    3. We found several old barrels in the <u>attic</u> in the <u>garage</u> and in the basement.

    4. My <u>great</u> grandfather quoted Psalm <u>119</u> <u>1</u> 8 by memory.

    5. <u>Self</u> denial is an important <u>virtue</u> no one can be Jesus' disciple without it.

    6. **Dear <u>Sirs</u>**

       I will not be able to keep my appointment of <u>2</u> 00 on March 12.

    7. <u>Boys</u> hurry <u>inside</u> it's going to rain.

I. Write whether each underlined item is an *adjective* or an *adverb*.

    1. We hit the nails <u>hard</u> to get them into the <u>hard</u> wood.

    2. The lady <u>in the kitchen</u> is my grandmother.

    3. My grandfather is visiting <u>in the living room</u>.

    4. The big truck, <u>which we had loaded</u>, broke down.

    5. They had just finished moving in the furniture <u>when it began to snow</u>.

J. Label the words in each pair as synonyms (*S*), antonyms (*A*), or homophones (*H*).

    1. silence—quietness   4. knew—new

    2. plane—plain   5. flammable—fireproof

    3. brightness—dimness

Index